CW00965871

Globe Law
and Business

Secured Finance Transactions

Taking Security, Deal Structures
and Emerging Markets
Second Edition

Consulting Editor **Dominic Griffiths**

Consulting editor
Dominic Griffiths

Managing director
Sian O'Neill

Secured Finance Transactions: Taking Security, Deal Structures and Emerging Markets, Second Edition
is published by

Globe Law and Business Ltd
3 Mylor Close
Horsell
Woking
Surrey GU21 4DD
United Kingdom
Tel: +44 20 3745 4770
www.globelawandbusiness.com

Printed and bound by CPI Group (UK) Ltd, Croydon CR0 4YY, United Kingdom

Secured Finance Transactions: Taking Security, Deal Structures and Emerging Markets, Second Edition

ISBN 9781787425149
EPUB ISBN 9781787425156
Adobe PDF ISBN 9781787425163

Table of contents

Introduction

Dominic Griffiths
Mayer Brown

When I think back to when I decided to become a banking and finance lawyer, I'm not sure I fully imagined what a varied and interesting career I would subsequently have. But what I had already come to realise, through the anecdotes of senior colleagues, was that practising finance law could lead to involvement in a myriad of different transactional scenarios and exposure to a plethora of client institutions whose involvement in the markets was each individual and unique. No one deal was exactly the same; and by the time I started practising in the 1990s, certain basic financing techniques and structures had developed and morphed into new product types and financing techniques that were supporting a fast-changing financial world (particularly since the deregulation of financial markets and the subsequent expansion of investment banking from 1986).

Before the 1990s, it was rare for a London City solicitor to be described as purely a 'finance lawyer' – with some notable exceptions, such as Bill Tudor John and Martin Hughes, two of the architects of the first syndicated loan agreement. Corporate lawyers would turn their hand to the drafting and negotiation of loan agreements and security when the occasion arose. After the 'Big Bang' in 1986, however, borrower demand for secured lending (and investment banking appetite) increased exponentially, and over the next few years loan agreements increased in length and complexity. We also saw the introduction to Europe of US-style financing techniques such as the high-yield bond and securitisation, expanding the international investor base and demand for leverage. Banks were growing and evolving, and advisers were becoming more specialised in their coverage of transactional work.

No time at law school or otherwise studying finance-related case law and precedent can prepare you for the reality of front-line deal structuring and negotiating. The modern-day experience for a junior lawyer in a City finance law practice is being faced with a number of different product areas and often the expectation that you will specialise early in your career in one, or maybe a maximum of two of those areas. Through hard work and deal experience, one becomes expert in a given area and able to understand and reflect the commercial needs of clients, who themselves will have probably specialised fairly early in their careers in that area of banking. In a market where it is less usual to have a broader outlook on transactions and markets, when a situation arises in a transaction which is outside of your specialised area, where do you turn for guidance? Certainly to colleagues with experience in that other area; but also to books and practice guides. In this updated edition of *Secured Finance Transactions*, we have attempted to provide such guidance; whether it is being read by an in-house bank or corporate counsel, private practice solicitor or interested student, the intention is to give a little flavour and direction to the different regimes governing security interests and the types of transactions (and jurisdictions) in which they are practically applied. It is not intended to be comprehensive in detail, but can be used as a base for further research.

I would also like to think that this book may inspire students of law and trainee solicitors in deciding which area of finance law may be attractive to pursue in their future career. I would even apply that element of curiosity and inspiration to those more senior solicitors, such as myself, who have an interest in what others do in this field. While writing my chapter on English law security this summer, overlooking Portofino Mountain from my study window, I received the first draft of the chapters on "Real estate finance" and "Project finance" for review. I have practised alongside lawyers involved in those areas for decades, but now have a bigger window onto their world: an environment where there is a tangible, real asset to be financed and secured – whether a wind farm in Southeast Asia, a shopping centre in Frankfurt or a significant London West End commercial property. Assets that you can see for yourself and help shape the process through which they are sold, rented, refinanced or developed. Aircraft and shipping finance have a similar draw – with the added complication of taking security over such large movable assets.

Techniques and documentation in acquisition finance will be in large part familiar to the real estate finance practitioner and not wholly different from those to which the fund finance lawyer is accustomed. Asset-based lending documentation shares some of the features of both acquisition finance and real estate finance agreements and security, but typically with more emphasis on specific security interests and control over assets. Each area has its own legal and market terminology, and varying types of security documentation; but at the same time, with some significant overlapping elements – like dialects of the same common language. Then you add the varying jurisdictional elements of emerging and developing markets in Africa, Central and Eastern Europe and South America, with their legal influences shaped by history – be it the Napoleonic Code developed in Central and Southern Europe 200 years ago, or English or Portuguese law promulgated during those countries' colonial histories. It is often the method of creating security interests, the way that security is perfected against the interests of third parties and the manner of enforcement that draw out the contrasts between, and peculiarities of, the laws of each individual jurisdiction. If you are lucky enough to be a cross-border secured lending lawyer, those differentials and your familiarity with them will define your value as an adviser and ensure that you are never bored by the same transaction features being replicated from deal to deal. I hope that some of this satisfaction – exemplified in the contributions made by colleagues and contemporaries who have authored these chapters – is shared with you as the reader.

I wish to thank all of those who have contributed so expertly and selflessly to this edition; as well as my wife Francesca and children Millie, Jack and Annie for their support and patience.

English law security interests

Dominic Griffiths
Mayer Brown

1. The history of security

The history of security being used as a way of ensuring that collateral can be seized or sold for the repayment of loans goes far back in time – probably to the inception of the use of currency to pay for goods and property. Medieval custom and law in England and Wales observed property rights and the use of a possessory claim over assets for the repayment of debts. As regards the usage of security interests in English law, this had traditionally been in the form of property mortgages or possessory interests over chattels. It was a long time before the law came to conceptualise the principle of non-possessory security over chattels and security over intangibles. The flexibility of our common law system, coupled with the exponential rise of trade and industry in the late 18th and 19th centuries, caused the forms and uses of security interests to expand organically, satisfying the need for capital on a massive scale. With the formation of joint stock companies – entrepreneurs having made their riches in coalfields, steel and cotton mills and the railroads sprawling across the country and empire – there was a need for more liquidity than could be provided by cash reserves; and the types and quantities of collateral being used for security for loans had substantially expanded. The banking system that had developed beyond the traditional function of bailing out governments and supporting the economy in the face of expensive wars in mainland Europe and the Americas was now serving this rising mercantile and industrial growth.[1] Private banks – which had taken security over the country estates of the rich to finance their ships and expeditions abroad – were now becoming commercial lenders, providing loans to companies for working capital to expand their operations and acquire other businesses. The rise of Western capitalism went hand in hand with the growth in size and sophistication of the banking market; ancient forms of security were being contorted and innovated to satisfy the demand for credit.

---

[1] As observed by David Kynaston in *Till Time's Last Sand: A History of the Bank of England 1694-2013* (Bloomsbury 2017, p107), in reference to the aftermath of the battle of Waterloo: "The year 1815 marks one of those attractively straightforward lines in the sands of modern British history: not only the end of the war, but the start of almost a century of peace (broadly speaking), of Britain's rise to becoming the workshop of the world, of London's increasing dominance as an international finance centre, exporting capital to all parts of the globe."

The forms and uses of security interests, and their documentation, thus developed in a chaotic fashion – partially derived from a historic law of property and partially through case law, which for many years took a benign and relatively *laissez-faire* view of the commercial transactions taking place in the new world of commerce and credit. Historically, land and buildings could be mortgaged – whether by way of giving up possession to the creditor or retaining possession until the loan was due; and the law in this area was predominantly focused on preventing usury – the unfair profit accruing from the possession or seizure of property worth far in excess of the consideration originally provided. Legislation did not intervene substantially until the Law of Property Act 1925. While the English courts had more or less enabled the use of security by way of mortgaged property to function effectively in an increasingly commercial and property-owning environment, while protecting both the interests of the landowning borrower and the lender, the 1925 act facilitated modern conveyancing of real property and enshrined in law the concept of mortgage by statutory charge.

Chattels had been used for centuries as security for the repayment of loans, through the owner retaining use but transferring title to a creditor through a bill of sale until repayment; but it was not until the 1854 Bills of Sale Act, repealed by the 1878 Bills of Sale Act ("An Act to Consolidate and Amend the Law for Preventing Frauds upon Creditors by Secret Bills of Sale of Personal Chattels"), that there was any statute requiring registration of security interests at the High Court, so that interested third parties could be made aware of the existence of security (in the form of 'security bills of sale'). The 1854 and 1878 acts were largely introduced to prevent fraud, but they led to a much wider usage of security bills of sale. The 1882 Bills of Sale Act was enacted in response to parliamentary concerns about unsuspecting borrowers entering into complex documentation with unscrupulous creditors resulting in unfair consequences – an early example of an attempt at consumer protection.

The concept of the floating charge as a form of security interest over the assets of a company was not substantively considered by the courts until 1870;[2] and floating charges were not required to be registered with Companies House until the Companies Act 1900 (this act for the first time also subordinated floating charge holders to preferential creditors). One must look to the second half of the 19th century for substantial evidence of judges trying to rationalise, explain and organise the varying natures of security interests and their effects through enforcement and insolvency – no mean task in the face of centuries of common usage, but necessary in the context of an increasingly litigious corporate world, where there was a lot to be gained or lost through one legal interpretation over another, with rippling effects of a decision across markets far

---

2   *Panama, New Zealand and Australia Royal Mail Company* [1870] 5 Ch App 318.

and wide (including British dominions through Privy Council decisions by judicial committee).

Against this patchwork backdrop of custom, case law and statute, how can the student or practitioner easily identify how security may be implemented and what consequences ensue for the lender and borrower or other obligor? Other chapters of this book deal in detail with the types of collateral that are typically used to secure credit in secured finance transactions and the method by which security is taken. The following is an attempt to sift through some of the mire of complexity surrounding English law security and give context to the contemporary legal position, with somewhat more of a historical context than is typical of other commentaries in this field.

2.   Pledges and liens

Outside of the trade finance environment, the English law practitioner will rarely, if ever, come across the concept of an English law pledge. The term itself has more context in civil law jurisdictions, where it is often used as either a generic term for a security interest or a form of security not dissimilar to the 'charge' in England and Wales, as a security interest distinct from an 'assignment by way of security'. However, it is worth examining the history of the English pledge, as it gives some background to the development of the law in relation to security.

Described by Goode and Gullifer[3] as "the oldest security device", the common usage of the pledge as a form of bailment can be explained by its intrinsically simple and practical application. The word 'pledge' probably has its origin in old French (deriving from the Frankish Latin word *'plevium'* (*'pingus'* in Roman law), meaning a 'security' or 'assurance'.[4] It relies on the concept of dispossession of the asset for satisfaction of a debt until such time as the debt is discharged. Thus, without the need for complicated documentation or archaic formulation, a creditor could possess an asset with a right to title on default. Practically speaking, this device was normally used in relation to physical chattels (before the common use of documentary intangibles). Beyond the ability to possess and potentially sell the asset on enforcement, a pledgee could also use the asset for its own purposes and sell on its interest in the asset obtained through the pledge.

The ability to create a pledge over land is theoretically possible, but of somewhat academic interest, as land is conveyed and mortgaged in the modern world by way of following statute.[5] Goode and Gullifer espouse the historical

---

3   *Goode and Gullifer on Legal Problems of Credit and Security* (Sweet & Maxwell, Sixth Edition, 2017), Chapter 1, para 47.
4   Philip R Wood, *Comparative Law of Security Interests and Title Finance* (Sweet & Maxwell, Third Edition, 2019), Chapter 4, para 10.
5   Law of Property Act 1925.

use of the pledge to secure land, citing AWB Simpson's *A History of the Land Law*,[6] on the basis that land is reducible to possession.[7] Geoffrey Fuller[8] is of the contrary view that land cannot be pledged, as a pledge requires actual delivery of the asset in question. No doubt 12th century landowners or London merchants would not have hesitated to consider themselves the beneficiary of rights under English law when taking possession of property from a counterpart who owed money or service, and cared not whether what they were doing constituted a 'pledge' or 'mortgage', or what the implication of such outcome might have been.

Donald v Suckling[9] is often cited as the leading authority, with the most extensive commentary, on the law relating to pledges. The case related to debentures used as security for the payment at maturity of a bill, with such debentures being utilised by the pledgee to secure a debt incurred by it to a third party prior to satisfaction of the original payment obligation. The use of language in the case is interesting – the word 'pawn' (as in 'pawnbroking' – the ancient but still common method of lending money in return for pawning or pledging goods, frequently jewellery) and an even more archaic word, '*vadium*', are used interchangeably with 'pledge' and in distinction to a lien or mortgage – a lien only giving a personal right to detain; a mortgage passing the absolute property on condition broken; and a pawn (or pledge) not transferring title on default, but giving a right to sell. Such a defined right to sell something pledged to you in possession on non-satisfaction of the payment due comes down from both English common law and Roman civil law. The pledgee can retain unused or use (at its own risk – the relationship with the pledgor is fiduciary) the asset taken as pledge. This is something that a mere bailment by way of lien does not confer. The right to sell on default of payment is also a special right given to the pledgee, whereby the security can be utilised by way of sale to discharge the obligation. As regards the ability to re-pledge in this particular case, while such an arrangement might be a breach of contract, depending on the terms of the pledge arrangement, the use of the pledged property prior to repayment of the debt (provided that it is not used to secure a debt larger than that subject to the original pledge) did not in itself invalidate the pledge.

Courts and commentators agree that for a pledge to exist, there must be delivery of possession to the goods subject to the security. Let us examine what that can encompass. Actual delivery of goods by way of pledge is not typically compatible with modern forms of business. Over the years, the concept of constructive delivery became relied upon. As stated in *Paget's Law of Banking*,[10]

---

6   AWB Simpson, *A History of the Land Law* (Oxford University Press, 1986).
7   Goode and Gullifer (n 3), Chapter 1, para 48.
8   Geoffrey Fuller, *Corporate Borrowing Law and Practice* (Jordans, Fourth Edition, 2009), Chapter 6, para 8.
9   [1866] LR 1 QB 585.
10   John Odgers QC, *Paget's Law of Banking* (Butterworths LexisNexis, 15th Edition, 2018), Chapter 16, para 3.

"In older cases this is usually described as the handing over of the key to the warehouse where the goods are stored"; the more modern practice being an acknowledgement (or 'attornment') by the warehouse keeper constituting a method by which there is proof that it is holding the goods to the order of the pledgee. This must be seen in distinction to the delivery of a documentary undertaking to hold goods to the order of a creditor, which could not work as a pledge unless the goods were in fact being held to order – and even then that would probably not be a pledge by virtue of the Bills of Sale Acts. A more common remaining usage of the pledge under English law is in the context of the delivery of a bill of lading. A bill of lading conveys the ability of the holder to actually possess the shipment of goods upon the delivery of the undertaking of the carrier. Even bills of lading are slowly being consigned to history, through demand for more immediate methods of evidencing rights and title to goods in transit, typified by waybills and electronic confirmations – none of which can convincingly be used to replicate the legal form of a pledge.

What of the lien? The English finance lawyer engaged in transatlantic work will be familiar with the term 'lien' used by US attorneys as referring to almost any form of security over an asset. In English law, it is quite distinct from a mortgage, charge or pledge (as confirmed in *Donald v Suckling*). It shares characteristics of a pledge only with respect to the creditor's possession of the asset. It confers no right of sale or title and is generally exercised over goods already delivered for a purpose other than the creation of security. English law students will be familiar with *Green v All Motors Ltd (1917)*,[11] where a garage owner had the right to retain a repaired vehicle until payment was made – the classic example of the use of a lien operating under English common law. Unlike the English law pledge, such lien can be applied to a variety of practical situations, such as horses detained for payment of stabling costs. As detailed by Fuller,[12] liens can also be derived through equity – for example, a vendor's lien over land which would give a vendor which has not been paid the full purchase price the ability to apply to court for sale of the land, with the unpaid amounts being recovered from the sale; and by statute (eg, a master's maritime lien under the Merchant Shipping Act 1995 for liabilities and disbursements). Possessory liens are also created through contract, although there is somewhat conflicting case law and commentary on whether attaching a power of sale to a contractual lien creates a form of possessory pledge or charge. Such situations usually derive from the poor drafting of contracts, where if the intention was to confer a registrable charge or other form of security, it would have been entirely possible to do so through the use of the right words in the contract.

---

11   1 KB 625.
12   Fuller (n 7), Chapter 6, para 10.

3. Mortgages and charges

The terms 'mortgage' and 'charge' are used so frequently in modern law as to almost infer no difference between the two. This congruence of terminology has arisen both due to alternate usage in case law and among commentators and through statute – for example, the Law of Property Act 1925 enabling the establishment of a registrable, statutory charge through the creation of a mortgage. The two, however, are distinct in legal meaning, although often created in tandem. As referred to above, the mortgage was for centuries the predominant means under common law to provide a loan against the value of property. Essentially, the creditor could gain legal title to the property pending repayment of the debt due. Other than the pledge, this was the sole fashion under common law for the creation of security. Mortgages may be legal or equitable,[13] and can entail any form of asset, whether tangible or intangible – as, unlike for a pledge, possession is not a prerequisite for the creation of the security. So an agreement to appropriate the asset in order to redeem the debt due by the creation of a mortgage is supported in equity as a mortgage; but in such circumstances, the agreement to appropriate also constitutes a charge (the transfer of ownership constituting the mortgage), and thus every equitable mortgage (and for that matter, legal mortgage, by virtue of it being a right to obtain title) is also a charge.[14] Here we have one of the more unusual elements of English security law, in the automatic creation of a charge through the implementation of a mortgage; and hence the interchangeable terminology.

How about the ubiquitous charge – the most common and recognisable form of English law security? A 'charge' in its most basic form is an agreement by contract to make an asset available as security for repayment of a debt. It is an equitable form of security interest, unless coupled with a mortgage giving rights to title of the asset (or where created by statute – for example, by the Law of Property Act 1925). The chargee does not have to obtain possession of the asset concerned in order to benefit from the security; and the asset can change hands, but still be subject to the charge (other than when transferred to a *bona fide* purchaser of the legal interest for value without notice, such situation being mitigated against through registration – in relation to which see the subsequent chapters of this book). For at least the past 150 years, the charge has been the most effective and practical manner of securing the assets of companies in favour of creditors. It can be created simply by way of contractual agreement and at *de minimis* cost (solely registration fees).

One of the better descriptions of a 'charge' in English law is to be found in the often-cited Court of Appeal judgment of Lord Justice Atkin in *National Provincial and Union Bank of England v Charnley* (1924).[15] Atkin's judgments are

---

13 *Tailby v Official Receiver* [1888] 13 AC 523.
14 *Shea v Moore* [1894] IR 158.
15 KB 431.

some of the most erudite, concise and comprehensible in the history of the English courts. He went on, eight years later, to deliver the famous judgment in the case of a snail in a bottle of ginger beer (*Donahue v Stevenson* (1932)),[16] which established for the first time the concept of professional negligence in English common law. The 1924 case centred on how a charge is created over assets of a company and the effect of that security interest, where the defendant – in this case being a creditor of the company – had seized vehicles on property purportedly subject to a registered security interest (including a charge over chattels on such property, although not expressly registered as such) in favour of the bank, which claimed the assets from the defendant under its security. There are peripheral elements of this case that exemplify the pragmatism of English courts in interpreting circumstances to the favour of commercial judgment for creditors. For example, the failure to specify security with regard to chattels when the security instrument was registered (most likely to come under the head of "a floating charge on the undertaking or property of the company" within the registration form) was not deemed to impede the effectiveness of the charge contractually agreed. In addition, the conclusion that the motor vans constituted 'plant' and were thus caught by the charging clause – "fixed and moveable plant machinery implements and utensils now or hereafter fixed to or placed upon or used in or about the said hereditaments and premises" – stretches somewhat the natural meaning of 'plant', which in the world of manufacturing and industry more meaningfully describes large mechanical equipment such as boom lifts, pile drivers or compressors (although courts had previously decided that horses used in the business of a company were 'plant', again exemplifying their willingness to stretch a natural meaning to suit an argument). But we digress; the purpose of referencing this case is to see how the definition of a 'charge' developed in the 20th century courts. Atkin decided that there is no need for a formal definition of a 'charge' – supporting a view of English security interests existing and evolving organically. He did, however, explain that where:

> both parties evince an intention that property, existing or future, shall be made available as security for the payment of a debt, and that the creditor shall have a present right to have it made available, there is a charge, even though the present legal right which is contemplated can only be enforced at some future date, and though the creditor gets no legal right of property, either absolute or special, or any right to possession, but only gets a right to have the security made available by an order of the Court.

This is by way of contrast with an agreement between the parties that there should be a future right, by a licence or other form of agreement, to seize assets, which Atkin made clear did not create a charge. Atkin deemed there to have

---

been a floating equitable charge over the chattels (including the motor vans) and therefore a valid security in favour of the bank.

4. Charge over future property

One defining element of the English law charge is its ability to secure future existing assets. For a considerable time, the English courts had accepted the concept of security in the form of a charge being effective as against property that was substituted or that otherwise changed in nature over time. Thus we see the efficacy and pragmatism of English law, and in a manner which facilitated trade and commerce, with the provision of funding by financiers which were protected in case of the insolvency of a debtor. This is in stark contrast to the position in many civil law jurisdictions where, in order to attach a security interest to a future existing asset, it is necessary to update the original security document – be it a pledge or assignment by way of security – with precise details of the newly existing asset. Alternatively, in jurisdictions where laws have evolved somewhat to enable the creation of more encompassing security, at a bare minimum a very detailed and precise description is required in the securing document of the future assets encompassed in the scope of the security (eg, it is often not enough in jurisdictions such as France or Italy to refer to "all book debts of a company, now or in the future existing"; instead, one needs to attach the security to the book debts owing from a current identified customer of the pledgor, albeit coming into existence in the future).

The 1862 case of *Holroyd v Marshall*[17] provided the opportunity for the House of Lords to confirm the principle in English common law of the charge over future assets. The facts examined nicely encapsulate a Victorian tale of fortune gained and lost. A Mr James Taylor – a manufacturer of damask in Yorkshire, who reportedly became 'embarrassed' and had his effects sold at auction – became indebted to his former employers (the Holroyds), who bought the machinery used at the mill. Thus, it appears that the respondent had improved himself and taken on his own mill and the production of damask, but had fallen on hard times. Although no detail is given as to his relationship with the Holroyds, it is evident that the former employers decided to help Taylor continue to run his business notwithstanding his 'embarrassment', the debt being created by indenture in which the Holroyds agreed to sell the machinery back to Taylor. However, as Taylor had no money currently available for consideration, he was permitted to use the assets which were held by a third party in trust for Taylor paying the sum due to the Holroyds. On default, the agent had the power to sell, with the proceeds going to the Holroyds to satisfy their debt and the balance reverting to Taylor. Perhaps inevitably, Taylor defaulted and an attempt was made to sell all the machinery and for the Holroyds to thereby recover their debt.

---

17   10 HL Cas 191.

The measure of whether an equitable charge over the assets as a whole had been created by the agreement contained in the indenture was in question due to the fact that, prior to enforcement, Taylor had replaced certain items of the machinery through sale and the purchase of other items. The first case decision held in favour of the Holroyds recovering to full value, with this being overturned on appeal. Now before the House of Lords, there was the opportunity for counsel and the lords to peruse previous case law in support of an argument that an equitable charge or mortgage could exist notwithstanding the lack of existence of the relevant assets at the time of execution of the indenture. The lord chancellor (Lord Westbury) stated:

> *if a vendor or mortgagor agrees to sell or mortgage property, real or personal, of which he is not possessed at the time, and he receives consideration for the contract, and afterwards becomes possessed of property answering the description in the contract, there is no doubt that a Court of Equity would compel him to perform the contract, and that the contract would, in equity, transfer the beneficial interest to the mortgagee or purchaser immediately on the property being acquired.*

This was supported by Lord Chelmsford:

> *At law property, non-existing, but to be acquired at a future time, is not assignable; in equity it is so. At law (as we have seen), although a power is given in the deed of assignment to take possession of the after-acquired property, no interest is transferred, even as between the parties themselves, unless possession is actually taken; in equity it is not disputed that the moment the property comes into existence the agreement operates on it.*

The overwhelming proportion of preceding relevant case law supported the argument that in an agreement of this sort, the beneficial interest passes in equity to a mortgagee or purchaser immediately upon the acquisition of the property.

5.   The floating charge (and the fixed by comparison)

The concept of the equitable charge 'floating' over all assets of a company, or an entire asset type, is one largely particular to English law. Certain civil law jurisdictions have attempted to apply the concept of an all-encompassing security interest through a 'corporate pledge' over all assets of a company; but financiers rarely rely on such security, it being somewhat uncertain how one would enforce such an interest and with the more common certainty derived from specific security over defined assets in such countries.

Goode and Gullifer[18] draw an interesting comparison between the attitude of the US courts (prior to the introduction of the Uniform Commercial Code in 1892) and those of the English courts towards the concept of permitting the debtor to deal with its assets in an unfettered fashion, purportedly secured in

---

18   Goode and Gullifer (n 3), Chapter 4, para 2.

favour of a creditor. The US courts took the position that such a dealing with assets would effectively defraud a creditor which was unable to exert control over the assets in question. The English courts took a more pragmatic view. It would be highly impractical, for example, for a debtor to have to give notice and obtain consent to the sale of individual items of stock charged to a creditor:

> *Thus in contrast to American law, English law permitted a form of security in which attachment was contractually postponed. It was not a specific security with a licence to the debtor company to deal with the assets in the ordinary course of business, but an ambulatory security dependent for its attachment on the fulfilment of a condition precedent, namely the occurrence of a crystallising event.*[19]

This concept was enshrined in common law by virtue of the judgment in *Re Panama.*[20]

English law students are always directed to *Re Yorkshire Woolcombers Association Ltd* (1903)[21] for the iconic description of Lord Justice Romer (note a 'description', not a 'definition') of a 'floating charge'. Romer was a judge of the Victorian era, having also sat on the Royal Commission on South African Hospitals during the Boer War. He was to retire from the bench five years after this judgment – I wonder whether he realised how the following words would echo down the ages:

> *I certainly think that if a charge has the three characteristics that I am about to mention it is a floating charge. (1.) If it is a charge on a class of assets of a company present and future. (2.) If that class is one which in the ordinary course of the business of the company would be changing from time to time; and (3.) If you find that by the charge it is contemplated that, until some future step is taken by or on behalf of those interested in the charge, the company may carry on its business in the ordinary way so far as concerns the particular class of assets I am dealing with.*

Any prudent solicitor acting for a financier and drafting the security interests to be granted by the debtor would seek to include as much of the debtor's assets as possible in the category of 'fixed charges', subject to the commercial intent of the parties. One of the undoubted benefits of the floating charge is the ability of the debtor to continue operating its business in as undisturbed a manner as possible; but the fixed charge holder is the beneficiary of rights that trump those holding only a floating charge. I have not attempted in this chapter to explain all the law regarding the priority of security interests and preferential creditors; but it should be noted that a fixed charge, duly registered at Companies House, will – with a few notable exceptions (ie, a registrable mortgage not registered under the Land Registry Act 2002; a prior

---

19   *Ibid*, p 127.
20   *Panama, New Zealand and Australia Royal Mail Company* (1870).
21   2 Ch 284.

equitable charge defeated by a subsequent legal charge where the legal mortgagee or charge has no actual or constructive notice of the prior charge; loss of priority of a prior legal charge through misconduct in the form of estoppel, fraud or gross negligence or a prior equitable charge by inequitable conduct; and charges falling foul of the rule of priorities in *Dearle v Hall* (1828),[22] being determined by whomever gives notice first in writing to the debtor or other person prescribed by statute)[23] – take priority over subsequent charges, as well as unsecured preferential creditors (including contributions to pension schemes, wages and salary (up to £800 per person), holiday pay and Crown preference for source taxes – meaning value added tax, pay as you earn income tax, national insurance contributions and Construction Scheme Industry deductions).

How does English law determine whether a charge, purported to be fixed, takes effect as an enforceable fixed charge? The judgment of Romer above is a useful starting point – in other words, identifying your charge as not likely to be a floating charge when considering his description of such. If only it were that simple. Owing in large part to the importance placed by banks on obtaining a fixed charge over the book debts and bank accounts of companies, there has been a great deal of litigation before the English courts (and Privy Council) on the subject, heightened in the early 2000s by the decisions in *Agnew v Commissioner of Inland Revenue* (2001)[24] and *Spectrum Plus Ltd (In Liquidation), Re* (2005).[25] Such decisions can be used by analogy to examine the method by which one can determine whether there is enough control actually taken over any asset in order to conclude that a fixed charge exists. Subsequent chapters explore this principle in more detail; but it is interesting to observe that in the English law environment, practitioners yearn for further clarification of the position through court decisions and will continue to debate the efficacy of drafting in security documents, in combination with the actions of the parties to a transaction, in establishing a fixed charge.

No doubt over time, through new ways of doing business and the introduction of different types of collateral used to secure debt, we will see the need for further evolution in the application of security interests in secured finance transactions. If history is anything to go by, the English courts will be accommodating to such evolution and will have an extensive prior base of laws on security upon which to determine such new concepts.

---

22   3 Russ 1.
23   Timothy Parsons, *Lingard's Bank Security Documents* (Butterworths LexisNexis, Seventh Edition, 2019), Chapter 8, paras 22 to 25.
24   2 AC 710.
25   UKHL 41 at 102.

Receivables

Charles Thain
Mayer Brown

1. Introduction

A company's accounts receivable (also commonly known as 'receivables', 'debts' or 'book debts') often form a large part of its current assets.

In order to better service its working capital needs, a company may look to monetise its accounts receivable by:

- selling them to a financier at a discount (known as 'factoring' or 'invoice discounting'); or
- borrowing against the value of its accounts receivable in exchange for granting security over them (known as 'asset-based lending' or 'borrowing base lending').[1]

Both forms of financing remain very popular and continue to grow in the UK market and further afield.

This chapter looks at the main legal principles applicable to taking security over accounts receivable.

For ease of reference, in the remainder of this chapter we will use the term 'receivables'. For the avoidance of doubt, this chapter does cover security granted by individuals (including sole traders) or partnerships.

2. What is a 'receivable'?

A 'receivable' is classified as a chose or thing in action, where the expression 'chose' or 'thing in action' is used to describe all personal rights of property which can only be claimed or enforced by action, and not by taking physical possession.[2]

In the case of a receivable, the chose or thing in action is the right to receive payment of a sum of money from the account debtor in consideration of goods supplied or services rendered. As a result of being a chose in action, a receivable is not a physical or tangible asset, but is instead an intangible asset.

---

1   These products are not limited to funding receivables and often comprise other fundable asset classes, such as inventory (including commodities), plant and machinery and real estate.
2   *Torkington v Magee* [1902] 2 KB 427 at 430.

A receivable can be seen as existing in two phases: first, the receivable; and second, once paid by the account debtor, its collected proceeds. However, for the avoidance of doubt, a receivable ceases to exist once paid, when all that remains are its proceeds. There is a vast amount of academic discussion on whether security over an asset automatically attaches to its proceeds. However, in practice, a well-drafted security agreement which expresses to take security over receivables should always also express to take security over the proceeds of the receivable. As such, we will not dwell on this matter; but we will revisit the proceeds of a receivable when discussing fixed versus floating charges over receivables later in this chapter.

A receivable rarely exists in isolation. There is typically a bundle of other rights or assets that may be related to a receivable over which a financier may also want to take security. These related rights may include (without limitation):

- documents of title in respect of the sold goods which have given rise to the receivable;
- rights arising from the contract with the account debtor, such as the benefit of indemnities granted by the account debtor, late payment interest or retention of title rights;
- guarantees and other security interests granted by the account debtor or its parent or an affiliate; and
- rights under a credit insurance policy.

In the remainder of this chapter, we will refer to these rights as 'related rights'.

Receivables arising from negotiable instruments such as bills of exchange and promissory notes are outside of the scope of this chapter, due to their tangible nature and the fact that the transfer of a negotiable instrument is effected through negotiation[3] and delivery[4] of the negotiable instrument, rather than through assignment.

3. What security is available?

Under English law, there are two options for taking security over a receivable: a mortgage or a charge. This section discusses the differences between the two in the context of security over receivables; but see also the "English law security interests" chapter for a more general discussion of mortgages and charges.

3.1 Mortgage

A 'mortgage' is the transfer by one person (the mortgagor) of the ownership of an asset or an interest in an asset by way of security to another person (the

---

3   Section 31 of the Bills of Exchange Act 1882.
4   *Ibid*, Sections 2 and s 21.

mortgagee) to secure an obligation owed to the mortgagee, subject to the condition that the mortgagee will transfer back the asset or the interest in the asset to the mortgagor upon the obligation being satisfied (this right of the mortgagor to redeem the asset or the interest in the asset is called the 'equity of redemption'). A mortgage may be effected by an assignment or by novation. A mortgage by assignment, as opposed to by novation, is by far the more common method for taking security over receivables in finance transactions. Accordingly, mortgages by novation are outside of the scope of this chapter.

Under English law, an assignment by way of security may be legal or equitable. The primary benefit of a legal assignment by way of security of a receivable is that the mortgagee has priority over subsequent interests obtained in the receivable; whereas an equitable assignment by way of security can be overreached by a third party which acquires a legal interest in the receivable as a *bona fide* purchaser for value and without notice of the equitable assignment. However, the security registration regime under the Companies Act 2006 has removed some of those risks for an equitable assignee, due to actual and/or constructive notice being deemed given to some third parties as a result of registration.[5]

Below we discuss the requirements for both a legal assignment and an equitable assignment of a receivable. These principles apply equally to assignments by way of security and assignments for outright transfers of a receivable. An analysis of the distinction between a security interest over, and an outright transfer of, a receivable is beyond the scope of this chapter.

(a)   *Legal assignment*

A 'legal assignment of a receivable' is an assignment which satisfies the requirements of Section 136 of the Law of Property Act 1925, and will vest in the assignee:

- the legal right to the receivable;
- all legal and other remedies for the receivable (including taking legal proceedings against the account debtor in its own name); and
- the power to give a good discharge for the receivable.

To satisfy Section 136:

- the receivable must be a legal chose or thing in action, as opposed to an equitable one – therefore, for example:
  - the receivable must be a present receivable (not a future receivable); and
  - the assignment can only be in respect of the whole of the receivable (not part only);[6] and

---

5   See section 5.1 for further discussion on the effect of registrations under the Companies Act 2006.
6   *Forster v Baker* [1910] 2 KB 636.

- the assignment of the receivable must:
  - be absolute (ie, without condition and in respect of the whole receivable);
  - be in writing under the hand of the assignor;
  - not purport to be by way of charge only; and
  - be notified to the account debtor in writing.

(b) *Equitable assignment*

The only requirement for the creation of an equitable assignment in respect of a receivable is the clear intention of the assignor to transfer the benefit of the receivable to the assignee.[7] Accordingly, an equitable assignment:

- may be in writing or made orally;
- may apply to equitable choses or things in action (eg, future receivables), as well as legal ones; and
- may relate to the whole or a part of a receivable.[8]

Further, the assignment need not be notified to the account debtor in order for it to be effective as between the assignor and assignee.

In the case of an assignment of future receivables, the assignment does not take effect at the point in time the assignor agrees to the assignment, because it is not possible to assign something that does not exist. Instead, the assignment is characterised as an agreement to assign the future receivable and – based on the maxim that equity looks on that as done which ought to be done – equity gives effect to the assignment immediately upon the future receivable coming into existence. It does not matter that the amount of the receivable is not known or ascertainable at the date the assignor agrees to assign it,[9] provided that the future receivable is capable of being identified.[10] Accordingly, an assignment which purports to assign, for example, either all present and future receivables of the assignor or all present and future receivables arising from a specific contract of the assignor will be valid in respect of the future receivables, because the future receivables are identifiable and capable of being ascertained once they come into existence.

Unlike a legal assignment, if the assignee of an equitable assignment over a receivable wishes to take legal proceedings against the account debtor, it will need to add the assignor (as owner of the legal title) to the legal proceedings. However, this is simply a procedural step (albeit an important one), and therefore can be easily complied with at the necessary time.

---

7   See Marcus Smith and Nico Leslie, *The Law of Assignment* (Oxford University Press, 3rd edition, 2018), Chapter 13, paras 90-94 for a discussion on whether consideration is required.
8   *Brice v Bannister* (1878) 3 QBD 569.
9   *Crowfoot v Gurney* (1832) 9 Bing 372 at 376.
10   *Tailby v Official Receiver* (1888) 13 App Cas 523 at 543.

3.2   Charge

Conceptually, a charge is very different from a mortgage. It does not involve the transfer of ownership of the asset, but instead creates an encumbrance on the asset. It creates a new interest in respect of the asset and it exists only in equity.

Due to its equitable nature, a charge can be overreached by a third party which acquires a legal interest in the asset as a *bona fide* purchaser for value and without notice of the charge. However, the security registration regime under the Companies Act 2006 has removed some of those risks for a chargee due to actual and/or constructive notice being deemed given to some third parties as a result of registration.[11]

Nevertheless, from a practical perspective, there is little difference between an assignment by way of security and a charge over a receivable, because the chargee enforces its security by serving notice on the account debtor and redirecting payment in the same way as an assignee. However, similarly to an equitable assignment, if the chargee of a receivable wishes to take legal proceedings against the account debtor, it will need to add the chargor (as owner of the legal title) to the legal proceedings; although as mentioned above, this is simply a procedural step (albeit an important one), and therefore can be easily complied with at the necessary time.

4.   Floating or fixed charge

Under English law, when taking security over receivables, it is important to understand the distinction between a fixed charge and a floating charge. The main reason for needing to understand such distinction is that in case of the insolvency of the chargor, a floating charge holder ranks – absent any contrary arrangements or restrictions on the chargor known to a subsequent security holder – behind both a fixed charge holder in respect of the same assets, certain preferential creditors and the prescribed part.[12] This becomes even more significant where the financier has provided a loan to the chargor based solely on the value of its receivables (eg, a borrowing base product). If, in case of the insolvency of the chargor, the financier will not be entitled to receive the full value of the secured receivables because there are preferential claims, the financier will be unable to advance the same level of credit to the chargor. Accordingly, in order to receive the best possible outcome upon the insolvency of the chargor and to be able to provide to the chargor the amount of credit it desires, a financier of receivables will often seek to obtain a fixed charge over the receivables.

Although most English literature and cases use the terms 'fixed charge' and 'floating charge', we think it is reasonable to assume that in the context of

---

11   See section 5.1 for further discussion on the effect of registrations under the Companies Act 2006.
12   Sections 175, 176ZA, 176ZB and 176A of the Insolvency Act 1986.

receivables, the principles of fixed and floating charges extend equally to equitable assignments by way of security; this was indicated in *obiter dictum* in *National Westminster Bank plc v Spectrum Plus Limited*.[13] Accordingly, in this section, references to 'fixed' and 'floating' charges should be considered equally in respect of an equitable assignment by way of security.

This section discusses the differences between a fixed and floating charge in the context of security over receivables, but see also the "English law security interests" chapter for a more general discussion on this topic.

4.1 Floating charge

There is no specific definition of a 'floating charge', although there is a volume of case law and literature considering its characteristics. In brief (as this is discussed in detail in the "English law security interests" chapter), it is generally accepted that a 'floating charge' is a charge taken over a class of assets or all assets of the chargor where the chargor remains free to deal with those assets in the ordinary course of its business until the occurrence of certain crystallisation events, following which the charge will crystallise on the assets and the company will no longer be able to deal with them.

It is very easy to take a floating charge over receivables and therefore, the remainder of this section will focus on the requirements for obtaining a fixed charge over receivables.

4.2 Fixed charge

It is well established that:

- in order to obtain a fixed charge over an asset, control of the asset must not be left with the company; and
- it is possible to create a fixed charge over present and future receivables.[14]

What has not always been clear, however, is what amounts to 'control' for the purposes of obtaining a fixed charge over a receivable.

It was previously understood from *Siebe Gorman*[15] that 'control' for the purposes of a fixed charge over receivables could be demonstrated where:

- the company was contractually prohibited from granting security over, or disposing of, its receivables; and
- the company was required to ensure that the proceeds of the receivables were paid into a bank account held with the security holder, from which the company could freely withdraw collections.

---

13   [2005] UKHL 41 at 102.
14   *Tailby v Official Receiver* (1888) 13 App Cas 523 and affirmed in *Spectrum Plus Ltd (In Liquidation), Re* [2005] UKHL 41.
15   *Siebe Gorman & Co Ltd v Barclays Bank Ltd* [1979] 2 Lloyd's Rep 142.

Following *Re New Bullas*,[16] it was also understood that a fixed charge could be taken over a receivable and a floating charge could be taken over its proceeds.

However, *Re New Bullas* was overruled by *Agnew*,[17] where the court made clear that in order to obtain a fixed charge over a receivable, the security holder must control both the receivable and its proceeds; and *Siebe Gorman* was overruled by *Spectrum Plus*,[18] where the court clarified that a charge over receivables could not be a fixed charge if the company was able to use the collected proceeds, because an ability to deal with the proceeds would be an ability to remove them from the charge, which is a characteristic of a floating charge.

Lord Hope in *Spectrum Plus*[19] went on to clarify that where receivables are being collected into a bank account of the company, in order to evidence control, the bank account must be blocked; and Lord Millet[20] also pointed out that it was not enough to provide in the security agreement for the bank account to be blocked if it was not in fact operated as a blocked account. Lord Walker[21] also made clear that it was necessary to exercise the necessary control in respect of a receivable and its proceeds from the commencement of the charge, and it was not possible to take control from a later date.

Noting the above cases, to obtain a fixed charge over receivables, a security holder will thus typically require:

- the company to grant a fixed charge over its receivables and their proceeds in favour of the security holder;
- the company to contractually agree not to dispose of, or deal with, the receivables or their proceeds without the consent of the security holder;
- the company to direct its account debtors to settle the receivables by making payment to a specified bank account which is also expressed to be subject to a fixed charge in favour of the security holder; and
- the company and the account bank to enter into a bank account control agreement with the security holder, pursuant to which the account bank agrees to not allow any withdrawals from the bank account unless consented to by the security holder.

What is not so clear from *Spectrum Plus*, however, is the extent to which a security holder can provide advance or standing consents to the account bank for the company to withdraw collected proceeds from the blocked account from time to time. Based on Lord Walker's statement that "so long as the charge remains unredeemed, the assets can be released from the charge only with the

---

16   *New Bullas Trading Ltd, Re* [1993] 12 WLUK 201.
17   *Inland Revenue Commissioner v Agnew, Agnew v Inland Revenue Commissioner* [2001] UKPC 28.
18   *Spectrum Plus Ltd (In Liquidation), Re* [2005] UKHL 41.
19   *Ibid* at 54.
20   *Ibid* at 140.
21   *Ibid* at 146.

active concurrence of the charge",[22] it is clear that a security holder can definitely provide consent on a case-by-case basis; but it is not necessarily clear whether, for example, an advance or standing consent which is periodically reviewed by the security holder would suffice to satisfy the strict control requirements with respect to collected proceeds. Accordingly, we have a good idea, but not a definitive position, as to what amounts to 'control' in order to achieve a fixed charge over a receivable, and there will likely be future cases which will have to consider this question again.

As a final note on fixed charges, certain case law indicates that an asset which is expressed to be subject to a fixed charge may be recharacterised as a floating charge asset if that asset is grouped into a charging provision which also covers assets that are subsequently characterised as floating charge assets.[23] We mention this because, as discussed in section 2, a receivable rarely exists in isolation and is typically supported by various related rights; and it is common for those related rights to be referred to in a security agreement within the definition of the 'receivable'. As it is usual to draft related rights broadly, and it may be hard for a security holder to evidence the necessary control of each related right, a common approach (when trying to create a fixed charge over receivables) is to charge the related rights separately from the receivable, in order to avoid any risk of the fixed charge over the receivable being recharacterised as a floating charge due to insufficient control of all related rights.

5. Perfection and priority

'Perfection' is the term used to describe the process of making the mortgage or charge enforceable against persons other than the mortgagor or chargor. However, particularly in respect of security over receivables, 'perfection' does not necessarily equate to 'priority' (albeit that the effects of a perfection step may be determinative in concluding whether a person has priority).

For ease, in this section we will refer to both a mortgagee and a chargee as a 'security holder'.

5.1 Registration at Companies House

To perfect a mortgage or charge over receivables so that it is enforceable if the

---

22   *Ibid* at 138.

23   First instance decision in *Re ASRS Establishment Limited (in administrative receivership)* [1999] 11 WLUK 298, where Justice Park stated: "It is all or nothing. Either it creates a fixed charge over all the other debts and claims, or it creates a fixed charge over none of them"; and *Beam Tube Products Ltd, Fanshawe v Amar Industries Ltd* [2006] EWHC 486 (Ch), 33, where Justice Blackburne stated:

      In my view it is all or nothing. Either the clause creates a fixed charge over all of the assets to which it refers or it creates a fixed charge over none of them. I do not consider that the clause is to be construed as a fixed charge over some of the assets but only a floating charge over the others. I consider that this construction is consistent with the approach taken by Lord Hoffmann in Smith (Administrator of Cosslett (Contractors) Ltd) v Bridgend County Borough Council *[2001] 1 AC 336 at 353 paragraph 44.*

company becomes insolvent, the mortgage or charge must be delivered for registration to the registrar at Companies House before the end of the period allowed for delivery[24] (which, at the time of writing, is 21 days beginning the day after the date of creation of the mortgage or charge).[25]

Registration of a mortgage or charge at Companies House has two effects:

- It makes the mortgage or charge enforceable against a liquidator, administrator or creditor of the company[26] if the company becomes insolvent; and

- It acts as actual notice of the mortgage or charge to any person that searches the charges register of the company (which will be the case for most prudent financiers proposing to provide credit to the company); and it may also act as constructive notice to such persons that could be reasonably expected to search the charges register (eg, financiers), irrespective of whether they have actually searched the register.[27] For the avoidance of doubt, the account debtor of a receivable would not be classified as someone that could be reasonably expected to search the register.[28]

As mentioned above, registration does not necessarily mean that the security holder will have priority over persons that may also have an interest in the receivable which is the subject of the security; but the effects of the points above are taken into account when determining who has priority.[29]

5.2   Notice to the account debtor

To perfect a mortgage or charge over a receivable against the account debtor, a notice of the security must be delivered to the account debtor. To the extent that such notice is being delivered to satisfy the requirements for a legal assignment, such notice must be in writing.[30] For the purposes of an equitable assignment or charge, there is no such requirement for the notice to be in writing; but a prudent security holder should seek to do so for evidential purposes.

The delivery of a notice of the security to the account debtor has the following effects:

- The account debtor can discharge the receivable only by making payment to the security holder or to its order.

- Certain equities (eg, certain rights of set-off) as between the assignor/chargor and the account debtor which arise after the date of

---

24   Section 859A(2) of the Companies Act 2006.
25   *Ibid*, Section 859A(4).
26   *Ibid*, Section 859H.
27   See Roy Goode and Louise Gullifer, *Goode and Gullifer on Legal Problems of Credit and Security* (Sweet & Maxwell, 6th edition, 2017), Chapter 2, para 31 for further insight on constructive notice.
28   See section 5.2 in respect of perfection against the account debtor.
29   See section 5.3.
30   Section 136 of the Law of Property Act 1925.

receipt of the notice will not be enforceable against the security holder.[31] As a reminder, the security holder will take subject to prior existing equities.[32]

- The security holder may obtain priority to other persons with an interest in the receivable.[33]

To the extent that a security holder wants to take security over a receivable free from all equities *vis-à-vis* the account debtor, the security holder will need to seek a waiver of those rights from the account debtor.

5.3   Priority

Under English law, the priority of competing interests in assets is a relatively complex area of law. In this section, we will briefly set out the main rules on priority relating to security over receivables.

(a)   *Security holder versus prior equities*

It is a well-established principle of law[34] that a security holder cannot obtain better title to a receivable than the title the company has. As such, a security holder will take subject to any prior equities affecting the receivable.

(b)   *Registered security holder versus unregistered security holder*

As between a registered security holder and an unregistered security holder, the registered security holder will take priority over the unregistered security holder.

(c)   *Registered security holder versus registered security holder*

As between two registered security holders, the security holder whose security interest was created first in time will take priority over the other, unless those security holders agree otherwise.

(d)   *Registered security holder versus an outright assignee*

The rules of priority set down in *Dearle v Hall*[35] state that where a receivable is assigned to more than one assignee, the assignee that gives notice to the account debtor first in time will take priority over the other assignee(s), provided that assignee did not have any actual or constructive notice of a previous assignment at the time it received its assignment. The rule in *Dearle v Hall* applies equally to a charge, save that in this case, the analysis should be viewed in the context of whether the outright assignee takes subject to the charge.

---

31   For a detailed analysis on equities that may affect a security holder, see Smith and Leslie (n 7), Chapter 26, Section D.
32   See section 5.3.
33   See section 5.3.
34   See for, example, *Mangles v Dixon* (1852) 3 HLC 702.
35   (1828) 3 Russ 1.

Applying *Dearle v Hall*:

- Prior outright assignee: A registered security holder will take priority over a prior outright assignee if the registered security holder delivers notice to the account debtor first and did not have knowledge of that prior outright assignee; and, vice versa, the prior outright assignee will take priority to the subsequent registered security holder if the outright assignee delivers notice to the account debtor first.
- Subsequent outright assignee: Irrespective of whether a registered security holder of a receivable has notified the account debtor of its security, the registered security holder may have priority over a subsequent outright assignee because the registration of its security acts as:
  - actual notice to the outright assignee if that assignee has searched the company's charges register; and
  - constructive notice if the assignee is considered to be a person that could be reasonably expected to search the charges register (which is believed to be the case for most sophisticated persons acquiring receivables from a company).

To the extent that it is determined that registration of the registered security does not constitute notice to the outright assignee (and it did not have any actual or constructive notice via any other means), priority will be determined by whoever delivers notice to the account debtor first. However, a floating charge holder will not take priority over a subsequent outright assignee by serving notice first, because in that case the security holder, by virtue of the floating charge, has consented to the disposal of the receivable free from its security interest.

6. Prohibitions on assignment

A prohibition or ban on assignment is a provision in a contract between a company and its account debtor restricting one or both parties from assigning (whether by way of outright transfer or by way of security) certain or all of their rights (including any receivables) under that contract or any other contracts between the company and its account debtor.

While there is considerable academic debate on what the effect of a prohibition on assignment provision should be under English law, the current English law position is that if a contract contains a clearly drafted prohibition on assignment, an assignment (including by way of security) in breach of such prohibition will be ineffective to vest the receivable in the assignee,[36] unless the Business Contract Terms (Assignment of Receivables) Regulations 2018 apply.[37]

---

36   *Helstan Securities Ltd v Hertfordshire County Council* [1978] 3 All ER 262; *Linden Gardens Trust Ltd v Lenesta Sludge Disposal Ltd/St Martins Property Corp Ltd v Sir Robert McAlpine & Sons Limited* [1994] 1 AC 85.
37   See section 6.4.

To the extent that a prohibition on assignment is effective, the account debtor may disregard any notice of assignment given to it by an assignee and continue to make payment to the company to obtain good discharge of the receivable; and its rights of set-off (if any) will also be unaffected.[38]

At first glance, this appears to be extremely detrimental to any security holder that takes an assignment by way of security over receivables. However, there is support for the view that a purported assignment in breach of a prohibition on assignment will still have contractual effects as between the assignor and assignee;[39] and further, that it does not necessarily restrict the company from charging the receivables or dealing with the proceeds of the receivables. This is examined further in the remainder of this section.

If a contract is silent on whether the rights arising from such contact can be assigned, other than in respect of personal contracts (ie, contracts where the rights are so personal to the parties that the rights are not capable of being assigned), a receivable arising from that contact may be assigned without requiring the consent of the account debtor and without condition.

In the remainder of this section, we will consider whether a prohibition on the assignment of a receivable may have wider effect, and also the effect of the Business Contract Terms (Assignment of Receivables) Regulations 2018.

6.1 The proceeds of a receivable

Although not definitive from case law,[40] academics such as Goode and Gullifer[41] contend that a person should be able to assign the proceeds of a receivable notwithstanding any provision which restricts the assignor from assigning the receivable or its proceeds, because such restriction is contrary to public policy as a restraint on alienation (ie, the right of a person to freely deal with and transfer its own property). Once a receivable has been paid by the account debtor, why should the account debtor be able to restrict how the creditor deals with those proceeds? Accordingly, an assignment by way of security over the proceeds of a receivable should be valid irrespective of a prohibition on assignment of the receivable or its proceeds. Therefore, where a security holder has taken security over the bank accounts of the company in addition to its receivables (which would be the case where trying to take fixed security anyway), the effect of a

---

38   *Helstan Securities Ltd v Hertfordshire County Council Ltd* [1978] 3 All ER 262.
39   In *Linden Gardens*, Lord Browne-Wilkinson stated that "in the absence of the clearest words [a prohibition on assignment] cannot operate to invalidate the contract as between the assignor and the assignee and even then it may be ineffective on the grounds of public policy"; Smith and Leslie (n 7), Chapter 25, para 21, citing with approval a comment in an article by Allcock (1983) to the effect that the assignee should have no difficulty in establishing that the assignor impliedly warranted its power to assign.
40   In *Linden Gardens*, Lord Browne-Wilkinson expressed no final view on whether a prohibition on assignment which purported to extend to the proceeds of a receivable was contrary to public policy.
41   Goode and Gullifer, (n 27), Chapter 3, para 40; Roy Goode, *Contractual Prohibitions against Assignment*, [2009] LMCLQ 300-318.

prohibition on assignment is reduced (although, as mentioned above, the account debtor would continue to be able to enforce all rights of set-off and other equities that it possesses).

Furthermore, the ability to declare a trust of the proceeds of a receivable notwithstanding any prohibition on the assignment of the receivable seems to be well settled. In *Re Turcan*,[42] the Court of Appeal held that the beneficiary of an insurance policy, which was expressed to be non-assignable, could validly make a declaration of trust of the proceeds. Accordingly, it is common for security holders to require their security agreements to contain a declaration of trust in respect of the proceeds of receivables which are subject to a prohibition on assignment.

6.2 Declaration of trust of the benefit of a receivable

With regard to a trust of the benefit of a receivable, in *Don King Productions Inc v Warren*,[43] Justice Lightman held that a provision that prohibits an assignment "is prima facie restricted to assignments of the benefit of the obligation and does not extend to declarations of trust of the benefit", quoting the words of Lord Browne-Wilkinson from *Linden Gardens* that "a prohibition on assignment normally only invalidates the assignment as against the other party to the contract so as to prevent the transfer of the chose in action: in the absence of the clearest words it cannot operate to invalidate the contract as between the assignor and assignee and even then it may be ineffective on the grounds of public policy". Accordingly, a prohibition on the assignment of a receivable should not restrict a company from declaring a trust of the benefit of the receivable to a third party. This view was supported in *Barbados Trust Co Ltd v Bank of Zambia*[44] and is also supported by academics such as Goode and McKendrick.[45] As such, it is common for security holders to require their security agreements to contain a declaration of trust in respect of the benefit of receivables which are subject to a prohibition on assignment. However, Smith and Leslie[46] consider that Lightman's analysis is analytically flawed, on the basis that such a trust would be identical in all respects to an equitable assignment of a legal chose in action; they therefore question whether an assignor should be able to circumvent a prohibition on assignment by describing the assignment as a declaration of trust.

For the avoidance of doubt, it is generally accepted that a provision which expressly prohibits a trust being declared in respect of a receivable will be effective to restrict the beneficial interest of the receivable vesting in the beneficiary of the trust.

42   (1888) 40 Ch D 5.
43   [2000] Ch 291.
44   [2007] EWCA Civ 148.
45   Roy Goode and Ewan McKendrick, *Goode and McKendrick on Commercial Law* (LexisNexis Butterworths, 6th edition, 2020), Chapter 29, para 41.
46   Smith and Leslie (n 7), Chapter 25, para 41.

6.3 Charge over a receivable

A contract that prohibits the assignment of a receivable will not prohibit the creation of a charge over the receivable.[47] Accordingly, it is common for a well-drafted security agreement to contain an assignment of the receivables and also a charge over the receivables to the extent that the assignment is ineffective. As there are minimal practical differences from a security holder's perspective between a fixed charge and an equitable assignment by way of security, certain security holders may consider dispensing with the assignment altogether.

For the avoidance of doubt, it is generally accepted that a provision which expressly prohibits a charge being granted over a receivable will be effective to render such charge ineffective.

6.4 Business Contract Terms (Assignment of Receivables) Regulations 2018

On 24 November 2018, the Business Contract Terms (Assignment of Receivables) Regulations 2018 came into force. They are intended to make it easier for small and medium-sized enterprises to access receivables-based finance by making ineffective any prohibitions, conditions and restrictions on the assignment of receivables arising under a contract. Consequently, not only do the regulations render a prohibition on assignment provision ineffective, but their scope also extends to related clauses, such as confidentiality clauses, to the extent that such clauses prevent the assignment of a receivable.

However, a security holder will be unable to rely on the regulations being applicable without further diligence at the time the receivable is assigned. This is because the regulations do not apply:

- to contracts entered into before 31 December 2018;
- if the supplier is a large enterprise (assessed, in the case of companies, on turnover, balance sheet and/or number of employees by reference to the company's most recent annual accounts), or a member of a large group, at the time of assignment;
- if the supplier is a special purpose vehicle with the primary purpose of holding assets (other than trading stock) or financing commercial transactions, which in either case involves it incurring a liability under an agreement of £10 million or more at the time of assignment; or
- to a contract where none of the parties to the contract have entered into it in the course of carrying on a business in the United Kingdom.

---

47   However, Goode and Gullifer (n 27; Chapter 3, para 45) flag that many charges are often drafted in such a way that they are likely to be construed as equitable mortgages, so care should be taken in this regard when drafting a security agreement if the purpose of the charge is to avoid the effect of a prohibition on assignment.

Inventory

Simon Fisher
Mayer Brown

1. Introduction

Many companies engaged in trading or manufacturing will maintain a level of inventory in order to run their businesses. While these assets will ultimately be used in generating revenue, they can also be used as collateral for financing transactions – either as part of a wider security package or as a more tailored inventory or 'asset-based' lending (ABL) financing arrangement. While each individual item may have little value on its own, together the relevant assets can be a significant source of value for a financier looking to advance credit.

In this chapter, we will examine the methods of taking security over inventory and certain practical concerns and issues that may arise in connection with such security. In this respect, the chapter deals with inventory in a commercial context (where the borrower is a corporate entity). In England and Wales, the position as regards security granted by individuals over assets is primarily governed by the Bills of Sale Acts[1] and is beyond the scope of this chapter.

1.1 Nature of inventory

'Inventory' is a category of chattels (defined in Section 4 of the Bills of Sale Act 1878 as "goods, furniture, and other articles capable of complete transfer by delivery"). More commonly, 'inventory' is the stock of a company which is used in its business.

Trade inventory can be broken down into three distinct categories:
- raw materials;
- work in progress; and
- finished goods.

Each category has distinct challenges when taking security. While raw materials will have a lower value, they may well have some resale value to another manufacturer in the same or a similar line of business. Finished goods, on the other hand, will be of higher value, but may be limited in the

---

1   The Bills of Sale Act 1878 and the Bills of Sale Act (1878) Amendment Act 1882.

opportunities for sale – for example, where items are branded or are manufactured to a particular customer's specifications.

1.2 Challenges with taking security over inventory

The purpose of this chapter is to examine some of the issues relating to taking security over inventory – both the forms of security that it is possible to take over inventory and some of the practical issues connected with inventory as an asset class.

The key considerations when looking to take, maintain and subsequently enforce security over inventory are as follows.

(a) *Revolving nature*

The borrower will invariably require access to the assets in order to run its day-to-day business. As such, the assets will invariably comprise a revolving pool, the make-up of which will change on a daily basis. This will make obtaining control or even keeping track of assets for the purpose of taking and ultimately enforcing security more difficult.

(b) *Location, location, location*

Consideration should be given to the location of the assets in the context of the form of security that can be taken, as well as the context of access upon enforcement.

In particular, where goods are stored on leased/other third-party premises, consent from the landlord may be required to access the premises upon an enforcement and consideration may need to be given to dealing with any liens the landlord may have.

(c) *Easily movable*

By its very nature, inventory is a movable asset. As such, the ability to locate the assets on an enforcement becomes important, as otherwise there will be a risk that the items over which the financier has security cannot be recovered.

Goods in transit, particularly if shipped internationally, pose a particular risk – not only in relation to the ability to locate and gain possession of, but also in relation to the form of security to be taken over, the assets and relevant shipping documentation.

(d) *Commingling*

Where the assets in question are not distinctive and may be hard to tell apart from other similar assets (eg, raw materials), there will be concerns surrounding the commingling of inventory subject to security with unsecured inventory and/or inventory of a third party.

2. Nature of security over inventory

2.1 Pledge versus charge versus mortgage

There are broadly three types of security it is possible to take over inventory:

- a charge;
- a mortgage; and
- a pledge.

Of these types of security, the charge is by far the most common in practice, save over certain specialised types of assets.[2]

2.2 Form of security – inventory

The most common form of security to take over inventory is a charge.

While it is theoretically possible for a financier to obtain fixed security over inventory, that would require contractually restricting the borrower from utilising and/or disposing of its inventory without the consent of the financier (and that the borrower complies with those restrictions in practice).

Due to the revolving nature of inventory in most businesses and a borrower's requirement to deal with its inventory on a daily basis, such control is likely to be impractical, not to mention burdensome for the financier to operate (either directly or through an appointed agent (sometimes the warehouse owner/operator)). The decision in *Re Beam Tube Products Ltd*[3] made it clear that the provisions in relation to control required for obtaining a fixed charge[4] apply equally to the questions of fixed versus floating security over assets. Furthermore, the House of Lords has held, in the context of plant and machinery, that the ability to replace such assets in the ordinary course of business would lead to that charge being floating, not fixed.[5] As such, a financier will typically only be able to obtain floating security over inventory in England.

This brings with it a number of considerations, not least to the value of any recoveries. Floating charge security ranks further down the waterfall on insolvency and behind a number of priority creditors; so – especially where the borrower is a trading company (as is likely where it has significant inventory to make a financing against the value of inventory worthwhile) – its recoveries are likely to rank behind the following:

- security holders with fixed charges over the same assets – this is unlikely

---

2   For more information on the different types of security available under English law, see the "English law security interests" chapter.

3   [2006] EWHC 486 (Ch) – in the context of plant and machinery.

4   As per the decisions in numerous cases in relation to receivables – in particular, *Agnew v Commissioner of Inland Revenue [2001] 2 AC 710 and Re Spectrum Plus Ltd* [2005] 2 AC 680.

5   *Re Cosselett (Contractors) Ltd* [2001] UKHL 58 and also consistent with the decisions in *Agnew* and *Spectrum Plus*.

in practice, owing to the difficulties involved in obtaining fixed charges over inventory; and the existence of negative pledge provisions (in order to prevent there being any such competing security) or priority/intercreditor arrangements with competing creditors (which would at least regulate the position as between the financiers) would limit the risk of there being such priority creditors and/or them being able to recover ahead of the financier's claim;

- moratorium debts and priority pre-moratorium debts;[6]
- costs and expenses of the insolvency process[7] – these would include any remuneration of administrators/liquidators and payment of disbursements and expenses properly incurred by them in performing their functions;
- preferential creditors[8] – as at the date of writing, these comprise:
  - employees' claims for arrears of wages (subject to a maximum of £800 per UK employee) and holiday pay;
  - certain unfunded pension contributions; and
  - secondary preferential debts – most commonly claims by Her Majesty's Revenue & Customs in respect of taxes including value added tax and pay-as-you-earn income tax, employee National Insurance (NI) contributions and Construction Industry Scheme deductions (but excluding corporation tax and employer NI contributions); and
- an amount equal to the prescribed part[9] – this is an amount of the assets which would otherwise be available to meet the floating charge, which is set aside for unsecured creditors and paid in priority to floating charge holders. The prescribed part is currently calculated as:
  - 50% of the first £10,000 of a company's assets; and
  - 20% of assets exceeding £10,000 up to a maximum of £800,000.

In certain specialised forms of financing (eg, ABL), the financiers may be able to impose a reserve (essentially a reduction in the amount of the funding) equal to the anticipated value of the priority claims.[10] In other types of deals, this mechanic is unlikely to be available and therefore potential deductions from the recoveries owing to priority creditors will need to be factored into any lending decisions and decisions as to the scope and composition of the security package.

6   Schedule 3, paragraph 13 of the Corporate Insolvency and Governance Act 2020, inserting a new Section 174A into the Insolvency Act 1986.
7   Section 176ZA and Schedule B1, paragraph 99 of the Insolvency Act 1986.
8   *Ibid*, Section 175, Section 386 and Schedule 6.
9   *Ibid*, Section 176A.
10 For more information on ABL transactions and specific mechanics available in such transactions to determine the assets against which such loans may be made (eg, eligibility criteria, borrowing base calculations and reserves), see the "Asset-based lending" chapter.

2.3   Form of security – other chattels

While a charge is the most common form of security over inventory, other forms may be more appropriate for other types of chattels. Where control can be taken in relation to specific, particularly high-value, assets, a mortgage might be a more appropriate form of security. Indeed, for ships and aircraft, mortgages expressly tailored to those assets are standard. Likewise, if taking security over artwork, mortgages are commonly used – albeit that where the financier can obtain possession of the item in question, a pledge will provide more effective security.

It is also possible to take a lien over inventory. This form of security is likely to arise where the assets are in the possession of the beneficiary of security, for a purpose other than that of the security. The most commonly given example is the mechanic's lien, which would attach to chattels in the possession of the mechanic (for the purposes of repair or maintenance) to cover payment of the mechanic's bill.

Other than in relation to a discussion of a landlord's lien,[11] these are specialist areas and are beyond the scope of this chapter.

3.   Issues on taking security over inventory

3.1   Location/access rights/landlord issues

While floating charge security can be validly taken without identifying the location(s) in which the assets are located, the location of the inventory will have a practical bearing on enforcement and other matters.

(a)   Warehouse

If the inventory is located in rented or leased commercial premises (eg, a warehouse), the landlord will have a common law lien giving it a right to seize, retain and then sell any inventory in the warehouse as security for the payment of any arrears of rent (or other services) or property damage. The landlord may also have a contractual right to security or possession set out in the lease or rental agreement with the borrower – this should be checked, as any specifically agreed contractual provisions would likely take precedence over the common law rights.

Such a lien would likely diminish the value of the inventory upon an enforcement as, outside an ABL transaction where a reserve may be imposed, a payment would need to be made to the landlord in respect of such rent in order to gain access to the inventory in order to be able to sell it.

In order to mitigate the risk of being unable to access significant assets on enforcement, the financier may require a waiver from the relevant landlord or,

---

11   See section 3.1(a).

as noted above in ABL transactions, may apply a reserve (so that there would be sufficient availability under the facility to enable the financier to discharge the rent arrears).

Any contractual agreement with the landlord (a collateral access agreement or landlord waiver agreement) may comprise an agreement:

- to maintain the borrower's assets separately from any assets of third parties which may also be storing assets in the same location;
- to allow the financier access to the assets on certain terms (usually notice and an agreement to make good any damage) for the purposes of recovery and sale; and
- to waive any right to assert a lien or other form of security.

Whether a landlord would be prepared to enter into such an agreement would be a commercial question.

If imposing a reserve, the amount is commonly set at three months' rent; although in certain jurisdictions, a landlord can have rights to payment over a longer period and so it may be appropriate to apply a larger reserve.[12] In any event, when calculating the amount that might be lost to such a lien, consideration must be given to the likely speed of enforcement and the length of time for which access would be required.

(b)   Retail

A more complicated situation is where the inventory is located in a retail setting – either where the borrower itself is a retail company (and is selling goods in its own shops) or where the borrower is supplying assets to third-party retail outlets.

In the case of the former, where the borrower's assets are in its own premises and are not commingled with assets of other entities, issues of access, identification and recovery will be made more easy for a financier, as it can be relatively certain that:

- it will be able to gain access to the premises;
- there will be no landlord lien issues to be dealt with; and
- there will be no identification issues in connection with the assets.

However, where the borrower is supplying to a third-party store, all of those considerations become relevant. Careful consideration will need to be given by financiers to taking security over/attributing value to such assets in the event

---

12   In Germany, for example, a landlord is entitled to entitled to a statutory lien on all assets owned by a tenant that have been brought onto the rented premises for claims which result from a lease relationship including claims for future rent (as well as outstanding rent). Pursuant to Section 562(2) of the German Civil Code, the maximum amount that can be claimed for future rent is for rent obligations for the remainder of the then current year and the following year.

that they are unable to engage the owner of the retail locations and agree some form of access rights or protections against commingling.

3.2 Identification of assets and commingling

When taking floating charge security, it is not necessary to provide lists of the assets; although if an attempt is being made to take fixed charge security or a chattel mortgage, identifying the assets will become more important as part of being able to evidence control.[13]

However, ideally, the financier should have the ability to request information in relation to the location of the inventory from time to time so that, on an enforcement, it can direct its agents to take possession of the relevant assets.

Care will particularly need to be taken to ensure that assets of the borrower which are subject to security in favour of the financier are not commingled with assets belonging to third parties. Any commingling will increase the difficulty of identifying the assets over which the financer has security upon an enforcement and may also jeopardise the security if the assets cannot be appropriately identified at the relevant time. This is especially an issue if security is being taken over assets which are not in and of themselves distinctive (eg, raw materials). A contractual obligation to segregate (contained in the security instrument) and (for valuable assets) appropriate labelling requirements may be imposed on the borrower in order to identify assets which are secured in favour of the financier.

3.3 Goods in transit

One question that can arise, particularly in ABL transactions where a financier is attributing value to specific items of inventory, is whether (and, if so, to what degree) effective security can be obtained over inventory while in transit (either from a supplier, between group entities or between different locations of the same entity).

(a) What are the issues?

The concerns are practical ones. Where inventory is being moved, there are a number of risks, from items going astray, being damaged or getting lost *en route* to the ability to track and trace the assets if an enforcement commences before the goods have arrived at their destination.

Where goods are moving across borders, the concerns increase as the distance and number of jurisdictions involved increase. The issues that a financier will need to consider include the following:

- When does ownership of the goods pass (as opposed to risk)?
- What security should be taken over the goods and when will this be

---

13   See section 2.2.

effective? The general position under English law is that title is determined by the domestic law of the place where the asset is located at the relevant time (the *lex situs* rule).[14] It follows that, in order to ensure minimal issues in relation to recognition and enforceability of the form of security taken, security governed by the laws of the jurisdiction in which the asset is located should be taken. However, where the goods are in transit on land, they may pass through several jurisdictions; and if they are travelling by sea, they will likely be in international waters for much of the journey.

- How can the financier take control of the assets given the more widespread locations (or none, if they are in international waters) in which the goods may find themselves at the time of an enforcement?
- What other parties (eg, shipping agents or hauliers) may have a claim over the assets, either contractually (by holding title documents) or pursuant to liens for fees?

(b)   *What are the options?*

Assuming that there is not simply a blanket exclusion on attributing value to goods in transit (or an acceptance of a certain amount of risk in light of the scale of the inventory that may be in transit at any one time), a number of options are available to a financier which is looking to obtain the benefit of the value of inventory in transit.

Take supporting documentation/additional perfection measures: A financier may ask for copies of bills of lading or other shipping documents (eg, sea waybills) to evidence the existence of and title to the goods. Even better would be to hold the originals (if they are negotiable, with an endorsement in favour of the financier); but this may be impractical, as they may take time to be received and are likely to be needed by the borrower's agent (eg, in order to permit the agent to recover the goods off the ship).

In such case, the financier may choose to enter into a tripartite agreement with the borrower and the relevant third-party agent in order to permit the borrower to run its business, but also allow the financier to take control of the shipping documents upon a trigger, with the third party holding the documents on trust for the financier.

Any such protections will be aimed at obtaining more control over the goods while in transit and also at the port of destination (when moving across borders).

In-depth analysis: Where there is a significant amount of goods in transit, a financier may be willing to conduct an in-depth analysis of the transport

---

14   Confirmed in *Blue Sky One Ltd v Mahan Air* [2010] EWHC 631 (Comm).

arrangements to fully assess the risks. By definition, this analysis must be comprehensive, so this option has timing implications.

The relevant considerations will vary on a case-by-case basis, but will generally require an analysis (both commercial and legal) of the following, among other things:

- each relevant transport route – point of departure, destination, duration and method;
- the relevant transport/shipping documentation:
  - whether an original is required to claim the goods and, if so, what happens to that in practice;
  - to whom is it sent; and
  - how long it takes to arrive at the destination;
- the point during the journey at which title passes to the borrower (and therefore the point at which the borrower is potentially able to grant security). This will depend in part on the terms and conditions of sale and also in part on the form of the transport/shipping documentation;
- what arrangements are made to get the goods from the port of arrival to their final destination (eg, the borrower's warehouse or factory);
- what laws may be applicable to the goods at each point and, accordingly, a consideration of the best laws to govern the security;
- whether the goods can be identified and/or tracked accurately; and
- what reporting can be made in relation to the goods while in transit.

Reserves: Financiers in ABL transactions will also have the benefit of being able to take reserves in relation to in-transit inventory. These may be taken to cover the fees of any third parties involved in the transport process (eg, hauliers, carriers, shipping agents), so that the financier can pay to release the goods from the possession of any such person and release any lien it may have.

In addition, ABL financers will have the option of either:

- excluding in-transit inventory from the borrowing base entirely; or
- limiting the value of the inclusion of such assets, so as to limit the risk of being unable to recover against the value of in-transit inventory.

3.4   Ownership

Establishing ownership of the assets which are to be the subject of the security is key to taking security.

As noted in section 4, retention of title (ROT) clauses may well have an impact on whether and when the borrower will possess title to the inventory, and establishing the point at which the borrower obtains title is important in any in-depth analysis of the ability to take security over goods in transit.[15]

---

15   See section 3.3.

However, there are other structures which could impact on the question and which, if they form part of the structure, should be investigated by any financier looking to take security over inventory. These may include the following.

(a) Tolling structures

Under a tolling structure, all raw material purchasing requirements for a group of companies are undertaken by a single entity (which may also undertake sales/billing and marketing functions) (the 'administration entity'). However, the processing and manufacturing of the raw materials will be undertaken by other group companies (each a 'tolling entity'), potentially located in different jurisdictions with a more established manufacturing base and closer to relevant markets. This arrangement will be governed by an agreement which will (or at least should) set out which entity owns the raw materials and resulting finished goods at which stage(s) of the process.

Under a tolling structure, it is invariably the administration entity that retains title to the raw materials and that holds title to the resulting finished goods – albeit that the assets will be in the possession (sometimes until point of sale) of the tolling entity.

Security can still be taken over the assets from the administration entity; but care will need to be taken to ensure that:

- title does indeed rest with that entity; and
- as a matter of local law, there is no overriding claim or lien over the assets in favour of the tolling entity while in its possession (eg, for payment of fees in connection with the tolling agreement) which might affect the priority of the financier's security interests.

In many ways, a tolling structure may actually be advantageous, as it could potentially be used to establish a degree of dispossession in jurisdictions where possessory security either is the only form of security available or confers certain benefits.[16]

(b) Commissionaire structures

Commissionaire structures, which are primarily a civil law agency construct, are in many ways the reverse of the tolling structures outlined above. In a commissionaire structure, the commissionaire entity will generally market and sell the goods in its own name, but on behalf of a principal. That principal will be the owner of the goods until title passes to the borrower at the point of sale. Such arrangements may also be referred to as 'consignment stock arrangements'.

The commissionaire agreement will set out key issues such as:

---

16   See section 5.

- how the commissionaire is paid for the sales;
- how the commissionaire will transmit any collections under the invoices generated to the principal; and
- liability as regards the goods and the end customer (which is usually unaware of this behind-the-scenes arrangement).

As with tolling structures, it is important to check the documentation to ensure that the entity that the financier thinks is the owner of the goods actually is (ideally, matters of title should be set out in the commissionaire documentation; but if not, it should be ascertained that there is nothing which establishes a contrary position). In cross-border situations, it should also be ascertained that there are no provisions of relevant local law that may give the commissionaire entity rights to the inventory at any point which might pre-empt the security taken by the financier.

3.5   Related security interests

(a)   *Insurance*
Where a significant proportion of a borrower's assets comprise inventory (and in any event, where there is a direct lending against the value of inventory, as in an ABL transaction), it is often a requirement of financiers that appropriate insurance be maintained by the borrower with a reputable insurer (with financiers often stipulating an appropriate rating for the insurer).

In addition (or as an alternative) to any commercial requirements in relation to the insurance set out in the financing documentation (eg, the requirement to make the financer loss payee or co-insured/joint insured), the financier will usually require security over the benefit of the insurance, or at least over the proceeds of any claim. This security will typically take the form of an equitable assignment. Appropriate due diligence should be undertaken in relation to the insurance policy to ensure that it is capable of being subject to the security.

(b)   *IP rights*
Certain inventory (eg, branded items or proprietary software or hardware) may require the benefit of IP rights or licences in order to effect a smooth sale and recovery outside of an administration or other form of insolvency proceeding. Where this is the case, it would be prudent for a financier to ensure that it takes security over such rights and/or that it is (or on a trigger can be) granted a licence to use or sell such items.[17]

---

17   See the "Intellectual property" chapter for more on IP rights and taking security.

(c) Rights under other agreements

Where there are tolling arrangements, commissionaire arrangements or goods in transit, it may be advisable for security to be taken over the borrower's interests in any documentation in relation to the arrangements (including, where possible, shipping documentation). Having such security would give the financier greater rights in relation to those arrangements and direct rights against relevant third parties, in each case enhancing the chances of recovering against the relevant assets.

3.6 Registration

Security interests (with certain exceptions) granted by an English company or limited liability partnership must be registered at Companies House within the period specified for delivery.[18] Failure to register the security within the specified period will result in the security becoming void as against third parties (specifically a liquidator, administrator or creditor of the entity)[19] – albeit that the contractual agreements as between the borrower and the financier will still be valid.

While registration at Companies House will likely be the only registration for most types of inventory, other registrations may be required for other asset types, such as ships and aircraft; although an examination of the requirements for those types of assets is beyond the scope of this chapter.

4. Contractual diligence and retention of title

If inventory forms a significant part of the asset base (and in ABL transactions, where funds are being advanced against the value of the inventory from time to time), a financier will often require a review of the relevant supply contracts.

Rather than being concerned with every commercial term that a borrower may have agreed with its supplier, the financier will be concerned with ensuring that the borrower has unfettered title to its inventory. In particular, in this regard, the financier will be concerned with determining what ROT rights, if any, the supplier may have in relation to the inventory, as any valid and enforceable ROT rights will limit the financier's ability to take security.

4.1 What is an ROT clause?

As a matter of English law, title to goods passes when the parties intend title to pass. Absent a specific intention, the Sale of Goods Act 1979 sets out a number of rules for determining intention – for example, where there is an unconditional contract for the sale of specific goods in a deliverable state, title

---

18   Part 25 of the Companies Act 2006 – in particular, Section 859A. In most cases, the period will be 21 days from the date of creation of the security.
19   Section 859H of the Companies Act 2006.

passes to the buyer at the time the contract is made or, for future or unascertained goods, at the time they become ascertained.[20]

An ROT clause (also referred to as a *Romalpa* clause after the leading case on the subject)[21] is a contractual provision that provides for the supplier to retain title to the inventory until payment has been made by the buyer. This enables the supplier, including in the event of insolvency of the buyer, to reclaim the inventory from the buyer (or its administrators or liquidators) ahead of the claims of any financier.

4.2   Common types of ROT clauses

There are a number of forms that an ROT clause can take, each of which has a different impact:

- Basic ROT: The supplier retains title to the inventory supplied until the buyer has paid for those particular items.
- All moneys ROT: The supplier retains title to the inventory supplied until the buyer has paid for those particular items and also for any other items supplied by the supplier to the buyer from time to time.
- Extended ROT (EROT): The supplier not only looks to retain title to the inventory, but also asserts a claim over the proceeds of any sale of that inventory.
- Mixed inventory ROT: The supplier aims to retain title to the inventory even where the physical state of that inventory has changed and/or has been mixed with other inventory. This is common where the inventory comprises components intended to be part of a manufacturing process.
- Double ROT: This arises where the inventory supplied on ROT terms is then sold on by the buyer to a third party on terms which also include a valid ROT clause. Provided that the assets can be traced and there are no estoppel arguments, the existence of a double ROT clause could give the supplier a right to recover inventory, which has not been paid for by the buyer, directly from the third party. Consequently, for a financier, a double ROT clause has a similar impact to an EROT clause, as the third party will not pay the buyer for the inventory if it has been reclaimed by the supplier.

4.3   Validity of ROT clauses

The English courts are generally willing to uphold ROT clauses as valid, provided that key elements of the claim can be evidenced as follows:

---

20   Section 17 of the Sale of Goods Act 1979 provides that title to specific or ascertained goods will pass when the parties intend it to be transferred, with consideration to be given to the terms of the contract, the conduct of the parties and the circumstances of the case. Section 18 of the Sale of Goods Act 1979 sets out the rules for determining when title will pass. Section 19 of the Sale of Goods Act 1978 permits the seller of goods to retain title after delivery until the fulfilment of certain agreed conditions (eg, payment).

21   *Aluminium Industrie Vaasen BV v Romalpa Aluminium Ltd* [1976] 2 ALL ER 552/[1976] 1 WLR 676.

- Incorporation: The ROT clause must be properly incorporated in the supply contract between the supplier and the buyer, and the buyer must have agreed/consented to those contractual terms. However, in certain cases, where a long-term course of dealings exists between the parties, terms could become incorporated without express agreement/consent.
- Validity: The ROT clause must not contain provisions that are inconsistent with the general commercial relationship between the parties.
- Identification: The inventory which is the subject of the ROT clause must be identifiable.

However, it is generally considered that certain types of ROT clauses – EROT, mixed inventory ROT and double ROT clauses – in fact amount to a security interest[22] and will therefore be void if not registered at Companies House.[23] It had been suggested that an all moneys ROT clauses also creates a charge; however, the House of Lords, on appeal from a Scottish decision, has held that such a clause does not create a charge.[24]

4.4 Impact of mixing and manufacturing of inventory on ROT clauses

Where the identity or character of the inventory remains distinct even after being mixed or incorporated with other inventory, an ROT clause may be effective (subject to the other tests). However, if the identity or original character of the inventory is lost as part of the process, such that the inventory sold forms part of, or becomes indivisible from, the new product, an ROT clause (other than a mixed inventory clause) may not be effective.

The rules in relation to the impact of mixing and manufacturing on the effectiveness of an ROT clause (even a mixed inventory ROT clause) are complex. This will often depend on the specific language of the clause, what the assets are and exactly what is being done to or with the assets in practice, and so will need to be assessed on a case-by-case basis. Nevertheless, certain broad themes can be identified, as follows.

(a) Mixing

Where inventory is a commodity, such as raw materials, it may be difficult to specifically identify the supplier's inventory in a mixed pool, so mixing can defeat a supplier's ability to identify its assets. However, this does not necessarily mean that the supplier loses title to that inventory in that pool in all cases. Rather, the supplier may retain title as a tenant in common with other suppliers

---

22   Various authorities, including *Borden (UK) Limited v Scottish Timber Products* [1979] 3 AER 961 as regards mixed inventory ROT.
23   See section 3.6.
24   *Armour v Thyssen Edelstahlwerke AG* [1990] 3 AER 481.

in respect of the mixed pool and a claim that is brought by all the suppliers whose assets have been mixed together may succeed.

(b)   Manufacturing

In a manufacturing process, inventory may be consumed (eg, raw materials converted into a new product) or incorporated (eg, a completed subassembly added to a number of others to produce a new, combined item). Where the inventory is incorporated with or consumed by another product such that it loses its separate identity and/or becomes indivisible from the new product, an ROT claim is likely to be defeated. However, if the item of inventory retains its essential character (even after processing) and/or can be easily identified and removed from the manufactured product (eg, a tyre put on a car), an ROT claim may still be successful.[25]

5.   Overseas inventory

While rules will vary, most jurisdictions will apply a variation of the *lex situs* rule noted in section 3.3(a). As such, a financier would be well advised to take security over assets under a governing law which matches the location of the asset. This, of course, assumes that the assets will still be located in the same jurisdiction at the time of enforcement. Financiers lending against assets may thus want to impose restrictions over the movement of inventory out of the relevant jurisdiction(s) in which it is originally located; and, in the case of ABL transactions, financiers will usually attribute value only to assets located in specified jurisdictions where they hold valid and effective security.

For inventory located overseas, even where owned by an English entity, a financier will normally require input from relevant local counsel to establish the appropriate form and formalities for the security. While, as noted above, English security most likely will take the form of a charge, the form of security for overseas assets will vary (eg, pledges are far more common forms of security in civil law jurisdictions). There also tends to be more emphasis on both identifying the assets and dispossessing the borrower of control over the assets.

5.1   Possessory versus non-possessory security

Many European jurisdictions will have a form of inventory security which requires possession of the inventory to be taken by the financier in order to create effective security. This may be the only available form of security in some jurisdictions, or may be coupled with an alternative non-possessory form. France, the Netherlands and Spain, for example, all have possessory and non-possessory forms of security.

---

25   Various authorities, including *Borden, Clough Mill Ltd v Martin* [1984] 3 ALL ER 982 and *Hendy Lennox (Industrial Engines v Grahame Puttick Ltd* [1984] 2 ALL ER 152.

As discussed in connection with the English position relating to control,[26] taking possession (or dispossessing the borrower) of the inventory can raise practical issues which may outweigh the benefit of taking the security in the first place. In jurisdictions with no alternative to the possessory form, this may mean not taking security at all or, where there is an alternative, accepting a less protective form of security or one which comes with other issues (eg, the possessory form of the Civil Code security in France is not subject to priority creditors, whereas the non-possessory form is).

5.2 Identifying assets

In certain jurisdictions, the inventory subject to any security interest will need to be specifically identified. This is often done by attaching lists of assets – either by scheduling lists of assets to the security agreement (which can be updated from time to time) or, as in Germany, scheduling a map to the security document which indicates a security area within which all assets owned by the borrower will be subject to security.

5.3 Future assets

While security can be taken in England over future assets, that is not possible in all jurisdictions. Where this is the case, supplemental security may need to be taken on a periodic basis to ensure that the financier retains security over all (or as much as possible) of the asset pool from time to time.

---

26   See section 2.2.

Real estate

Andrew Hepner
Mayer Brown

1. Introduction

Lending on the basis of security created over land is an important part of many lenders' businesses, whether a loan is being made available for investment or development purposes or in connection with the purchase of residential property. This chapter looks at the types of security commonly created over land in England and Wales; the principles which apply to the taking of such security; and the manner in which security over land is perfected. We also discuss how the priority of competing security interests created over land is determined.

We will focus in this chapter primarily on the law as it relates to commercial real estate. We refer to the person taking the security (the mortgagee or chargee) as the 'lender' and the person creating it (the mortgagor or chargor) as the 'borrower'. In some cases, however, the mortgagor or chargor may differ from the borrower where the former is providing third-party security for the indebtedness of the borrower.

2. Estates and interests in land in English law

In England and Wales, the only estates in land which are capable of existing or of being conveyed or created at law are an estate in fee simple absolute in possession or a term of years absolute – the former being freehold land and the latter leasehold.[1] Certain interests and charges in or over land are also capable of existing at law, including a charge by way of legal mortgage (as to which see below).[2] All other estates, interests and charges in or over land take effect as equitable interests.[3]

A freehold interest is an estate that is indefinite in its duration, which means that the estate itself and ownership thereof endure in perpetuity. Freehold titles are generally preferred by lenders, as there is little risk of interference with a borrower's title or ownership which might otherwise prejudice the lender's security.

---

1   Section 1(1) of the Law of Property Act 1925. Commonhold, as introduced by the Commonhold and Leasehold Reform Act 2002, does not constitute a new legal estate, but is a type of freehold estate that permits fractional ownership of the freehold of a single property within a building. It is outside the scope of this chapter.
2   *Ibid*, Section 1(2).
3   *Ibid*, Section 1(3).

Leasehold estates are interests that are limited to a certain term of years. Longer-term leases of up to 999 years and which are granted in consideration of a premium are tantamount to a freehold interest and are preferred by lenders, as they hold a capital value. Shorter-term (or 'rack rented') leases reserving a periodic rent have no intrinsic value and are not typically accepted by lenders as security in non-recourse real estate financing transactions.

3. Types and nature of security

3.1 Types of security

While guarantees and other security taking the form of sureties hold some attraction for lenders, security over real property often offers greater benefits for lenders in the context of the insolvency of a borrower or other default by it of its obligations to a lender.

Security and quasi-security (ie, a generic term for the methods employed by a lender to seek to replicate the creation of an actual security interest, which include guarantees, indemnities, set-off, retention of title arrangements and similar) over real property may:

- be created by contract;[4]
- arise by operation of law;
- arise by an order or act of the courts; or
- arise under certain statutes.

Security created by contract will usually take the form of a mortgage, a pledge or a charge; and where it arises by operation of law, it is known as a lien.[5] Pledges and liens are beyond the scope of this chapter.

3.2 Nature of security

While the characteristics of the security interests outlined above differ significantly, they have certain features in common:

- a right of the creditor to make the property which is subject to the security answerable for the debt or other obligation;
- a right of the debtor to redeem the property by paying the debt or performing the obligation; and
- a liability on the part of the creditor on payment or performance to restore the property to the owner.[6]

---

4   See *Re Cosslett (Contractors) Ltd* [1998] Ch 495, in which Lord Justice Millett identified the four kinds of contractual or 'consensual' security under English law.
5   In the well-known authority of *Halliday v Holgate* (1868) LR 3 Exch 299, applied in subsequent cases, Justice Willes set out the three classes of real security: "the first, a simple lien; the second, a mortgage passing the property out and out; the third, a security intermediate between a lien and a mortgage: viz, a pledge, where by contract a deposit of goods is made a security for a debt, and the right to the property vests in the pledgee so far as it is necessary to secure the debt."

4. Mortgages

4.1 Characteristics of a legal mortgage

A mortgage is created by contract to secure the payment of an amount due to a lender or the performance of some other obligation. It confers on the lender an interest in the asset which is the subject of the mortgage. As explained above, a feature of mortgages and other real security is a condition (which may be express or implied) that, on payment of the debt or discharge of the secured obligation, the asset will be transferred to the borrower. As Master of the Rolls Lindley in *Santley v Wilde*[7] explains in his description of a mortgage:

> *...a mortgage is a conveyance of land or an assignment of chattels as a security for the payment of a debt or the discharge of some other obligation for which it is given. This is the idea of a mortgage: and the security is redeemable on the payment or discharge of such debt or obligation, any provision to the contrary notwithstanding. Any provision inserted to prevent redemption on payment or performance of the debt or obligation for which the security was given is what is meant by a clog or fetter on the equity of redemption and is therefore void.*

An actual transfer or conveyance of the asset may be made by the borrower to the lender under a mortgage. Prior to changes in the statutory landscape in the last century, it was also possible for a mortgage of land to be created by a transfer or conveyance; but with the entry into force of the Law of Property Act 1925 on 1 January 1926, a mortgage of land must now be created by a charge by way of legal mortgage or by demise – that is, by lease.[8] Mortgages may be granted by demise or sub-demise, but only in respect of unregistered freehold or leasehold land. In practice, nearly all mortgages of land are now created by a charge by way of legal mortgage and must be created by deed.[9]

The statutory framework now applicable to the creation of mortgages of land also provides, as a substitute for the prior practice of actual conveyances of interests in land, for the equivalent of a 3,000-year lease to be granted to the lender in the case of freehold land. In relation to leasehold land, the equivalent of a sub-demise of the land for a term one day less than the borrower's lease is granted to the lender.[10] Accordingly, following the grant of the mortgage, the borrower retains its estate, encumbered by the mortgage.[11]

---

6   See Fisher and Lightwood's *Law of Mortgage*, 15th edition, LexisNexis, 2019, Chapter 1.
7   [1899] 2 Ch 474.
8   The relevant statutory provisions are to be found in Section 85(1) of the Law of Property Act 1925 for freehold land and in Section 86(1) for leasehold property.
9   Section 52(1) of the Law of Property Act 1925.
10   *Ibid*, Section 87(1).
11   See Fisher and Lightwood (n 6), Chapter 1.

4.2 Equitable mortgages

Equitable mortgages are created by:

- mortgage of an equitable interest in land;
- an agreement to create a legal mortgage (including mortgages of future acquired land); or
- a mortgage which does not comply with the formalities required to create a legal mortgage.

(a) Mortgages of equitable interests in land

A mortgage of an equitable or beneficial interest in land is made by assignment of that interest subject to an express or implied condition that, on the discharge by the borrower of the obligation in question, the equitable interest will be reconveyed to the borrower.[12] As a matter of statute, a mortgage of an equitable interest in land must be made in writing.[13]

(b) Agreements to create mortgages over land

In the case of an agreement to create a mortgage over land, any contract entered into since 27 September 1989 must be made in writing and by incorporating all the terms expressly agreed by the parties to that contract. Those terms must be incorporated in a single document or, where there is an exchange of contracts, in each document. Each party must sign the contract.[14]

The statutory provisions relating to agreements for the creation of mortgages over land do not apply to the creation of a mortgage itself.[15]

(c) Mortgages of future acquired property

It is not possible to grant a legal mortgage over future acquired property – that is, property which is not in existence at the time the mortgage is created or which is not owned by the borrower at the time the mortgage is granted.

An equitable mortgage over future property may be created so that the mortgage will be an equitable mortgage over the relevant property once that property is in existence and owned by the borrower.[16]

---

12   See also *Downsview Nominees Ltd v First City Corp Ltd* [1993] 3 All ER 626 at 634, in which Lord Templeman explained the settled law that "an equitable mortgage is a contract which creates a charge on property but does not pass a legal estate to the creditor. Its operation is that of an executory assurance, which, as between the parties, and so far as equitable rights and remedies are concerned, is equivalent to an actual assurance, and is enforceable under the equitable jurisdiction of the court".

13   Section 53(1) of the Law of Property Act 1925. See also *Helden v Strathmore Ltd* [2011] EWCA Civ 542, in which Master of the Rolls Lord Neuberger discussed the distinction between these requirements and those contained in Section 2 of the Law of Property (Miscellaneous Provisions) Act 1989.

14   Section (2) of the Law of Property (Miscellaneous Provisions) Act 1989.

15   *Murray v Guinness* [1998] NPC 79.

16   *Tailby v Official Receiver* (1888) 13 App Cas 523.

(d)   Mortgages lacking requisite formalities

A document purporting to create a legal mortgage may instead create an equitable mortgage. This may result from:

- defects in form or other failures to observe formalities;
- a failure to perfect the security purported to be taken; or
- a lack of title of the borrower.

If a legal mortgage is not granted by deed or is not properly executed in the manner required by law, it will take effect as an equitable mortgage, provided that it complies with the requirements of the Law of Property (Miscellaneous Provisions) Act 1989 discussed above. In *Bank of Scotland v Waugh*,[17] a legal charge which was void under Section 52 of the Law of Property Act 1925 because of the borrowers' failure to ensure their signatures were attested was nevertheless held to be valid and to take effect as an equitable mortgage.

A legal mortgage which otherwise complies with the requisite formalities may also take effect as an equitable mortgage for want of registration. Under Section 27 of the Land Registration Act 2002, the grant of a legal charge constitutes a disposition requiring completion by registration at Her Majesty's Land Registry and a legal charge does not operate at law until the relevant registration requirements are met.

4.3   Mortgages as distinguished from charges

The terms 'mortgage' and 'charge' are often used interchangeably, but they are different animals and carry different rights and benefits. That distinction is not aided by the confusing terminology in some areas – notably arising from the statutory framework discussed above in the context of the creation of mortgages of land (under the Law of Property Act 1925) by a charge by way of legal mortgage.

While both a mortgage and a charge constitute security for the payment of a debt or other obligation, a mortgage confers an interest in property to a lender, whereas a charge involves the appropriation of property without giving the lender possession of the property or any interest in it.

In *Re Cosslett (Contractors) Ltd*,[18] Lord Justice Millett, discussing the various contractual security interests capable of creation under English law, made it clear that:

> ...a pledge and a contractual lien both depend on the delivery of possession to the creditor. The difference between them is that in the case of a pledge the owner delivers possession to the creditor as security, whereas in the case of a lien the creditor retains possession of goods previously delivered to him for some other

---

17   [2014] EWHC 2117 (Ch).
18   [1998] Ch 495 at 508.

purpose. Neither a mortgage nor a charge depends on the delivery of possession. The difference between them is that a mortgage involves a transfer of legal or equitable ownership to the creditor, whereas an equitable charge does not.

As regards the distinction between an equitable mortgage and an equitable charge, some commentators have suggested there is now little or no difference between the two. The authorities do not necessarily support this proposition, however. In *Swiss Bank Corporation v Lloyds Bank Ltd*,[19] Lord Justice Buckley said that:

An equitable charge may, it is said, take the form either of an equitable mortgage or of an equitable charge not by way of mortgage. An equitable mortgage is created when the legal owner of the property constituting the security enters into some instrument or does some act which, though insufficient to confer a legal estate or title in the subject matter on the mortgagee, nevertheless demonstrates a binding intention to create a security in favour of the mortgagee, or in other words evidences a contract to do so... An equitable charge which is not an equitable mortgage is said to be created when property is expressly or constructively made liable, or specially appropriated, to the discharge of a debt or some other obligation, and confers on the chargee a right of realisation by judicial process, that is to say, by the appointment of a receiver or an order for sale.

Further, there remain fundamental differences between the two security interests, principally in the context of the rights and remedies available to a lender holding the benefit of an equitable mortgage which reserves to the lender a right of foreclosure and an entitlement to possession.[20]

5. Perfection of security over land

Certain formalities must be complied with, and registrations made, in order to perfect security granted over land in England and Wales. The steps required to be taken vary depending on:

- the nature of the security;
- whether the property is registered or unregistered; and
- whether title to the property in question is held legally or beneficially by the borrower.

Compliance with these requirements is often necessary to render the security valid against third parties or to achieve a particular priority position.

---

19   [1980] 2 All ER 419 at 426.

20   See *Carreras Rothmans Ltd v Freeman Mathews Treasure Ltd* [1985] Ch 207 at 227, in which Justice Peter Gibson said of an equitable charge:

The type of charge which it is said was created is an equitable charge. Such a charge is created by an appropriation of specific property to the discharge of some debt or other obligation without there being any change in ownership either at law or in equity, and it confers on the chargee rights to apply to the court for an order for sale or for the appointment of a receiver, but no right to foreclosure (so as to make the property his own) or take possession.

5.1 Basic formalities

(a) Execution as a deed
A mortgage over property must be executed as a deed by the borrower if:

- it is to take effect as a legal mortgage granted over registered or unregistered land;[21]
- it contains certain powers afforded to a lender by statute;[22] or
- it grants a power of attorney in favour of the lender.[23]

(b) Law of Property (Miscellaneous Provisions) Act 1989
As we have discussed above, the Law of Property (Miscellaneous Provisions) Act 1989 applies to contracts for the sale or other disposition of land, including agreements to create a legal mortgage. A legal mortgage is not caught by Section 2 of this act, but certain security interests – including equitable mortgages in respect of future acquired property which provide for a right in favour of a lender to call for a legal mortgage in due course – are subject to the act.

(c) Execution by lender
The lender need not execute or sign the mortgage unless Section 2 of the Law of Property (Miscellaneous Provisions) Act 1989 applies.

(d) Security over equitable interests
Security over an equitable interest in land must be in writing and signed by the borrower.[24]

5.2 Registration at Companies House

(a) Section 859D statement of particulars
A company registered in England and Wales, Scotland or Northern Ireland which has created a mortgage or charge, or any person interested in that mortgage or charge, may deliver a statement of particulars in respect of the security to the registrar of companies.[25] Although registration is voluntary, in practice most if not all lenders will deliver a Section 859D statement of particulars to ensure that the security is enforceable against certain persons.

(b) Period allowed for delivery of statement of particulars
The registrar must register the security if, before the "end of the period allowed

---

21 Sections 85 to 87 of the Law of Property Act 1925.
22 *Ibid*, Section 101.
23 Section 1(1) of the Powers of Attorney Act 1971.
24 Section 53(1) of the Law of Property Act 1925.
25 Section 859(A)(2) of the Companies Act 2006.

for delivery", the company or any person interested in the security delivers a Section 859D statement of particulars for registration. The period allowed for delivery is 21 days beginning with the day after the date of creation of the security.[26]

(c)   ***Consequences of failure to register***
If the relevant security is not registered, the security is void as against a liquidator, administrator or creditor of the company on its insolvency.[27] The Companies Act 2006 provides, however, that when security becomes void, the money secured by it immediately becomes payable.[28]

5.3   Registration at Her Majesty's Land Registry

Registration of legal mortgages: A legal mortgage granted over land which is registered in England and Wales must be registered at Her Majesty's Land Registry against the title number under which the property is held. If a mortgage must be completed by registration, it does not operate at law until the relevant registration requirements are met.[29]

An application, using the relevant forms accompanied by the requisite supporting documentation, should be submitted to Her Majesty's Land Registry within the period of priority conferred by an official search of the relevant title carried out prior to grant of the mortgage.

On completion of the relevant registration requirements, a charge created by means of a registrable disposition of a registered estate has effect, if it would not otherwise do so, as a charge by deed by way of legal mortgage.[30]

Pending registration at Her Majesty's Land Registry, any mortgage over registered land takes effect in equity only.[31]

In practical terms, completion of registration results in the lender and the date of the legal mortgage being entered in the charges register of the relevant title number. An application to register a restriction on the title is also invariably made, preventing disposition of the legal title to the property by the borrower without the consent of the lender. Such an entry is made in the proprietorship register of the relevant title.

Registration also confers on the lender priority over certain interests, discussed below.

---

26   *Ibid*, Section 859(A)(4).
27   *Ibid*, Section 859(H)(3).
28   *Ibid*, Section 859(H)(4).
29   Section 27(1) of the Land Registration Act 2002.
30   *Ibid*, Section 51.
31   *Mortgage Corporation Ltd v Nationwide Credit Corporation Ltd* [1994] Ch 49.

Registration of equitable mortgages: An equitable mortgage granted in respect of a legal interest in registered land may be protected by notice only. Registration is important so as to protect the priority of such a security interest. If not protected by notice, an equitable mortgage will be postponed to a registrable disposition which includes a subsequent legal mortgage.[32]

5.4   Registration at Land Charges Department

(a)   *General principles*

It is increasingly uncommon to come across unregistered commercial real estate, but large tracts of agricultural land and property held in settled estates remain unregistered.

The Land Charges Act 1972 governs the position in relation to unregistered land. If a mortgage is granted over unregistered land and is protected by the deposit of title deeds with the lender, it need not be registered at the Land Charges Department. If security is not protected by the deposit of title deeds, it will need to be registered.

(b)   *Equitable mortgages of legal interests in unregistered land*

An equitable mortgage of a legal interest in land which is not protected by the deposit of title deeds with the lender (referred to in the Land Charges Act 1972 as a 'general equitable charge')[33] should be registered as a Class C(iii) land charge.

An equitable mortgage protected by the deposit of the deeds is not registrable as a Class C(iii) land charge,[34] but it may nevertheless fall to be considered also as a Class C(iv) land charge.[35] It is not the general practice of conveyancers to register an equitable mortgage as an estate contract unless there is an express (as against implied) agreement to create a legal mortgage. However, given the uncertainty of the legal position, it would be prudent to effect registration in all cases – although the better view is that a protected equitable mortgage is not registrable.[36]

---

32   See Section 29(1) of the Land Registration Act 2002, which provides that: "If a registrable disposition of a registered estate is made for valuable consideration, completion of the disposition by registration has the effect of postponing to the interest under the disposition any interest affecting the estate immediately before the disposition whose priority is not protected at the time of registration."

33   Section 2(4)(iii) of the Land Charges Act 1972.

34   *Ibid*, Section 2(4)(iii)(a).

35   In Section 2(4)(iv) of the Land Charges Act 1972, an 'estate contract' is defined as "a contract by an estate owner or by a person entitled at the date of the contract to have a legal estate conveyed to him to convey or create a legal estate, including a contract conferring either expressly or by statutory implication a valid option to purchase, a right of pre-emption or any other like right".

36   See Fisher and Lightwood (n 6), Chapter 4.

(c) Agreements to create legal mortgages

As discussed above, where an equitable mortgage contains an express or implied agreement to create a legal mortgage, practitioners should consider registering such interests under both Class C(iii) and Class C(iv).

(d) Consequences of failure to register land charges

The consequences of failing to register a land charge depend on the class in question. Failure to register a Class C(i) or C(iii) land charge renders the charge void against a purchaser of any interest in the property. Any failure to register a Class C(iv) land charge makes the charge void against a purchaser (including a lessee and a lender) of the legal estate for money or money's worth.[37]

6. Priority of security created over land

Provided that the perfection requirements discussed above are satisfied, priority in respect of a lender's security will be conferred on it as regards certain other interests affecting property. This is especially important in the context of an enforcement in determining how any proceeds resulting from realisation of a property are applied among lenders whose debt is secured over the same asset.

The rules in relation to priority differ for registered and unregistered land.

6.1 Registered land

(a) Registered mortgages

Registered mortgages created in respect of the same registered title rank in the order in which they are shown in the charges register of that title.[38] The order in which the charges were created is not relevant.

The Land Registration Act 2002 acknowledges that the order of priorities may be varied by agreement – that is, by the parties entering into a deed of priority or intercreditor arrangement – and that this is effective to alter the usual order of priority, provided that the registrar makes an entry to this effect (typically in the charges register).[39]

As we have seen above, a lender does not become the registered proprietor of, or acquire a legal interest in, the security until registration has been completed.[40] In the absence of registration, the lender enjoys an equitable interest only, which means that the priority of such interest may be adversely affected by a subsequent disposition for valuable consideration. Thus, a subsequent registered charge has priority over any prior charge not registered or protected on the register.[41]

---

37   Sections 5 and 6 of the Land Charges Act 1972.
38   Section 48 of the Land Registration Act 2002.
39   *Ibid*, Section 48(2)(a).
40   *Ibid*, Sections 27 and 29.
41   See Fisher and Lightwood (n 6), Chapter 36.

As a result of the statutory framework discussed above, a registered mortgage has priority over:

- any subsequent registered mortgage which takes effect at law, even if the latter was created before the former;
- any equitable charge created after the date of the registered mortgage; and
- any equitable charge created before the date of the registered mortgage, but which was not protected by an entry on the register.[42]

(b) *Equitable mortgages*

Equitable mortgages rank in order of the date of their creation.

As we have seen above, an equitable mortgage may and should be protected by noting it on the title to the property. In doing so, the priority of an equitable mortgage is protected against a subsequent registered disposition.[43] The Land Registration Act 2002 provides, however, that: "The fact that an interest is the subject of a notice does not necessarily mean that the interest is valid, but does mean that the priority of the interest, if valid, is protected for the purposes of sections 29 and 30."[44]

If an equitable mortgage is not noted on the register, it does not lose priority to a subsequent equitable mortgage, even where the subsequent security interest is noted and the 'first in time' rule prevails.

If an equitable mortgage has not been protected by a notice on the register, it will be postponed to a registrable disposition of the property for valuable consideration if that disposition is registered including the grant of a subsequent legal mortgage.[45]

An equitable mortgage protected by a notice on the title register has priority over the holder of a subsequent legal mortgage entered into.[46]

(c) *Further advances*[47]

The question of whether a lender with the benefit of a registered mortgage may also make a further advance on the security of a mortgage ranking in priority to a subsequent mortgage is now governed by the Land Registration Act 2002.[48]

---

42   See Fisher and Lightwood (n 6), Chapter 36 and Section 29 of the Land Registration Act 2002.
43   Sections 29 and 32 of the Land Registration Act 2002.
44   *Ibid*, Section 32(3).
45   *Ibid*, Section 29(1).
46   *Ibid*, Sections 28 and 29.
47   In *Urban Ventures Ltd v Thomas* [2016] EWCA Civ 30, the meaning of 'further advances' was at issue. In that case, it was held that further advances do not include rolled-up interest and fees, even where rolling-up was not envisaged by the original finance documents. It was also held that facilities that became subject to new terms but where no new funding had been advanced and no amounts had been repaid did not constitute further advances. The Court of Appeal did not address the question of whether further fees paid on renewal of the original facility that fell within the charging provisions of the first ranking mortgage, but that were not envisaged under the original terms in fact constituted further advances.
48   Section 49 of the Land Registration Act 2002.

The act provides that the 'first lender' may do so in the following circumstances:[49]

- if the further advance is made at a time when the first lender has not received notice of the creation of the subsequent mortgage from the subsequent lender.[50] Notice must be served on the first lender's address for service as shown on the registered title;
- if the further advance is made pursuant to an obligation and, at the time of the subsequent mortgage, the obligation was entered in the register in accordance with the rules – that is, the Land Registration Rules 2003.[51] The usual method of applying to the registrar for such an entry to be made is to use Form CH2;
- if the parties have agreed a maximum amount to be secured by the first lender's mortgage and, at the time of creation of the subsequent mortgage, the agreement was entered on the title register in accordance with the Land Registration Rules 2003;[52] or
- by agreement between the first lender and subsequent lender.[53]

With the exception of tacking[54] with the agreement of the subsequent lender, the provisions of the Land Registration Act 2002 apply only to proprietors of registered mortgages. Thus, the ability to maintain priority with respect to further advances applies only to legal mortgages. However, the priority conferred by the statutory provisions is effective against subsequent mortgages and therefore confers priority whether the subsequent mortgage is legal or equitable.[55]

If the first lender has only noted the benefit of its security and has not registered it as a legal mortgage, the first lender requires the consent of subsequent lenders for further advances made by it to take priority over amounts advanced by subsequent lenders.

6.2   Unregistered land

(a)   *Possession of title deeds*
A lender that holds the title deeds to a property which is mortgaged can rely on

---

49   See Fisher and Lightwood (n 6), Chapter 38 for a detailed examination of the relevant grounds.
50   Section 49(1) of the Land Registration Act 2002.
51   *Ibid*, Section 49(3) and Rule 108 of the Land Registration Rules 2003.
52   Section 49(4) of the Land Registration Act 2002 and Rule 108 of the Land Registration Rules 2003.
53   Section 49(6) of the Land Registration Act 2002.
54   See *Urban Ventures Ltd v Thomas* [2016] EWCA Civ 30, in which Lord Justice Richards proffers the following definition of 'tacking': "'Tacking' describes the means by which a creditor, with a charge securing an original advance, is able to use the charge to secure a further advance and so obtain priority for the further advance over sums secured by any second or subsequent charge. Because of the potential prejudice to the interests of the holders of second or subsequent charges, first equity and then statute have severely restricted the circumstances in which tacking will be permitted."
55   See Fisher and Lightwood (n 6), Chapter 38.

possession of those deeds for priority whether the mortgage is legal or equitable. As explained above, a lender that is protected by the deposit of title deeds cannot register a mortgage as a land charge.

(b)   Land charges

Registered land charges rank in the order in which they are registered.[56] As with security over registered land, the parties may agree to vary the usual priorities.[57]

(c)   Further advances

A lender that makes a further advance secured over a mortgage has priority over a subsequent mortgage in the following circumstances:

- The first and subsequent lenders agree;
- The first lender has no notice of the subsequent lender's mortgage when the further advance was made; and
- The first lender's mortgage obliges the first lender to make a further advance even if it has notice of the subsequent mortgage.[58]

A lender cannot tack further advances if it has notice (whether actual or constructive) of a subsequent mortgage, unless the prior mortgage contains an obligation to make further advances. Where a subsequent lender has registered its mortgage, this amounts to notice and, unless the prior mortgage contains an obligation to make further advances, will prevent the first lender from tacking. The effect of Section 94(3) of the Law of Property Act 1925 is to abolish tacking other than as expressly permitted above.[59]

---

56   Section 97 of the Law of Property Act 1925.
57   See Fisher and Lightwood (n 6), Chapter 35, para 14.
58   Section 94(1) of the Law of Property Act 1925.
59   Fisher and Lightwood (n 6), Chapter 38.

Intellectual property

Mark Prinsley
Mayer Brown

This chapter provides an overview of key aspects of intellectual property (IP) rights and rights in personal data for the purposes of security over these rights. It covers the following issues:

- the nature of IP rights and rights in personal data;
- the mechanics of taking security over IP rights;
- good stewardship of IP rights;
- good stewardship of personal data; and
- insolvency.

1.   The nature of IP rights

For a lender taking security, it is important to understand the nature of the protection that IP rights give and therefore the significance of IP rights to the business. The lender will also need to understand the value of the intellectual property should it ever become necessary to take control of the assets.

All IP rights are the product of laws designed to protect, in one way or another, intellectual creation. IP laws have grown out of national policy decisions as to how best to protect individual creators or to stimulate or protect industry. Inevitably, different legal systems have come up with different solutions to the same problem. For example, the UK/European patent system is based on the principle that the inventor first devising an invention should be entitled to apply for and benefit from the grant of patent protection. By contrast, in the United States, the patent system evolved originally on the principle that the inventor first filing an application for a patent for an invention should be entitled to the patent, even if at some later date another inventor emerges which can prove that it invented substantially same thing as the invention covered by the patent before the date of the application filed by the other 'inventor'.

Over time, many national differences in the protection of IP rights have been harmonised across a number of countries or accommodated by way of international treaties. In Europe, for example, the European Patent Convention (EPC) provides for a central examination of inventions for patentability across all member states, so that the test as to what inventions qualify for patent protection are the same in each country; although each country still grants its own national patent, assuming that the central examination establishes that the invention meets the requirements for a patentable invention.

In the case of copyright works, a series of international conventions have the effect of granting the same protection enjoyed by copyright works created in and protected under the domestic laws of one country to works created in another country and protected by copyright in that country.

1.1   Registered IP rights

(a)   Patents

Patents are rights granted by statute. The basic principle is that in exchange for making public the nature of the invention in the patent specification or description, the patent owner is given a monopoly in products or methods that fall within the scope of the patent for the term of the patent, which is generally 20 years. The monopoly applies in the countries covered by the patent.

Unless specifically excluded from patent protection, patents can be obtained for inventions in all fields of technology which are new, involve an inventive step and are capable of industrial application.[1] Under many patent regimes, certain types of inventions are excluded from patentability. Methods of doing business and computer programs as such are frequently excluded from patent protection.[2] The extent to which patents can be used to protect inventions implemented by means of a computer program as opposed to protecting the underlying computer program as such has been hotly debated around the world. It also seems clear that for an invention to be capable of protection, it must have a human inventor. Pure artificial intelligence-generated inventions are not capable of protection in the United States or in Europe.[3]

As part of the process of filing an application for a patent, the invention is examined for novelty over the existing state of the art, which includes a review of previously granted patents and the general state of technology in the same or related fields. Inventions which seem to lack novelty over common general knowledge will not be protected by the patent system.

Once granted, a patent lasts for a term of 20 years. For some medicinal products, it is possible to extend this 20-year period for a maximum of a further five years through supplementary protection certificates[4] (SPCs), reflecting the fact that it may take many years to obtain regulatory approval to market a pharmaceutical product and that, absent the SPC, the effective period of

---

1   Article 52(1) of the EPC.
2   See, for example, Article 52(2) of the EPC.
3   See European Patent Office Decisions in Applications EP 18 275 163 and EP 18 275 174 and US Patent and Trademark Office Decision on Application 6/524,350 (Dabus applications).
4   See EU Regulations 469/2009 and 2019/933 concerning supplementary protection certificates for medicinal products.

protection, during which the invention will be protected from copies in the market, might be considerably less than 20 years.

From the point of view of a lender, it is important to understand the following at a basic level.

Extent of territorial protection: This concerns the countries covered by a patent or family of patents and therefore the extent of the market for which the business has protection by way of patents.

Remaining term of the patent protection: At the end of the 20-year term, competitors are entitled to launch clone or generic products using the knowledge disclosed in the patent and can generally undercut the price of the product marketed with the benefit of the patent protection. Understanding the remaining term of the patent protection is an important element of the value of the security. It may also be important to understand the extent to which a competitor can take steps during the term of the patent to prepare to launch a competitive product on expiration of the patent.

Licensees: If the business has granted licences over the patent, the value of the patent to the business will be dictated, at least to some extent, by the terms of the licence and it will be important to understand the terms of any licences.

Scope of patent: The patent will only protect against competitor products that fall within the scope of the patent. Part of the value of the security will involve an assessment of the scope of the patent in terms of the extent to which it really acts to monopolise a part of the market.

(b)   *Registered trademarks*

Trademarks protect the goodwill that a business generates in its trading style or the brands that it uses in its business (eg, in logos). Many countries give a business the right to protect itself against unfair competition from third parties taking advantage of the reputation it has established in its trading style or in the brands it uses for its goods or services. In the United Kingdom and other Commonwealth countries, there is a common law right to restrict unauthorised third parties from 'passing off' their business or products and services as those of a competitor. A registered trademark creates a presumption that the trademark owner owns the relevant goodwill in the brand for the goods and services for which the mark is registered and similar goods and services. This makes restraining 'knock-off' competitors much easier. It also means that the business has a registered right which is relatively easy to license to third parties and therefore use to generate revenue.

Registered trademarks are available for marks that distinguish a business or its goods and services from others. The EU Trademarks Directive, which has been implemented into the domestic laws of all EU member states and the United Kingdom, provides that a trademark may consist of any signs – in particular words, including personal names or designs, letters, numerals, colours, the shape of goods or the packaging of goods or sounds that:

- are capable of distinguishing the goods or services of one business from those of others; and
- are capable of being represented on the trademark register in a manner which enables the authorities and the public to determine the clear and precise subject matter of the protection given by the registered trademark.[5]

The registered trademark system is generally national, so a business must obtain separate trade registrations in all relevant countries. In the European Union, there is a Community trademark system, under which a single registration covering all EU member states can be obtained. Following the United Kingdom's departure from the European Union, existing Community trademarks were cloned into UK national trademarks insofar as the United Kingdom was concerned, to protect such rights in the United Kingdom as well as in the remaining EU member states through the Community trademark.

Properly policed registered trademark rights grow stronger over time as the brand becomes more distinctive. Unlike other registered IP rights, registered trademarks can last forever. However, if a registered trademark is not used for a continuous period of five years, it is susceptible to challenge and removal from the register in respect of those goods or services for which there has been no use in the relevant five-year period.

From the point of view of a lender, it will be important to understand:

- the extent to which the trademark portfolio in fact protects the products and services of the business; and
- the extent to which the trade registrations substantially cover the activities of the business. Exact overlap is not important; but if the goods or services of the business have evolved in way which is substantially different from the goods and services covered by trademark registrations, a further trademark registration programme may be necessary.

Territorial coverage of registered trademarks: Are the trademarks registered in all important territories in which the business operates?

Third-party use: If unauthorised third parties have been allowed to use brands which are the same or similar, the mark may cease to be distinctive of the business and is therefore at risk of being challenged by a third party.

---

5   Article 3 of the EU Trademarks Directive (2015/2436/EU).

Trademark licences: If third parties have been licensed to use the trademark, it will be important to understand whether those licences comply with competition law, which in the European Union in particular is concerned to ensure that IP rights are not used to create barriers to the free movement of goods and services within the European Union.

(c)   *Other registered rights*

Another potentially significant registered IP right is the registered design, which protects aspects of the shape or decoration of a product. Registered design protection is similar to patent protection, although it generally subsists for a shorter period than patent protection. The factors relevant to assessing the value of a patent will be similar for registered designs from the perspective of a lender.

1.2   Unregistered IP rights

(a)   *Copyright*

Copyright protects literary, dramatic, artistic and musical works. The precise scope of works protected is determined by national law – in the European Union, a series of directives have contributed to the creation of a broadly harmonised landscape as to the scope of works protected by copyright in EU member states (and the United Kingdom). Computer programs, for example, are protected as literary works in the European Union, the United Kingdom and elsewhere in the world.

The Agreement on Trade-Related Aspects of Intellectual Property Rights (TRIPs) describes copyright as a system which extends to protect "expressions and not... ideas, procedures, methods of operation or mathematical concepts as such".[6]

International treaties have provided reciprocal protection for works recognised as copyright-protected works in one country in other member countries of the various treaties for many years – for example, the TRIPs Agreement between all member nations of the World Trade Organization. Essentially, a work protected by copyright in one country will be protected in other countries which belong to the treaty as if the work had been created in those other countries.

There are generally no formalities surrounding the creation of a copyright work – for example, there is no need to register copyright with a national IP office to claim the rights. Often, creators will want to date stamp an original work to show its date of creation and identify the author on copyright works for evidential purposes.

---

6   Article 9 of the Agreement on Trade-Related Aspects of Intellectual Property Rights, World Trade Organization 1994.

Some works will have a number of copyrights which will have potential value to a business. In the music world, for example, there are separate copyrights in the original score and lyrics and the sound recordings; and publication of the finished work is likely to involve the use of different copyrights, which in turn may require permission from a number of different copyright owners.

Copyright protection is given to human authors and generally the term of copyright is measured by reference to the life of the author plus a number of years. Copyright protection can last for very long periods of time, which influences the potential value of the protection.

From the point of taking security over copyright works, it will be important for a lender to have a general understanding of:

- how the business acquired ownership of the copyright;
- the different rules by which employers acquire ownership of copyright in works created by employees, which vary from country to country; and
- whether ownership is open to challenge.

Joint ownership issues: Where copyright is owned jointly, the rights of each individual owner to exercise rights of ownership – such as licensing to a third party – will be limited by law or the terms of the agreement between the joint owners.

Nature of the work: The nature of the work will dictate the duration of the copyright and the unexpired duration of the copyright will influence the value of the security.

Scope of any licences over the work: It is common for copyright interests to be licensed, and the scope of licences granted to customers or third parties will be relevant to the value of the copyright over which security is taken.

(b) Confidential information

Business know-how, extending from clear trade secrets to simple undocumented methods of doing business, might fall within the general description of 'confidential information'. The extent to which any of this confidential information can be truly protected will largely depend on national laws – particularly around restrictions on the use of information acquired by employees or contractors following termination of their relationship with the business.

The European Union implemented the Trade Secrets Directive in 2016 with a view to harmonising the protection afforded to trade secrets throughout the EU member states.[7] The directive was to be transposed – to the extent that any

---

7   EU Directive 2016/943 on the protection of undisclosed know-how and business information (trade secrets) against their unlawful acquisition, use and disclosure.

changes were necessary – into domestic law in all member states, including the United Kingdom, by June 2018. For confidential information to qualify for protection in line with the directive it must be secret, in the sense that it:

- is not generally known by people in the relevant field of activity;
- is commercially valuable because it is secret; and
- has been subject to reasonable steps to keep it confidential.

The directive makes clear that trade secret protection should not be given to information which could be used to restrict the post-employment mobility of individuals to use experience and skills honestly acquired in the normal course of their employment.[8]

From the point of view of taking security over trade secrets, a lender will want to understand:

- the national laws relating to this area in the country in which the trade secrets are used; and
- the steps to which the borrower has gone to keep that information secret and confidential in order to assess the value of the rights over which it is taking security.

A problematic aspect of confidential information from the perspective of the lender is that the confidential nature, and therefore the protection, of the information can be destroyed easily.

(c) **Rights in personal data**

'Personal data' is generally regarded as information relating to the characteristics of a living individual which enable him or her to be identified.[9] Legislation – at least in Europe – was originally directed at controlling the way in which personal data could be collected, held or used, and not necessarily at protecting the investment of the business that collected the data. The potential value of personal data became more recognised with the explosion of digital media and the ability to collect and manipulate data to profile individuals and target advertising and the like at them on a personalised basis. This, in turn, has led to greater regulation of the ways in which this data may be collected and used.

Laws regulating the collection and use of personal data are largely national – or in the United States, largely state based rather than federal based – and not all countries have laws which could be described as regulating the collection or use of personal data. Often, the applicable domestic law of a country will extend to regulate the collection and use of personal data about residents of a country

---

8   *Ibid*, Article 1.3.
9   See, for example, Article 4 of the EU General Data Protection Regulation (2016/679) (GDPR).

by a business which is established outside that country – especially where that business is targeting consumers within the country with the products and services it offers. For businesses that collect data on a multinational basis, there is therefore a risk that personal data laws applicable in the country where the individuals from whom the data is collected are resident will apply even if, in a commercial sense, it is clear to everyone that the 'collector/controller' of the data is located in a completely different country.

The value of a database of personal data will be heavily influenced by the ways in which the relevant data has been collected and used. If the data has not been collected in a lawful way – which in general terms means that the business collecting the personal data has been transparent with the individual from whom the data has been collected – then not only may possible use of the data be limited, but the controller may also be open to significant administrative fines imposed by local data protection authorities and possible class action claims from affected individuals.[10] Correcting a database of personal data which has been created in a non-compliant way may be practically no less expensive than starting to assemble the database from scratch.

A lender taking security over a database of personal data will want to understand:

- how the data was collected;
- whether the individuals from whom the data has been collected have been given accurate information about how the data has been collected by the controller and how it will be used by the controller;
- the quality of the processes that the controller has in place for handling personal data – for example:
  - whether the controller conducts appropriate assessments of the ways in which it uses personal data; and
  - whether the arrangements that it has in place with contractors or other third parties with which it shares personal data comply with legal requirements; and
- the controller's data breach history – in particular, whether the controller has been subject to data breaches which indicate poor data governance; and
- how the controller has satisfied itself that any international transfers of personal data are being conducted under robust and lawful means. The ability to transfer data internationally may well be a significant issue for the lender to consider if it must exercise its rights under the security.

---

10   For example, in July 2021 the National Data Protection Commission of Luxembourg announced an intention to fine Amazon Europe Core Sàrl €746 million for failing to comply with the GDPR.

2. Mechanics of taking security and providing notice

2.1 Registered IP rights

The legal nature of registered IP rights in the United Kingdom is spelled out in the domestic legislation.

UK patents and patent applications are personal property – which means that the owner has the right to possess, enjoy or sell the property and prevent others from doing so (without being a thing in action)[11] – and as such, may be assigned or mortgaged. They will vest by operation of law in the same way as any personal property.

A registered trademark is also personal property (in Scotland, incorporeal movable property).[12] UK registered trademarks, like patents, are transmissible by assignment or operation of law in the same way as any other personal or movable property.

The EU Trademarks Directive also provides that a trademark may, independently of the undertaking, be given as security or be the subject of rights *in rem*[13] (ie, rights that relate to the property rather than an individual). The directive requires member states to have procedures in place to record rights *in rem* in their registers. It is therefore possible to give notice of a security interest over trademarks through registration in EU member states and in the United Kingdom. Lenders will want to confirm whether to take this step; and to confirm the position as to the ability to give notice of their security interest in registers maintained in the countries where the trademark subsists.

2.2 Unregistered IP rights

The UK Copyright, Designs and Patents Act 1988 provides that copyright is treated as personal or movable property and can be dealt with by assignment or transmission by law as any personal or movable property.[14] However, an important difference for the lender from the position in relation to patents or registered trademarks is that, by definition, no register is kept of unregistered rights and there is nothing copyright specific that the lender can do to give general notice of its security interest over the copyright – at least in the United Kingdom.

For common law rights, such as rights in unregistered trademarks or confidential information, in reality there is no certainty as to the scope of the borrower's rights at any particular point in time. Also, exactly how the security interest can be effected will be a matter for bespoke consideration.

---

11   Section 30 of the Patents Act 1977.
12   Section 22 of the Trade Marks Act 1994.
13   Article 23 of EU Directive 2015/2436.
14   Section 90 of the Copyright, Designs and Patents Act 1988.

2.3 Personal data

Taking and exercising security over personal data is not straightforward. Where a party becomes a controller of personal data and is in a position to make decisions as to how that data is to be used or 'processed', obligations to notify the affected individuals – or 'data subjects' – will be triggered in the European Union and the United Kingdom under the EU General Data Protection Regulation (GDPR). There may also be notification obligations to the local data protection authority. Under the GDPR, the obligation to notify the data subjects must be satisfied within 30 days of the transfer to the new controller, unless a specific exemption applies. The borrower is unlikely to want to notify the individuals whose data it holds that it has granted security interest in favour of the lender; and equally, the lender may well want to resist the obligations of becoming a controller of the personal data unless and until it exercises the security interest. The tight regulation of international transfers of personal data may also add to the complexity of a lender exercising its security over a database consisting of personal data.

3. Good stewardship of IP rights by the borrower

A lender will want to ensure that the borrower takes the reasonable steps that any owner of IP rights would take to preserve the value of those rights and therefore the lender's security.

These obligations will include the following.

3.1 Dealing promptly with all formality requirements

Payment of registration and renewal fees for all registered rights is important. While there is generally a short grace period which enables the recovery of registered rights, ultimately, non-payment of renewal fees leads to the irrevocable loss of registered rights. There may well be good commercial reasons for non-payment of patent renewal fees – in particular, in countries where there is no market for the patented product or methods. The lender may well want have advance notice or the right to overrule decisions by the borrower to allow rights to lapse through non-payment of renewal fees.

For patent applications, the borrower may have used a filing system which allows the applicant to nominate a large number of countries in which applications will be made for a patent if the invention meets all criteria of a patentable invention as determined through a central examination process. This is a common and cost-effective approach to multi-country patent filing. The lender may well want to have notice of, and be involved in, any process by which the borrower limits the countries in which a patent is eventually applied for off the back of the successful central examination. The costs of the national phase of these applications can be significant in terms of national filing expenses and local language translations.

3.2 Appropriate policing of infringements

The lender will be concerned that appropriate steps are taken to police infringement of any IP rights. This is particularly important in relation to registered rights, where failure to police infringements appropriately can lead to a total loss of the IP right over which security has been taken – not just diminution in value of the IP right. For patent infringements, a standard approach from a defendant is to argue that the patent is invalid and should be revoked. A lender may well want to be kept informed as to decisions to commence infringement proceedings which might result in the invalidity of the patent.

For trademarks, the risk of not taking proceedings to restrain infringements may be that the trademark ultimately ceases to be distinctive of the goods or services of the borrower's business and, as such, the trademark ceases to have any value.

All IP disputes come with risk and cost which will be of concern to the lender.

3.3 Licensing by the borrower

For many businesses, the value of the intellectual property in the business is extracted by licensing that intellectual property to customers of the business. An example would be a software business. The lender will want to ensure that all licences granted by the borrower are enforceable and properly protect the underlying intellectual property. The lender may wish to be assured that certain minimum protections are included in all IP licences granted by the borrower, such as restrictions on assignment of the licence.

3.4 Product development and use of open source code

For the security to remain valuable, it must continue to relate to the products or future plans of the business. Ideally, the security should extend to developments and enhancements of the intellectual property in existence at the date the security is taken.

For businesses which develop software, one concern will be to ensure that where open source code is used in the business, care is taken to ensure that it is not used in a way which exposes key development work to free access to other users of the open source code. The use of open source code is likely to give the business the ability to innovate rapidly and cheaply with robust code; but the lender will be interested to confirm that appropriate policies are in place in the business surrounding the use of open source code.

4. Good stewardship of personal data by the borrower

As mentioned above, the value of a database of personal data is dependent on 'good hygiene' in the collection and use of that personal data. The lender will want assurance that the borrower will collect data in a transparent manner insofar as the individual data subjects are concerned, and that appropriate data protection notices are made available to those individuals. Good data governance will depend on the policies applied by the borrower to the personal data used in its business. Depending on the nature of the business, there could be changes in policies relating to the use of personal data, of which the lender will want to be given advance notice.

5.   Insolvency

Insolvency will be a trigger for the exercise of security over intellectual property. In some cases, such as retail businesses, the key IP assets needed to carry on the business can be separated relatively easily from the other assets and liabilities of the business, and a new business can emerge from the insolvency trading under the established brands of the business. In many situations, this ability to extract an easily realisable asset is just the protection that the lender will wish to have.

The lender will also want to ensure that appropriate controls are put in place to prevent the borrower from moving key IP assets around a group of companies such that they are somehow outside the companies within those parts of the group over which security has been taken.

As discussed in section 3, the nature of relevant IP rights means that often customers of a business are in fact licensees of the intellectual property relating to the goods or services supplied to the customer. In software arrangements – in particular, where the customer typically takes an ongoing licence and maintenance and support arrangements from the licensor so that it has the right to receive updates and the like – the customer will need protection against the administrators of the insolvent licensor disclaiming the ongoing obligations and depriving the customer of effective ongoing support and maintenance. In software licensing arrangements, this is generally covered through escrow arrangements whereby the source code required to maintain the licensed software is released to the customer by an escrow agent on the insolvency of the licensor. Where key intellectual property is licensed to a customer – for example, the right to apply for a trademark to goods embodying the customer's intellectual property but not yet manufactured – careful consideration will need to be given to the rights that any lender to the customer will need in order to carry on the business of the customer in the event of the insolvency of the licensor of the third-party intellectual property.

Security interests in bank accounts under the UNCITRAL Model Law on Secured Transactions

Spyridon V Bazinas
Lecturer, author and consultant

1. Introduction

In 2016, the United Nations Commission on International Trade Law (UNCITRAL)[1] adopted the Model Law on Secured Transactions ('Model Law').[2] The Model Law implements in statutory language the recommendations of the UNCITRAL Legislative Guide on Secured Transactions, which UNCITRAL adopted in 2007 ('Secured Transactions Guide').[3]

With respect to the registration of notices of security interests in a general security interest registry, the Model Law implements the legislative recommendations of the UNCITRAL Guide on the Implementation of a Security Rights Registry, which UNCITRAL adopted in 2013 ('Registry Guide'). With respect to security interests in intellectual property, the Model Law implements the legislative recommendations of the UNCITRAL Legislative Guide on Secured Transactions: Supplement on Security Rights in Intellectual Property, which UNCITRAL adopted in 2010 ('IP Supplement').

With respect to security interests in and outright transfers of receivables by agreement, the Model Law contains the provisions of the United Nations Convention on the Assignment of Receivables in International Trade, which UNCITRAL prepared and the United Nations General Assembly adopted in 2001. Most importantly, with respect to the treatment of security interests in insolvency, the Model Law is accompanied or supplemented by the UNCITRAL Legislative Guide on Insolvency Law, which UNCITRAL adopted in 2004.

The Model Law is accompanied by the UNCITRAL Model Law on Secured

---

1   For a brief description of UNCITRAL and its work, see https://uncitral.un.org/en/about.
2   All texts of UNCITRAL on security interests are available at https://uncitral.un.org/en/texts/securityinterests. For a bibliography on the UNCITRAL texts on security interests, see https://uncitral.un.org/en/library/bibliography.
3   For a discussion of the treatment of security interests in rights to payment of funds credited to a bank account under the Secured Transactions Guide, see *Spiros V Bazinas*, "Security interests over key assets: bank accounts", in Paul U Ali (ed), *Secured Finance Transactions: Key Assets and Emerging Markets* (Globe Law and Business, 2007), p101.

Transactions: Guide to Enactment, which is an article-by-article commentary of the Model Law and which UNCITRAL adopted in 2017 ('Guide to Enactment'). In addition, the Model Law is accompanied by the UNCITRAL Practice Guide to the Model Law on Secured Transactions, which provides practical guidance to parties involved in secured transactions in states that enact the Model Law, and which UNCITRAL adopted in 2019 ('Practice Guide').

With all these texts, the Model Law constitutes a comprehensive and modern uniform law applying to security interests (defined in a functional way to cover all transactions serving security purposes) in all types of movable assets (with limited exceptions, such as intermediated securities and financial contracts).[4] Thus, the Model Law applies to security interests in rights to payment of funds credited to a bank account, which is the topic of this chapter.[5]

Section 2 of this chapter considers the scope and terminology of the Model Law; section 3 the creation of a security interest; section 4 the effectiveness against third parties of a security interest; section 5 the registry system; section 6 the priority of a security interest; section 7 pre-default rights and obligations of the parties and third-party obligors; section 8 post-default rights of parties; section 9 conflict of laws; section 10 transition issues; and section 11 security interests in insolvency.

2. Scope and terminology of the Model Law

The Model Law applies to security interests in movable assets (Article 1(1)). The term 'security interest' is defined in a functional way to cover any consensual property right in a movable asset that secures payment or other performance of an obligation, regardless of whether the parties have denominated it as a security interest (Article 2(kk)). The term 'movable asset' is defined as any tangible or intangible asset other than immovable property (Article 2(u)), and thus includes the right to payment of funds credited to a bank account. This right is the encumbered asset, not the entire bank-client relationship. Although this right to payment is in general terms a receivable, it is excluded from the definition of the term 'receivable' (as is a right to payment under a negotiable instrument or under a non-intermediated security; Article 2(dd)). The reason is that the asset-specific rules that apply to a receivable under the Model Law do not apply to a right to payment of funds credited to a bank account.

---

4   For a comparison of the Model Law with the Model Inter-American Law on Secured Transactions, see Spyridon V Bazinas, "Uniform secured transactions law: the Model Inter-American Law and the UNCITRAL Model Law on Secured Transactions compared", in David Morán Bovio (ed), *Ley Modelo Interamericana sobre Garantías Mobiliarias: su implementación* (organización de los Estados Americanos Marcial Pons, 2020, pp321–351 (www.oas.org/es/sla/ddi/docs/publicacion_Ley_Modelo_Interamericana_sobre_Garantias_Mobiliarias_Su_Implementacion.pdf).

5   In the five years since its completion in 2016, the Model Law has been enacted in eight states (https://uncitral.un.org/en/texts/securityinterests/modellaw/secured_transactions/status). It is also being considered for enactment in a number of other states; and its main provisions reflect the provisions of the laws of many more states.

The term 'bank account' is generally defined as an account to which funds may be credited or debited, and which is maintained by any institution authorised (licensed) by each state enacting the Model Law ('enacting state') to receive deposits (Article 2(c)). The term includes any type of bank account (eg, current or checking and savings account), but it does not include a right against a bank to the payment of funds evidenced by a negotiable instrument drawn on that bank (because different asset-specific rules of the Model Law apply to these types of assets).[6] While the term is defined in a general way, it is up to the enacting state to adjust this definition (and other definitions) to its relevant national law.

The term 'grantor' means the person that creates a security interest in its assets (Article 2(o)). The term 'debtor' means the person that owes the secured obligation, whether or not that person is the grantor of the security interest (Article 2(h)). The term 'debtor of the receivable' means the person that owes payment of a receivable that is subject to a security interest (Article 2(i)). The term 'secured creditor' means the person in whose favour a security interest is created (Article 2(f)). The term 'encumbered asset' means the asset in which a security interest is created (Article 2(k)). The term 'secured obligation' means an obligation secured by a security interest (Article 2(gg)).[7]

Several chapters of the Model Law have two parts: a part with general provisions that apply to security interests in all types of movable assets; and another part with asset-specific provisions that apply, in addition to the general provisions, specifically to certain types of assets (ie, receivables, negotiable instruments, negotiable documents, rights to payment of funds credited to a bank account, intellectual property and non-intermediated securities).

Thus, security interests in rights to payment of funds credited to a bank account are regulated by the general provisions and the asset-specific provisions that deal with security interests in rights to payment of funds credited to a bank account.

The Model Law also applies to outright transfers of receivables by agreement in all respects except enforcement (Article 1(2)). The reason is that outright transfers of receivables are part of receivables finance transactions and it is important that the same third-party and priority rules apply to all receivables finance transactions, as it is often difficult for third parties to determine whether an outright transfer, a security transfer or a security interest in receivables is involved in a particular transaction.

As already mentioned, rights to payment of funds credited to a bank account are excluded from the definition of the term 'receivable' (Article 2(dd)). Thus, the Model Law does not apply to outright sales of those rights of funds

---

6   Guide to Enactment, para 39.
7   Further terms are defined in subsequent chapters.

credited to a bank account and the asset-specific provisions on security interests in receivables do not apply to security interests in those rights.

For different reasons, the Model Law does not apply to security interests in letters of credit, intellectual property (only in certain cases), intermediated securities and payment rights arising from or under financial contracts covered by netting agreements (Article 1(3)).

Letters of credit are not covered because they are not the typical assets offered and accepted all over the world as security for credit; and those states that have that practice could implement the recommendations of the Secured Transactions Guide.[8] Intellectual property is not covered only to the extent that the Model Law is inconsistent with the law relating to intellectual property, to avoid interfering with fundamental policies of that law.[9] Intermediated securities and payment rights arising from or under financial contracts covered by netting agreements are not covered because they are part of capital market transactions, rather than commercial finance transactions, and they raise complex issues that are addressed in other laws.[10]

3. Creation of a security interest

A security interest in any asset, including in a right to payment of funds credited to a bank account, is created by a security agreement (Article 6(1)). Once a security interest is created, it is effective as between the grantor and the secured creditor. Effectiveness as against third parties is, in principle, subject to further requirements (see section 4 below).

By splitting the property effects of a security interest in such a way, the Model Law simplifies the creation of a security interest, as, if upon its creation a security interest is effective only between the parties, the formal requirements for its creation can be reduced. In addition, by subjecting third-party effectiveness, in principle, to registration, the Model Law provides secured creditors with a simple, easy and inexpensive way to establish third-party effectiveness and third-party creditors with an objective criterion to determine priority before they extend credit. Moreover, the concept of priority makes it possible for grantors to create more than one security interest in their assets, as long as their assets have enough value to satisfy all secured obligations, thus allowing grantors to use the full value in their assets to obtain credit. With this approach, the Model Law achieved some of the key objectives of an effective and efficient secured transactions law.[11]

The main substantive requirement is that the grantor granting the security interest has rights in the asset or the power to encumber it (Article 6(1)). In the

---

8   Guide to Enactment, para 24.
9   *Ibid*, para 25 and Intellectual Property Supplement, paras 1 and 61.
10   Guide to Enactment, paras 26 and 27.
11   Secured Transactions Guide, Recommendations 1 (b), (c) and (f).

case of a security interest in a right to payment of funds credited to a bank account, this person is the account holder (or holders) or a secured creditor transferring its security interest to another person.

If, at the time of the conclusion of the security agreement, the right to payment of funds credited to a bank account to be encumbered exists and the grantor has rights in it, the security interest is created at that time. If the right to payment of funds credited to a bank account to be encumbered does not exist at that time or the grantor acquires its rights in that right thereafter, the security interest is created when that right comes into existence or the grantor acquires its rights in that right (Article 6(2)). Thus, the grantor need not amend the same security agreement each time it acquires an asset.

The security agreement must be concluded or evidenced in[12] a writing signed by the grantor and, at a minimum:

- identify the grantor and the secured creditor;
- describe the secured obligation and the encumbered asset; and
- if the enacting state chooses to add this requirement, state the maximum amount for which the security interest may be enforced (Article 6(3)).[13]

'Writing' and 'signature' generally include their electronic equivalents, but the Model Law leaves those matters to other relevant law of the enacting state. However, the Model Law deals with the standard that must be met for the description of the secured obligation and the encumbered asset in a security agreement to be effective. They both must be described in a manner that reasonably allows their identification (Articles 9(1) and (2)). This means that the description may be generic or specific, depending on whether a category of assets or a specific asset is encumbered.[14]

Unless otherwise agreed by the parties, a security interest in an asset automatically extends to its identifiable proceeds (Article 10(1)). Thus, when encumbered inventory is sold, the security interest automatically extends to the right to payment of the purchase price and, if that price is deposited in a bank account, to the right to payment of the funds credited to the bank account. If those funds are commingled with other funds in the account, the security interest automatically extends to the commingled funds, even though they have ceased to be identifiable; but the security interest is limited to the funds immediately before they were commingled. Moreover, if funds are withdrawn after the

---

12 Depending on which expression is chosen by an enacting state, a security agreement that is not in writing will be ineffective or will be effective if its terms are evidenced by a written document signed by the grantor (Guide to Enactment, para 88).

13 The reason for this requirement is to facilitate the grantor's access to credit from other creditors, if the value of the assets exceeds the maximum amount agreed by the parties. But this may lead the parties to agree on an excessively high maximum amount; and in states in which parties tend to obtain credit from one and the same financial institution, this requirement may not be needed (Guide to Enactment, para 89).

14 Guide to Enactment, para 96.

proceeds are commingled so that, at some point in time, the total amount of funds is less than the amount of the proceeds, the security interest extends only to the lowest amount between the time when the proceeds were commingled and the time when the security interest right in the proceeds is claimed (Article 10(2)). The same rule applies where funds in a bank account that are subject to a security interest are transferred to another bank account of the grantor and mixed with other funds in that other account; in such case, the funds transferred to that other account will be 'proceeds' of the original encumbered assets.[15]

A security interest in a right to payment of funds credited to a bank account is effective between the grantor and the secured creditor despite the existence of an agreement between the grantor and the deposit-taking institution prohibiting the creation of a security interest (Article 15). However, the creation of such a security interest does not affect the rights and obligations of the deposit-taking institution without its consent and, in particular, does not oblige the deposit-taking institution to pay the secured creditor or provide any information about the bank account to the secured creditor (Article 69). The position of the deposit-taking institution does not change without its consent even if the security interest is made effective against third parties by registration (Article 18(1)). If, however, the security interest is made effective against third parties essentially with the cooperation of the deposit-taking institution (ie, by the creation of a security interest in favour of the deposit-taking institution; by a control agreement between the account holder, the secured creditor and the deposit-taking institution; or by a transfer of the account to the secured creditor after which the secured creditor is the account holder), the position of the deposit-taking institution may change (Article 25).

4.   Third-party effectiveness of a security interest

A security interest in any type of asset, including a right to payment of funds credited to a bank account, may be made effective against third parties (ie, competing secured creditors, buyers of the encumbered asset, judgment creditors or the grantor's insolvency administrator (Article 2(e)), mainly by registration of a notice in a general security interest registry (Article 18(1)).

While registration of a notice provides an objective way of informing third parties about the possible existence of a security interest for which they can obtain more information from the secured creditor on record with the consent of the grantor, it may not be imposed on deposit-taking institutions without delaying or adding costs to normal banking transactions. So, additional methods of third-party effectiveness are introduced for security interests in rights to payment of funds credited to a bank account – namely, the creation of a security interest in favour of the deposit-taking institution, a 'control agreement' and the transfer of the account to the secured creditor (Article 25).

---

15   *Ibid*, para 102.

Upon the creation of a security interest in a right to payment of funds credited to a bank account in favour of the deposit-taking institution, it is automatically effective against third parties without any further act (third parties know that if the deposit-taking institution has a security interest, it has priority and can find out from the account holder before extending credit). A control agreement requires the participation of the deposit-taking institution and requires its consent to following instructions with respect to the account from the secured creditor (Article 2(g)(ii)). Similarly, a transfer of the account to the secured creditor requires the consent of the deposit-taking institution. This covers situations where:

- an existing account is transferred to the secured creditor; or
- the secured creditor agrees with the grantor that funds from the account of the grantor should be transferred to an account in the name of the secured creditor, either existing or to be opened.

If a right to payment of funds credited to a bank account (which is an asset that can be encumbered and transferred) is the proceeds of another asset (eg, goods where the sales price of encumbered goods is paid by a funds transfer to a bank account), a security interest in such proceeds is effective against third parties when the proceeds arise, which means that there is no need to have a separate act of registration or other third-party effectiveness method (Article 19(1)). This rule reflects the normal expectations of the parties and avoids overburdening them with additional registration or other requirements. This rule may always be derogated from or varied by the parties by agreement (as Article 19(1) is not among the mandatory law provisions set out in Article 3(1)).

Once a security interest becomes effective against third parties, it remains effective against them even if there is a change in the method of achieving third-party effectiveness (Article 21). For example, if the secured creditor registers a notice and later obtains a control agreement, third-party effectiveness dates from the time of registration. This means that third-party effectiveness is continuous and does not depend on the particular way in which it is achieved. However, if there is a time lapse, third-party effectiveness may be re-established; but it begins as of the time it is re-established (Article 22).

5. The registry system

The purpose of the registry system is to provide a method to achieve third-party effectiveness, an objective basis for determining priority and an alert for potential third-party financiers about the possible existence of a security interest, which should lead them to require more information essentially from secured creditors on record with the consent of the relevant potential borrowers. Registration of a notice about the security interest in the general security interest registry is the main method to render a non-possessory security interest effective against third parties (Article 18(1)). The Model Law foresees the establishment of a general security interest registry (Article 28). The details of the registration process are regulated in the Model Registry Provisions (MRP) which are part of the Model Law, and may be enacted with the Model Law or separately in another law or administrative regulations.[16]

For reasons of simplicity and efficiency, the registry envisaged in the Model Law provides for registration by grantor rather than by asset and is notice based rather than transaction based. The legal consequence of registration is not the creation, but the third-party effectiveness of a security interest. Some of the key features of the registry are set out below:

- Off-record authorisation must be in writing and may be given even after registration. The security agreement constitutes sufficient authorisation; without it, a registration is ineffective and the grantor may seek the registration of an amendment or cancellation notice (MRP, Articles 2 and 20).
- A registration may relate to multiple security interests and take place even before the creation of a security interest or the conclusion of a security agreement (MRP, Articles 3 and 4).
- Anyone may register a notice, as long as that person:
  - uses the prescribed notice form;
  - has a user account or otherwise identifies itself; and
  - pays or arranges to pay the prescribed fee (MRP, Article 5).
- The registry is under no obligation to verify the information contained in a notice (MRP, Articles 7(2) and (3)).
- The notice must contain a limited amount of data, such as:
  - the name and address of the grantor and the secured creditor;
  - a specific or general description of the encumbered asset; and
  - if an enacting state decides to enact the option offered in the MRP, the maximum amount secured by a security interest (MRP, Article 8).
- The grantor and the secured creditor are to be identified in similar ways (MRP, Articles 9 and 10).
- The description of the encumbered assets in the notice may be specific or generic, as long as it is sufficient to reasonably identify the assets (MRP, Article 11).
- The information in the notice must be expressed in the language specified by the state enacting the Model Law (with the exception of the names and addresses of the grantor and the secured creditor), and in the character set specified and publicised by the registry (MRP, Article 12).
- Registration is effective once the information has been entered in the

---

16   Model Law, footnote 8.

public registry record and becomes accessible to searchers (MRP, Article 13(1)).

- With respect to the duration of registration, options are offered from which enacting states may choose, ranging from periods of time set out in the law to periods of time selected by the parties, without any limit or up to a maximum number of years; in all cases, the registration may be renewed more than once (MRP, Article 14).
- The registry is obliged to send to the person identified in the notice as the secured creditor a verification notice, and that person must forward it to the person identified in the notice as the grantor (MRP, Article 15).
- The notice may be amended or cancelled by the registrant at any time (MRP, Article 16).
- Amendment notices must contain in the designated fields the registration number of the initial notice to which they relate and the information to be amended (MRP, Article 17).
- A registrant or the registry may enter a single amendment notice to amend the secured creditor identifier and address in multiple notices (MRP, Article 18).
- Cancellation notices must contain in the designated field the registration number of the initial notice to which they relate (MRP, Article 19).
- The secured creditor must register an amendment or cancellation notice in certain situations (eg, absence of authorisation; upon the performance of all secured obligations). If the secured creditor fails to do so in a timely fashion, the grantor may seek an order for the registration of an amendment or cancellation notice through a summary administrative or judicial proceeding (MRP, Article 20).
- With respect to the effectiveness of an unauthorised amendment or cancellation notice, options are offered from which enacting states may choose, ranging from the effectiveness to the ineffectiveness of an unauthorised notice (MRP, Article 21).
- The registry must have an electronic database in which notices will be indexed by the name of the grantor and authorised users with a confidential key may have remote electronic access (MRP, Article 22(1)).
- The registry must organise the information in the registry record in a way that makes searches possible according to the secured debtor or grantor name (the MRP also provides for indexing and searching by registration number), and issue a search result (MRP, Articles 22 and 23).
- The post-registration change of the grantor identifier does not affect the third-party effectiveness or priority of a security interest (MRP, Article 25).
- With respect to the effect of the post-registration transfer of an encumbered asset, options are offered to enacting states, ranging from

no effect to limited effect on the third-party effectiveness and priority of a security interest (MRP, Article 26).

- With respect to the way in which information in the registry record should be organised so that it may be retrieved, options are offered to enacting states, ranging from the retrieval of only exact matches to the retrieval of close matches of the search criterion (MRP, Article 28).

- In principle, the registry may not amend or remove information from the public registry record, except as provided below (MRP, Articles 30 and 31).

- The registry may remove information from the public registry record only if the registration is no longer effective or a cancellation notice is registered; although the MRPs also provide for an option under which cancelled notices remain on the public registry record with an indication that they have been cancelled (MRP, Article 30).

- The registry may correct errors it has made, but options are offered with respect to the way in which this correction may be made and its effect (MRP, Article 31).

- With respect to the liability of the registry, options are offered to enacting states, ranging from limited liability to limited or no liability at all (MRP, Article 32).

- With respect to registry fees, options are offered to enacting states, ranging from no fees to fees according to a fee schedule that the registry may amend, but must publicise (MRP, Article 33).

6.   Priority of a security interest

One of the key objectives of an effective and efficient law on secured transactions – including the Model Law[17] – is to allow debtors to use the full value inherent in their assets to obtain credit and, as a result, to be able to create more than one security interest in the same asset. This raises the question of which claim has priority, that is, which claim will be paid first in case of default. Thus, another key objective of the Model Law is to establish clear and predictable priority rules (Secured Transactions Guide, Recommendations 1(b)) and (g)).

The term 'priority' is a key concept and is defined in the Model Law to mean the right of a person in an encumbered asset in preference to the right of a competing claimant (Article 2(aa)). The term 'competing claimant' is defined to mean:

- another secured creditor with a security interest in the same encumbered asset (whether as an original encumbered asset or proceeds);

---

17   The key objectives and fundamental policies of the Model Law are the same as those of the Secured Transactions Guide (Guide Enactment, paras 5 and 16).

- another creditor of the grantor that has a right in the same encumbered asset (eg, by operation of law, attachment or seizure or similar process);
- the insolvency administrator in the insolvency of the grantor; or
- a buyer or other transferee (including a lessee or licensee) of the encumbered asset (Article 2(o)).

The main priority rule of the Model Law is based on the time of registration of a notice in the general security interest registry (Article 29). However, in view of the nature of a right to payment of funds credited to a bank account and the debtor of that right (a deposit-taking institution) that is subject to special rules, registration does not give the highest priority ranking. In the case of a priority competition of security interests in rights to payment of funds credited to a bank account, priority ranks as follows. First is the security interest made effective against third parties by the secured creditor becoming the account holder (eg, by way of the transfer of an account or by the opening of a new account in the name of the secured creditor). Next is a security interest with respect to which the deposit-taking institution is the secured creditor and the rights of set-off of the deposit-taking institution. Then follows a security interest made effective against third parties by way of a control agreement and, in the case of multiple control agreements, the first control agreement. And last in priority is a security interest made effective against third parties by the registration of a notice in the general security interest registry (Articles 47(1) to (5)).

These rules reflect normal banking law and practice, recognising the privileged position of deposit-taking institutions as compared to other creditors with a security interest in a right to payment of funds credited to a bank account.

A transferee of funds credited to a bank account acquires its rights free of a security interest, unless the transferee had knowledge that the transfer violated the rights of the secured creditor under the security agreement (Article 47(6)). The burden of proof is on the person challenging the transfer and is high, in order to ensure that bank transfers are not undermined. In any case, with respect to the rights of transferees of funds from bank accounts, the Model Law defers to the relevant banking or other law of the enacting state (Article 47(7)).

Where the grantor becomes insolvent, the question arises as to the priority ranking of the insolvency administrator or the mass of creditors. This is a matter of insolvency law (see section 11 below). However, to ensure legal certainty, the Model Law requires that any right that is given priority over a security interest be clearly set out in the relevant insolvency law (ideally, with a cross-reference in secured transactions law) for prospective secured creditors to be able to calculate the potential risk involved in a secured transaction (Article 35).

Furthermore, certain rights are at times given priority over security interests by law even outside of insolvency (eg, short-term claims of unpaid suppliers of goods; rights of retention of unpaid creditors that have rendered services such as repair services with respect to encumbered assets; claims of the grantor's employees for employment benefits; and tax claims). To alert prospective secured creditors to the existence and the maximum amounts of such claims before lending, the Model Law requires that they be limited and set out in the law enacting the Model Law (Article 36).

The Model Law recognises that unsecured creditors that have obtained a judgment ordering the grantor of a security interest to pay and that have taken steps to have that judgment enforced deserve some protection. Thus, if they take those steps before a security interest is made effective against third parties, they have priority; otherwise, they do not have priority (Article 37). This rule also applies where the encumbered asset is a right to payment of funds credited to a bank account.

Recognising the need for flexibility in the regulation of priority to meet the needs of financing practices, the Model Law permits a secured creditor to subordinate its priority unilaterally or by agreement in favour of an existing or future competing claimant, as long as the rights of third parties are not affected (Article 43).

The priority of a security interest extends to all obligations secured by a security agreement, including obligations incurred after a security interest became effective against third parties (Article 44(1)). However, if the registered notice mentions a maximum amount, priority is limited to that amount (Article 8(e)). Similarly, the priority of a security interest extends to all encumbered assets described in a notice, including assets that were acquired by the grantor or that came into existence after registration of a notice in the general security interest registry (Article 44(2)).

Whether a competing claimant has knowledge of the existence of a competing security interest is irrelevant for the priority position of that competing claimant's interest (Article 45). However, knowledge that a transfer of funds out of bank account violates the rights of a creditor under a security agreement results in the transferee taking the funds subject to the security interest (Article 48(1)).

7.   Pre-default rights and obligations of the parties and third-party obligors

The Model Law confirms the freedom of the parties to structure their security agreement in any way they wish so as to address their needs (Article 3(1)). At the same time, the Model Law recognises that party autonomy may have to be limited to avoid affecting the rights of third parties (Article 3(2)). Thus, for example, the provisions on general standards of conduct of the parties (Article 4), the requirements for a security agreement (Article 6) and the conflict-of-laws rules (Articles 85–100), with the exception of the rule dealing with the law applicable to the rights and obligations of the parties to the security agreement (Article 84), may not be derogated from or varied by agreement.

In addition to recognising the terms and conditions of the security agreement as the source of the mutual rights and obligations of the parties, the Model Law gives legislative strength to trade usages agreed by the parties and practices that they have established between themselves, which may not be generally recognised in all states (Article 52).

The Model Law also provides a set of mandatory rules that deal with issues such as:

- the duty of care of the person in possession of the encumbered assets; and
- the duty to return the assets or terminate any notice on the record of the registry upon full payment and termination of all credit commitments (Model Law, Articles 53 and 54; and MRP, Article 20(1), (2) and (3)).

In addition, the Model Law includes a set of non-mandatory rules that are applicable prior to default in the absence of agreement of the parties. Those rules deal with issues such as:

- the right of the secured creditor to use encumbered assets in its possession and to be reimbursed for reasonable expenses incurred for their preservation;
- the right of the secured creditor to inspect assets in the possession of the grantor; and
- the right of the grantor to regularly obtain information about the obligation owing and the assets encumbered at a particular point of time (Articles 55 and 56).

To coordinate with other relevant law, the Model Law includes a number of provisions dealing with the rights and obligations of third-party obligors, such as the debtor in the case of encumbered receivables; and the deposit-taking institution in the case of an encumbered right to payment of funds credited to a bank account.

With respect to the rights and obligations of the deposit-taking institution, the Model Law provides that the creation of a security interest in a right to payment of funds credited to a bank account does not affect the rights and obligations of the deposit-taking institution against its consent or oblige the deposit-taking institution to provide information about the account to third parties (Article 69).

The rationale for protecting deposit-taking institutions in this manner is that imposing duties on such an institution or changing the rights and duties of the institution without its consent may subject that institution to risks that it is not in a position to manage appropriately, unless it knows in advance what those risks might be; and to the risk of having to violate obligations imposed by other law, such as sanctions law.

At the same time, recognising the need for flexibility, the Model Law permits a deposit-taking institution to negotiate and agree to obtain instructions about the funds in a bank account from a secured creditor by entering into a control agreement with the grantor/account holder and the secured creditor or by accepting a transfer of the funds in the grantor's bank account to the secured creditor (Articles 25 and 47).

8.   Post-default rights of the parties

The Model Law gives an indicative definition of the term 'default' by referring to "the failure of a debtor to pay or otherwise perform a secured obligation and any other event that constitutes default under the terms of an agreement between the grantor and the secured creditor" (Article 2(j)). It thus leaves the exact meaning of the term 'default' to the security agreement and the law governing that agreement. However, to enhance certainty with respect to the enforcement of a security interest, which may affect the availability and cost of credit, the Model Law sets out in detail the remedies available to the secured creditor and those available to the grantor of the security interest in the case of default.

Generally, the secured creditor may:

- take over the enforcement process, if its security interest has priority over the security interest of the enforcing secured creditor (Article 76);
- obtain possession of a tangible encumbered asset (Article 77);
- sell or otherwise dispose of, lease or license an encumbered asset (Article 78);
- use the sales proceeds to satisfy the secured obligation (Article 79);
- propose to the grantor that the secured creditor accept an encumbered asset in total or partial satisfaction of the secured obligation (Article 80);
- collect payment where a security interest exists in a receivable, negotiable instrument, right to payment of funds credited to a bank account or non-intermediated security (Article 82); or
- exercise any other remedy provided in the security agreement except to the extent inconsistent with the secured transactions or other relevant law (Articles 72(1)).

Similarly, the grantor may:

- apply to the court or other authority for relief if the secured creditor is not complying with its obligations (Article 74);
- pay in full the secured obligation, including interest and reasonable costs, until disposition, collection or acceptance of encumbered assets, and obtain the release of the encumbered assets from the security interest (Article 75);
- propose to the secured creditor or reject the proposal of the secured creditor to accept the encumbered assets in total or partial satisfaction of the secured obligation (Article 80); or

- exercise any other right or remedy provided in the security agreement except to the extent inconsistent with the secured transactions or other relevant law (Article 72(1)).

Remedies may be exercised in parallel, as long as the exercise of one remedy does not make impossible the exercise of another (Article 72(2)). For example, a secured creditor that obtains possession of an encumbered asset with the initial intention of disposing of it may thereafter propose to acquire it in satisfaction of the secured obligation. But this remedy cannot be exercised if the secured creditor has already sold or agreed to sell the asset.

In recognising the security agreement as a source of remedies, the Model Law gives appropriate recognition to party autonomy, which is essential for parties in structuring their transactions so as to address their particular needs. At the same time, the Model Law sets the appropriate limits of the principle of party autonomy. The general standard of conduct (good faith and commercial reasonableness) cannot be waived or varied (Articles 3(1) and 4). In addition, to avoid abuse of the secured creditor's dominant position at the time of default and enforcement, no post-default remedy may be waived unilaterally or varied by agreement (Article 72(3)).

The secured creditor may exercise these remedies by applying to a court or other authority or without such an application (Article 73(1)). Judicial enforcement is subject to the provisions of the Model Law and other relevant law of the enacting state, and should include expeditious proceedings (Article 73(2)); extra-judicial enforcement is subject to the provisions of the Model Law (Article 73(3)). Where extra-judicial enforcement is permitted, the Model Law refers to safeguards to avoid abuse of power by the secured creditor (eg, Article 77(2)), and to the right of the debtor or other grantor to challenge the actions of the secured creditor before a court or other authority (Article 74).

More concretely, for the secured creditor to be able to obtain possession of an encumbered asset out of court:
- the security agreement must provide for extra-judicial repossession of the encumbered asset;
- the secured creditor must give notice of default and its intention to obtain possession out of court to the grantor and any other person in possession of the encumbered asset; and
- the person in possession of the encumbered asset must not object at the time of repossession (Article 77(3)).

If any of these conditions are met and, in particular, if the person in possession objects, the secured creditor must obtain the assistance of a court or other authority to obtain possession of the encumbered asset (Article 74).

If the secured creditor chooses to dispose of an encumbered asset without an application to a court or other authority, the secured creditor must notify the grantor, the debtor (if it is a different person from the grantor) and other competing claimants of record or claimants that notified the enforcing secured creditor (Articles 78(3)–(8)).

Once the encumbered assets are disposed of out of court and the secured obligation has been satisfied, any surplus must be returned to subordinate claimants that gave prior written notice to the enforcing secured creditor and any balance remaining to the grantor. In any case, the secured creditor may pay any surplus to a judicial or other authority. In the case of a judicial disposition, distribution of proceeds takes place in accordance with the relevant law applicable to execution proceedings. The debtor is liable for any shortfall still owing after application of the proceeds to the secured obligation (Article 79).

If the secured creditor chooses to propose the acquisition of an encumbered asset in full or partial satisfaction of the secured obligation out of court, the secured creditor must notify the same persons just mentioned (Article 80(2)). In the case of full satisfaction of the secured obligation, the secured creditor acquires the encumbered asset unless it receives a written objection from one of the persons notified (Article 80(4)). If an objection is made, the secured creditor may enforce its security right only by disposition (or collection if the encumbered asset is a receivable, right to payment of funds credited to a bank account, negotiable instrument or non-intermediated security (Article 82)). In case of partial satisfaction of the secured obligation, the secured creditor acquires the encumbered asset only if it obtains the consent in writing of all persons notified (Article 80(5)). This positive consent requirement is intended to protect the debtor since, in the case of a partial satisfaction of the secured obligation, it would remain liable for the balance of the obligation (Article 79(3)). It is also intended to protect any lower-ranking claimant whose rights would be extinguished under Article 81(3) of the Model Law. If the proposal is unsuccessful, the secured creditor may enforce its security interest only disposing of the encumbered asset (or by collecting it if the encumbered asset is a receivable, right to payment of funds credited to a bank account, negotiable instrument or non-intermediated security).

If the secured creditor chooses to enforce its security interest by applying to a court or other authority, a buyer of an asset will normally acquire the asset free of any security interest and a lessee or licensee may have the benefit of the use of the asset unaffected by any security interest. It is left to the court to protect the interests of third parties. However, in the case of extra-judicial enforcement, a buyer will acquire the asset free of, and a lessee or licensee may have the benefit of the use of the asset unaffected by, only security interests that are subordinate to the security interest of the enforcing secured creditor (Article 81).

Specifically, with respect to a security interest in a right to payment of funds credited to a bank account, the Model Law provides that the secured creditor may collect or otherwise enforce (eg, retain or assign) its security interest

(Article 82(1)). If the grantor consents, this right of collection may be exercised even before default and operates as a repayment of the secured obligation (Article 82(2)). Out-of-court collection, however, is not permitted if the security interest has been made effective against third parties by registration. A control agreement or some other form of consent of the deposit-taking institution will be required to ensure that the deposit-taking institution does not violate its obligations under banking law to accept orders with respect to a bank account only from the account holder (Article 83(4)). Generally, for the same reason, the right of the secured creditor to collect may not change the position of the deposit-taking institution under its account agreement and the applicable law (Article 82(5)). Of course, the grantor may always go to court to prevent out-of-court collection or seek other relief (Article 74).

9. Conflict of laws

The Model Law contains a chapter on conflict of laws that includes rules for determining the law applicable to the mutual rights and obligations of the grantor and the secured creditor, to the creation, third-party effectiveness, priority and enforcement of a security interest, as well as to the rights and obligations between a third-party obligor – such as a deposit-taking institution – and a secured creditor. The reason is that one of the key objectives of an efficient and effective secured transactions law is to harmonise secured transactions laws, including conflict-of-laws rules, and to provide certainty with respect to the rights of parties involved or affected by a secured transaction, including with respect to the law applicable to secured transactions.[18]

In addition, this chapter is useful in that it:
* clarifies the state in which a secured creditor must register or otherwise make its security interest effective against third parties; and
* helps to determine the territorial scope of application of the substantive law rules of the Model Law.

Following the approach of international texts, such as the Hague Principles on Choice of Law in International Commercial Contracts, the Model Law provides that the mutual rights and obligations of the grantor and the secured creditor with respect to a security interest arising from the security agreement are governed by the law governing the security agreement (Article 84). For example, this law may be:
* the law of the state with which a credit transaction is most closely connected (eg, the state in which a credit agreement is entered into and performed and in which the parties are located); or
* the law of the state in which the characteristic performance of a

---

18 Secured Transactions Guide, Recommendation 1(k).

transaction takes place (eg, the delivery of goods in a retention-of-title sale or the extension of credit in a credit agreement).

This approach is intended to align the law governing the security agreement with the law applicable to the purely contractual rights and obligations of the parties, and thus be in line with the expectations of the parties. Matters relating to the property aspects of secured transactions are outside the scope of Article 84 of the Model Law. The parties cannot select the law that is to govern these matters (with the exception of matters relating to a security interest in a rights to payment of funds credited to a bank account (Article 97, option B) and matters relating to a security interest in non-intermediated debt securities (Article 100)). Other matters – such as the ability of the parties to choose different laws for different aspects of their contractual relationship or to modify their choice of law – are left to other conflict-of-laws rules of the enacting state (eg, Articles 2(2) and (3) of the Hague Principles).[19]

With respect to security interests in tangible assets, the Model Law refers the creation, third-party effectiveness and priority to the law of the state where the assets are located (*lex rei sitae*) (Article 85); and enforcement to the law of the state in which the asset is located at the time of commencement of enforcement (Article 88(a)). Special rules are provided for security interests in:

- goods covered by negotiable documents (ie, the law of the state in which the negotiable document is located);
- mobile goods that cross national borders in the course of their normal use (ie, the law of the state of the grantor's location); and
- goods in transit and export goods (ie, the law of the state of origin or the state of destination).

With respect to security interests in intangible assets, the Model Law refers all issues to the law of the grantor's location (Article 86). This recommendation is consistent with the principle in Articles 22 and 30 of the United Nations Assignment Convention and provides legal certainty as to the law applicable to receivables, as:

- it provides for the application of a single law to all issues;
- the law applicable is easy to determine (the law of the state in which the grantor has its place of business or, in the case of no place of business, his or her habitual residence, and in the case of places of business in more than one state, its central administration); and
- the law applicable is the law of the state in which the main insolvency proceedings with respect to the grantor are most likely to be commenced (as the place of central administration is generally accepted to be the

---

19   Guide to Enactment, para 471.

same with the centre of main interests, in which a main insolvency proceeding is typically commenced).[20]

With respect to rights to payment of funds credited to a bank account, the Model Law has a special rule (Article 97). The scope of that rule is very broad and covers the creation, third-party effectiveness, priority and enforcement of a security interest. It also covers the rights and obligations between the deposit-taking institution and the secured creditor. The law applicable is not the law applicable to other intangibles. Two alternatives are offered. The first alternative refers to the law of the state in which the deposit-taking institution has its place of business. In the case of places of business in more than one state, reference is made to the law of the state in which the branch that maintains the relevant account is located. This alternative is based on the premise that a bank account can be located and the law applicable to security interests in rights to payment of funds credited to bank accounts should be the law that would be generally applicable to that bank or branch.

The second alternative refers to the law of the state expressly stated in the account agreement, provided that the deposit-taking institution has a branch in that state. This alternative is based on the assumption that, like cash in a securities account, cash in a bank account cannot be linked to a certain location and thus the law applicable to security interests in intermediated securities under the Hague Convention on the Law Applicable to Certain Rights in Respect of Securities Held with an Intermediary should apply.

The creation of a security interest in proceeds is governed by the law governing the creation of the security interest in the assets from which the proceeds arose (Article 89(1)). So, for example, if the original encumbered assets are goods and the proceeds take the form of a right to payment of funds in a bank account, the creation of a security interest in the right to payment of funds credited to a bank account is governed by the law of the location of the goods. In this way, creditors obtaining a security interest in goods will know that their right will extend to proceeds of goods subject to the law of the same state where the goods are located.

However, the third-party effectiveness and priority of a security interest in proceeds are governed by the same law as the law governing those issues with respect to assets of the same kind as the proceeds (Article 89(2)). So, if the proceeds of goods take the form of a right to payment of funds credited to a

---

20   For a discussion of the convention, see Spiros V Bazinas, "UNCITRAL's Contribution to the Unification of Receivables Financing Law: The United Nations Convention on the Assignment of Receivables in International Trade", *Revue de Droit Uniforme* 2003- 1/2, 49; and "Multi-jurisdictional receivables financing: UNCITRAL'S impact on securitization and cross-border perfection", *Duke Journal of Competition & International Law*, Volume 12, p365. For a comparison of the conflict-of-laws rules of the convention and a draft regulation proposed by the European Commission, see Spyridon V Bazinas, "The law applicable to third-party effects of assignments of claims: the UN Convention and the EU Commission Proposal compared", *Uniform Law Review*, Volume 24, Issue 4, December 2019, pp609-632.

bank account, these issues will be subject to the law of the state in which the relevant branch is located or the law specified in the account agreement, depending on which alternative the enacting state adopts. This approach ensures that the rights of third parties in the proceeds as original encumbered assets will be subject to the same law, at least with respect to the issues of third-party effectiveness and priority. But it has the disadvantage that the law that applies to the creation of a security interest in proceeds is different from the law that applies to the third-party effectiveness and priority of that security interest. Where the states whose laws apply have a different concept of proceeds, this bifurcated approach may lead to problems.[21]

10.   Transition

The importance of efficient transition rules for a new law that will also regulate existing rights cannot be overemphasised – in particular, as one of the main concerns associated with law reform is the impact of the new law on rights existing before the new law comes into force. In recognition of the importance of fair and efficient transition rules, the Model Law contains a set of detailed transition provisions. These rules are summarised in the following paragraphs.

The law governing security interests (as defined in the new law) before the entry into force of the new law ('prior law') is repealed or amended as provided in the Model Law (Article 101).

The new law applies in principle to all matters relating to a security interest, with the exception of matters that are the subject of proceedings commenced before the entry into force of the new law (Articles 102 and 103).

Prior law determines whether a security interest created before the entry into force of the new law is and remains effective between the parties (Article 104).

A security interest effective against third parties under prior law continues to be effective until the earlier of:

- the time it could have ceased to be effective against third parties under prior law; or
- the expiration of a short period of time after entry into force of the new law (Article 105).

Exceptionally, the priority of a security interest created under prior law is determined under prior law if:

- that security interest and all competing interests arose before the entry into force of the new law; and
- the priority status of all competing interests has not changed after the entry into force of the new law (Article 106).

---

21   Guide to Enactment, para 487.

The new law is to go into effect on a date, or according to a mechanism, to be specified by the enforcing state (Article 107).

11.   Insolvency

As already mentioned, the Model Law contains only two insolvency-related rules. The first rule provides that, in principle, the third-party effectiveness and priority of a security interest are respected in the case of the grantor's insolvency (Article 35).[22] The second rule provides that, in principle, commencement of insolvency with respect to the grantor of a security interest does not change the law applicable to that security interest (Article 94).

However, the Model Law is accompanied by the Secured Transactions Guide and the UNCITRAL Legislative Guide on Insolvency Law ('Insolvency Guide').[23] The Secured Transactions Guide reiterates the recommendations of the Insolvency Guide that are relevant to the treatment of security interests in insolvency. It also includes a few additional recommendations to clarify matters of interest to secured creditors that are not specifically addressed in the Insolvency Guide. Thus, these two guides provide a basis for the modernisation and harmonisation of insolvency law, and for the coordination of insolvency law with a modern secured transactions law, such as the Model Law.

In principle, encumbered assets – including an encumbered right to payment of funds credited to a bank account – are part of the estate of the insolvent grantor (Insolvency Guide, Recommendation 35). Thus, individual actions even by secured creditors to perfect or enforce their security interests are stayed (Insolvency Guide, Recommendations 39(a) and 46(b)). If, however, a security interest was already effective against third parties at the time of commencement of an insolvency proceeding, the secured creditor may take action to preserve the third-party effectiveness of the security interest to the extent and in the manner permitted by secured transactions law (Secured Transactions Guide, Recommendation 238).

The stay of individual actions remains effective throughout the insolvency proceedings until:

- the court grants relief from the stay;
- a reorganisation plan becomes effective; or
- in liquidation proceedings, a fixed time period expires, unless it is extended by a court (Insolvency Guide, Recommendation 49).

A secured creditor may apply to a court to provide protection of the value of the encumbered assets through, for example:

---

22   Reference is made to the insolvency of the grantor because, if the debtor is a different person and becomes insolvent, the creditor is an unsecured creditor in this insolvency proceeding.
23   See www.uncitral.org/uncitral/en/uncitral_texts/insolvency/2004Guide.html.

- cash payments by the estate;
- provision of additional security interests; or
- other means determined by the court (Insolvency Guide, Recommendation 50).

A secured creditor may also seek from a court the lifting of the stay if, for example:
- the encumbered assets are not necessary for the reorganisation of the grantor's business;
- the value of the encumbered assets is diminishing, while the secured creditor is not protected against diminution of value; or
- in reorganisation, a plan is not approved within the prescribed time limits (Insolvency Guide, Recommendation 51).

The insolvency administrator may use or dispose of the encumbered assets free of any security interests in the ordinary course of business, except cash proceeds. Cash proceeds may be used or disposed of if:
- the secured creditor consents;
- the secured creditor was given notice and an opportunity to be heard by a court; and
- the interests of the secured creditor will be protected against diminution in the value of the cash proceeds (Insolvency Guide, Recommendations 52 and 59).

The insolvency administrator may also use and dispose of encumbered assets even outside the ordinary course of business, subject to certain conditions. Such conditions include:
- the provision of adequate notice to creditors;
- the provision of an opportunity for them to be heard by a court; and
- the preservation of the priority of the security interests in the proceeds of the sale of the encumbered assets (Insolvency Guide, Recommendations 52, 55 and 58).

The insolvency administrator may also give further security interests in already encumbered assets to secure post-commencement finance. In principle, such further security interests do not have priority over existing security interests unless:
- the existing secured creditors agree to subordinate their rights to the rights of the post-commencement financiers; or
- the court authorises the creation of post-commencements security interests with priority over pre-commencement security interests.

The court may authorise the creation of post-commencement security interests with priority, provided that certain conditions are satisfied, including the following:

- Existing secured creditors were given an opportunity to be heard by the court;
- The debtor can prove that it cannot obtain necessary finance in any other way; and
- The interests of existing secured creditors are protected (Insolvency Guide, Recommendations 53, 65, 66 and 67).

Furthermore, the insolvency administrator may relinquish assets, provided that notice is given to creditors and they have an opportunity to object. Such notice is not necessary where:

- a secured claim exceeds the value of the encumbered assets; and
- the assets are not required for the reorganisation or the sale of the business as a going concern (Insolvency Guide, Recommendation 62).

Finally, the insolvency administrator may acquire new assets and those assets are not subject to security interests created by the insolvent grantor before commencement of insolvency proceedings, unless they constitute proceeds of encumbered assets (Secured Transactions Guide, Recommendations 235 and 236). For example, if receivables encumbered before the commencement of insolvency are paid into a bank account after the commencement of insolvency, the security interest in the original encumbered assets (ie, the receivables) extends to the proceeds (ie, the right to payment of the funds credited to the bank account).

While insolvency law recognises the effective creation of a security interest, which is a matter of secured transactions law, a security agreement may be subject to avoidance on the same grounds as any other transaction under the applicable insolvency law if, for example, it is a preferential or fraudulent transfer taking place in the suspect period (Insolvency Guide, Recommendation 88).

In addition, while insolvency law recognises the priority of a security interest under secured transactions law, in the case of the grantor's insolvency, another claim may be given priority under insolvency law. To ensure certainty and avoid a negative impact on the availability and the cost of credit, these claims with priority over a security interests should be limited and clearly stated in the insolvency law (Secured Transactions Guide, Recommendations 239 and 241). The Model Law includes the same rule (Model Law, Article 35).

As encumbered assets are part of the estate, subject to stay and other limitations, secured creditors should have a right to participate in the insolvency proceedings and be heard on any issue that affects their rights and obligations. For example, a secured creditor may:

- object to any act that requires court approval;
- request review by a court of any act for which court approval was not required or not requested; and
- request any relief available to the secured creditor in the insolvency proceedings (Insolvency Guide, Recommendation 137).

If voting on approval of a reorganisation plan is conducted by reference to classes, the Insolvency Guide leaves it to each insolvency law to determine how the vote will be treated. However, at least one class of creditors whose rights are modified or affected by the plan must approve it. In addition, if the insolvency law requires court confirmation of an approved plan, the court can confirm the plan, provided that:

- the necessary approvals have been obtained and the approval process was properly conducted;
- creditors will receive under the plan at least as much as they would have received in liquidation, unless they have specifically agreed to receive less;
- the plan does not contain provisions that are contrary to law;
- administrative expenses will be paid in full, unless otherwise agreed by the holder of such a claim; and
- unless otherwise agreed, the ranking of a class of creditors that has voted against the plan will not be changed and distribution to that class under the plan will be in line with that ranking (Insolvency Guide, Recommendation 152).

In determining the liquidation value of encumbered assets in a reorganisation proceeding, consideration should be given to the use of the assets and the purpose of the valuation (Secured Transactions Guide, Recommendation 242).

With respect to applicable law issues, the Insolvency Guide provides that all aspects of the commencement, conduct, administration and conclusion of insolvency proceedings should be determined by the conflict-of-laws rules of the state in which the insolvency proceedings are commenced (*lex fori concursus*). It also provides that the law of the state in which the insolvency proceeding is commenced should govern, among other things, the treatment of secured creditors; the treatment and ranking of claims; and the distribution of proceeds (Insolvency Guide, Recommendations 30 and 31).

The Insolvency Guide recognises that an exception may be made to this rule to avoid changing the law applicable to security interests.[24]

---

24   Insolvency Guide, Part 2, I, para 88.

The Secured Transactions Guide provides that the commencement of insolvency proceedings should not displace the law applicable to the creation, third-party effectiveness, priority and enforcement of a security interest. However, this rule should not affect the application of the law of the state in which insolvency proceedings commenced (*lex fori concursus*) to issues such as avoidance, treatment of secured creditors, ranking of claims or distribution of proceeds (Secured Transactions Guide, Recommendation 171 of the). The Model Law repeated essentially the same rule (Model Law, Article 94).[25]

12. Conclusions

The Model Law discusses in a comprehensive and systematic way most of the key issues to be addressed in legislation on security interests in tangible and intangible assets, with the exception of a few types of assets, such as intermediated securities and rights to payment under financial contracts. The Model Law applies to all transactions that serve security purposes irrespective of their name, including fiduciary transfers of title, retention of title sales and financial leases.

In particular with respect to security interests in rights to payment of funds credited to bank accounts, the Model Law codifies current law with respect to the creation of a security interest, and introduces novel provisions with respect to the third-party effectiveness of such a security interest by registration of a notice in a public registry or by conclusion of a tripartite control agreement by the grantor, the secured creditor and the deposit-taking institution.

While the priority rules of the Model Law are structured around third-party effectiveness methods that will be new in many jurisdictions, their application will lead to results that are consistent with current law governing bank accounts. The main premise of this law is that the rights of the deposit-taking institution under the account agreement and the law governing the agreement and banking activities in general should not be interfered with.

The Model Law also includes comprehensive rules dealing with the enforcement of a security interest in a right to payment of funds credited to a bank account, in and outside insolvency proceedings. The rules dealing with the treatment of a security interest in insolvency proceedings are contained in the Insolvency Guide and in Chapter XII of the Secured Transactions Guide, and reflect the consensus achieved in UNCITRAL between the international insolvency, banking and secured lender communities.

The only issue relating to security interests in rights to payment funds credited to a bank account with respect to which the Model Law does not have a single rule is the law applicable to such a security interest. This means that, depending on where an issue arises and the alternative that the forum has

---

25   Guide to Enactment, para 500.

chosen to enact, the law of the state in which the deposit-taking institution maintaining the account has its place of business or the law of the state expressly stated in the account agreement as the state whose law governs the account agreement may be applicable.

Thus, the Model Law provides a basis for the modernisation and harmonisation of secured transactions law, including conflict-of-laws rules relating to secured transactions. Its rules are coordinated with law applicable outside the Model Law, such as the law governing bank accounts. They are also coordinated with insolvency law based on the legislative recommendations of the Secured Transactions Guide and the Insolvency Guide, and prepared with the assistance of the international secured finance and insolvency communities.

Security interests in receivables under the UNCITRAL Model Law on Secured Transactions

Spyridon V Bazinas
Lecturer, author and consultant

1. Introduction

This chapter discusses security interests in and outright transfers of receivables under the UNCITRAL Model Law on Secured Transactions ('Model Law').[1] As the Model Law has incorporated the key provisions of the United Nations Convention on the Assignment of Receivables in International Trade (CARIT), this chapter also compares the Model Law with CARIT.[2]

Section 2 of this chapter considers the scope and the relevant terminology of the Model Law; section 3 the creation of a security interest; section 4 the effectiveness of a security interest against third parties; section 5 the registry system; section 6 the priority of a security interest; section 7 the pre-default rights and obligations of the parties and third-party obligors; section 8 the post-default rights of parties; section 9 conflict-of-laws issues; section 10 transition issues; and section 11 security interests in insolvency.

2. Scope of application and terminology

The Model Law applies to security interests in and outright transfers (pure or for security purposes) of receivables by agreement (Model Law, Articles 1(1) and (2)). The reason for this approach is that the same third-party effectiveness and priority rules have to apply to all receivables finance transactions (whether they involve outright transfers of or security interests in receivables), as it is difficult for third parties to know which type of transaction is involved in each particular case.

In addition, the Model Law applies to consumer transactions (ie, transactions for personal, family or household purposes), but without overring consumer protection law where the grantor (assignor) or the debtor of the receivable is a consumer (Model Law, Article 1(5)).

---

1   The Model Law, CARIT and all texts of UNCITRAL on security interests are available at https://uncitral.un.org/en/texts/securityinterests.

2   For a discussion of CARIT, see Spiros V Bazinas, "International receivables", in PU Ali (ed), *Secured Finance Transactions: Key Assets and Emerging Markets* (Globe Law and Business 2007, pp83–99).

CARIT also has the same broad scope, even though it achieves this result in a different way. The Model Law defines the term 'security interest' in a functional way to include transfers of receivables for security purposes (Model Law, Article 2(kk)). CARIT defines 'assignment' in a broad way to include outright and security transfers of receivables, as well as security interests in receivables (CARIT, Article 2(a)).

However, there are also some differences in the scope of application of the Model Law and CARIT, as CARIT is intended to facilitate international receivables finance transactions, while the Model Law is intended to facilitate receivables finance transactions in general.

First, unlike CARIT – which applies only to contractual rights to payment (CARIT, Article 2(a)) – the Model Law applies to any right to payment, contractual or not, even though different rules of the Model Law apply to certain types of payment rights (ie, rights to payment evidenced by a negotiable instrument, rights to payment of funds credited to a bank account and rights to payment under a non-intermediated security; Model Law Article 2(dd)).

Second, unlike CARIT – which applies to assignments of international receivables and to the assignment of international receivables (CARIT, Article 1(a)) – the Model Law applies to all receivables finance transactions, whether domestic or international, provided that a law enacting the Model Law is the applicable law under the conflict-of-laws rules of the forum.

Third, unlike the Model Law – which applies to security interests in rights to payment of funds credited to a bank account and non-intermediated securities (Model Law, Articles 1(1) and (3)) – CARIT excludes rights to payment arising from a bank deposit or any securities, intermediated or not (CARIT, Article 1(2)).

Finally, unlike CARIT – which deals with selected issues (eg, statutory limitations and contractual limitations on the assignment of receivables) by way of substantive law rules and with other issues (eg, third-party effectiveness and priority of an assignment) by way of conflict-of-laws rules – the Model Law deals with all relevant issues by way of substantive law rules and, in addition, contains a complete set of conflict-of-laws rules.

3.   Creation of a security interest

Under the Model Law, a security interest in a receivable is created in the same way as in any other type of asset – that is, by way of a security agreement between the grantor and the secured creditor (Model Law, Article 6(1)). The grantor must have rights in the receivable or have the right to encumber it; and, as the security interest secures payment or other performance of an obligation, there must be consideration given by the secured creditor to the grantor (eg, a loan).

If, at the time of conclusion of the security agreement, the receivable exists and the grantor has rights in it, the security interest is created at that time. If the receivable to be encumbered does not exist at that time or the grantor acquires its rights in that right thereafter, the security interest is created when that receivable comes into existence or the grantor acquires its rights in that right (Model Law, Article 6(2)).

The security agreement must:

- be concluded or evidenced[3] in writing signed[4] by the grantor; and
- at a minimum:
    - identify the grantor and the secured creditor;
    - describe the secured obligation and the encumbered asset; and
    - if the enacting state so chooses, state the maximum amount for which the security interest may be enforced (Model Law, Article 6(3)).

Upon its creation, a security interest is effective as between the grantor and the secured creditor. Effectiveness as against third parties is, in principle, subject to further requirements (see section 4 below). The reason for this approach is to achieve two of the key objectives of an efficient and effective secured transactions law – that is, to enable parties to obtain security interests in a simple and efficient manner; and to enhance certainty and transparency by providing for registration of a notice of a security interest in a general security interest registry as the main method for achieving third-party effectiveness.[5]

For the security agreement to be effective, the secured obligation and the encumbered receivable must be described in a manner that reasonably allows their identification (Model Law, Articles 9(1) and (2)). This means that the description may be generic (eg, 'all my receivables') or specific, depending on whether a category of assets or a specific asset is encumbered.

A security interest in an asset extends to its identifiable proceeds (Model Law, Article 10(1)). Thus, when encumbered inventory is sold, the security interest extends to the right to payment of the purchase price and, if that price is deposited in a bank account, to the right to payment of the funds credited to the bank account, even though they have ceased to be identifiable; but the security interest is limited to the funds immediately before they were commingled (Model Law, Article 10(2)).

A security interest in a 'trade receivable' is effective between the grantor and the secured creditor despite the existence of an agreement between the grantor and the debtor of the receivable prohibiting the creation of a security interest (Model Law, Article 13(1)). However, if the debtor of the receivable suffers a loss

---

3   Depending on which expression is chosen by an enacting state, a security agreement that is not in writing will be ineffective or will be effective if its terms are evidenced by a written document signed by the grantor (Guide to Enactment, para 88).

4   'Writing' and 'signature' generally include their electronic equivalents but the Model Law leaves those matters to other relevant law of the enacting state.

5   Secured Transactions Guide, Recommendations 1(c) and (f).

as a result of the creation of the breach of the anti-assignment agreement, the debtor of the receivable may seek compensation from the grantor, but not from the secured creditor; and if the receivable is a contractual receivable, the grantor may not seek to avoid the contract giving rise to the receivable on the sole ground of breach of the anti-assignment agreement (Model Law, Article 13(2)).

However, the creation of such a security interest in a receivable does not affect the rights and obligations of the debtor of the receivable without its consent (Model Law, Article 61). This means essentially that the payment terms of a contractual receivable do not change and the debtor of the receivable may raise against the secured creditor all the defences and rights of set-off that it had against the grantor, with the exception of rights of set-off arising from contracts with the grantor after the debtor of the receivable receives notification of the security interest (Model Law, Article 64(1)).

As a result, the Model Law allows a person to use its trade receivables as security for credit, which is extremely important for small and medium-sized enterprises, at the cost of an inconvenience to those powerful debtors that have the bargaining power to negotiate anti-assignment agreements (consumer debtors do not have such power; in any case, the Model Law does not override consumer protection legislation (Model Law, Article 1(5)).

As mentioned above, the application of the rule on contractual limitations to the creation of a security interest in receivables is limited to 'trade receivables', broadly defined (Model Law, Articles 13(1) and (3)). As a result of this limitation, under the Model Law, a security interest in a non-trade receivable (eg, a sovereign receivable) created despite an anti-assignment agreement would be ineffective.

An accessory, personal or property, security interest (eg, a guarantee or a pledge) securing payment of the encumbered receivable is transferred to the secured creditor without a new act of transfer; and the grantor is obliged to transfer to the secured creditor an independent security or other supporting right, such as an independent guarantee or a standby letter of credit (Model Law, Article 14).

CARIT does not deal generally with the effectiveness of an assignment agreement. It only sets aside statutory limitations on the assignment of:

- future receivables;[6]
- parts or undivided interests in receivables; and
- receivables that are not identified individually at the time of the assignment (CARIT, Article 8).

---

6   A receivable is a 'future receivable' if the contract from which it may arise does not exist at the time of the conclusion of the contract of assignment (CARIT, Article 5(b)). Whether a receivable is mature or payable, or whether it has been earned by performance, is irrelevant.

Apart from these statutory limitations, CARIT does not affect other statutory limitations, such as statutory limitations relating to sovereign receivables (to the contrary, it allows states to exclude the application of the rule on anti-assignment agreements (CARIT, Article 8) to sovereign receivables (CARIT, Article 40).

With respect to the form of assignment agreement, CARIT contains only a conflict-of-laws rule, which generally refers to the law of the state in which it is concluded (CARIT, Article 27). However, form of an assignment as a condition of third-party effectiveness and priority is referred to the law of the assignor's location (CARIT, Articles 5(g) and 22); and to the extent that notification of the debtor is a requirement for the effectiveness of an assignment as between the assignor and the assignee, it is set aside (CARIT, Article 14(1)).

With respect to contractual limitations to the assignment of receivables and the treatment of rights securing or supporting payment of an assigned receivable, CARIT follows the same approach as the Model Law (CARIT, Articles 9 and 10). However, as the rule of CARIT dealing with anti-assignment agreements applies only to the assignment of contractual trade receivables, CARIT leaves the effectiveness of an assignment of contractual non-trade receivables made despite an anti-assignment agreement in the contract giving rise to the receivables to other law. This law is the law governing the receivable (CARIT, Article 29). If, under that law, the assignment is not effective, there is no assignment to which CARIT (with the exception of Article 29) could apply. As a result, for example, sales of loans or insurance policies would, in effect, be excluded from the scope of CARIT.

4. Third-party effectiveness of a security interest

Under the Model Law, the main method of making a security interest in a receivable effective against third parties is the registration of a notice in the general security interest registry (Model Law, Article 18(1); other methods, such as the conclusion of a control agreement, are foreseen for other types of payment rights, such as the right to payment of funds credited to a bank account; Model Law, Article 25(b)).

If receivables are proceeds of other types of assets (eg, inventory), a security interest in those receivables as proceeds is effective against third parties when they arose, without the need to have a separate act of registration or other third-party effectiveness method each time that proceeds arise (Model Law, Article 19(1)). This rule, which reflects the normal expectations of the parties and avoids overburdening parties with additional registration requirements, is subject to a contrary agreement of the parties.

CARIT deals with this matter only by way of a conflict-of-laws rule (CARIT, Articles 5(g) and 22), referring it to the law of the state of the assignor's location (for the discussion of conflict-of-laws issues, see section 9 below).

5. The registry system

The Model Law establishes a general security interest registry (Model Law, Article 28) and includes a set of Model Registry Provisions (MRP) that deal with all registration-related issues. For the discussion of those issues, see the chapter "Security interests in bank accounts under the UNCITRAL Model Law on Secured Transactions".

6. Priority of a security interest

The main priority rule of the Model Law that regulates the priority of competing security interests in the same receivables, whether they have been created by the same or by different grantors, is the 'first-to-register' priority rule (Model Law, Articles 29(1) and 30). This priority rule applies also to competitions between a security interest in receivables and the right of a transferee of those receivables (as the term 'secured creditor' includes a transferee under an outright transfer by agreement; Model Law, Article 2(ff)).

Thus, if A transfers its receivables by agreement to X on 1 September and on 5 September creates a security interest in the same receivables in favour of Y, the priority between X and Y will be determined not on the basis of the *nemo dat* rule (essentially, the time of the conclusion of the relevant transaction, which is a fact not easily ascertainable by third parties), but on the basis of the time of registration of a notice in the general security interest registry. As a result, if Y registers first, Y will have priority over X, even though Y obtained a right in the receivables after X.

The fact that Y may have known about the transfer of the receivables to X does not affect Y's priority, as this is a subjective criterion that is difficult to prove; and a priority rule based on subjective criteria would introduce uncertainty and prolong litigation, and thus most likely have a negative impact on the availability and the cost of credit (Article 45).

What has been said with respect to the discussion of priority of a security interest in a right to payment of funds credited to a bank account over the grantor's insolvency administrator, preferential creditors and judgment creditors (Model Law, Articles 35–37), as well as to the subordination of priority and the priority of a security interest in future encumbered assets to secure future secured obligations (Model Law, Articles 43 and 44), also applies with respect to the priority of a security interest in receivables (see the chapter "Security interests in bank accounts under the UNCITRAL Model Law on Secured Transactions").

CARIT deals with priority only by way of a conflict-of-laws rule (CARIT, Articles 5(g) and 22), referring it to the law of the state of the assignor's location (for a discussion of conflict-of-laws issues, see section 9 below).

7. Pre-default rights and obligations of the parties and third-party obligors

7.1 The relationship between the grantor and the secured creditor

Under the Model Law, the grantor and the secured creditor may structure their transaction as they wish to address their particular needs (Model Law, Articles 3(1) and 52(1)). However, the parties may not deviate or vary by agreement certain mandatory law rules, such as the rule providing that the parties must exercise their rights and perform their obligations in good faith and in a commercially reasonable manner (Model Law, Articles 3(1) and 4). In addition, any agreement of the parties may not affect the rights of third parties (Model Law, Article 3(2)). The Model Law also recognises trade usages agreed upon and trade practices established between the parties (Model Law, Article 52(2)).

Security agreements are usually elaborate agreements that address a broad range of issues. In recognition of this fact, the Model Law includes only a few mandatory and a few non-mandatory law rules that regulate matters arising in the context of the relationship between the grantor and the secured creditor. For example, upon payment and extinguishment of the secured obligation (Model Law, Article 12), the secured creditor must register a cancellation notice in the general security interest registry releasing the encumbered receivable from the security interest (MRP, Article 20(3(c)); and the grantor has the right to request from the secured creditor information as to the outstanding amount of the secured obligation and the assets encumbered at a certain point of time (Model Law, Article 56).

In addition, in order to fill gaps left in the security agreement and to provide a list of issues to be addressed, the Model Law contains a number of default rules dealing with matters such as representations of the grantor, notification of the debtor and contractual rights to proceeds from the payment of receivables.

With respect to the representations of the grantor, the Model Law follows generally accepted principles and attempts to establish a balance between fairness and practicality. The risk of hidden defences of the debtor, for example, is placed on the assignor (Model Law, Article 57(1)(b)). The reason for this approach is that the grantor is in a better position to know whether it will perform the contract giving rise to the receivables properly and will not give rise to debtor defences. If the Model Law provided that the risk of hidden defences were on the secured creditor, the secured creditor would include that risk in the calculation of the cost of credit. In any case, parties are free to agree to a different risk allocation.

In addition, the Model Law introduces an independent right of the secured creditor to notify the debtor of the receivable and to request payment (Model Law, Article 58 (1)). Such a right is essential in situations where a notification is most needed (ie, where the grantor defaults and is unlikely to cooperate with the secured creditor). In practice, parties try to address this problem by including in the security agreement an authorisation for the secured creditor to notify the debtor of the receivable. Even if parties agree that the debtor should not be notified, the notification triggers a change in the way in which the debtor is to discharge its debt, but does not have any other effects (Model Law, Article 58(2)). The reason for this approach is that the debtor's discharge should not be made subject to agreements to which the debtor is not a party, while the party notifying in breach of an agreement should not unduly benefit from such a notification.

Moreover, as between the grantor and the secured creditor, the secured creditor may retain the proceeds of payment of receivables (and returned goods) if payment is made to the secured creditor, and claim them if payment is made the grantor or to another person over which the secured creditor has priority (Model Law, Article 59).

7.2 The relationship between the assignee and the debtor of the receivable

The Model Law explicitly elevates debtor protection to one of the basic principles underlying the Model Law (Model Law, Article 61(1)). As a result, any uncertainty or gap in the Model Law is to be resolved in a way that is favourable to the debtor of the receivable (Model Law, Article 5(2)). In any case, the assignment cannot change the currency and the country of payment (Model Law, Article 61(2)). Whether the debtor of the receivable can agree to such a change is left to other law.

As notification changes the way in which the debtor of the receivable may discharge its debt and limits the debtor's rights of set-off, for a notification to be effective,[7] it must be received by the debtor of the receivable and be "in a language that is reasonably expected to inform the debtor of the receivable about its contents"; and may also be given with respect to future receivables (Model Law, Articles 62(1) and (3)). To facilitate international factoring, the Model Law also provides that notification of a security interest (which includes the right of an outright transferee; Model Law, Article 2(kk)(ii)) constitutes notification of prior security interests and transfers (Model Law, Article 62(4)).

In order to avoid invalidating notifications that do not include a payment instruction and are given, for example, for the purpose of limiting the debtor's rights of set-off, the Model Law does not require that a notification include a payment instruction. However, notifying parties would be well advised to include a payment instruction even if they wish the debtor of the receivable to continue paying the assignor, since otherwise the debtor of the receivable may not know how to discharge its debt (Model Law, Articles 63(1) and (2)).

---

7   "Notification of a security interest in a receivable" means a notice (a communication in writing; Model Law Article 2(x)) by the grantor or the secured creditor informing the debtor of the receivable that a security interest has been created in the receivable (Model Law, Article 2(y)).

The Model Law makes debtor discharge subject to an objective criterion – that is, notification (Model Law, Articles 63(1) and (2)). It deals with the issue of multiple notifications and notification of security interests in parts or undivided interests of receivables (Model Law, Articles 63(3) to (7)), and gives the debtor of the receivable the right to seek adequate proof in case of doubt as to how to pay to discharge its obligation (Model Law, Articles 63(8) and (9)). Most importantly, it allows the debtor of the receivable to discharge its debt under other law by paying the person entitled to payment or to a competent judicial or other authority, or to a public deposit fund (Model Law, Article 63(10)).

With the exception of rights of set-off that arise from contracts unrelated to the contract giving rise to the encumbered receivables and are not available to the debtor of the receivable at the time of notification, the Model Law preserves all the defences and rights of set-off that the debtor of the receivable can raise (Model Law, Article 64). The Model Law allows in principle, but also introduces strict conditions with respect to, waivers of defences by the debtor of the receivable (Model Law, Article 65), and deals with the third-party effects of modifications to any contract giving rise to the encumbered receivables, provided that they are effective against the secured creditor until notification of the debtor of the receivable and thereafter only if the secured creditor consents (Model Law, Article 66).

All the above-mentioned rules of the Model Law provisions are based on the relevant rules of CARIT (CARIT, Articles 11 to 21).[8]

8. Post-default rights of the parties

If the grantor defaults in the payment of the secured obligation,[9] the secured creditor may sell, otherwise dispose of or collect the encumbered receivable directly from the debtor of the receivable (Model Law, Articles 78 and 82(1)). The secured creditor may exercise these remedies by applying to a court or other authority or without such an application (Model Law, Article 73(1)). Judicial enforcement is subject to the provisions of the Model Law and other relevant law of the enacting state, and should include expeditious proceedings (Model Law, Article 73(2)). Extra-judicial enforcement is subject to the provisions of the Model Law (Model Law, Article 73(3)).

Where extra-judicial enforcement is permitted, the Model Law refers to safeguards to avoid abuse of power by the secured creditor. For example, the secured creditor must notify the grantor and other claimants before an extra-judicial disposition (Model Law, Article 78(4)), and return any surplus remaining after payment of the secured obligation to the grantor (Model Law,

---

8   For a discussion of the relevant rules of CARIT, see Spiros Bazinas, *supra* note 2.
9   For the meaning of the term 'default', see Model Law Article 2(j).

Article 79); and the grantor may always go to court to prevent out-of-court collection or seek other relief (Model Law, Article 74).

The Model Law also provides that if the grantor consents, the secured creditor may collect the receivable directly from the debtor of the receivable even before default. In essence, this operates as a repayment of the secured obligation (Model Law, Article 82(2)). In any case, the right of the secured creditor to collect is subject to the provisions of the Model Law dealing with debtor protection (Model Law, Articles 61 to 71 and 82(5)).

9.   Conflict of laws

The Model Law contains a conflict of laws chapter, which discusses the rules determining the law applicable to the mutual rights and obligations of the grantor and the secured creditor, to the creation, third-party effectiveness, priority and enforcement of a security interest, as well as to the rights and obligations between the debtor of the receivable and the secured creditor. In addition, this chapter clarifies where a secured creditor must register or otherwise make its security interest effective against third parties, and determines the territorial scope of application of the substantive law rules of the Model Law.

Under the Model Law, the law applicable to the mutual rights and obligations of the grantor and the secured creditor arising from the security agreement is the law chosen by them and, in the absence of a choice of law, the law governing the security agreement (Model Law, Article 84). For example, the law governing the security agreement may be the law of the state which is most closely connected to the security agreement (eg, the state in which a security agreement is entered into and performed, and in which both parties are located).[10]

With respect to security interests in receivables, the Model Law refers all issues (ie, creation, third-party effectiveness, priority and enforcement) to the law of the grantor's location (Model Law, Articles 86 and 88(b)). This approach is consistent with the approach followed in Articles 22 and 30 of CARIT.[11] The value in this rule is in the fact that it refers all issues to the law of the state of the grantor's location, which is one law that is easily ascertainable and is likely to be that of the state in which the main insolvency proceeding with respect to the grantor is most likely to be opened (as in the case of places of business in more than one state, the grantor's place of business is the state in which the grantor has its central administration, which is generally accepted to be the same as the state of the grantor's centre of main interests; Model Law, Article

---

10   Guide to Enactment, para 472.
11   For a comparison of the approach of CARIT with the approach followed in a Draft Regulation being prepared by the European Commission, see Spyridon V Bazinas, "The law applicable to third-party effects of assignments of claims: the UN Convention and the EU Commission Proposal compared", *Uniform Law Review*, Volume 24, Issue 4, December 2019, pp609–632. See also Spyridon V Bazinas, "International trade receivables finance at a crossroads: the UN Convention and the EU Draft Regulation", *Butterworths Journal of International Banking and Financial Law*, April 2020, pp241–244.

90). Thus, the law governing all issues with respect to a security interest outside insolvency and the law governing all insolvency matters (including avoidance, ranking of claims and distributions) will be the law of one and the same jurisdiction.

However, the Model Law refers the priority of a security interest in a receivable that either arises from the sale or lease, or is secured by, immovable property as against the right of a competing claimant that is registrable in the relevant immovable property registry to the law of the state under whose authority the immovable property registry is maintained (Model Law, Article 87). While this rule is an understandable exception to the rule of the application of the law of the grantor's location, it introduces an element of uncertainty, as for a person to be certain which state's law is applicable to the priority of a security interest in a receivable, that person must determine whether the receivable arose from a sale or lease of, or is secured by, immovable property.[12]

In addition, the Model Law refers the creation of a security interest in proceeds to the law governing rights in assets of the same type as the original encumbered assets and the third-party effectiveness of such a security interest to the law governing rights in the same assets as the proceeds (Model Law, Article 89). For example, where the original encumbered assets are receivables and the proceeds a right to payment of funds credited in a bank account, the question of whether the security interest in the receivables extends to the right to payment of funds credited in the bank account is subject to the law applicable to security interest in receivables – that is, the law of the state of the grantor's location; and the third-party effectiveness and priority of that security interest are subject to the law applicable to security interests in rights to payment of funds credited to a bank account – that is, the law of the state in which the relevant bank is located (if option A of Article 97 of the Model Law is chosen by the enacting state). This may lead to problems in cases where the two applicable laws have a different notion of what constitutes 'proceeds'.

Moreover, the Model Law refers the rights and obligations of the debtor of the receivable and the secured creditor, the conditions under which the security interest may be invoked against the debtor and whether the debtor's obligations have been discharged to the law governing the receivable. This is the universally accepted approach and also reflects the principle of debtor protection embodied in the Model Law. It does not necessarily lead to the application of a law other than the grantor's location. For example, in the case of a receivable arising from a sales contract, the law chosen by the seller/grantor and the buyer/debtor of the receivable to govern the sales contract will apply to these matters, and this law is usually the law of the seller/grantor.[13]

---

12 Guide to Enactment, para 482.
13 Guide to Enactment, para 505.

10. Transition

For a discussion of the transition rules of the Model Law, see the chapter "Security interests in bank accounts under the UNCITRAL Model Law on Secured Transactions".

11. Insolvency

For a discussion of the treatment of security interests in insolvency under the Model Law and the UNCITRAL Legislative Guide on Insolvency Law and the UNCITRAL Legislative Guide on Secured Transactions, see the chapter "Security interests in bank accounts under the UNCITRAL Model Law on Secured Transactions".

12. Conclusions

The Model Law discusses in a comprehensive and systematic way most of the key issues to be addressed in legislation on security interests in tangible and intangible assets, including receivables. The Model Law applies to all receivables finance transactions (including those involving fiduciary transfers of title and outright transfers of receivables by agreement). It thus deals with the issue of fragmentation of receivables finance law in one law per type of practice (eg, factoring law, financial leasing law), which is bound to create gaps and inconsistencies, and thus have a negative impact on availability and the cost of credit on the basis of receivables.

With respect to security interests in receivables, the Model Law incorporated the key provisions of CARIT on issues such as:

- the validity of an assignment of future receivables;
- an assignment of receivables not identified individually; and
- an assignment made in breach of an anti-assignment agreement, as well as on issues related to debtor protection and conflict of laws.

It thus facilitates receivables finance transactions by:

- eliminating a number of obstacles to receivables finance transactions, relating mainly to certain statutory limitations and to contractual limitations;
- dealing with debtor-protection issues in a comprehensive way;
- preserving all the debtor's rights and defences;
- separating debtor discharge from issues of priority;
- promoting the transparency of through the registration of notices of security interests in receivables; and
- coordinating receivables finance with other relevant law, such as contract law.

In addition, the Model Law promotes the harmonisation of conflict-of-laws rules and enhances certainty as to the law applicable to security interests in receivables by referring the creation, third-party effectiveness, priority and enforcement of a security interest in receivables to the law of the state of the grantor's location, defining 'location' in such a way that this is most likely to be the same as the state that would govern these matters in case of the grantor's insolvency, and thus dealing with the issue of a change of the applicable law in case of the insolvency of the grantor.

Moreover, by dealing with conflicts of laws in time – that is, issues of transition from prior law to new law – the Model Law promotes certainty with regard to security interests created and made effective against third parties before the enactment of a new law based on the Model Law.

Finally, the Model Law and UNCITRAL's Legislative Guide on Insolvency Law and Legislative Guide on Secured Transactions enhance certainty as to the rights of a secured creditor when it matters most – that is, on the grantor's insolvency.

Acquisition finance

Stuart Brinkworth
Ignacio Mirasol
Mayer Brown

1. Background

In providing debt facilities to a prospective borrower in support of an acquisition (or refinancing debt incurred in relation to a previous acquisition), there are a number of commercial and legal considerations for lenders. While the commercial terms of the debt (eg, financial covenants and certain permissions, including debt incurrence and further acquisitions) will likely be the most heavily negotiated points between principals, the lenders' individual credit decisions will also consider, among other things:

- their overall exposure to a specific sector or industry;
- their relationship with the borrower or the sponsor backing the transaction; and
- the protections that they will receive for the repayment of the debt.

In leveraged finance transactions in particular, the security that the lenders will hold for the underlying debt is an essential component of their commercial analysis.

At a basic level, the negotiated security package is an element of the lenders' credit approval to enable them participate in a transaction. Should the borrower default on its obligations under the credit agreement or become insolvent, the security package will determine the ability of the lenders to recover value against the debts owing to them. However, the grant of security also has practical implications during the life of the facilities and it is in this regard that the interests of borrowers typically diverge: among other specific negotiating points, borrowers will generally prefer leaner security packages with delayed enforcement triggers, while lenders will generally prefer more robust security packages with earlier enforcement triggers. With these divergent interests, the final security package for a transaction accordingly represents the commercially agreed position in relation to risk allocation for the underlying debt. As with all commercially agreed positions, the negotiating power of each side plays a major role in determining the outcome.

This chapter will provide an overview of the key commercial issues in taking security in leveraged finance transactions, with a particular focus on the principles that apply to European and cross-border acquisition finance transactions. It will not provide a technical or legal summary of the different types of security, the methods of taking security or the steps required to perfect security. Instead, it will consider transaction security from a commercial, deal-driven lens and highlight the typical negotiation points in commercial and legal discussions around a security package. It will aim to provide insight into customary security structures in transactions involving stronger sponsors, as well as recent market developments in leveraged finance transactions.

The chapter will begin by describing a typical leveraged acquisition finance structure and will highlight its key features that make it appropriate for financing structures. It will then discuss a typical transaction timeline for taking security prior to and after completion. The chapter will then discuss in detail the agreed security principles in a credit agreement and their role in providing a negotiated framework for the security and guarantees to be given by the relevant obligors to the lenders, analysing the key themes which frame discussions around negotiating security packages and describing how security is typically taken over specific asset classes in leveraged finance transactions. It will also identify specific issues to consider in cross-border transactions, using short case studies for France, Germany and Israel. Finally, it will offer brief insight into developments around leveraged finance security packages over recent years in the context of wider developments in the debt finance market.

This chapter assumes, as is customary in leveraged finance transactions, that all guarantors under facility documents are also security providers. The terms 'guarantor', 'security provider' and 'chargor' are accordingly used interchangeably.

2. Typical structures

Figure 1 sets out a typical post-completion leveraged finance structure used in private equity acquisition finance transactions. While the precise structure of each transaction will be bespoke, a number of features of this structure make it appropriate for finance transactions and secured lending more generally. For the purposes of this section, the names given to each entity in Figure 1 will be used for ease of reference.

A typical pre-acquisition banking group structure consists of two companies: 'Parent' and 'Bidco'. Each of these entities is a wholly owned indirect subsidiary of the sponsor and any reinvesting shareholders or members of management. Parent is the sole direct shareholder of Bidco and the shareholding in Bidco creates an unbroken chain of ownership upward towards the sponsor funds and any reinvesting management.[1] Both Parent and Bidco are holding companies,

---

1   The shareholdings of reinvesting management need not be at Topco but may be lower in the structure. However, any shareholdings of reinvesting management will rarely be below Parent in the structure or otherwise within the banking group, as any minority shareholdings in Bidco or in any entity below Bidco will prevent a clean sale of the entire group on enforcement of security.

Figure 1. A typical post-completion leveraged finance structure

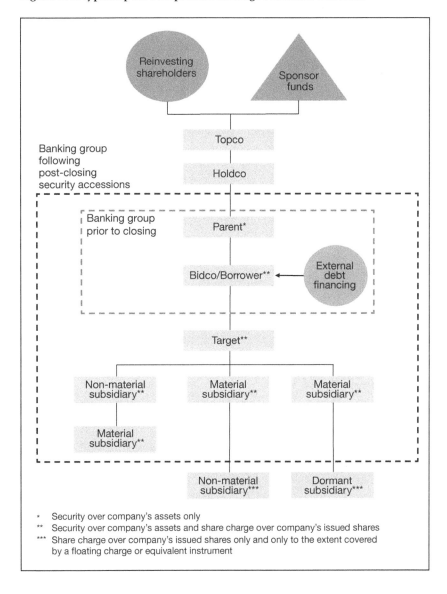

* Security over company's assets only
** Security over company's assets and share charge over company's issued shares
*** Share charge over company's issued shares only and only to the extent covered by a floating charge or equivalent instrument

typically prohibited from trading and limited to engaging in holding company activity; they are accordingly subject to holding company covenants under the credit agreement. Parent and Bidco will also often be off-the-shelf companies or companies newly incorporated solely for the purpose of the transaction. This limits the risk of claims into the banking group from third-party creditors which might compete with lenders' claims under the finance documents.

Parent and Bidco will each grant security over their assets. Where possible, each of Parent and Bidco will grant all-asset security in the form of a general security agreement. However, as these two entities are holding companies, they will not hold operational-type assets such as intellectual property or real estate. Security at this level will thus typically be limited to shares, intercompany receivables and bank accounts.

In the case of Bidco, this will include security over the shares in the target. In jurisdictions such as England and Wales, where security can be given over present and future assets, the shares of the target will automatically be subject to security at completion; in jurisdictions where security may not be granted over future assets, security over the target may be provided at or shortly after completion. Following the closing of the transaction and after completing the post-closing security accessions (where certain members of the target group become security providers and guarantors), the security structure will also include share charges over the material companies within the group which were not previously obligors under the finance documents and company-level security given by those material entities over their assets, on the same or analogous terms as the security provided by Parent and by and over Bidco. The security at this operating company and subsidiary level may be extended beyond the type provided by Parent and Bidco to include certain asset classes that are pertinent for the type of business being financed, such as material intellectual property in the case of a tech company. Sponsors, however, will be focused on keeping the scope of assets covered by the security package as narrow as possible.

A key feature of the security package worth identifying at this stage is the principle of a single point of enforcement. One of the key factors for lenders is to be able to enforce security over the target group at a single point in the structure, meaning speed and efficiency of enforcement in one single jurisdiction. Lenders will be keen to avoid having to enforce multiple security agreements in multiple jurisdictions. Lenders will want to able to realise value quickly – for instance, by selling the shares in a holding company or in the target.

In the structure set out in the diagram, the lenders would have the ability to sell the entire group through the sale of Bidco's shares alone and through the enforcement of the share charge over Bidco under the relevant all-asset security agreement or share charge given by Parent. Those advantages of the single point of enforcement to lenders make it an important practical tool in the security package. Lenders are accordingly focused on the single point of enforcement and often require that it feature in the security package as a condition to the debt facilitates.

As mentioned earlier, this structure represents one of the most common structures in leveraged finance transactions and which lenders are comfortable funding into. However, the precise structure and the choice of jurisdictions of the holding companies in a banking group will inevitably vary between transactions. Broader deal structuring is largely driven by tax considerations, including:

- the tax implications of sponsor distributions;
- the ability of the selling shareholders to reinvest in the new deal;
- withholding tax on loan interest payments to lenders; and
- the tax consequences upon the subsequent exit by a sponsor.

Those factors are analysed in detail and dealt with prior to or alongside term sheet discussions to ensure that the structure is appropriate for the needs of the sponsor's investment and the needs of the lenders to fund into the banking structure; and ultimately feed into the final banking and corporate structure of the transaction.

3. Timeline for taking security

The point in a transaction at which security is taken, as with the negotiated security package, is deal specific. However, the broad underlying principle is that security must be in place at the time when lenders fund the debt facilities under the credit agreement. The timing is intended to avoid any gap in the funding process during which the lending may be unsecured. Only in rare scenarios will lenders be able to fund commitments under a credit agreement with the initial security package being granted as a post-closing obligation.

In this regard, it is relevant to distinguish between closing security and post-closing security. Closing security consists of the security package which is taken no later than the moment immediately before completion. The initial security (which is provided by Parent and Bidco only) may be taken when the credit agreement is executed or, if signing and closing are split, prior to or simultaneously with completion. In acquisition finance transactions involving competitive bid scenarios, for instance, it is common for a credit agreement to be executed without the closing security in place or indeed without agreed form security agreements with limited time to agree a full suite of finance documents or where the availability of financing must be demonstrated as part of the time-critical bid offer. To meet these compressed timescales, security is instead taken as a condition to closing.

Post-closing security, conversely, involves security accessions by material companies to enable them to become guarantors under the finance documentation and provide the same or similar security as the security in the closing security package. The post-closing accessions will ensure that two criteria are satisfied:

- Each company in the group which contributes a material proportion of the group's earnings before interest, taxes, depreciation and amortisation (EBITDA), turnover and/or assets guarantees and provides security for the obligations owing under the credit agreement; and

- Those guarantors collectively account for an adequate proportion of guarantor coverage group in the form of EBITDA, turnover and/or assets.

The established market standard for materiality is a contribution of 5% or more of the group's consolidated EBITDA, turnover and/or gross assets; while the market standard for guarantor coverage is 80% to 85% in mid-market transactions. However, the guarantor coverage threshold may increase in lower mid-market transactions or transactions with a lower debt quantum. Sponsors will also seek to narrow the application of the test by limiting it to EBITDA only, or EBITDA and gross assets.

Taken together, the closing security package and the post-closing security package represent the ongoing security package of the lenders against which they can directly enforce their security in the event of a default. Materiality and guarantor coverage are ongoing compliance requirements typically tested annually by reference to the annual audited financial statements of the group. Further guarantor accessions may be required over the life of the debt facilities as group entities become material, as acquisitions are made and, more generally, as the business grows.

Market practice has evolved substantially since the 2007-2008 financial crisis. Immediately following the financial crisis, post-closing security over a target group was customarily taken at or immediately following completion on very short timescales. However, this compressed timescale presented significant logistical issues with the parallel corporate process of the acquisition. Issues such as changes to the board of directors at closing and the accompanying legal formalities, coupled with the already complex documentary corporate and finance conditions precedent process required to complete an acquisition, meant that attending to post-closing accessions at or immediately following completion was administratively burdensome and commercially unrealistic. It is also true that it takes some time to identify the assets at the local subsidiary level in order to complete the security process accurately. Immediately following the closing of an acquisition, the focus of the sponsor is on implementing its immediate ownership plan for the business. For these reasons, and also because of a shift towards more sponsor-friendly terms in finance documents, the practice in taking post-closing security has also developed.

It is now accepted market practice that there will be a reasonable gap between closing and the post-closing accessions. Stronger sponsors will expect to have a period of at least three to four months following closing to complete the post-closing accessions process, particularly in a cross-border acquisition financing. However, market practice differs slightly in other types of leveraged financings, such as refinancings and dividend recapitalisations. In these types of financings – which do not involve an acquisition or change of control and which, accordingly, do not give rise to the distinct logistical issues of acquisition – the period in between completion and the post-closing accessions is often shorter. In some limited circumstances (particularly in the absence of a change of ownership which can otherwise justify a longer gap), lenders may still expect post-closing accessions to occur on the same day as closing, with only minimal time periods given for security which cannot legally or practically be taken until after closing due to jurisdiction-specific issues or formalities.

4.   The agreed security principles

The agreed security principles (ASPs) represent a negotiated framework for the security and guarantees which lenders will benefit from as part of their security package. The ASPs will appear as a schedule to the credit agreement and will be referenced throughout the credit agreement as the overarching framework for the security and guarantees from which the lenders will benefit (and which will limit the obligation to grant security) in respect of the closing security package and the post-closing security package.

There is no set format for the ASPs, as they are often driven by sponsor precedents. Sponsors will typically expect that their precedent ASPs will be used as a base and then subsequently negotiated and adapted for the relevant transaction. Well-advised sponsors would look to agree the ASPs at the term sheet stage, to avoid renegotiating the scope of security when moving to the formal documentation stage of a transaction and potentially reopening negotiation points. Agreeing a security package early in the life of a transaction is particularly important in cross-border financings involving jurisdictions with specific nuances, including tax and financial assistance consequences relevant to the grant of security such as limitations concerning the creation of security over future assets. Tax and, in the context of cross-border financings, local advice is accordingly important not just in deal structuring, but also in agreeing the appropriate security package to be offered to lenders. Specific jurisdiction-related nuances will be discussed later by reference to selected jurisdictions.

While there is no set format for ASPs in the market, the ASPs can be grouped into two broad categories: the first series of sections describes the overarching principles governing the taking of security, while the remaining sections of the ASPs describe in more detail the principles for taking security over specific asset classes. These two categories are explored in more detail below.

The general principles in the ASPs will provide that all guarantees and security will be upstream, cross-stream and downstream guarantees, and will extend to all obligations of all obligors pursuant to the credit agreement and the other finance documents. While the scope of guaranteed and secured obligations is extensive at first glance, the ASPs will often explicitly recognise that such overarching principles must be subject to certain qualifications and will not apply absolutely. Those qualifications will also be identified in the general principles of the ASPs. Several representative examples of those qualifications are selected for discussion in this section – security:

- must comply with applicable law;
- must not adversely affect the business's trading and commercial relationships; and
- must be granted having regard to proportionality in assessing the benefit of the security to the lenders against the cost and administrative burden to the borrower's group of granting the security.

The sections below briefly describe how each of these considerations is typically addressed in the ASPs.

4.1 Legal requirements

The ASPs will recognise that security and guarantees must be granted subject only to general statutory limitations and regulatory rules, including limitations and requirements relating to or arising from:

- financial assistance;
- adequate capital maintenance;
- corporate benefit;
- illegal dividends;
- use of capital;
- prohibited loans;
- 'interest stripping';
- transfer pricing;
- fraudulent preference;
- regulatory approvals;
- directors' duties and fiduciary obligations; and
- similar or analogous concepts.

The ASPs therefore recognise that the scope of the guarantees and security may need to be limited in accordance with applicable law and regulation. As the general principles relating to legal requirements often state matters that would apply as a matter of law, and as security granted in breach of applicable law and regulation risks being set aside or considered invalid, the general security and guarantee limitations in the ASPs are typically subject to minimal negotiation.

An example of where these types of limitations would prohibit security being taken would be where the group being financed is regulated and where the regulator or rules implemented by the regulator prohibit regulated entities from guaranteeing debt or granting security over their assets. Additionally, even where a regulated entity can generally incur debt and grant security, it may lead to a breach of some form of balance-sheet test that is key to its regulatory approval. The ASPs in such circumstances would accordingly operate to prohibit security and guarantees from being given.

4.2   Trading and business relationships

The ASPs will also recognise that where security is granted, it should not interfere with or restrict the ability of a business to trade in the ordinary course. In particular, the security should not interfere with the ability of a business to deal with suppliers, customers and other third parties or otherwise prejudice its commercial relationships with them. To the extent that security over an asset would restrict the ability of a business to trade or adversely affect its commercial relationships, a different type of security, such as a floating charge or equivalent, may be granted. Alternatively, security may remain unperfected until an agreed enforcement trigger – typically the acceleration of the debt by the lenders – if perfection would prevent a guarantor from dealing in the relevant asset or negatively impact its commercial relationships.

A typical example here would be book debts. Prior to an enforcement scenario, a borrower would not want lenders serving notice on debtors stipulating that the relevant debts had been assigned by way of security, as the service of notices could then be damaging to the borrower's commercial relationships or could cause delays in payment.

4.3   Proportionality and practical considerations of cost and legal formalities

The ASPs will provide that security should be granted only where the benefit of that security to the lenders is proportional to the cost to, and the administrative burden on, the borrower or a guarantor in providing that security. This consideration is particularly relevant in jurisdictions where an individual security agreement is required for each secured asset class, as is common in a number of continental European jurisdictions. Multiple security agreements can quickly increase the legal costs of the borrower. In this regard, the ASPs will provide that the option to enter into a single all-asset security agreement such as an English law debenture or other general security agreement should be the appropriate method of taking security, unless local customary practice or legalities require otherwise.

The security package must also be agreed in a way that minimises statutory fees such as documentary taxes, notarial fees and the costs of similar legal formalities. In some jurisdictions, such as Germany, notarial fees are payable for each notary appointment and as a statutory percentage of the amount of the secured obligation. As legal processes such as notarisation can also increase transaction costs significantly – particularly on deals of a larger quantum – it is sensible to avoid incurring or duplicating such costs where possible, and the ASPs will articulate this principle. Taxes may also be payable in respect of certain types of assets over which security is granted, such as real estate.

4.4 Security limited to material companies and specified jurisdictions

Security at the subsidiary level will be required to be given only by a material subsidiary and only in respect of the specific jurisdiction where it trades or is incorporated. Furthermore, share security will typically be granted and required to be perfected only over material subsidiaries; share security will rarely be given over non-material entities in the structure, other than under a general security agreement (and if so given over non-material entities, will remain unperfected). In order to facilitate an unbroken chain of security, the materiality test in this regard will extend to a shareholder of a material subsidiary irrespective of the EBITDA, turnover or assets contribution of that shareholder. Similarly, a guarantor which is required to accede to the finance documents to satisfy guarantor coverage will also be regarded as a material subsidiary irrespective of the EBITDA, turnover or assets it accounts for.

In practice, there is typically minimal negotiation of these general principles or limitations expressed in the ASPs, as they are often articulated as broad statements which inform the subsequent sections of the ASPs that relate to specific asset classes. As the subsequent sections of the ASPs will be more prescriptive as to the scope of security to be taken and will attempt to explicitly describe the perfection requirements for each asset class, negotiation instead focuses largely on the latter sections of the ASPs and their application to different asset classes.

5. Security over specific asset classes

This section will provide an overview of a typical security package taken over specified asset classes. It will also identify key limitations on the scope and perfection of security granted, based on the considerations referred to in previous sections of this chapter.

5.1 Shares

Share security is one of, if not the most important piece of the security package for lenders. Share security facilitates the most direct route of enforcement over an entity and all of its assets, including any shares in subsidiaries. As an asset of particular importance and as the asset class relevant to a lender's single point of enforcement, it is one of several asset classes over which security is formally perfected. Perfection typically occurs through the delivery of share certificates and blank share transfer forms to effect a transfer of those shares on enforcement. In certain jurisdictions, the lenders' security interest may even be noted expressly in the shareholder register of a charged entity. As referenced earlier, fixed security in a leveraged finance transaction will be taken over wholly owned material subsidiaries and will be perfected accordingly; security over non-material subsidiaries or dormant subsidiaries will customarily be subject only to floating security and will remain unperfected until enforcement.

Share certificates and share transfer forms thus will not be required in respect of non-material subsidiaries until enforcement.

5.2   Bank accounts

As is consistent with the principle that security should not interfere with the ordinary course trading of a chargor, the main principles that apply to security over bank accounts are as follows:

- Security agreements should not require the chargor to change its banking arrangements with its existing bankers; and
- The chargor should remain free to deal with its operational accounts until the security becomes enforceable.

As a result, it may be that security is not granted over accounts where a bank's standard terms and conditions restrict charging or where the relevant account bank refuses to give its consent to the creation of the fixed security; or security may need to be granted subject specifically to any underlying restriction on charging the relevant bank account. Furthermore, as perfecting fixed security over an account will often require or result in the chargor ceasing to exercise control over the bank account and being unable to operate it, the ASPs will often provide that bank account security will be perfected only upon the occurrence of the relevant enforcement trigger.

5.3   Intercompany receivables

The principle in relation to intercompany receivables is analogous to that for bank accounts: a chargor must remain free to deal with its intercompany receivables and collect them in to its own accounts until the security has become enforceable. Prior to enforcement, lenders will not have the ability to require that receivables be paid into specific accounts designated by them, other than requiring that receivables be paid into accounts that are subject to general bank account security and which, as discussed previously, a chargor would be free to operate in the ordinary course. For the same reason, perfection steps such as the service of notices on debtors are similarly not undertaken if perfection would interfere with the ability of a security provider to collect in and deal with its receivables.

5.4   Real estate

Unless real estate is a key asset in a business or is of material value, specific fixed or floating security over real estate assets is rarely taken in leveraged finance transactions and the ASPs will provide that security over real estate assets will not generally be taken. In practice, it is typical for the underlying businesses in pure leveraged finance transactions to have no real estate assets or very limited real estate assets. Instead, security over real estate may be taken as part of a general security agreement.

5.5   Intellectual property

Fixed security over intellectual property will rarely be given by a chargor, unless there is specifically identifiable intellectual property that is of significant value to the business. In such cases, stronger sponsors will wish to limit fixed security to material intellectual property. General intellectual property will instead be subject to a floating charge or equivalent with any specific restrictions on the disposal of material intellectual property included in the credit agreement. Furthermore, security over intellectual property will rarely be perfected through the registration of the lenders' interests at trademark registers, IP bodies and their equivalent. Such security registrations are more common in debt restructuring and work-out transactions.

5.6   Acquisition agreements

In acquisition finance transactions, it is customary for an assignment of rights under acquisition documents to be included in the security package. Value may lie in claims under acquisition agreements – for instance, for breach of seller warranties. Where security is taken over acquisition agreements, lenders will ordinarily expect that the security will be perfected by service of a notice of assignment on the seller.

5.7   Fixed and floating security

A chargor will not typically object to general security being granted over all or substantially all of its assets, provided there are no adverse tax consequences for granting the security and there are adequate carve-outs for assets with legal restrictions on charging; and, from a practical perspective, the chargor will remain able to deal with its assets in the ordinary course of business. As fixed security will not always allow a chargor to deal with its assets freely in the ordinary course of business, borrowers will generally prefer to have assets covered by floating security instead of fixed security.

6.   Cross-border transactions

The principles expressed in the ASPs are especially relevant in the context of cross-border transactions, where customary security packages and the implications of granting security can vary across jurisdictions. In multi-jurisdictional deals, the ASPs will be amended to include jurisdiction-specific limitations that reflect both the commercial will of the sponsor and local law requirements and formalities. Alongside an analysis of the legal issues and tax issues from each relevant jurisdiction in the proposed banking structure, negotiations around the security to be given to lenders should also take into account practical issues such as transaction timescales and legal costs.

In formulating an appropriate security package, it is important for borrowers and lenders to identify material subsidiaries and material jurisdictions in the banking group at the due diligence stage of a transaction and, where possible, prior to beginning negotiations with prospective lenders. This will enable principals to seek appropriate tax structuring and local law advice from their professional advisers, particularly where prospective lenders are expected to fund into an unfamiliar jurisdiction. Seeking appropriate advice at the outset and involving local legal and tax advisers will allow jurisdiction-specific issues to be considered early and avoid unexpected issues delaying negotiations.

7.   Jurisdiction-specific issues
In the sections that follow, this chapter will highlight key issues relevant to borrowers and lenders when taking security in three jurisdictions: France, Germany and Israel.

7.1   France
Security packages in French leveraged finance transactions will typically consist of a pledge over the target's and a guarantor's equity, intra-group loans, bank accounts and any acquisition claims. Security must be taken by asset class, as French law does not have the concept of a floating charge.

French law is particularly protective of the rights of a debtor or guarantor, as demonstrated by the examples that follow. As such, the ability of lenders to enforce their security is more limited than in other jurisdictions such as England and Wales. For instance, the French pledges will be exercisable only in the event of an actual payment default under a credit agreement, rather than following the occurrence of any event of default generally. Furthermore, the beneficiary of a share pledge will not have any specific voting rights prior to the actual appropriation of the shares following the enforcement of the pledge. The blocking of pledged accounts will similarly be possible only upon enforcement of the relevant account pledge. French law also enables a debtor or guarantor to prevent the enforcement of security by the filing of pre-insolvency proceedings as a judicial safeguard and to obtain a court-mandated rescheduling of the relevant underlying loan.

French corporate benefit and financial assistance rules generally prevent the granting of upstream or cross-stream guarantees, or will limit such guarantees to the portion of the loan which is actually downstreamed or cross-streamed by the relevant borrower to the guarantor. In practice, these rules effectively prevent an entity from granting security over its assets in order to secure the debt subscribed for by a parent or sister company.

For syndicated deals, in particular, the way in which security is held by a security trustee or security agent on behalf of multiple lenders has several nuances under French law. Until recently, the French legal system had no equivalent concept to a security trust. At the same time, the existing regime of parallel debt did not offer an adequate solution to the absence of the security trust concept. However, following certain legislative amendments in 2017 (see Articles 2488-6 and following of the Civil Code), French law now recognises that a security agent may be appointed to take, register, manage and enforce security interests (including personal guarantees), and to bring legal action before a court, for the benefit of all creditors of the relevant secured obligations, acting in its own name on behalf of those beneficiaries.

In addition to recognising the function of a security agent, the new security agent regime establishes a form of trust (derived from the French *fiducie*) which is more similar to the security trustee concept customary in common law jurisdictions such as England. Prior to the introduction of this form of trust, the rules concerning security trust property were complex and somewhat unclear. For instance, security property held on trust as part of a secured lending transaction was subject to appropriation in the event of the security agent's insolvency and thus a commercial risk to the parties. The new form of trust, however, creates a distinct asset class (*patrimoine affecté*) under which all rights and assets acquired by the security agent in performing its duties in that capacity are treated as separate and distinct from its own assets, and are therefore protected in the event of its own insolvency. These recent developments in French law have simplified the process for taking security, particularly in cross-border financings.

7.2 Germany

Leveraged finance transactions with credit support from German group companies or which involve taking security over German assets broadly follow the same mechanism as in the United Kingdom, subject to specific nuances.

The granting of upstream security for the benefit of the creditors of an entity's shareholder or cross-stream security for the benefit of the creditors of entity's sister company is subject to certain restrictions. The overarching principle is that German law restricts directors from providing credit support where doing so would adversely affect the registered share capital of the relevant entity providing security – for instance, in the form of an unlawful distribution. In practice, prior to granting any upstream or cross-stream security, directors will need to form the view that the security under consideration may be properly granted in favour of the relevant shareholder or sister entities in light of the economic condition of the guarantor. In addition, directors will be protected through limitation language relating to the grant of guarantees and security. The principal aim of such language is not to restrict enforcement as such, but rather to limit enforcement to a degree where it would not subject the directors to personal liability.

German law also includes so-called 'anti-blocking' or 'anti-boycott' laws, which restrict the application of foreign sanctions. In order to avoid any conflict between the sanctions provisions in a credit agreement and German anti-blocking laws, German law requires that the application of sanctions which are not based on German or EU law or UN sanctions not extend to entities resident in Germany. The provisions of security agreements governed by German law or under which German entities are security providers should accordingly reflect this position.

In Germany, there is no concept of an all-asset security agreement, so security must be taken over individual asset classes. A standard security package would include a share pledge over the target and any subsidiary shares, and the assignment of certain receivables. Receivables security will typically be taken over German law-governed intercompany receivables; on occasion, security will additionally be taken over insurance receivables and receivables under acquisition agreements. A more extensive security package would also include individual security over fixed and movable assets, real estate and intellectual property.

Cost is a particularly pertinent consideration in taking security. For instance, the grant of share pledges and land charges can give rise to substantial costs with notarisation; the cost of notarisation is determined by reference to the value of the encumbered assets and the loan amount (with the lower of those amounts typically forming the basis of the notarisation fee). In the case of real estate assets, a separate security purpose agreement will also be required in addition to the completion of post-closing registrations with the land register.

Further noteworthy formalities in Germany relate to security over bank accounts. As account pledges become valid only following registration with the relevant account bank, a chargor will typically serve a notice of pledge which will include a form of acknowledgement of the security interest. In practice, however, some account banks prefer to use their own form of acknowledgement instead of the *pro forma* acknowledgement included with the notice. While account bank standard form acknowledgements may be acceptable to lenders, these additional steps can lead to further negotiations.

7.3   Israel

With the boom in the Israeli technology sector in recent years, there has been increased deal flow from tech-focused private equity houses acquiring Israeli businesses and a corresponding increase in leveraged finance transactions to debt fund those acquisitions. With this trend, local law issues relating to granting security and guarantees by Israeli entities have been brought into sharper focus. Several of those key issues are summarised below.

In leveraged finance transactions with an Israeli nexus, the grant of guarantees and security applies in broadly the same way as in standard leveraged finance transactions, but is subject to certain Israeli-specific nuances. The issues surrounding security and guarantees in Israel centre mainly on avoiding potential claims around financial assistance or unlawful distributions and minimising potential tax liabilities from any deemed taxable distributions.

Standard upstream, downstream and cross-stream guarantees can generally be granted by Israeli entities, provided that they are structured and limited in a manner that would avoid such guarantees being set aside for lack of corporate benefit or for constituting financial assistance. Guarantee limitations apply in a slightly different way to overseas subsidiaries of Israeli guarantors than they would tend to apply in standard transactions. In respect of overseas subsidiaries of Israeli guarantors, Israeli guarantee limitations will apply irrespective of the overseas guarantee limitations in the jurisdictions of those overseas subsidiaries. Furthermore, guarantees given by Israeli entities in favour of the obligations of a shareholder may, as mentioned above, be limited by potential distribution issues. The beneficiary of the guarantee will typically mitigate this risk by paying each guarantor an arm's-length guarantee fee.

The grant of fixed and floating charges by Israeli entities is similarly subject to certain limitations. Due to financial assistance restrictions and unlawful distributions, a target will typically carve out from the scope of the secured obligations any of those obligations arising from the tranche of debt used to acquire it, to the extent that the securing of those obligations would constitute an unlawful distribution under Israeli law. In addition, in order to avoid any tax deemed distributions as a result of the grant of security, any charge to secure acquisition financing will often be granted by way of floating charge and not by way of fixed charge. It is accordingly more typical for a target to grant security over its assets in the form of a floating charge (which is similar to an English floating charge) combined with a negative pledge.

However, the combination of a floating charge and negative pledge granted by the target does not provide the same first-ranking position in the insolvency waterfall that lenders might expect in other jurisdictions, such as England and Wales. Under an Israeli insolvency waterfall, the enforcement of a floating charge and negative pledge will entitle the lenders to up to 75% of the value of the security proceeds. The remaining 25% of the recoveries will be set aside into a pool for unsecured creditors and any remaining balance owing to the lenders will rank *pari passu* to those unsecured creditors. However, under Israeli law, negative pledges (if properly registered) do have the force of statute and bind third parties.

The same corporate and tax restrictions on the creation of security do not apply to non-acquisition debt incurred by the target or any other entity in the structure. Accordingly, fixed and floating charges can and often are required by lenders to be granted in respect of other (non-acquisition) tranches of debt.

In practice, it is therefore important to have clearly identifiable tranches of debt in a credit agreement and for this distinction to be clear in the drafting of the secured obligations under a security agreement. More broadly, it is important that lenders are aware of these nuances of Israeli security and insolvency rules, as their expectations of the security package and their potential enforcement may differ from more standard transactions.

8. Movement of the market and concluding remarks

Following the financial crisis and the tightening of financing terms as a reaction to it, the general leveraged finance market has more recently shifted markedly away from lenders and towards sponsors. The shift towards sponsor-friendly security packages has accompanied the shift towards sponsor-friendly commercial terms in credit agreements and finance documentation more generally.

With this movement in the market, stronger sponsors have likewise improved their finance documents to better accommodate their commercial concerns and the operational practicalities for their portfolio companies. This shift has resulted in leaner and more focused security packages over a smaller selection of key assets, which can be granted more quickly and with lower legal expense or reduced administrative burden for the banking group. It has furthermore resulted in a shift in enforcement triggers under security agreements simply from events of default to declared default triggers requiring positive action to accelerate the underlying debt.

For as long as the debt capital markets remain favourable to sponsors, and with stronger sponsors gradually improving their positions under their financing documents, the security principles in those documents and the negotiated security packages will continue to shift in a more favourable direction to accommodate the concerns of sponsors.

The authors would like to acknowledge Clifford Davis (S Horowitz & Co, Tel Aviv), Martin Philipp Heuber (Mayer Brown, Frankfurt), Patrick Teboul and Constance Bouchet (Mayer Brown, Paris) for their assistance in drafting this chapter.

Asset-based lending

Alex Dell
Mayer Brown

1.   What is asset-based lending?

Asset-based lending (ABL) is a well-established feature of the US loans landscape, having become mainstream around 30 years ago; it is now also rising in prominence both within Europe and, more specifically, the United Kingdom. ABL has traditionally been used by corporates as a form of primary working capital, but is increasingly appearing in more complex capital structures, including on, or following, an acquisition.

ABL is fundamentally different from traditional forms of working capital debt. Conventional lending primarily focuses on a corporate's balance sheet, historic trading performance and/or financial projections; whereas ABL primarily focuses on a corporate's assets, providing finance against receivables, inventory, plant and machinery and/or real property, where advances are calculated by reference to the value of the asset base.

An asset-based lender rarely funds the full value of an asset to ensure that it is over-collateralised at all times. Accordingly, it will set an advance rate and will advance funds only if such funds do not exceed the asset value multiplied by the advance rate. The credit agreement may specify a single advance rate for all asset classes or different advance rates for each asset class.

An asset-based lender sets eligibility criteria, operational covenants and reporting requirements which are designed to evaluate and monitor the fluctuating performance of the asset classes against which funding has been provided. It is this regular monitoring and reporting that enables ABL to deliver a competitive pricing model, given that this level of scrutiny and control enables ABL to benefit from favourable capital treatment.

An asset-based lender will undertake specific diligence prior to the commencement of a transaction, focusing on how it will enforce its rights against the assets it is funding to ensure that anything which might prevent it from realising the full value of those assets upon an enforcement (eg, prior ranking creditors) is taken into consideration when determining the quantum and availability of the facilities.

2. ABL receivables financing

ABL receivables financing is invariably (but not always) used by corporates as a form of cash-flow/working capital financing. It allows a company (or group of companies) to unlock the value of its receivables and receive the financial benefit of a receivable earlier rather than having to wait for it to be paid by its customer (a 'debtor') when it matures.

It is also established practice in the United States and the United Kingdom for investment-grade corporates (typically with a selection of investment-grade debtors) to use ABL receivables facilities to derecognise their receivables from their balance sheet (see section 2.2(k)).

In the United Kingdom, an ABL receivables finance facility can be structured as either:

- a receivables purchase facility, where the asset-based lender (typically in this context called a 'receivables purchaser') purchases receivables outright from its customer (often in this context called a 'client' or 'seller') in consideration for a purchase price; or
- a revolving loan secured against the value of receivables, where the asset-based lender makes loans to its customer (the 'borrower') by reference to the fluctuating value of the borrower's receivables in consideration of the borrower granting priority, perfected security over those receivables.

If the facility is structured as a loan, standard lending terminology will be adopted in the finance documents (eg, 'lender', 'borrower', 'loans/advances' and 'interest'). However, if it is structured as a receivables purchase facility, true sale terminology (eg, 'receivables purchaser', 'client/seller/supplier' (rather than 'borrower'), 'purchase price' and 'pre-payments' (rather than 'loans' or 'advances') and 'discount' (rather than 'interest')) must be used, to avoid recharacterisation issues (see section 2.1).

If the facility is structured as a loan, the asset-based lender will look to take fixed security over all the borrower's receivables. If it is structured as a receivables purchase facility, the asset-based lender will look to take fixed security over the client's non-vesting receivables which it has purported to purchase, but title to which has failed to vest effectively in the asset-based lender for any reason.

An asset-based lender will only fund against 'eligible' receivables and the facility agreement will typically contain detailed eligibility criteria and representations and warranties in respect of receivables. An asset-based lender will also apply 'reserves' to mitigate known risks and dilutions by suppressing the amount of funding available.

It is essential that the asset-based lender regularly monitors the fluctuating value of the receivables. The facility agreement will typically provide for a number of monitoring rights and reporting obligations, such as:

- an obligation on the client/borrower to:
  - regularly (daily or weekly) notify the asset-based lender when new receivables are created, or if the value of any receivable has reduced for any reason or the collectability of a receivable has changed (receivables purchase facility); or
  - regularly (monthly or weekly following a trigger) provide a certificate to the asset-based lender, identifying the present value of the borrower's receivables (a 'borrowing base certificate') (receivables loan);
- a right for the asset-based lender to access and audit the client's/borrower's book, records and ledgers; and
- various operational covenants which measure the performance of the client's/borrower's receivables by reference to its ageing, dilutions and concentration.

If the client/borrower has credit insurance, the benefit of the policy is typically assigned to the asset-based lender. Often, but not always, it is noted on the policy as joint insured or co-insured as well as sole first loss payee.

2.1   Distinguishing purchase of receivables from lending on security

While the commercial effect is substantially similar, there are fundamental legal differences between, and consequences arising from, purchasing receivables and lending against security over receivables.

Security over receivables granted by an English company must be registered at Companies House within 21 days of the date of creation of the security; otherwise, the security is void against a liquidator, administrator or creditor of the company with an interest in the secured property.[1] If receivables are purchased, there are no registration requirements (unless the receivables purchase agreement is a whole turnover type of agreement (see section 2.2(c)) entered into by a sole trader or partnership, in which case it must be registered under the Bills of Sale Act 1878 – which is more relevant to the small and medium-sized enterprise sector of the factoring market).

If an asset-based lender purchases receivables, the provisions of the Insolvency Act 1986 on priority of payment of creditors in the event of the insolvency of the client has no application on the receivables purchaser or the receivables, because the receivables do not form part of the client's insolvent estate.[2] As such, the receivables purchaser can collect the receivables directly from the debtors without permission from any appointed insolvency

---

1   Section 859A of the Companies Act 2006.
2   This is subject to Insolvency Act provisions which might be used to challenge the ABL transaction, such as Sections 238, 239 and 423.

practitioner. Conversely, an asset-based lender which has loaned money against the security over receivables is subject to the normal insolvency rules relating to the enforcement of the security. The appointed insolvency practitioner will be responsible for controlling the collection or sale of the assets of the insolvent corporate, including distributing any realisations/collections of receivables to creditors in accordance with the statutory insolvency waterfall.

In order to be able to distinguish a purchase from a lending arrangement, an analysis of English case law is required.[3]

Purchase agreements should be evaluated in accordance with the approach taken by Lord Justice Millett in *Orion Finance* (but taking heed of the two-stage approach articulated by Lord Justice Millett in Agnew and followed by the House of Lords in *Spectrum Plus*) as follows:

- Not a sham: Is the purchase agreement a 'sham' (as that expression is used in *Welsh Development Agency*)?
- Parties' characterisation:
    - Is the purchase agreement structured on a sale transaction basis rather than a secured loan basis?
    - Does the terminology used in the documents consistently support a sale transaction basis?
- Rights and obligations: Ignoring the terminology used in the purchase agreement, are the rights and obligations of the parties consistent with a sale characterisation and inconsistent with a secured loan characterisation? In this regard, we consider the following (without limitation):
    - Are all rights, title and interest in the receivables assigned absolutely to the receivables purchaser without any equity of redemption or other proprietary right remaining with the client?
    - Is the amount which is paid by the receivables purchaser to the client in respect of the receivables paid by the receivables purchaser without any right for the client to repay it? If there is a right or obligation to repay, this may constitute an equity of redemption.
    - Is there any obligation on the receivables purchaser to resell the receivables to the client at any time or any right of the client to repurchase the receivables at any time? If so, this may constitute an equity of redemption.
    - Does the receivables purchaser have the sole right to collect receivables? If a receivables purchaser entitles the client to deal with

---

3   See *Re George Inglefield Limited* [1933] 1 Ch 1, *Welsh Development Agency v Export Finance Co Limited* [1992] BCLC 148, *Orion Finance Ltd v Crown Financial Management Ltd* (1996) 2 BCLC 78 and *Agnew v Commissioner of Inland Revenue* [2001] 2AC710, which are the leading cases with respect to characterising an absolute assignment versus an assignment by way of security. Other cases which have considered this include *Olds Discount Co Ltd v John Playfair Ltd* [1938] 3 All ER 275, *Chow Yoong Hong v Choong Fah Rubber Manufactory* [1962] AC 209, Lloyds and *Scottish Finance Ltd v Cyril Lord Carpets Sales Ltd* [1992] BCLC 609 and *Curtain Dream plc v Churchill Merchanting Ltd* [1990] BCC 341.

collections as if they were the client's own property, this may be inconsistent with the receivables purchaser's purported ownership of such receivables. However, this does not prevent a client from collecting receivables on behalf of the receivables purchaser, provided that it promptly (ie, within one working week) accounts to the receivables purchaser for them. In this regard, the receivables purchaser typically appoints the client as its agent, on either a disclosed or undisclosed basis, to collect the receivables from the client's debtors on behalf of the receivables purchaser; and the client declares that while it holds any such collections, it will hold them on trust for the receivables purchaser.

2.2   Receivables purchase facilities

(a)   *Distinguishing between 'invoice discounting' and 'factoring'*
A receivables purchase facility will typically be classed as either an invoice discounting facility or a factoring facility.

The principal difference between the products is whether the sales ledger administration and collection functions are retained by the client (invoice discounting) or outsourced to the receivables purchaser (factoring). As such, factoring is more suitable for smaller companies which have less sophisticated internal sales ledger and debt collection processes; whereas invoice discounting is more suitable for larger companies with reliable sales ledger and debt collection processes.

(b)   *Disclosed versus confidential*
A 'disclosed' facility means that the debtor has been notified of the assignment of receivables to the receivables purchaser.

A 'confidential' facility means that the debtor is not aware of the financing arrangements and has not been notified of the assignment. Under a confidential invoice discounting facility, the client is responsible for maintaining its sales ledgers and collecting the receivables as agent for the receivables purchaser. It is only upon the occurrence of a termination event that the client's agency to collect receivables on behalf of the receivables purchaser is terminated and the assignment disclosed to the debtor.

Although confidential facilities are typically preferred by clients, because their debtors remain unaware that their receivables have been assigned, the main drawback for the receivables purchaser is that if a client subsequently assigns the same receivable to another assignee in breach of the terms of the facilities agreement, the rule in *Dearle v Hall*[4] provides that the assignee whose

---

4   (1828) 38 ER 475.

notice of assignment is served first on the debtor will have priority over each other assignee, provided that such assignee acted in good faith and was not aware of any earlier assignment.

(c)   Facultative versus whole turnover

The assignment is typically documented as either a 'facultative' or 'whole turnover' arrangement (or sometimes a combination of both).

Under a facultative facility, the client is obliged to offer to assign to the receivables purchaser all receivables to which the facility applies; but title to a receivable is not transferred to the receivables purchaser until the receivable is offered to, and the offer is accepted by, the receivables purchaser.

Under a whole turnover facility, the client assigns all receivables existing at the commencement date of the facility and also all future receivables to the receivables purchaser. Future receivables automatically vest in the receivables purchaser immediately upon their creation without any further formality. As common law does not recognise a present assignment of property not yet in existence (ie, future receivables), the assignment of future receivables operates by way of equitable assignment, provided that the receivables are identifiable from and bound by the receivables purchase agreement.[5]

Whole turnover facilities are more commonly used by receivables purchasers where the client's requirement is for primary working capital, as they have certain advantages over facultative facilities. For example, under a whole turnover facility:

- the receivables vest automatically upon their creation in the receivables purchaser irrespective of whether the client has notified the receivables to the receivables purchaser; and
- all receivables (present and future) are sold at the commencement of the facility and not when the receivable comes into existence and so, should the client become insolvent, the sale of the receivables will not be deemed to be a disposition of property for the purposes of Section 127(1) of the Insolvency Act 1986.

Investment-grade corporates, whose primary objective is balance-sheet management rather than working capital, will almost always use the facilitative offer and acceptance model, albeit without the obligation to make offers.

(d)   Discount

A receivables purchaser does not charge interest because it is not providing a loan and the accrual of interest on an outstanding principal sum is a typical feature of lending. Instead, the finance cost to the client is called a 'discount' and is deducted from the purchase price of a receivable (see section 2.2(e)).

---

5   See *Holroyd v Marshall* (1862) 10 HL Cas 191 and *Tailby v Official Receiver* (1888) 13 AC 523.

The discount will typically be a fixed rate calculated by reference to:

- the notified value of the receivable (ie, the value of the receivable in the relevant invoice and as notified to the receivables purchaser by the client); and
- the number of days between:
  - the receivables purchaser paying the pre-payment (as defined below) to the client; and
  - the receivable being paid or discharged by the relevant debtor.

(e) *Purchase price*

The purchase price of a receivable is its notified value less the discount and any other fees and charges payable to the receivables purchaser. It consists of:

- an initial amount paid on the date of notification (the 'pre-payment'); and
- the balance of the purchase price paid on the maturity date of the receivable.

The pre-payment is calculated by applying an agreed percentage (the 'pre-payment percentage') to the notified value of the receivable.

Receipt of the pre-payment on the date of notification provides the cash-flow finance sought by corporates.

Receivables purchasers use a deferred purchase mechanism (ie, they pay only for a proportion of the receivable upfront (the pre-payment), with the balance of the purchase price paid on maturity of the receivable), to create a buffer to:

- mitigate dilutions (ie, anything that creates a shortfall between the notified value of a receivable and the amount which is actually collected); and
- ensure that if the client becomes insolvent, amounts collected from debtors should exceed the aggregate of pre-payments which have been paid to the client.

(f) *Availability*

Notwithstanding what is set out in section 2.2(e), for administrative ease, a receivables purchaser will typically run a receivables purchase facility using an 'availability' mechanism rather than continually calculating a purchase price for each individual receivable. On a daily basis, the client will be permitted to draw down against availability where availability is calculated on a rolling basis by:

- applying the pre-payment percentage to the value of all notified eligible receivables outstanding at that time;
- deducting an amount which the receivables purchaser has set to mitigate known risks and dilutions (a 'reserve'); and
- deducting an amount equal to any debit balance on the ledger that the

receivables purchaser uses to run the facility, where it debits any pre-payments, discount and fees, and credits any collections received, to provide a net position of amounts outstanding under the facility at any time.

Availability will always be limited by the facility limit, irrespective of the aggregate value of notified receivables.

Typically, discount accrues on a daily basis by reference to the aggregate value of pre-payments which have been paid in relation to any outstanding notified receivables and, for administrative convenience, at the end of the month, it is deducted from availability.

(g)   Dilutions

As mentioned above, a 'dilution' is the difference between:
- the notified value of a receivable; and
- the amount actually paid by the debtor.

A receivables purchase facility will typically provide for receivables-specific warranties to be given by a client to confirm, among other things, that:
- the receivables are not subject to any set-off, counterclaim or retention rights;
- the contract of sale between the client and its debtor contains no bans on assignment; and
- the receivable has not been assigned (by way of security or otherwise) to a third party.

To the extent that these warranties are breached, the receivables purchaser has the right to recourse (ie, to require the client to repurchase the receivable).

(h)   Trusts

To the extent that the assignment fails and any receivables do not vest absolutely in the receivables purchaser, the facility agreement will contain a declaration from the client that it holds any such receivables ('non-vesting debts') on trust for the receivables purchaser.

To the extent that a debtor does not pay a receivable into the account which has been designated for collections, the facility agreement will also include a declaration that the client holds the proceeds of such receivables on trust for the receivables purchaser, and will keep them separate from its own moneys and pay them over to the designated account promptly following receipt.

(i)   Power of attorney

A well-drafted receivables purchase agreement should contain a provision appointing the receivables purchaser, as attorney for the client, to sign all documents and do anything necessary to preserve and/or perfect the receivables purchaser's title to the receivables or collect the receivables. This is of particular importance for non-vesting debts.

A power of attorney can be granted only pursuant to a deed, which is why receivables purchase agreements are executed as deeds.[6]

(j) Recourse versus non-recourse

A receivables purchase facility can be provided either:

- with recourse (or on a recourse basis), where the receivables purchaser has the right to require the client to repurchase a receivable if it remains unpaid by the debtor after a certain number of days, for whatever reason; or
- without recourse (or on a non-recourse basis), where the receivables purchaser assumes the credit risk of a debtor's insolvency that arises post-notification of the receivable.

The additional risk to the receivables purchaser providing a non-recourse facility will be priced into the economics of the facility through a combination of the discount rate and the fee structure, and as mitigated by credit insurance.

(k) Off balance sheet

The term 'off balance sheet' refers to a transaction whereby the client is entitled to derecognise the receivables it has sold to the receivables purchaser on its balance sheet by complying with applicable accounting standards in the facility agreement structure.

A receivables purchase facility does not automatically create an off-balance-sheet transaction just because it operates by way of sale and purchase. It is important not to confuse a legal true sale and an accounting true sale. To achieve off-balance-sheet treatment, both are required.

The principal aim of off-balance-sheet receivables purchase facilities is for a client to obtain financing against its receivables, but structured in such a way that the finance cost is not shown as a liability on the client's balance sheet. A detailed analysis of a corporate's applicable accounting reporting standards is required to ensure that the legal arrangements meet the necessary accounting requirements.

2.3 Receivables loan facilities

Receivables loan facilities operate as revolving loans made to the borrower by

---

6   See Section 1(1) of the Powers of Attorney Act 1971 as amended by Section 1(18) and Schedule 1 of the Law of Property (Miscellaneous Provisions) Act 1989.

reference to the fluctuating value of its receivables. These facilities will always be secured facilities.

The borrower will be required to submit borrowing base certificates regularly to the asset-based lender detailing the value of its outstanding receivables. The amount of the loan available to be drawn at any time is calculated by applying an agreed advance percentage to the aggregate value of 'eligible' receivables detailed within the borrowing base certificate, less any reserves which have been set by the asset-based lender. As with receivables purchase facilities, loan facilities use an availability mechanism for drawing.

Interest accrues on a daily basis by reference to the amount of the loans which have been advanced to the borrower.

Loans can be repaid in either of the following ways, depending on the commercial agreement between the parties:

- The asset-based lender sweeps the proceeds of receivables collected into the collection account to another account owned and operated by the asset-based lender where such proceeds are applied to repay the outstanding loans. This in turn increases availability against which the borrower can draw new funds; or
- The asset-based lender applies new drawings made by the borrower to repay old loans (ie, the same mechanism as is used in a standard revolving loan facility) and the proceeds of the receivables which have been collected into the collection account are, at the asset-based lender's discretion and on its instruction, paid over to the borrower for its own account. A facility operating on this basis will often include a right for the asset-based lender to transition to the process described in the first bullet above following certain trigger events (eg, a breach of headroom or an event of default).

Asset-based lenders often require a certain level of headroom or excess availability to be maintained throughout the life of the facility, breach of which may be a trigger event for more stringent controls, including increased reporting requirements and/or disclosure of the security over the receivables to the debtors.

If a receivables loan facility is operated in accordance with the first bullet above, the asset-based lender is said to have 'cash dominion'; whereas if a receivables loan facility is operated in accordance with the second bullet above, the asset-based lender is said to have 'springing cash dominion'.

It is important to differentiate between the existence of:

- cash dominion/springing cash dominion; and
- control of the proceeds of receivables for the purposes of attempting to obtain fixed security over the receivables.

An asset-based lender can operate an ABL with springing cash dominion and still have control. Please see the "Receivables" chapter for more detail on what is required to obtain fixed security over receivables.

3. Other ABL asset classes

3.1 Inventory financing
An inventory facility is typically structured as a revolving loan facility where the amount available for drawdown is calculated by reference to one of the following values of the borrower's inventory at any time, depending on the commercial agreement between the parties:
- the cost value;
- the market value; or
- the net orderly liquidation value (NOLV) – that is, the estimated value that a company would receive if assets were liquidated in an orderly manner over a reasonable period, generally six to nine months, and not as part of a 'fire sale'.

The asset-based lender will regularly monitor the inventory and have rights to request independent valuations.

Due to the fluctuating, impermanent nature of inventory and the borrower requiring the ability to sell its inventory in the ordinary course of business, only floating charge security is granted to the asset-based lender over the inventory.

An asset-based lender will only fund against 'eligible' inventory, and the facility agreement will typically contain detailed eligibility criteria and representations and warranties in respect of inventory. An asset-based lender will also apply 'reserves' to mitigate known risks (eg, landlord liens) by suppressing the amount of funding available. Inventory will become a receivable once it has been sold by the borrower; such receivable can then be funded under the receivables facility, provided that the value of the inventory is first deducted from amounts available under the inventory facility to avoid double counting.

Relevant insurances must be maintained by the borrower, the benefit of which is typically assigned by way of security to the asset-based lender; and the asset-based lender is noted on the policy as joint insured or co-insured as well as sole first loss payee.

3.2 Plant and machinery financing
A plant and machinery facility can be structured as a revolving loan facility or an amortising term loan facility. In either case, the amount available for drawdown is calculated by reference to the NOLV of the borrower's plant and machinery at any time.

Valuations and regular monitoring are key and valuations will be periodically updated (eg, every six months or annually) by a third-party field examiner expert.

An asset-based lender will only fund against 'eligible' plant and machinery, and the facility agreement will typically contain detailed eligibility criteria and representations and warranties in respect of plant and machinery. An asset-based lender will also apply 'reserves' to mitigate known risks (eg, landlord liens) by suppressing the amount of funding available.

The facility agreement will also typically contain a number of undertakings about the plant and machinery in relation to its condition and maintenance so as to preserve its value.

Relevant insurances must be maintained by the borrower, the benefit of which is typically assigned by way of security to the asset-based lender; and the asset-based lender is noted on the policy as joint insured or co-insured as well as sole first loss payee.

The asset-based lender will typically require a fixed charge over the plant and machinery against which funding has been provided.

3.3   Real property financing

A real property facility is typically structured as an amortising term loan, where the amount available for drawdown is calculated by reference to the value of real property owned by the borrower at commencement of the facility. The asset-based lender will take a mortgage over the real property and the security will need to be registered at the land registry (as well as Companies House).

Valuations and regular monitoring are key. Typically, a valuation will assume that the asset is sold within a certain amount of time (eg, 180 days), to reflect realistic realisations on enforcement. This is determined by a third-party field examiner expert.

An asset-based lender will obtain a 'certificate of title' or 'report on title' prior to lending, and the facility agreement will contain a number of undertakings about the real property in relation to its condition and maintenance so as to preserve its value.

Relevant insurances must be maintained, the benefit of which is typically assigned by way of security to the asset-based lender; and the asset-based lender is invariably noted on the policy as joint insured or co-insured as well as sole first loss payee.

4.   Eligibility criteria and operational covenants

All ABL facilities will contain eligibility criteria in respect of the assets being funded and may also contain operational covenants which test the client's/borrower's assets by reference to a number of factors.

4.1 Eligibility criteria

The facility agreement will expressly set out the eligibility criteria for each applicable asset class. Set out below are some example eligibility definitions (often drafted in the negative):

'*Eligible Receivables*' *are any receivables which the Receivables Purchaser/Asset-based Lender determines is eligible which excludes, by way of examples, a receivable:*

which is not subject to first priority security in favour of the Asset-based Lender;[7]

which is subject to security in favour of a third party (unless permitted);

which is overdue;

with respect to which any covenant, representation, or warranty contained in the finance documents has been breached or is not true;

which (i) does not arise from the sale of goods or performance of services in the ordinary course of business, (ii) is not evidenced by an invoice or other documentation satisfactory to the Receivables Purchaser/Asset-based Lender, (iii) represents a progress billing, (iv) is contingent upon the Client/Borrower's completion of any further performance, (v) represents a sale on a bill-and-hold, guaranteed sale, sale-and-return, sale on approval, consignment, cash-on-delivery or any other repurchase or return basis, or (vi) relates to payments of interest;

for which the goods giving rise to such receivable have not been shipped to the Debtor or for which the services giving rise to such receivable have not been performed by the Client/Borrower or if such receivable was invoiced more than once;

with respect to which any cheque or other instrument of payment has been returned uncollected for any reason;

which is owed by an insolvent Debtor or a Debtor which is subject to insolvency proceedings;

which is owed by a Debtor domiciled in an unapproved jurisdiction;

which is due in a currency other than an approved currency;

which is owed by any 'affiliate' of the Client/Borrower;

which, for any Debtor, exceeds a credit limit determined by the Receivables Purchaser/Asset-based Lender, to the extent of such excess;

which is subject to any counterclaim, deduction, defence, set-off or dispute;

which is evidenced by any promissory note, chattel paper or instrument;

which is for goods that have been sold under a purchase order or pursuant to the terms of a contract or other agreement or understanding (written or oral) that indicates that a third party has or has had an ownership interest in such goods, or which indicates any such third party as payee or remittance party; or

which was created on cash on delivery terms.

---

7   Applicable only for a receivables lending structure.

'**Eligible Inventory**' is inventory which the Asset-based Lender determines in its permitted discretion is eligible and, by way of examples, excludes inventory:

which is not subject to first priority security in favour of the Asset-based Lender;

which is subject to security in favour of a third party (unless permitted);

which is, in the Asset-based Lender's opinion, slow moving, obsolete, unmerchantable, defective, used, unfit for sale, not saleable at prices approximating at least the cost of such inventory in the ordinary course of business or unacceptable due to age, type, category and/or quantity;

with respect to which any covenant, representation, or warranty contained in the finance documents has been breached or is not true and which does not conform to all standards imposed by any governmental authority;

in which any third party shall (i) have any direct or indirect ownership, interest or title or (ii) be indicated on any purchase order or invoice with respect to such inventory as having or purporting to have an interest therein (ie, retention of title rights);

which is not finished goods or which constitutes work-in-process or raw materials;

which is not located in an approved warehouse;

is in transit;

in respect of which there is insurance satisfactory to the Asset-based Lender;

which is the subject of a consignment by the Borrower as consignor; or

which has been acquired from a sanctioned third party.

'**Eligible Plant & Machinery**' is plant & machinery owned by the Borrower and meeting each of the following typical requirements:

the Borrower has good title to such plant & machinery;

the Borrower has the right to subject such plant & machinery to security in favour of the Asset-based Lender; such plant & machinery is subject to first priority security in favour of the Asset-based Lender and is free and clear of all other security of any nature;

the full purchase price for such plant & machinery has been paid by the Borrower;

such plant & machinery is located in approved warehouses and where such warehouse is leased by the Borrower the lessor has delivered to the Asset-based Lender an access agreement waiving standard liens or a Reserve for rent, charges, and other amounts due or to become due with respect to such facility has been established by the Asset-based Lender;

such plant & machinery is in good working order and condition (ordinary wear and tear excepted) and is used or held for use by the Borrower in the ordinary course of business of the Borrower;

such plant & machinery (i) is not subject to any agreement which restricts the ability of the Borrower to use, sell, transport or dispose of such plant & machinery or which restricts the Asset-based Lender's ability to take possession of, sell or otherwise dispose of such plant & machinery and (ii) has not been purchased from a sanctioned third party; and

such plant & machinery does not constitute 'Fixtures' under the applicable laws of the jurisdiction in which such plant & machinery is located.

Eligible real property is typically only those real properties which have been due diligenced and approved by the Asset-based Lender and its legal counsel and over which the Asset-based Lender has first priority perfected security.

4.2 Operational covenants

As previously mentioned, an asset-based lender closely monitors the assets against which it is providing funding to ensure that it is not under-collateralised at any time and that it does not become overexposed to a particular type of asset (or a sub-class of asset).

This monitoring is undertaken by:

- the client/borrower regularly providing information to the asset-based lender;
- third-party valuers periodically valuing the assets; and
- the asset-based lender or its appointed agents periodically undertaking audits of the client/borrower.

Receivables are distinct from the other classes of asset as they are intangible and are therefore monitored differently. An asset-based lender will often monitor the following and apply covenants, which may be either formal covenants in respect of which the client/borrower provides covenant certificates and breach of which has certain remedies (more common for receivables purchase structures) or incorporated as thresholds within the eligibility criteria:

- Debtor concentration: The value of receivables due by any one particular debtor as a percentage of all receivables. If the pre-agreed debtor concentration threshold is breached, any receivables notified in excess of that threshold will not be eligible for funding (or will be the subject of a reserve). This prevents the asset-based lender from becoming over-exposed to a single debtor, thereby mitigating risk by spread.
- Export concentration: The value of receivables due by debtors domiciled outside England and Wales as a percentage of all receivables. If the pre-agreed export concentration threshold is breached, any receivables in excess of that threshold will not be eligible for funding (or the subject of a reserve). This prevents the asset-based lender from becoming overexposed to receivables due by debtors located outside England and Wales, where it may be more challenging to collect receivables if local law perfection requirements have not been complied with.

- Dilutions: The value of dilutions in any period as a percentage of all receivables notified in that period. If the pre-agreed dilution threshold is exceeded, this indicates to the asset-based lender that there may be something adverse occurring with regard to the client, its products or services, the sector in which it operates or its debtors. Any breach of such covenant will typically allow the asset-based lender to reduce the pre-payment percentage (receivables purchase) or the advance percentage (receivables loans).
- Debt turn: The average number of days it takes for debtors to pay. If the pre-agreed threshold is exceeded, this indicates to the asset-based lender that there may be something adverse occurring with regard to the client, its products or services, the sector in which it operates or its debtors. Any breach of such covenant will typically allow the asset-based lender to reduce the pre-payment percentage (receivables purchase) or the advance percentage (receivables loans).

Aircraft finance

Jane Man
Richard Stock
Mayer Brown

1. Introduction

Powered aircraft are a relatively recent invention, but the techniques used to finance aircraft date back centuries. This is because the concepts, structures and documentation used to finance aircraft are largely derived from their maritime equivalents – ships.

One key difference is that, while English maritime law ascribes a unique set of proprietary interests to a ship, English law treats an aircraft like any other chattel – albeit a chattel that often crosses international borders. As a consequence, while the concepts, structures and documentation applicable to the financing of ships and aircraft share many similarities, the different legal nature of the underlying asset requires a different approach when creating security.

This chapter considers the security interests created in a range of commonly adopted financing structures:

- pre-delivery financing of commercial aircraft (designed to fund the advance payments due under an aircraft purchase agreement while the aircraft itself is being manufactured);
- delivery financing of commercial aircraft (including direct loans to airlines, structures involving special purpose vehicles and structures involving third party aircraft lessors); and
- corporate jet financing.

These financing structures are not the only structures adopted to finance aircraft,[1] but they provide a useful set of examples of secured lending transactions involving aircraft.

2. Pre-delivery financing

Manufacturing an aircraft is a complex task involving the sourcing of thousands of items of equipment over a reasonably long timeframe. An aircraft

---

1   For example, we have not sought to address export credit financings, Japanese operating leases and asset-backed securitisations.

manufacturer needs to order and pay for components many months (sometimes years) before the aircraft is delivered. In addition to presenting formidable supply chain challenges, this endeavour ties up a significant amount of working capital.

2.1 Advance payments/pre-delivery payments

To address both the aircraft manufacturer's working capital needs and the risk that a contracted buyer may fail to purchase the newly manufactured aircraft, the aircraft manufacturer typically requires the buyer to pay a portion of the purchase price before delivery, often in stages. Advance payments (also known as pre-delivery payments (PDPs)) can amount to up to 30% of the list price of the aircraft and can become payable by the buyer many months (and sometimes years) before the aircraft is delivered.

However, the buyer of an aircraft may not wish to use its own cash to settle its PDP commitments. The relevant aircraft will not start generating revenue for many months (if not years), and the buyer may have better uses for its working capital.

2.2 A typical PDP financing

The buyer can instead request a financial institution to advance funds to finance the PDPs payable to the aircraft manufacturer under the purchase agreement (see Figure 1).

Figure 1. A typical PDP financing

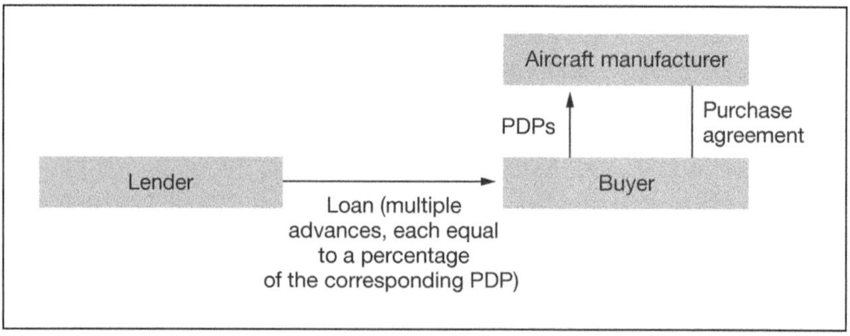

A lender seldom finances the entirety of the PDPs payable for an aircraft; the lender will want the buyer to pay a portion of the PDPs so that some of the buyer's own funds remain at risk if the purchase does not proceed. It is common for the buyer to pay from its own funds the first PDP instalment and a portion of each subsequent PDP instalment.

To remove the risk of the airline using the loan for other purposes, the lender will usually pay the advanced amounts directly to the manufacturer. The buyer then pays interest on the PDP loan throughout its term and repays the principal upon delivery of the aircraft (often from the proceeds of the delivery financing).

No security can be granted over the aircraft itself, as it is still in production. Instead, the buyer grants to the PDP lender a security assignment over the buyer's rights in the purchase agreement, including the buyer's right to take title to the aircraft in return for paying the balance of the purchase price. Weaknesses with a purchase agreement assignment include the following:

- The manufacturer often has the right to terminate the purchase agreement if the buyer defaults, making the assignment of questionable value to a lender;
- The pricing incentives given to the buyer cannot be used by the lender (meaning that if the assignment is enforced, the lender must pay the full 'sticker price' for the aircraft without the benefit of discounts customarily granted by a manufacturer to the buyer); and
- The purchase agreement assignment often requires the prior written consent of the manufacturer.

For these reasons, it is common for a lender to enter into negotiations with the manufacturer (in the context of obtaining the manufacturer's consent to the assignment) for improved terms. It is common for the manufacturer's consent to the assignment of the purchase agreement to be bundled with a parallel 'step-in' arrangement, which permits the lender to step into the shoes of the buyer and pay a price for the aircraft which is pre-agreed with the aircraft manufacturer. This right to step into the shoes of the buyer does not constitute security, but it has a similar effect. This is often referred to as the lender's 'step-in right' while the price payable by the lender is referred to as the lender's 'step-in price'.

2.3 The step-in right and the step-in price

One of the key issues negotiated between the parties is the step-in price. This is not the same as the price payable by the buyer (which is confidential and often includes discounts granted by the manufacturer). The step-in price is a function of several factors:

- The aircraft specification and configuration: Since a change to the specification or configuration will affect the step-in price, a lender will want to approve changes or make the relevant change conditional upon the buyer pre-paying to the lender an amount equal to the increase in price payable to the manufacturer as a consequence of the change.
- The delivery date: The lender will want to have a right to approve any change to the delivery date. It will also want to ensure that in case of any delivery delay, the step-in price does not continue to escalate. Furthermore, in case of a non-excusable delay, the lender should (if it

'steps in' to the purchase agreement) become entitled to receive (from the manufacturer) liquidated damages resulting from the delivery delay.

- The PDPs already paid by the buyer: The lender will usually ask the manufacturer to certify the amount of PDPs previously received from the buyer, and will seek to ensure that the manufacturer does not reimburse these PDPs to the buyer or apply them towards other liabilities owed by the buyer.

In some jurisdictions, the PDPs paid by the buyer for the aircraft can be claimed by a liquidator appointed to the buyer (for general distribution to the buyer's creditors). The lender should obtain a legal opinion from counsel in the jurisdiction of incorporation of the airline regarding the nature and extent of this risk. Where necessary, the lender could require the buyer's rights under the purchase agreement to be transferred to a bankruptcy-remote special purpose vehicle (SPV) before those rights are assigned to the lender as security.

2.4 Exercising rights upon the buyer's default: standstill period

In addition to assessing the above factors, the lender will need time (after the buyer defaults) to decide whether to exercise its step-in right. This is typically addressed by agreeing a 'standstill period' with the manufacturer, during which the manufacturer will undertake not to terminate the purchase agreement. During the standstill period, the lender will try to find an alternative buyer for the aircraft. The marketability of the aircraft is a function of various factors, including:

- the delivery position of the aircraft;
- the maximum take-off weight;
- the engine configuration; and
- the cabin and avionics equipment installed.

After the lender steps into the shoes of the buyer, the lender will wish to have a right to exercise all rights of the original buyer, including changing the aircraft specification or configuration to cater to the market preferences or airworthiness requirements.

2.5 Buy-out right

The manufacturer will naturally be wary of a lender exercising its step-in right, because if the lender then seeks to sell the aircraft to another buyer, this may interfere with the manufacturer's efforts to market the same aircraft type to that buyer. For this reason, a manufacturer may insist on having the right to buy out the lender's interests by paying a pre-agreed price. The lender will want to ensure that the buy-out price is sufficient to repay all amounts advanced by the lender (together with interest).

The manufacturer has a right to buy out the interests of a lender, but has no obligation to do so. This means that the lender cannot (in circumstances where the lender does not have sufficient cash to pay the step-in price) compel the manufacturer to buy out its interest. If a lender is unable to pay the step-in price, the manufacturer may try to resell the aircraft to another buyer (but may be able to do so only at a reduced price). A manufacturer may insist that these resale proceeds be applied first to compensate the manufacturer for its loss and only second to reimburse the lender for the advance payments made. This means that the amount recovered by the lender may fall far short of the amount of principal and interest owed by the buyer to the lender.

3. Delivery financing

A variety of structures are adopted for the delivery financing of commercial aircraft.[2] Some common structures are illustrated below.

A lender may make a loan directly to an airline to fund a portion of the purchase price payable to the aircraft manufacturer (typically, less than 85%) (see Figure 2).

Figure 2. Delivery financing through direct loan

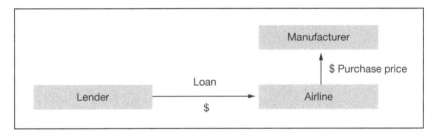

Alternatively, an airline may choose to use an SPV as borrower (see Figure 3).

Figure 3. Delivery financing through SPV

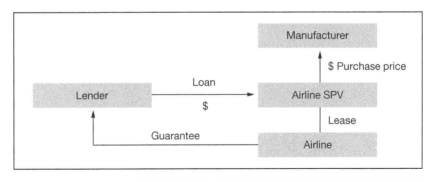

---

2   Different considerations apply for corporate jets – please see section 4.

If the airline has insufficient liquidity to fund the equity portion of the purchase price, the airline may request a third-party lessor to purchase and leaseback the aircraft (see Figure 4).

Figure 4. Delivery financing through sale and leaseback

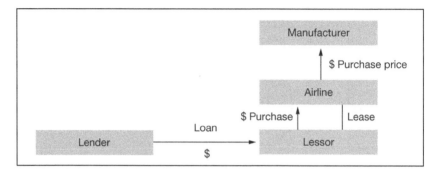

A lender will invariably require the owner to grant security over:

- the aircraft, including the engines, the component parts and maintenance records;
- the manufacturer warranties related to the airframe and the engines and, less commonly, the auxiliary power unit (access to the warranties provides to a lender some protection against design flaws and manufacturing flaws);
- insurance proceeds resulting from any damage to, or loss of, the aircraft; and
- where the loan is advanced to an SPV or an intermediary (eg, a third-party lessor) and leased to an airline:
  - an assignment of the lease;
  - a charge over the bank account into which the airline pays rent under that lease; and
  - if the SPV is a company owned by the airline, a charge over the shares of that company.

Less commonly (and only where a third-party lessor is involved), a lender may require a charge over the bank accounts in which the lessor holds the security deposit and maintenance reserves paid by the airline.

An English law aircraft mortgage document can address all of these security interests, although it is more common for English law documentation to address security over the aircraft separately from the other security (eg, warranties, insurance). Each is considered below.

3.1   Aircraft mortgage and other security

In this section, we will first introduce the basic features of an English law mortgage (section 3.1(a)). We will then survey the other property over which a lender typically takes security, such as an assignment of manufacturer warranties and insurance (section 3.1(b)). We will then consider the adjustments to a lender's security package required when the financing involves an SPV or a third-party lessor (section 3.1(c)). Our focus will then shift to consider, at a high level only, two technical aspects relating to the validity of an English law aircraft mortgage:

- the validity problems highlighted by the *Blue Sky* decision (section 3.1(d)) and
- the more positive impact of the Cape Town Convention (section 3.1(e)).

We will then complete our review with a few remarks on enforcement (section 3.1(f)).

(a)   *Basic features of an English law aircraft mortgage*

The term 'mortgage' is actually misleading. A legal mortgage would involve the transfer of legal title, but an English law aircraft 'mortgage' does not actually involve any transfer of title. Transferring title to the lender is usually impracticable, for three reasons. First, local laws often impose certain responsibilities and liabilities on an aircraft owner.[3] Second, in some jurisdictions, a title transfer may attract transfer taxes. Third, an English law legal mortgage cannot automatically extend to cover replacement aircraft engines and parts which are installed on the aircraft; nor can it automatically extend to cover new maintenance records. This is problematic, as the engines can comprise up to half the value of an aircraft and regulatory requirements mean that an aircraft without complete maintenance records is nothing more than an expensive paperweight.

Instead, an English law aircraft 'mortgage' actually functions as a fixed charge over the aircraft. In other words, the aircraft owner creates, in favour of the lender, an equitable proprietary interest in the aircraft as security for the discharge of the loan. The fixed charge will automatically extend to each replacement engine or part and each new maintenance record as and when the owner of the aircraft also becomes the owner of that part or maintenance record, without the need for any further act.[4] This charge is then released automatically when the secured debt is discharged.

---

3   For example, local laws sometimes contemplate strict liability for damage caused during the operation of the aircraft.

4   As a matter of practice, the charge may be confirmed in writing by the airline in case of an engine replacement.

Assets covered by an English law mortgage: The practice for English law aircraft mortgages differs from the practice for New York law aircraft mortgages. The scope of an English law aircraft mortgage is typically limited to:

- the airframe;
- the engines;
- the airframe and engine parts;
- all replacement parts and engines; and
- the manuals and technical records for the aircraft.

By contrast, a New York law aircraft mortgage often expressly extends to property ancillary to the aircraft, such as:

- the warranties for the aircraft;
- insurance over the aircraft; and
- earnings generated by the aircraft.

The reasons an English law aircraft mortgage does not typically address these ancillary rights might include the following:

- Each manufacturer has its own form of warranty agreement, making it inefficient to update an aircraft mortgage to reflect the requirements of a particular manufacturer;
- In some cases, the warranties reside with the airline rather than the SPV/lessor that is entering into the aircraft mortgage; and
- In the case of a multi-tiered structure, adding additional parties to the mortgage (eg, to document an assignment of insurance from the airline to the SPV) can make the English law aircraft mortgage unwieldly; it is often more efficient to document a multi-tiered assignment through a series of individual documents.

(b)   *Other security and protections for a delivery financing*
While an aircraft mortgage is the centrepiece of any security package in a secured aircraft financing transaction, a lender providing delivery financing will also typically seek security over other aircraft-related property, including the following.

Warranties: Each airframe and engine manufacturer provides certain contractual warranties relating to the condition and continued airworthiness of the airframe, engines and components installed on an aircraft. If any warranty is breached, the manufacturer must repair or replace the relevant parts or pay compensation.

Component warranties (ie, warranting the fault-free operation of individual components) are the most straightforward of the available warranties, but these warranties also tend to expire relatively quickly. Of greater potential value to a lender are the service life policies and ultimate life warranties for the structure of the airframe and high-value components within each engine; these warranties tend to have both a longer expiration period and greater value to a lender (because the costs of rectifying a faulty airframe or high-value engine components can be significant).

The extension of the warranties to the lender used to be documented by way of an assignment of warranties, but is now more commonly documented by an independent contractual arrangement with the relevant manufacturer or by way of a deed poll using the manufacturer's form. An airline typically retains the use of these warranties until a default occurs, at which time the lender is given the benefit of these warranties.

Insurance: Airlines typically obtain the following types of insurance for an aircraft:

- Hull insurance, which protects the airline against the risk of physical damage to the aircraft (both in flight and on the ground).[5] Hull insurance is usually obtained on an 'agreed value' basis; and
- Liability insurance: Whenever an aircraft is operated, there is an inherent risk that the aircraft will cause personal injury or property damage, resulting in third-party claims. For this reason, most jurisdictions require an operating aircraft to be covered by liability insurance exceeding a minimum liability limit.

If the aircraft is subject to a mortgage, the lender will require the airline's insurance policy to be modified by Airline Finance/Lease Contract Endorsement AVN67B. AVN67B was designed to streamline the procedure for arranging insurance coverage in financing and leasing transactions. A lender named in an AVN67B endorsement as a 'contracting party' becomes an additional insured on the airline's insurance policy. If an aircraft is destroyed (ie, a total loss occurs), the insurance proceeds will be paid to the party specified in the transaction documents (usually, the lender). The addition of the lender as an additional insured also means that if an aircraft accident occurs, any third-party claims against the lender will also be covered by the liability insurance. The lender also benefits from 'breach of warranty' protection, which provides that a breach of the policy by the airline will not invalidate the policy in relation to the lender (unless the lender had caused or knowingly condoned the relevant breach).

In addition, the lender can obtain political risk insurance. This type of insurance covers the risk of government confiscation or requisition of the aircraft.

---

5   The term 'hull insurance' is an example of the use of maritime concepts in an aviation context.

(c)   ***Delivery financing involving an SPV/third-party lessor***

So far, our discussion has focused on the most basic form of delivery financing: a direct loan to an airline. In practice, it is also common for the parties to use an intermediate entity to own the aircraft and lease it to the relevant airline.

For example, an SPV may be used to own the aircraft and borrow the funds because it is located in a 'creditor-friendly' legal system (while the airline is not), or because of tax considerations. Alternatively, a third-party lessor might be asked to purchase the aircraft from the airline (thus releasing working capital that might otherwise have been committed by the airline towards the 'equity' component of the aircraft financing).

If an SPV is involved, the SPV will acquire ownership of the aircraft and lease it to the airline for a rental designed to cover repayments scheduled to be made by the SPV to the lender under the loan. In return for the lender granting the loan to the SPV, the SPV (being the aircraft owner) will grant a mortgage (together with the usual assignment of insurance and warranty assignment) to the lender. If the SPV is owned by the airline, the airline may guarantee the obligations of the SPV. In addition, the lender will typically obtain a security interest over the following property to secure the repayment of the loan:

- Assignment of lease: The SPV will assign to the lender the SPV's rights under the lease (or, less commonly, only the right to receive rent and other amounts from the airline).
- Account charge: The SPV will grant a charge over the bank account into which the airline makes payments of rent (or, alternatively, direct the airline to make payments directly to the lender).
- Share charge: If the SPV is a company owned by the airline, the airline will grant a charge over its shares in the SPV to secure the SPV's obligations towards the bank, including the repayment of the loan.

If a third-party lessor is involved, that lessor will acquire ownership of the aircraft and lease it to the airline. If this structure is used, then the airline will not guarantee the obligations of the lessor (it being a third party). Depending on the nature of the loan, a lender may additionally request the following from a lessor:

- Charge over security deposit account: An aircraft lessor typically collects a security deposit from the airline to protect itself against the risk of an airline default. If the aircraft is mortgaged, a lender may require the lessor to grant a charge over the account in which the security deposit is held.
- Charge over maintenance reserves account: Airframes and engines require scheduled maintenance and refurbishments, while life limited parts require replacement from time to time. This can be costly. For this reason, lessors typically collect a further stream of payments from the

airline (known as 'maintenance reserves') to ensure that sufficient cash is reserved to pay for future maintenance.[6] If the aircraft is mortgaged, a lender could consider requiring the lessor to grant a charge over the account which holds the maintenance reserves as security for the repayment of the loan.

In addition, the lender will need to be satisfied that the lessor's right to terminate the lease and repossess the aircraft will be recognised and enforceable. The lessor will have rights to inspect the aircraft and the aircraft documentation, and these rights will need to be extended to the lender.

(d) The law governing the validity of the mortgage and the Blue Sky decision

Where the parties choose English law to govern an aircraft mortgage contract, this means that English law will govern the contractual aspects of the aircraft mortgage. However, the aircraft mortgage also creates proprietary rights (or rights in rem) over the aircraft. Which law governs the validity of the mortgage?

In the Blue Sky decision,[7] the English court confirmed that proprietary rights over movable assets (eg, aircraft) are governed by the law of the place where the asset is located at the time when the mortgage is granted (the 'lex situs'). The English court also confirmed that the lex situs is the domestic law of the situs (without reference to its conflict of law rules). In other words, the English court rejected renvoi.[8]

The application of this rule is straightforward if the aircraft is located in England when the mortgage is granted: the lender will simply take the steps required under English law to ensure the validity of the mortgage and preserve its priority. This involves (if the aircraft is registered in the United Kingdom) registering the mortgage in the UK Register of Aircraft Mortgages maintained by the Civil Aviation Authority and (if the mortgagor is a UK company) filing the mortgage with the UK Companies House.

The situation becomes less clear if the aircraft is located outside England when the mortgage is granted. In some jurisdictions, it is possible to obtain straightforward legal advice on the validity of the mortgage and the local registrations necessary to perfect the mortgage.[9] However, in other jurisdictions, local counsel may respond that domestic conflict of law rules point to the laws

---

6   Maintenance reserves may not be required from a top-tier airline.
7   Blue Sky One Ltd v Mahan Air [2009] EWHC 3314 (Comm) and [2010] EWHC 631 (Comm).
8   Renvoi is a conflict of law doctrine which applies when:
     • a court in one jurisdiction is directed (by its own conflict rules) to determine a particular issue by reference to the law of a second jurisdiction, including the conflict rules of that second jurisdiction; and
     • the conflict rules of the second jurisdiction requires that issue to be determined by the law of the first jurisdiction or by a third jurisdiction.
9   Depending on the jurisdiction, this may involve registration on a mortgage register, operator register and/or a company register.

of another jurisdiction (eg, the jurisdiction where the aircraft is registered). This creates a conundrum because the *Blue Sky* decision states that the domestic laws (rather than the conflict rules) of the *situs* will apply.

In many cases, the solution has been to fly the aircraft into English airspace or to another jurisdiction where it is possible to obtain clear advice on the validity of the mortgage. However, this can be costly and disruptive.

To address the uncertainties inherent in an English law mortgage, a lender can look to the Cape Town Convention (which is the subject of the next section).

(e) Creation and registration of international interests under the Cape Town Convention and the Aircraft Protocol

The Cape Town Convention[10] was established to facilitate the financing and leasing of mobile equipment, and the Aircraft Protocol[11] applied the Cape Town Convention to high-value airframes, aircraft engines and helicopters (collectively, 'CTC').[12, 13]

In order for the CTC to apply to a secured financing transaction, there must be a connecting nexus: either the aircraft owner must be situated in a contracting state or the aircraft must be registered in a contracting state.[14] Where the CTC applies, it primarily assists a lender in three ways:

- The CTC established an International Registry for the registration of certain interests in aircraft, including security interests. As a consequence, the lender can:
  - search the International Registry to ascertain whether any pre-existing security has been filed against the aircraft;
  - require the aircraft owner to create an 'international interest' in favour of the lender, which must constitute an interest "granted by a chargor under a security agreement".[15] An English law aircraft mortgage usually satisfies the CTC requirements for an international interest; although the validity of the CTC international interest is determined independently from the validity of the English law

---

10 The Convention on International Interests in Mobile Equipment signed at Cape Town on 16 November 2001.
11 The Protocol on International Interests in Mobile Equipment on Matters Specific to Aircraft Equipment signed at Cape Town on 16 November 2001.
12 The Cape Town Convention applies only to 'aircraft objects', a term which covers high-value airframes, aircraft engines and helicopters that satisfy certain requirements specified in the Aircraft Protocol, including minimum requirements as to capacity or thrust (please see Article II.1 of the Protocol and the relevant definitions in Article I(2) of the Protocol).
13 Given the length of this chapter, the aim of this section is to provide an introduction to the CTC, rather than a comprehensive guide.
14 Article 3(1) of the convention and Article IV(1) of the protocol.
15 Article 2(2)(a) of the convention. The term 'chargor' is not defined in the convention, but the Official Commentary to the Cape Town Convention states that it denotes the grantor of any form of security interest, possessory or non-possessory. The term 'security agreement' means an agreement by which a chargor grants or agrees to grant to a chargee an interest in or over an object to secure the performance of any existing or future obligation of the chargor or a third person (Article 1(ii) of the convention).

aircraft mortgage. Thus, the CTC international interest is a parallel security interest whose validity does not depend on any national law and should be recognised by all contracting states; and

- upon creation of its mortgage, register the resulting international interest with the International Registry (and obtain first-to-file priority over subsequent security).[16] However, registered international interests will rank behind categories of non-consensual rights or interests (eg, mechanics' liens or airport liens)[17] if the relevant contracting state has made a declaration to that effect.

- The lender can benefit from the enforcement options available in each contracting state.[18]
- If the aircraft is to be registered in a contracting state, the lender should also require the party in whose name the aircraft is registered to sign an irrevocable de-registration and export request authorisation (IDERA) and submit it to the registry authority for recordation.[19] If the relevant contracting state has opted in to the de-registration arrangements in the CTC, the registry authority in that contracting state has an obligation to process each IDERA request in a timely manner (thus allowing the lender to avoid the delay and uncertainty which often accompanied the de-registration process under local systems).

Because an English law aircraft mortgage usually satisfies the requirements for an international interest, the CTC can help to circumvent some of the problems highlighted by the *Blue Sky* case. However, the CTC is not a panacea. In many contracting states, the enforcement of security interests created under the CTC remains a developing area of law. In addition, it is not always possible to repossess the aircraft in a state which is a contracting state. As a result, many lenders still prefer to have a fully enforceable local law mortgage which exists in parallel with any security interests created under the CTC.

(f)   *Enforcement*

The method and process of enforcing an aircraft mortgage will depend largely on the location of the aircraft at the time of enforcement. Enforcement regimes can vary significantly from one jurisdiction to the next, and so a lender will first need to seek advice from lawyers in the relevant jurisdictions. A survey of the different enforcement regimes is, unfortunately, beyond the scope of this chapter.

---

16   Articles 29(1) and 29(2)(a) of the convention.
17   To mitigate the risk of liens imposed by airport and air navigation authorities, it is common for airlines to authorise the relevant authorities to provide (at the lender's request) a statement of the charges owed by the airline.
18   Space constraints prevent a review of the enforcement options.
19   Article XIII(2) of the protocol.

4. Corporate jet financing

Many of the structures and documents used to finance a corporate jet will be familiar to anyone that has documented the financing of a commercial aircraft. However, one key difference in corporate jet financing is the absence of an airline. The majority of corporate jets in operation are owned and operated for the benefit of high-net-worth individuals or corporate entities that do not have the licences and certifications necessary to operate an aircraft.[20]

This presents a new set of challenges for a lender: in the absence of a certified airline, who should be responsible for overseeing the maintenance, operation and insurance of the aircraft?

Figure 5. Corporate jet financing

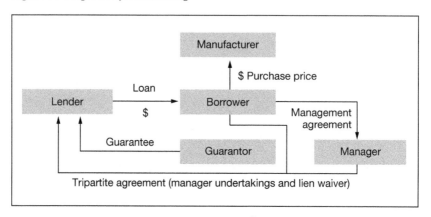

Typically, the owner of the corporate jet delegates responsibility for overseeing the maintenance, operation and insurance of the aircraft to a third-party aircraft management company. That manager must be acceptable to the lender (audits are common, even for reputable managers), and must enter into supplemental documentation to provide comfort to the lender.

For example, it is common for a lender providing funds to finance a corporate jet to require the manager:

- to enter into a tripartite agreement (among the owner/borrower, the manager and the lender) in which, among other things, the manager agrees:
  - to ensure that the aircraft is operated, maintained and insured in accordance with the arrangements agreed between the lender and the owner/borrower;

---

20   For the purpose of this section, we have confined our comments to the financing of a corporate jet operated on a private basis by a high-net-worth individual or a corporate entity not involved in the provision of charter services to unrelated entities.

- to waive (as against the lender) any lien or encumbrance that the manager may obtain against the aircraft; and
- to follow instructions from the lender should the owner/borrower default;

- in circumstances where the aircraft is insured under the manager's fleet policy, to provide to the lender an assignment of insurances relating to the aircraft. In order to prevent a situation in which the manager is underwriting repayment of the owner's/borrower's debt, that assignment is typically given on the basis that recourse against the manager is limited to the assigned property; and
- to the extent that the manager has entered into maintenance service contracts with respect to the aircraft, to provide the lender with the right to 'step in' to those maintenance service contracts.

Two further features distinguish the financing of a corporate jet from a commercial aircraft transaction:

- Corporate jet financing is often provided within a package of private banking services offered by the lender to the relevant high-net-worth individual. As a result, the lender may also seek security over the assets deposited in the account of the borrower or its beneficial owner maintained with the lender.
- A corporate jet is typically owned by an SPV. To circumvent the difficulties of enforcing security over the aircraft, a lender usually takes security over the shares of the SPV. Upon default, the lender may be able to take control the aircraft by assuming control of the SPV.

5.   Conclusion

The security instruments used to document the financing of an aircraft will be familiar to many English lawyers, particularly those with experience in ship finance. However, the inherent mobility of an aircraft, the frequent exchange of high-value components and the legal characteristics of an aircraft under English law introduce complexity that can make aircraft finance deals satisfying to structure, negotiate and document.

Shipping finance

Bill Amos
Maggie Cheung
Conor Warde
Mayer Brown

1. Introduction

Since ancient times, the shipping industry – essentially consisting of the businesses of building, purchasing, owning and trading ships – has been one the most important cornerstones of trade. Over time, ships have become significantly larger, more specialised and durable; and the huge number of ships floating on the oceans and other waterways around the world at any one time is enough to cause one to wonder how it is possible for so many ships to be in existence and operating at any one time.

1.1 The business of shipping

One thing that has been constant throughout the history of shipping is that ships are expensive to build, purchase and operate – which means that financial assistance in some form is usually needed by their owners. Typically, the modern business of financing ships involves a financial institution – often a bank or a leasing company – which provides funding to an owner to finance the construction of a ship or to purchase a second-hand ship from another owner. Often, the funds loaned by the financial institution are also used by the owner to maintain and operate the ship going forward, and perhaps for use by the owner or its affiliate for other non-shipping purposes. The funds advanced by a bank or other lender are then typically secured by a mortgage and other security over the ship and its related earnings from its employment.

Recent years have seen a significant surge in the use of leasing structures rather than (or in addition to) traditional bank-provided loans. This is predominantly evident in Asia, and particularly in China, through the growth of leasing houses which are owned by financial institutions or other large corporate groups. The leasing house will set up a special purpose company in a recognised onshore or offshore jurisdiction – such as Hong Kong, the Marshall Islands, Panama, Liberia or Ireland – and then lease the ship to the 'real' owner. In connection with that lease financing arrangement, the leasing house will typically obtain refinancing of its own acquisition costs incurred in purchasing the ship from a bank in order to reduce its direct exposure.

Ship financing differs from other types of lending and secured financings in the fact that shipping transactions are almost always international in nature. A Greek or Hong Kong ship owner may obtain funding from a Chinese leasing company or a Japanese bank to purchase a ship from a German seller, for example; or to build a ship in China, South Korea or Japan with funding provided by a French lender. Despite the multi-jurisdictional and cross-geographical nature of shipping transactions, the one near-constant is the use of US dollars as the currency for the shipping industry. Typically charter hire is paid in US dollars and loans are made in US dollars, although there may be some circumstances where euros or other currencies are utilised.

1.2 Risks and rewards

The shipping industry is competitive and capital intensive. It is also exposed to many factors outside of its control, including oil price shocks, global and regional politics, currency fluctuations and the changing size of the world's shipping fleet. In recent years, there has additionally been a significant increase in regulatory pressures involving environmental regulations as well as restrictions on financial institutions that impact their ability to finance the shipping industry compared to previous years. As a result, there has been a partial, but significant, withdrawal by European and North American lenders from the shipping finance market. At the same time, Asia-based lenders and leasing companies have rapidly increased their market share to fill the gap.

Volatility in the shipping industry is often the norm rather than the exception, with swings from good times to bad times a well-known part of the history of the industry. For those lending money or otherwise advancing funds to the shipping industry, it is critical to ensure that those loans, credit facilities or other financial arrangements are properly secured.

1.3 Overview

This chapter considers the key types of security that one would expect in a shipping finance transaction, for both traditional bank financings and leasing finance structures. While the documents themselves may vary depending on the relevant jurisdictions involved and other factors, the security package for an English law governed financing will typically be based on at least some of the documentation described in this chapter.

2. Ship registries and their role in secured transactions

Unlike land or real estate, in which title is typically registered at the location in which the property is located, an internationally trading ship is usually on the move and is either on the high seas beyond the territorial jurisdiction of any country or only briefly in the waters of a country when it arrives to conduct loading/unloading or other operations in port. Ships are instead registered in a jurisdiction chosen by the ship owner, which is known as the 'flag state' of that ship. There are almost as many flag states as there are countries in the world, with varying regulatory regimes and standards. The quality of these flag states and of their oversight of the ships registered with them can differ substantially.

From a secured financing perspective, the flag state is also relevant, as the ship mortgage will be governed by the law of that flag state and typically must be registered with the flag state or some regulatory authority thereof. This can lead to complications and misunderstandings, as there is no uniform standard of a ship mortgage that may be registered in every flag state. Instead, there are many different versions and styles – not to mention the use of different languages and formalities for registering the mortgages.

Some lenders have little concern about the flag state chosen, provided that local lawyers have assured them that their security is adequate. Others place great emphasis on the flag states of their customers and will require the flag state to be one of their 'approved' flag states before agreeing to proceed with the financing. However, at the very least, lenders should be confident that the flag state of a ship financed by those lenders is reliable and offers well-tested security. The various forms of mortgage and related issues and security documents are described in more detail in the following sections.

3.   Security for ship financing transactions

3.1   Documentation overview

Once the terms of the ship finance facility are agreed between the borrower and the lender, the parties will negotiate and agree on the terms of the facility agreement and the security documents for the ship finance facility. The facility agreement will typically be based on Loan Market Association/Asia Pacific Loan Market Association templates, but with modifications made to reflect the various vessel and insurance-related certificates and other documentation that are common in the shipping industry.

In addition to the facility agreement, a typical ship finance package includes the following security documents:

- ship mortgage;
- assignment of charterparties or other employment contracts, earnings and requisition compensation;
- assignment of insurances;
- account charge/pledge;
- share charge/pledge; and
- in the case of ships under construction, assignment of the shipbuilding contract and the refund guarantee(s).

There may also be other credit support and subordination undertakings.

As described earlier, another common form of ship financing is a financial leasing structure, rather than a traditional bank or other lender financed structure. Although the documentation regarding the financing arrangements and repayments under a traditional loan structure versus a financial leasing structure is different (eg, instead of a facility agreement, the key financing terms in a financial leasing structure will usually be contained within a bareboat charter along with other traditional bareboat charter provisions, and there will not be any ship mortgage), the security provided under a financial leasing structure will be quite similar to that of a traditional lender financing.

3.2   Security documents

(a)   *Ship mortgage*

A ship mortgage is inevitably the primary form of security in a ship financing transaction and creates a fixed security over the ship, even if there is a change of ownership of the ship.

The form and content of a ship mortgage vary according to the flag state in which the ship is registered. Often, the mortgage will be in a statutory form in those common law jurisdictions in which the law is derived from English statutory maritime law (including Malta, the Bahamas, Hong Kong and Singapore), and will provide security on an 'account current' basis (which allows security over additional amounts advanced by a lender and is most common), or on the basis of a fixed amount plus accrued interest thereon. A separate deed of covenants made between the owner (as mortgagor) and the lender (as mortgagee) is customary to supplement a statutory ship mortgage, to oblige the owner to comply with the vessel-related undertakings concerning registration, maintenance, operation, insurances and other usual ship-related covenants.

The common alternative form of mortgage is the long form of mortgage (usually described as a 'preferred ship mortgage'), which includes the security granting provisions and the vessel-related undertakings in one document, removing the need for a separate deed of covenants. This form of preferred ship mortgage is utilised in jurisdictions such as the Marshall Islands, Liberia, Panama and the United States. There is no prescribed form for a preferred ship mortgage, although the flag state will generally require the mortgage to contain certain provisions, including:

* a description of the ship;
* references to relevant local legislation;
* the inclusion of a maximum amount secured; and
* perhaps, a maturity date.

Other jurisdictions require alternative forms which are often essentially a hybrid between the statutory form and the long form.

The formalities for registering and perfecting a ship mortgage vary for each jurisdiction and must be followed. Although a registered ship mortgage confers a secured creditor status on the lender (as mortgagee), the priority of a mortgagee varies between jurisdictions and may rank behind certain classes of liens (which can include maritime liens, statutory liens and possessory liens). Under English law, for example, a mortgagee will receive its share of the sale proceeds before suppliers of bunkers and provisions, repairers and cargo owners (which may have claims for damaged or lost cargo); but will rank after claims for wages of crew, port dues, salvage and collision damage. Further information on the priority of claims is found in section 4 below.

(b)   *Assignment of charterparties or other employment contracts, earnings, insurances and requisition compensation*

Assignment of charterparties or other employment contracts and earnings: The lender or (in the case of a financial lease, the owner) will generally require an assignment of the charters and earnings of the ship. The principal source of earnings for a vessel will be the sums payable by charterers to either the owner or perhaps a bareboat charterer as disponent owner. It is these earnings that the financier will look to as the source of repayment of its loan and any interest or other expenses. The following relates to an assignment in a traditional bank financing structure, but the principles are the same for a financial lease structure where the owner is the financier of the bareboat charterer.

Where a ship is employed or deployed under medium to long-term employment contracts (eg, charters, consecutive voyage charters, contracts of affreightment, drilling contracts), the lender will additionally require an assignment of such employment contracts to have a secured interest in:

- the income of the ship (which will be the key source of cash flow for debt servicing); and
- the rights and interests of the borrower/owner/charterer in the employment contracts.

The lender will typically require that the owner ensure that its charterer pay the charter hire relating to the ship to a bank account of the owner established with the lender or another financial institution acceptable to the lender. The earnings will usually be applied for debt service and released to or to the order of the owner after satisfaction of certain pre-agreed conditions set out in the facility agreement or the security document (eg, no event of default having occurred and continuing). Retention, cash build and dividend lock-up mechanisms may also be incorporated for debt servicing and operational purposes.

Before taking an assignment of any employment contract or any other vessel-related securities, the lender should review and confirm whether there is any:

- guarantee granted by any person to guarantee the obligations of the charterer under the charter or other employment contract (eg, charter guarantee);
- security interest granted by the charterer or any other person to secure the obligations of the charterer under the charter or other employment contract, such as an assignment of insurances and sub-charter by the bareboat charterer;
- prohibition on any ship mortgage, assignment of the employment contract, earnings, requisition compensation and insurances relating to the ship by the owner; or
- quiet enjoyment undertaking required by the charterer from any mortgagee of the ship or assignee of the charter or other employment contract.

If any guarantee or security interests are granted in favour of the owner, the lender should determine whether it requires an assignment of that guarantee or assignment of those security interests in its favour.

If there is any prohibition on assignment, the lender should ensure that all requisite consents and other conditions can be and will be satisfied, to ensure that its assignment will be valid and not challenged by the charterer or any other relevant person.

If there is no prohibition on assignment, the lender's interest (as assignee of the employment contract under English law) will be perfected by service of the notice of assignment on the charterer or any other relevant person.

Where the charters or other employment contracts oblige the owner to procure that the mortgagee of the ship will enter into a quiet enjoyment undertaking in favour of the charterer, the lender should review the restrictions to be imposed on the mortgagee and assess whether these are acceptable. A quiet enjoyment undertaking usually restricts the rights of the mortgagee to take enforcement actions against the ship and the owner, which may interfere with the charterer's right of peaceful and quiet enjoyment of the ship.

When agreeing to any quiet enjoyment undertaking, the lender should ensure that it is subject to no event of default (or equivalent) having occurred under the employment contract. The lender should also consider requiring step-in rights as assignee of the employment contract to substitute itself (or its nominee) in place of a defaulting owner in the event of the occurrence of certain defaults or repudiatory breaches (which can include insolvency of the owner) by the owner under the charter or other employment contract, so as to preserve the employment contract and the cash flow/income stream for debt servicing.

Assignment of insurances and requisition compensation: The lender will also typically require an assignment of all insurances and requisition compensation relating to the ship. If a mortgaged ship becomes an actual or constructive total loss, the primary security that generates cash flow for debt service will no longer be available. The owner loses its ability to receive income generated from the asset and the lender will have to look towards the total loss insurance proceeds to cover the loan exposure.

The lender generally requires the insurance cover to be the greater of the market value of the ship and the loan outstanding (often with an additional buffer), to ensure that the loan exposure will be covered at all times by the insurances.

The main types of marine insurances taken out by an owner of ship are:

- hull and machinery insurances (including increased value cover);
- war risks insurances; and
- protection and indemnity insurances.

Where a ship is designated for deployment for certain projects, the lender may also require loss of hire/earnings insurances to cover any loss of income (which will be necessary for debt service) as a result of any off-hire events under the employment contracts.

In addition, the lender may require the borrower to cover the costs of mortgagee's interest insurance and mortgagee's additional perils (pollution) insurance, to protect the lender against non-payment of insurance proceeds under the insurance policies taken out by the borrower/owner as a result of any act or omission to act by the borrower/owner (eg, non-payment of insurance premiums, misrepresentation or non-disclosure of material events or breach of any express or implied warranty or condition by the owner). Such insurances will be taken out by the lender (as mortgagee) in its name directly, with the insurance premiums to be paid or reimbursed by the owner.

In the case of an assignment of insurances under English law, notices of assignment of insurances will be served on the relevant insurers or insurance brokers as well as the protection and indemnity clubs. Letters of undertaking from the foregoing and (in the case of protection and indemnity insurance) updated certificates of entry should be obtained to confirm that the lender or mortgagee will be notified if the insurance premium is not paid or if the insurance policy is not renewed, and also to reflect the mortgagee's interest in the insurances.

Requisition compensation is the compensation paid by the flag state in the event that it requisitions title to a ship registered with that flag state for its own purposes (eg, in a time of war). This differs from requisition of the ship for hire, which occurs when the flag state compulsorily takes on hire a ship registered with it and pays hire to the owner, as the proceeds from a requisition for hire will be assigned under the assignment of earnings. Although requisition of title is an unusual occurrence, it does occur and a lender should insist that an assignment over requisition compensation be obtained.

(c)   Account charge/pledge

In addition to the above assignments, the lender will usually obtain a charge/pledge over the bank account into which earnings and other income associated with the ship are paid.

Any such account charge/pledge will typically be governed by the law of the jurisdiction in which the account is situated and relevant local laws will apply for the perfection of the charge/pledge over account. The amount of control to be exercised by the lender over the account is a matter of negotiation between the parties.

(d)   Shares charge/pledge

A lender may also require a charge/pledge over the shares in the borrower/owner. This is appropriate for ship finance transactions whereby the ship is owned by a single purpose company established for the purpose of owning the ship.

Further information on the enforcement of a charge or pledge over shares and the potential risks of such enforcement is set out in section 5.4.

(e)   Assignment of shipbuilding contract and refund guarantee

Apart from providing financing for existing vessels, the lender may also provide funding for owners to acquire vessels that are under construction, often referred to as a 'pre-delivery ship finance transaction'.

For pre-delivery ship finance transactions, assignments of the owner's rights under the shipbuilding contract and any refund guarantees will typically be additionally required during the construction phase of the ship. The shipbuilding contract will typically require instalment payments to be made at certain milestones during the pre-delivery period. There will also typically be one or more refund guarantees issued by the shipbuilder's bank in favour of the owner to secure the obligations of the shipbuilder to refund payments advanced by or on behalf of the owner should the shipbuilder default under the shipbuilding contract.

If the borrower defaults under a shipbuilding contract under which pre-delivery instalments have already been paid, an assignment of shipbuilding contract enables the lender to remedy the default of the owner and continue with the construction of the ship.

If a shipbuilder defaults under the shipbuilding contract, an assignment of the refund guarantee(s) enables the lender to recover the moneys already paid to the builder and apply them towards the loan exposure.

It is important that the lender is aware that any recourse to the moneys covered by the refund guarantee is limited to circumstances of a shipbuilder's default. If the owner is the party in default under the facility agreement only, the lender will have to consider any other security or any form of credit support that it may require to mitigate such credit risk during the construction phase of the ship. As such, pre-delivery ship finance transactions typically also include other forms of credit support by or recourse to the sponsors or parent of the borrower.

3.2 Credit support and subordination undertakings

(a) Credit support

Common types of credit support for a ship finance transaction include one or more of the following:

- corporate guarantee;
- sponsor's undertaking; and
- others (eg, remarketing agreement, standby charter, put option deed, keep well deed).

The forms of credit support that may be provided are generally heavily negotiated and influenced by:

- the bargaining power of the parties;
- the leverage of the transaction;
- the type of financing (ie, pre and/or post-delivery financing); and
- the transaction structure (ie, pure asset based and ring fenced or hybrid structures).

(b) Subordination undertakings

A lender will usually require subordination undertakings from any ship managers, which may have rights and interests in and to the insurances of the ship, and also right of claims against the borrower/owner and/or the ship. It may be difficult to obtain subordination undertakings or assignments of insurances from third-party managers, but managers which are affiliates of the owner should be required to provide these undertakings or assignments whenever possible.

If the financing is provided to a single purpose company, a lender may also require the shareholder or any other financier (affiliated with the owner or otherwise) to subordinate its rights to the rights of the lender.

3.3 Registration requirements for securities

When taking security in a ship finance transaction, it is critical to check and ensure that the security perfection requirements can be and are duly complied with, so as to perfect and maintain the security interests of the lender.

Apart from ship mortgage registrations, in certain jurisdictions (eg, England, Hong Kong and Singapore), security interests created by a company incorporated or registered in such jurisdictions must be registered with local companies or other government registries, failure of which may render such security interest void against a liquidator or third-party creditors of the owner as debtor.

4.   Priority of claims

A ship may be the subject of a host of different types of claims and debts. Imagine a situation where one ship negligently collides with another and must be salvaged. The ship owner goes bankrupt and fails to pay the wages of its crew, not to mention its suppliers. Consequently, the mortgagee bank asserts its own claim against the ship. In such case, the chances are that the total amount of all those claims will exceed the value of the ship.

After a ship has been the subject of a judicial sale, the court does not distribute the sale proceeds equally between all claimants. Instead, the court will follow a recognised order of priority of claims, while retaining discretion to do what is just in any particular case. As a result, some claims are met in full before other claimants receive anything.

English law recognises four types of claim which give rise to maritime liens:
- salvage;
- collision damage;
- crew wages; and
- master's disbursements.

Maritime liens have a number of special features:
- They attach to the ship, in the sense that they survive any private sale of the vessel;
- They enable the claimant lien holder to arrest the ship in order to obtain payment; and
- Most significantly from the perspective of a ship financier, they have priority over a ship mortgage.

What constitutes a 'maritime lien' will vary from jurisdiction to jurisdiction. For example, jurisdictions such as the United States and South Africa may in certain circumstances grant maritime lien status to suppliers of goods and services.

Another class of lien which ranks ahead of a mortgage is a shipyard's possessory lien in respect of work carried out to the vessel. However, if the shipyard relinquishes possession and allows the vessel to depart, the shipyard will lose its lien. In that event, the shipyard's claim will be relegated to the status of a 'statutory' lien.

In addition to maritime liens, the Senior Courts Act 1981 lists several types of claims which are known as 'statutory' liens, given that they are derived from statute. These liens rank below a mortgage and include claims for cargo damage, breach of charter, unpaid bunkers and other supplies, and so on.

The priority of claims is a vital factor for a ship financier to take into account when it is considering enforcement of its rights.

5.   Enforcement

A mortgagee may well not have the luxury of choice as to which jurisdiction to select for enforcement. The ship may be arrested by other claimants such as bunker suppliers, agents, tugs, pilots or stevedores that have been unpaid. There may be cargo claims against the vessel leading to its arrest. Although most such cargo claims will be covered by the protection and indemnity club, which can be called upon to provide security for the claim so as to have the ship released, they do not cover all claims (eg, claims for misdelivery of cargo); and it may well be that the owner has not paid its insurance premiums or calls.

If any other claimants have arrested the ship in a particular jurisdiction, the mortgagee should think carefully whether that is also a convenient jurisdiction from its point of view, or whether those claims will enjoy priority over the mortgagee's claim – in which case it may well be advised to settle those competing claims to enable the ship to be taken to a better jurisdiction. The usual form of mortgage conditions and detailed deeds of covenants give power for the mortgagee to advance such funds on behalf of the owner and include them in the amount outstanding under the mortgage. If the vessel calls frequently at jurisdictions where the mortgagee can easily enforce its mortgage through arrest of the vessel, then that may well provide a useful option for the mortgagee. However, if the vessel is continually trading between jurisdictions with undeveloped legal systems or where the mortgagee's claim does not enjoy priority status, the mortgagee may well be advised to employ alternative methods.

5.1   General considerations

In general terms, a mortgagee is entitled to take steps which affect the contractual obligations of the vessel only when either the owner is itself unable to perform the charterparty (eg, it needs a further advance from the mortgagee to meet the running expenses) or the contract imperils the security of the mortgagee. This second category does not include simply the charterparty being a bad commercial bargain which does not cover the cost of the vessel or the vessel ending up in a jurisdiction which is unfavourable for the enforcement of the mortgagee.

Cargo owners also usually require their cargo to be on-carried to destination if at all possible. Although in English-type jurisdictions, if the vessel is arrested, the cargo interests must bear the costs of transshipment and on-carriage of the cargo (which form a non-priority claim against the owner, which is likely to be insolvent anyway), other jurisdictions have different rules of procedure and priorities.

Also, in the case of high-bulk but low-value cargo, the cargo owner may prefer simply to abandon it, leaving the mortgagee faced with the cost of financing discharge of the cargo and its storage pending sale to try to recover the cost of doing so – always assuming that this is physically possible.

In general terms, it is much more convenient if the ship is empty of cargo when the mortgagee comes to enforce its security.

5.2   Arrest of the vessel and sale through the courts

This option will depend on the vessel being in an appropriate jurisdiction which has a favourable procedure and grants the mortgagee priority over the majority of the competing claims.

As noted previously, a registered mortgagee generally enjoys a substantial degree of priority, ranking behind only the cost of enforcement, crew wages, salvage and damage claims. Other potential claimants – such as cargo owners, suppliers of equipment or services to the vessel and repairers – rank below a mortgage. Also, as indicated above, the obligation for the discharge and on-shipment of any cargo on board the vessel falls in the first instance on the owners of cargo.

There are two important advantages of a court sale:

- The vessel is sold free and clear of all encumbrances, whether registered or not, such that it should, by convention, be protected in the hands of new owners from any claims against the old owners, even if those claims have the status in any jurisdiction of a maritime lien or were protected by the issuance of proceedings before the sale took place; and

- A court sale, properly advertised and conducted, will usually protect the mortgagee against any claim for sale at an under-value or in breach of its duty of good faith to the mortgagor to obtain the best price for the vessel.

There is generally no prohibition on a mortgagee purchasing the ship itself (usually by means of a subsidiary company) and then selling at arm's length on private terms. Generally, vessels sold through court sale do not achieve the best possible price; but a mortgagee can substantially protect its interests by this method. The distribution of the proceeds of sale paid into court will be the subject of a determination of priorities in accordance with the rules in that jurisdiction.

5.3   Entering into possession

Most mortgages or deeds of covenants will give this right to the mortgagee. However, by doing so, the mortgagee becomes liable to perform the contracts of the owner (eg, the charterparty) and also becomes personally liable for all future debts of the vessel. Generally, therefore, this is likely only to be a fairly short-term remedy to enable the mortgagee to give instructions to the master to take the vessel to an appropriate jurisdiction for arrest and sale.

There can also be practical difficulties in taking physical possession if, for example, the ship is not in port at the time or the master on instructions from the borrower refuses to cooperate. However, it is frequently the case that the master and crew are owed substantial arrears of wages by the time the mortgagee comes to enforce its mortgage, and a promise of prompt payment of those arrears of wages can often secure cooperation from the master and crew.

5.4 Exercise of pledge

This allows the mortgagee to take over the control of the ship-owning company, appoint its own shareholders and directors and control the vessel. This can often be useful for the purpose of retaining a favourable charterparty, although a charterer in those circumstances is likely to seek every possible avenue for termination. Future liabilities of the ship remain the responsibility of the shipowning company (rather than the mortgagee personally).

However, there can be certain statutory obligations and liabilities which could make a mortgagee personally liable for claims arising out of the operation of the ship, whether it is in possession or controlling the ship-owning company through its nominees. The most serious potential liability is within the United States under the Oil Pollution Act of 1990 or similar state legislation, where a mortgagee may well be determined to be a 'responsible person', particularly under the deep pocket concept.

6. Conclusion

Taking security in connection with a ship financing transaction – whether under a traditional bank financing structure, a financial leasing structure or otherwise – requires careful attention and adherence to the formalities not only of English law typically, but often also of the jurisdiction in which the ship itself is registered and wherever the owner's earnings or other bank accounts are situated. Failure to comply with, for example, the registration requirements for a ship mortgage or the perfection of security interests in the ship's insurances may result in dire consequences for any financier. Competent legal advice in relation to each of the relevant jurisdictions and a strong understanding of, or advice in relation to, marine insurance and regulatory matters are critical whenever a lender or other financier is contemplating entering into or operating within the ship financing industry.

Real estate finance

Charles Malpass
Mayer Brown

1. Introduction

1.1 The market in Europe

'Real estate finance' is a broad term encompassing several different financing structures applied to fund a wide range of real estate investments. These include:

- investment properties (commercial or residential);
- operating businesses (including care homes, student accommodation and hotels);
- retail;
- industrial;
- warehouses and logistics (or sheds);
- development properties; and
- other types of real estate assets.

English law governed loan agreements and finance techniques are used for transactions throughout Europe – particularly for larger financing transactions or for facilities which may ultimately be syndicated. The use of English law governed facility agreements has largely been unaffected by Brexit, although this remains an area of self-inflicted uncertainty.[1]

---

1   While the United Kingdom formed part of the European Union, it benefited from, and was subject to, the Recast Brussels Convention, which regulated matters such as service of process and automatic recognition of judgements between EU member states. The Lugano Convention also applied to the United Kingdom by virtue of its membership of the European Union. The Lugano Convention regulated equivalent issues between the EU and Norway, Switzerland and Iceland. The United Kingdom has applied to become part of the Lugano Convention post Brexit (in other words, so that it is treated the same as Norway, Switzerland and Iceland), but the European Union has not yet accepted this, and it is unclear whether it will do so. Since there is currently no bespoke agreement between the United Kingdom and the European Union on these matters, and the Lugano Convention currently does not apply, the United Kingdom enacted the Hague Convention on 1 January 2021. This is not considered to be as comprehensive as the Recast Brussels Convention or the Lugano Convention, as there are certain areas of uncertainty around its applicability, and it only applies where the English courts have exclusive jurisdiction (as opposed to non-exclusive jurisdiction), but it does at least provide a framework for recognition of judgements between the signatories. If the Hague Convention does not apply (which it may not to agreements entered into before 1 January 2021), then the relevant EU country will reference its own rules on recognition of judgements, which may make enforcement more complicated. None of this impacts arbitration: arbitration clauses will continue to be recognised and enforced under the New York Convention.

Apart from the ease of syndication, the benefits of English law governed loan agreements are as follows:

- English law and the choice of English jurisdiction are relatively creditor friendly;
- There is a large and well-developed body of common law which can be relied on in order to help determine a dispute;
- Lenders can standardise English law governed loan agreements, which can then be used in various jurisdictions across Europe, subject only to such amendments as are required by local law; and
- Enforcement of English law judgments in courts across Europe was previously relatively straightforward, as a result of the United Kingdom being a member of the European Union. This meant that local courts within Europe were previously bound to give effect to English law judgments. While the position post-Brexit is less clear, the market view is that the benefits of English choice of law and jurisdiction outweigh the downsides, and European loan agreements continue to be subject to English choice of law and exclusive jurisdiction clauses (exclusive jurisdiction is required in order for the parties to be able to rely on the Hague Convention).

2. Principal types of real estate finance transactions

2.1 Investment finance

'Investment finance' refers to the financing of a commercial tenanted building. There is a regular and predictable source of income which can be used to pay interest and other costs incurred in connection with a financing. The lenders will look primarily to the underlying property for the source of its payments under the loan, rather than to the covenant strength of the borrower.[2] In fact, advance rates and financing terms are generally better if the income from the property can be isolated in a property-owning special purpose entity (SPE). An SPE will represent and covenant that it:

- has not owned any other business since its incorporation other than ownership of the property;
- has no employees; and
- has not incurred any other indebtedness.

Interest is typically paid current on a monthly or quarterly basis. Since quarterly rent payments are a common feature of the UK real estate market,[3]

---

2   The lender will rely primarily on the covenant strength of the underlying tenant(s) and will most commonly expect an 'FRI lease' to be in place – in other words, a full repairing and insuring lease, where the tenant bears all the costs of the building, including insurance and repair. This means that the cash the landlord receives should be free cash which is available for payment of financing costs.

payments of interest and financing costs are made a number of business days after the relevant rental quarter day in relation to English commercial real estate.

Key financial covenants in investment finance loans refer to the interest cover ratio (ICR) and/or a loan to value (LTV) test. The ICR test is usually tested on a 12-month look-forward basis, and the LTV is tested annually or more frequently if the loan is in default or potentially in default. The ICR tests total net income from the property (less void costs and other irrecoverable costs, and assuming that all tenant break clauses are exercised on the first available date) against the outstanding balance of the loan. LTV tests the ratio of the outstanding balance of the loan to the value of the property.

A breach of either the ICR or the LTV covenant can be cured by a pre-payment under the loan. In addition, if the borrower knows or anticipates an upcoming breach, it can pre-pay before the covenant test occurs. Care should be taken when acting for either the lenders or the borrower to determine whether this pre-payment can be made without incurring a pre-payment fee, and to ensure that the restrictions on pre-payment do not prevent a part pre-payment from being made in order to cure a breach or a potential breach of financial covenant.

Loan agreements typically impose restrictions on the number of times that a financial covenant can be cured (eg, the borrower can only cure a breach of financial covenant on four occasions during the life of the loan, and on no more than two consecutive occasions). These restrictions are included to prevent a deterioration of the credit quality of the property on a long-term basis without the lenders being able to call an event of default under the facility, and to increase the lenders' control over whether to continue to be exposed to a deteriorating asset. Pre-payments are possible to cure a potential event of default (see above); and such pre-payments will not reduce the limited number of cures available (since the restrictions on cures refer to an actual, rather than a potential, breach).

A further benefit of the SPE nature of the property-owning entity is that its shares can be sold on enforcement, which can result in a substantial stamp duty saving for the purchaser as against a sale of the asset. This translates into a higher sale price and therefore a higher valuation. It is therefore key that the SPE which owns the asset does not incur any other liability (including tax liabilities),[4] as the purchaser will not want to buy an entity which has unpaid or potential liabilities at a higher price than it would buy the asset itself.

---

3   Rent is usually paid quarterly on the usual quarter days, which are 25 March, 24 June, 29 September and 25 December in each year, but this can vary.

4   Care should be taken in relation to tax liabilities. For example, entities which are incorporated in other jurisdictions or which are managed by directors in other jurisdictions in practice (regardless of where the entity is incorporated) may incur tax liabilities in those other jurisdictions. It is important that tax liabilities are diligenced, as they cannot be subordinated or secured in the same way that intra-group liabilities can.

It is important that any third-party liabilities which arise from property ownership and are owed by the SPE are also fully subordinated and/or charged to the lenders or their agent. This means that any equity or other debt which is injected initially or in order to cure any potential or actual defaults (or otherwise) must be fully subordinated to the secured debt.

The stamp duty saving associated with a transfer of shares means that real estate transactions are frequently structured as sales of shares rather than assets. Restrictions on financial assistance[5] in some jurisdictions can affect the structure of the sale and/or the initial advance rate. A sale of shares will mean that the borrower will acquire the target property-owning vehicle, which will then accede to the facility as a borrower/guarantor. The structure of the acquisition will therefore have a material effect on the terms and structure of the financing.

2.2 Development finance

The principal differences between investment and development finance are as follows:

- The disbursement of the advance is made in stages. The first part of the moneys which are to be advanced under the facility agreement pays for the costs incurred in connection with the acquisition, with subsequent staged drawdowns used to pay for ongoing development costs. Those ongoing drawdowns are dependent on there being no event of default under the facility agreement. Central to this is the appointment of a project monitor on behalf of the lenders or their agent, whose job it is to monitor the progress of the development and costs against budget. If a cost overrun (an increase in costs over budgeted costs) is incurred, then additional moneys must be made available by the sponsor/shareholder to pay for this, or it must be covered by available amounts in the budget representing contingency or cost savings, in order to be able to continue to fund the development.
- The lenders will require a guarantee, letter of credit, equity commitment letter or a deposit of moneys in order to fund the payment of interest and other budgeted financing costs in the absence of an income stream from the underlying property.

---

5   Rules on financial assistance are restrictions or a prohibition on the ability of a target entity to grant security in order to finance the purchase price for the acquisition of its shares. This means that a property-owning entity cannot be acquired by a purchaser, and immediately grant security to the lender which has financed the acquisition. Financial assistance was largely abolished for all practical purposes in England, meaning that financial assistance is no longer relevant to real estate acquisitions where the target entity is an English company, but it is an issue in a number of other jurisdictions. There are frequently ways in which to structure the transaction in order to mitigate the effects of the rule against financial assistance, but this may involve a delayed drawdown or other structural features which will have a material impact on the financing transaction. Enquiries should be made about whether financial assistance applies to the target entity early in the transaction, and prior to finalisation of the term sheet for the financing, in order to understand how the financing will need to be structured.

- The lenders will expect consent rights in relation to the appointment of material development parties (eg, the main building contractor).
- The facility agreement will contain a number of development covenants which should include:
  - a long stop date for practical completion;
  - reporting requirements in relation to the development;
  - a requirement to obtain and comply with relevant permissions; and
  - a minimum specification for the development (eg, a minimum floor area for the various components of the development).
- Additional due diligence in relation to development contracts and security over the relevant third-party contracts entered into in respect of the development will be required.
- The lenders will expect consents in relation to proposed sales, lettings or other disposals, including a requirement that part of the loan be repaid on a disposal (to the extent that the disposal is not the grant of a lease at full market rent).

Development financing is therefore likely to involve a greater degree of ongoing involvement and management time for the lender as against an investment facility.

2.3 Operating businesses versus tenanted properties

A significant number of operating businesses (eg, hotels and care homes) may include Opco/Propco structures. Both the Opco and the Propco are subsidiaries of a common parent, but the Opco retains the operational business and the Propco retains the ownership of the property.

The Opco may employ staff, incur liabilities and enter into management contracts, franchise agreements or leases with third parties in order to outsource the day-to-day management of the business.

The separation of the operating and property sides of the business can be considered to be form over substance to some extent, since the borrower will ultimately still rely on income from the operating business in order to pay finance costs. Well-advised lenders should therefore be concerned with the operating business irrespective of the structure.

This will involve, for example:
- conducting due diligence in respect of the management of the operating business, including (for hotels) approving the form of hotel management agreement; and
- including financial covenants in the facility agreement which reference the performance of the operating business in place of a straightforward interest cover test.

The lenders will usually require security over the benefit of agreements with third parties, and may be involved in a negotiation over the extent to which their requirements affect or restrict the operating business.

Hotel managers or lessees who are appointed for a long term will expect the lenders or their agents to enter into non-disturbance agreements with the hotel operator where it agrees that the hotel management agreement will continue to the extent that it takes enforcement action, and requiring the security agent to notify the hotel manager if it does so.

Any such third-party agreements may include step-in rights giving the lenders or their agent the ability to assume control over the way in which the contract is discharged. Hotel management agreements (or equivalent) may grant the hotel manager the right to acquire the hotel if it is sold.

The non-disturbance agreement will need to be negotiated in order to ensure that the lender and the hotel manager exercise appropriate levels of control.

The lender will want to understand the effect of the insolvency of the Propco and/or the Opco on the underlying franchise agreement, management agreement or lease, since the insolvency of the Opco may allow third parties which have contracted with the Opco to terminate their agreement. This may have an adverse impact on the Opco, and therefore the Propco.

Financial covenants may be subject to a ramp-up period. For example, operating income may only be tested once a hotel is developed, or care home income may only be tested once the care home has reached a certain occupancy level (which may be some time after it has been opened). Operating income is generally tested on a 12-month look-back period, rather than a 12-month look-forward, as it relies on being able to assess the earnings before interest, taxes, depreciation and amortisation of the business, rather than a fixed amount of rent over a future period. It can also test net operating income against the outstanding amount of the loan.

2.4 Term loan versus revolving facilities

'Term loans' are loans with a single drawdown at the commencement of the facility agreement or with a defined or projected drawdown profile (eg, for development loans) over a fixed term.

Revolving loans are used where there is an element of a facility which can be used for operational or other purposes on an ongoing basis, repaid or pre-paid, and then fully re-drawn. A revolving loan may require a clean-down period, or may require that a loan be fully repaid immediately before it can be re-drawn. A 'clean-down period' is a defined time during which the loan cannot be drawn or cannot be drawn above a specified amount, and is intended to ensure that the revolving part of the loan facility is not used to fund long-term debt.

Revolving facilities are typically used in real estate finance as an ancillary facility alongside a term facility in connection with an operating business which may have ongoing cash-flow requirements.

For example, a care home business may require:

- a revolving facility for its operating business;
- a development facility in respect of new care homes it acquires and develops; and
- an investment facility once the care homes have been built and have reached a certain occupancy level.

These facilities may be from different lenders or the same lender, and this will impact on their terms.

2.5   Loan on loans

Loan on loan transactions involving real estate refer to the financing of underlying loans which are made between an underlying lender and an underlying borrower in order to finance underlying real estate. While terms vary, these transactions generally have the following characteristics which are not present in direct real estate finance transactions between lenders and borrowers:

- Loan on loan transactions are generally considered to be securitisation transactions,[6] and are therefore subject to the EU Securitisation Regulations and/or their UK equivalent. This has a number of knock-on effects, including:
  - requirements in respect of ongoing reporting;
  - a requirement that exposure to ongoing risk be retained by an originator or sponsor by holding a vertical or horizontal strip of not less than 5% in the economics of the financing transaction; and
  - the preparation of a memorandum for the parties to the financing setting out how the requirements of the relevant regulations are complied with.
- The covenants will be focused on a portfolio. They may therefore reference eligibility criteria, with the loans that fail to meet those criteria no longer considered eligible assets. Financing covenants are then tested on the basis of the eligible assets in the portfolio, meaning that those financial covenants could be breached to the extent that a significant part of the portfolio becomes ineligible.
- For larger portfolios, security over the loan is taken by the lender or its agent, but that security cannot be perfected by registration of a sub-charge at the Land Registry until after an event of default.

---

6   It may be possible to structure the transaction so that this is not the case.

- The underlying debtor may not be served with notice of the sub-charge until after an event of default.
- The covenants around management of the underlying portfolio may be subject to wide materiality qualifiers for larger portfolios in order to allow the borrower under the loan on loan to service its loans in the ordinary course.
- Specified performance triggers may allow the lender to require the borrower under the loan on loan to replace the servicer rather than default the loan. Similarly, the insolvency of the servicer may trigger a servicer replacement obligation only (or an event of default if the servicer is not replaced by an acceptable servicer within a defined period).
- A lender may take a more relaxed approach to due diligence, since there is a portfolio which secures the underlying loan. It may therefore be more willing to accept a 'red flag' report, rather than a full due diligence report on each asset.

2.6 Understanding the impact of the financing type

The key to each type of facility (investment, development, loan on loan, revolving or term or a combination, and/or whether for an operating business or for investment) is an understanding of the transaction structure and the proposed route to enforcement. This will help to inform the level of due diligence which needs to be undertaken, in respect of which entities, and the identity of the obligor group.[7] The focus of the lenders should be on ensuring that sufficient due diligence on the proposed structure is carried out to allow them to make a commercial assessment of the risks to enforcement or to cash flow. This may involve sampling or red flag due diligence on larger portfolios, and/or negotiations with third parties. Any material risks which are identified should be provided for.

3. Structuring the real estate finance transaction

3.1 Senior loan or note issuance facility

'Senior loans' are loans which are secured over real estate assets by way of a first-ranking charge or mortgage. Senior lenders expect to have control over the

---

7   The obligor group references the parties which enter into the facility agreement as primary obligors, or which are referred to in the facility agreement as transaction obligors. It is important to determine the parties which should directly covenant with the lender (the primary obligors, such as the borrower and the target property owning entity), and the transaction obligors and other material companies (eg, the hotel operator, whose insolvency may trigger an event of default, but which will not contract directly with the lender). Similarly, it is important to understand how far up the chain of companies the obligor group should extend. It is therefore advisable to request a structure chart of the proposed obligor group early in the transaction so that this can be analysed and properly understood.

enforcement process, with security granted in favour of the lender or (more typically) a security trustee or security agent.

Senior loans can be structured as straight loans between a senior lender and a borrower or an obligor group, or as secured notes. In the case of secured notes, the borrower is termed the 'issuer' (since it issues notes, or debt instruments, to the lender), and the lender is termed the 'noteholder'.

If the loan has been syndicated, then decisions may be made by an instructing group of lenders to the security agent or security trustee,[8] or by all lenders. In the case of a note issuance facility, this concept is replaced by a meeting of noteholders, which must be quorate and which will be subject to minimum notification requirements for calling the meeting.

Aside from these and other similar structural differences,[9] the terms of a senior loan or a note issuance facility should largely amount to form over substance; but the change in form will nevertheless materially impact the form of the term sheet and the finance documents.

A note issuance facility can be required where there are regulatory or other restrictions in the relevant jurisdiction which mean that a senior loan cannot be entered into.

3.2 Mezzanine loans and debt tranching

Mezzanine loans generally share in the security over the real estate asset and are therefore beneficiaries of the security trust (if the security is in a common law jurisdiction); or their debt is taken into account in a parallel debt obligation (if security is taken in a civil law jurisdiction). Control over the enforcement of the security is retained by the senior lenders until the senior debt has been repaid in full,[10] but the mezzanine lenders share in the proceeds of enforcement of the security over the property. The mezzanine lenders generally lend at a higher LTV ratio than the senior lenders and therefore receive a higher margin to compensate for the increased risk.[11]

This can be achieved in one of two ways: by contractual subordination or by structural subordination of the mezzanine debt.

---

8   Typically the majority lenders make certain decisions, with more material decisions (eg, changing the margin payable on the loan) being made by all lenders in the syndicate. The threshold for majority lender decisions is usually two-thirds of the parties entitled to vote, although in certain instances this can be changed – for example, where a concept of super majority decisions is included which may require a higher threshold.

9   Other structural differences include the fact that a note must be for a minimum denomination, and notes are then transferred in those denominations, whereas there is no such restriction at law on the transfer of participations in loans. The lender and its counsel will need to discuss the amount of the minimum denomination which should apply to the transaction.

10   In certain instances, standstill arrangements may be negotiated which allow the mezzanine lender to take control of the enforcement process if the mezzanine facility is in default and a defined period of time has passed, but these arrangements are not frequently seen in the real estate finance market.

11   In a number of cases mezzanine lenders have advanced both a senior and a mezzanine loan initially, and have then sold a participation in the senior so that they only continue to hold the mezzanine loan. This allows them to control the origination process and build volume.

Contractual subordination is much less common than structural subordination, as it means that the mezzanine lender lends directly to the senior borrower and the perception is that this may adversely affect enforcement. The market has therefore almost invariably adopted structural subordination as the method by which mezzanine loans are made.

'Structural subordination' means that a mezzanine loan is made to an entity which sits above the senior obligor group and which becomes the mezzanine borrower. There will be restrictions under the terms of an intercreditor agreement on amendments to the terms of the senior loan and the mezzanine loan (eg, to prevent an increase in the amount of the senior facility which would adversely impact the mezzanine loan). Enforcement of the mezzanine-only security should be permitted under the terms of the intercreditor agreement (ie, a sale of the shares in the mezzanine borrower), although the mezzanine lender should consider the extent to which this would trigger an event of default under the senior facility as a result of a change of control in the borrower group.

Real estate facility agreements normally permit debt tranching. Debt tranching should be distinguished from mezzanine finance in that the tranched debt is held by part of the group of senior lenders and the holder of a tranche is therefore in the same position as any other senior lender. The blended rate on the debt tranching remains the same, although the margin paid to each holder of a tranche of debt may differ between tranches. It may be that different lenders are paid ahead of other lenders in a waterfall between the various senior lenders; but this is (typically) a contractual arrangement between the lenders, rather than between the lenders and the borrower.[12]

4. Post origination: the transfer of risk

There are a number of reasons why a lender may wish to reduce its exposure to a particular loan. These include the following:

- In order to increase the internal rate of return (IRR), a lender may finance the loan it has made by entering into a back-to-back financing transaction with a third party under which it pays a reduced margin to that finance provider when compared with the margin it receives under the facility agreement;
- Following an event of default, its cost of capital may increase (on a risk weighted basis), and/or it may decide that it does not want to take enforcement action;
- It may wish to manage its balance sheet (eg, in order to reduce the cost

---

12   Lawyers acting for the lenders should consider the extent to which the lender which is entitled to a higher margin runs a credit risk in relation to a senior lender within the group, since tranching relies on a contractual agreement only with that party in relation to the excess over the contracted margin it is entitled to receive from the borrower.

of capital charge it incurs) while retaining some or all of the fees (eg, the arrangement fee and the right to the pre-payment fee);[13]

- It may wish to manage its exposure to avoid breaching country or sector concentration limits;
- It may seek to sell non-performing loan pools in order to clean up its balance sheet; or
- It may do so as part of a *Pfandbrief*[14] or other public securitisation, where cheaper cost of funds can be passed on to borrowers through lower margin.

An understanding of these techniques is important in real estate finance transactions, since it can affect the way in which decisions are made in relation to an underlying loan, including whether to enforce following an event of default. While there are restrictions on assignment and sub-participations in many loan agreements, a borrower may not appreciate that the risk has been wholly or partially laid off to another entity, and that its lender of record may be constrained from making decisions by a third-party arrangement.[15]

These back-to-back financing techniques are also important to understand for lenders, as they may permit the lender to:

- increase its IRR above the margin in the facility agreement;
- lend at lower margins while maintaining its IRR; or
- build volume using a smaller balance sheet.[16]

4.1 Syndication and debt trading

'Primary syndication' refers to the initial syndication of a facility by the arranger/initial lender[17] by assigning or transferring[18] participations in the loan to an incoming lender.

In a syndicated facility, the facility agreement includes language pursuant to which the borrower agrees to provide assistance in relation to the syndication

---

13 Pre-payment fees were retained as a matter of course by conduit lenders which sold loans into commercial mortgage-backed securities (CMBS) structures on an ongoing basis. The originator could thus divest itself of risk while retaining potential fee income. This is the reason the arranger may not want to include the amount of the fees in the facility agreement itself, but rather in a separate fee letter between the arranger and the borrower.
14 *Pfandbrief* is a German covered bond programme where the originator retains the loan on its balance sheet.
15 The practical effects of this are perhaps less than might be expected in most situations.
16 An example of this is Northern Rock, where the volume of loans it originated, and market share, increased quickly over a short period of time. It then entered into regular securitisations of its mortgage book. CMBS and residential mortgage-backed securities loan conduit programmes were more common in Europe before the financial crisis in 2008.
17 Due diligence reports are routinely addressed to the facility agent and the initial lenders which acquire a participation in a loan on primary syndication within six to 12 months of the date of the facility agreement.
18 A transfer of rights and obligations can be achieved by including a form of transfer certificate in the loan agreement, with a provision that the borrower will be bound by the transfer to the extent that the agent signs the certificate. While it is usually necessary under English law for all the parties to a contract to enter into a novation of that contract, this is not required where these provisions are contained in the loan, under the rule in *Carlill v Carbolic Smoke Ball Company* [1892] EWCA Civ 1, [1893] 1 QB 256 (CA), where a binding offer capable of acceptance can be made to the whole world.

process, which can include making personnel available in order to meet with potential lenders.[19]

Some facilities are subject to market flex provisions, where the financial terms or (potentially) the structure and other terms can be amended in order to facilitate a successful syndication and help to protect the arranger from a change in market conditions. These provisions are typically heavily negotiated, since a borrower is naturally resistant to any changes being made to the agreed terms.

By contrast, 'debt trading' refers to the sale of debt often as part of a large volume of trades and other than by way of primary syndication. It is generally carried out on the terms of the Loan Market Association's (LMA) Standard Terms and Conditions for Par and Distressed Trade Transactions (Bank Debt/Claims), although deviations from those terms are often agreed between the parties.

The standard LMA terms for par and distressed trades are often also used as part of an assignment or transfer of debt on an assignment or transfer of a single loan, whether or not as part of a larger debt trade.

A transferee of debt will be bound by the term of the facility agreement, including the restrictions on assignment and transfer that have been negotiated; but the attitude of an incoming lender to a default may differ from the lender which has arranged the loan, and with which the borrower may have a relationship. Borrowers therefore focus on to whom the debt can be transferred (particularly prior to an event of default), and may treat assurances from the arranger in negotiations that it has no current intention to syndicate with a reasonable degree of caution.

4.2   Repurchase transactions and total return swaps

'Repurchase transactions' are a financing technique under which the repo seller is the borrower under the related documentation and the repo purchaser is the lender.

The lender of record under the original loan transfers its participation to the repo buyer by entering into a form of repurchase agreement.[20] The repo purchaser may be able to obtain favourable regulatory capital treatment, as the repo may be deemed to satisfy the relevant conditions to allow it to be treated as part of the repo buyer's trading book.[21] One of the requirements for this is that the repo facility provide for daily margining and there will therefore be limited scope to negotiate this from the seller's perspective. Daily margining can

---

19   These provisions may be negotiated by the parties, as the borrower may not want to commit excessive management time to a protracted syndication process.

20   For example, it is possible to adapt the Global Master Repurchase Agreement issued by the International Capital Markets Association so that it applies to real estate finance transactions.

21   The arguments around whether or not it should be considered part of the trading book are not straightforward.

mean that the seller is compelled to cash collateralise changes in the value of the loan calculated by the repo buyer, which can lead to frequent margin calls on short notice. If those margin calls are not met immediately, the repo facility will go into default. These provisions are therefore often negotiated with a requirement that the margin call must exceed a minimum specified threshold before it can be made.

The repo buyer can have control and/or consultation rights over the way in which decisions are made on the underlying loan, and this could potentially impact on the underlying borrower.[22]

A repo transaction constitutes a sale and purchase for English law purposes,[23] involving a transfer of the interest in the loan to the repo purchaser. An undated and signed transfer certificate is delivered to the repo purchaser, which it can date and complete to the extent that the seller under the repo is in default.

These arrangements are typically not disclosed to the underlying borrower, which may therefore be unaware of the consent or control rights which the repo purchaser has.

An alternative to a repurchase transaction is a total return swap, which is structured as a derivative transaction, but which is otherwise similar in many respects.

4.3   Public securitisation transactions

Public securitisation can take a number of forms, including a *Pfandbrief* programme or a true sale securitisation, where the sale is intended to isolate the loan from the risk of insolvency of the originator, so that investors only have reference to the credit quality of the loan itself.

Securitisations can also be used to finance portfolio acquisitions of debt, as they allow the originator to access the capital markets and achieve a cheaper cost of capital.

In the case of a rated securitisation, a rated servicer must typically be appointed to service the loan(s) which are being securitised. This may be a third-party professional servicer which is unrelated to the lender. So, while the facility agent and security agent may seek instructions from the lender of record in respect of proposed consents which are to be issued under the loan, the lender may be a securitisation issuer with professional directors who have delegated their decision-making powers to a nominated servicer. The servicer may be constrained by the terms of the servicing agreement and the other

---

22   In many cases the repo purchaser's approach is relatively accommodating, as it can ultimately rely on its margining rights.

23   The position is less straightforward under a New York law governed master repurchase agreement, since it may not constitute a sale for Chapter 11 purposes in all relevant states in the United States. Back-up security may therefore need to be taken in addition to the sale, in case the sale is not effective.

securitisation documents, which can place restrictions on the ability of the servicer to agree amendments to the underlying transaction documentation.[24]

Some originators have sought to continue to influence decision making by the appointment of an operating adviser or a noteholder committee, which can provide guidance to the servicer and the issuer.

A securitisation can therefore have an impact on the ability of a lender group to restructure a loan or agree to an extension of a maturity date, but the securitisation market nevertheless forms a key part of the real estate finance market.

5.   Conclusion

Lenders and borrowers in the real estate finance market should be aware of the various financing techniques that are used in the market, since they can:

- deliver improvements in IRR;
- result in a cheaper cost of funds for the borrower; and
- help drive the amount of liquidity in the market which is available.

Those financing techniques are a key part of the market and essential to its proper functioning; but a borrower should be aware of their potential impact and should treat assurances from lenders that they have no current intention to syndicate the loan, and that a particular position can therefore be accepted on the underlying financing, with a certain degree of scepticism.

---

24   An example is where the loan is to be extended beyond its maturity date. It may be that this cannot be done without the consent of the trustee in practice, and that the trustee will not make a decision to extend without a vote by the noteholders. Obtaining a vote from a quorum of noteholders can prove problematic in practice.

Fund finance

Aimee Sharman
Mayer Brown

1. Introduction to fund finance: basic concepts

The concept of 'fund finance' refers to a broad array of liquidity solutions, as this chapter demonstrates. The common feature, however, is that fund finance products provide liquidity to a private fund at the top of its fund structure (ie, at fund level), rather than to a special purpose vehicle (SPV) structure, below the level at which investors commit. Most typically, fund finance involves lending to a partnership structure (noting that the specific nature of partnership vehicles differs across jurisdictions); while this chapter primarily deals with partnership structures, it is becoming increasingly common for fund financing solutions to be made available to corporate entities (eg, partnerships or companies limited by shares and umbrella/portfolio companies).

For the purposes of this chapter, a 'fund' will be construed as an English limited partnership vehicle, which consists of:

- at least one or more 'limited partners' (ie, third-party investors in the fund, which are not involved in the management of the fund), each of whose liability is limited to the amount of its unfunded limited partner commitment to the fund; and
- a general partner, which is a sponsor vehicle and is responsible for the day-to-day affairs of the fund, and whose liability is unlimited.

The fund is constituted by a limited partnership agreement (LPA), which is the contract between, among others, the investors and the general partner; this is the governing document of the fund. The LPA – together with, most notably, the subscription agreement (also known as an 'application form', 'commitment letter', 'deed of adherence' or other similar terms) and management agreement (discussed below) – constitutes the 'fund documentation'. By subscribing to the fund, an investor commits to provide capital (up to an agreed maximum amount) to the fund over an agreed period as and when called for by the fund.

In this chapter, we discuss the process and considerations involved in taking security on fund finance transactions; and some of the key issues and features of some of the different liquidity solutions that fall within the broad category of fund finance.

2. Taking security in fund finance transactions: structural considerations

Security packages in fund finance transactions typically fall within one of two structural categories (or on occasion, a combination of both): on the one hand, where the lender's recourse is to the uncalled investor capital commitments of the fund (ie, 'upward-looking' security); and on the other, where the lender's recourse is to the fund's portfolio and/or underlying assets (ie, 'downward-looking' security). Before discussing the key characteristics of upward-looking and downward-looking security – and the differences between them – we introduce the most commonly seen forms of financing products pursuant to which such security is taken.

2.1 Subscription credit facilities

The most ubiquitous liquidity solution in the fund finance market is the subscription credit facility (also commonly referred to as a 'capital call facility', 'equity bridge facility' or simply a 'sub-line'). This form of liquidity solution is a facility provided by one or more lenders to a fund for the purpose of bridging the fund's investment and other activities in lieu of capital being drawn from the investors in the fund. As collateral for such a facility, the fund, its general partner and/or manager will grant in favour of the lenders (or a security trustee on their behalf) security over the investor commitments and the rights to issue capital call notices to the investors, and receive the proceeds thereof (referred to as 'capital call security'). The security package in a subscription credit facility will also include security over the bank accounts into which the proceeds of such capital calls are to be paid (the 'account security').

As in any financing transaction, the general rule is that the law governing the security will follow where the secured asset is located; for the capital call security, this will be the governing law of the capital call rights (ie, the governing law of the LPA and/or fund documents that provide for the manner in which capital calls can be made), which ordinarily is the jurisdiction where the fund is established/registered; and for the account security, this will be the law of the jurisdiction where the secured account is physically located. Practically speaking, this means that one or more jurisdictions may be involved on a subscription credit facility:

- The credit agreement may be governed by English or New York law;
- The fund may be established in a jurisdiction such as Luxembourg, the Cayman Islands, Delaware, Jersey or Guernsey; and
- The secured accounts may be held in a different jurisdiction altogether.

While there are different models for assessing and calculating the amounts that can be borrowed under a subscription credit facility (largely between so-called 'coverage ratio' models and 'borrowing base' models),[1] the key feature of

Figure 1. Fund structure, subscription credit facility

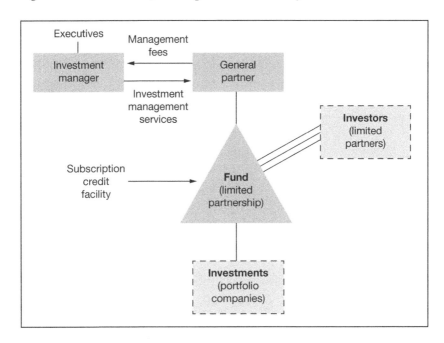

a subscription credit facility is the amount of debt which the fund can incur (whether this is limited to debt under the subscription credit facility or all fund-level debt, including the subscription credit facility, varies from transaction to transaction), tested against the amount of uncalled investor capital commitments in the fund; and the financial covenants or borrowing base in a subscription credit facility is focused on this relationship. Over the life of the fund and its subscription credit facility, as the fund calls capital from its investors, both the amount of uncalled investor capital commitments available to the fund (and thus the size of the lenders' collateral pool) and the amount available to the fund under the facility will decrease in proportion to each other. For this reason, subscription credit facilities tend to be put in place by funds early in their lifecycle, when the fund is likely to have called minimal capital from its investors and the collateral available to lenders under a subscription credit facility (and therefore the amount available to be drawn by the fund under such a facility) is at its greatest.

---

1   Please note that while a discussion of these models is beyond the scope of this chapter, we refer you to another article published by Mayer Brown: Kiel Bowen, Todd N Bundrant, Mark C Dempsey and Christopher N Ellis, "Subscription Credit Facilities: A Comparison of Borrowing Base Structures" (2019), www.mayerbrown.com/-/media/files/perspectives-events/publications/2019/10/subscription-credit-facilities—a-comparison-of-borrowing-base-structures.pdf.

2.2   Net asset value and hybrid transactions

As the fund finance market continues to grow and diversify globally in parallel with funds being raised with increasing amounts of capital and with more complex structures, so too have fund finance liquidity solutions been required to evolve. While fund finance was initially considered an upward-looking form of financing, it is becoming increasingly common for funds to seek out – and, consequently, for lenders to offer – alternative forms of liquidity. Two common products within this category are net asset value (NAV) and hybrid facilities.

In contrast with subscription credit facilities, NAV facilities are loans secured by recourse to the assets of the fund, which typically include:

- equity held by the fund in holding and/or portfolio companies (in the case of a private equity fund or similar) or the ownership interests in debt instruments held by the fund (in the case of a credit fund); and
- security over income and receivables from the fund's investments.

Figure 2. Fund structure, NAV/hybrid facility

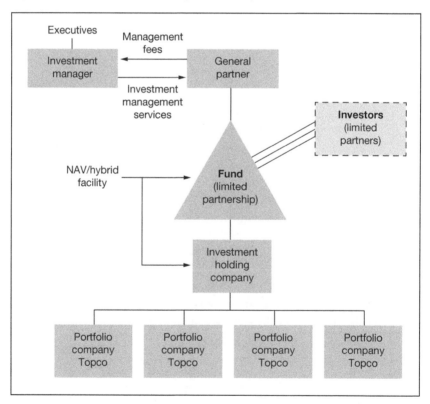

Hybrid transactions, as the name suggests, combine features from a subscription credit facility and a NAV facility. Specifically, this tends to entail that lenders have recourse on a downward-looking basis (as in a NAV facility), in addition to upward-looking capital call security and related controls in the credit agreement, to ensure that a certain level of uncalled investor capital commitments to debt is being maintained (as in a subscription credit facility). While NAV facilities and hybrid facilities can differ significantly (and, admittedly, oftentimes the words are used interchangeably), for our purposes the key aspects of them are that NAV facilities are purely downward looking, while hybrid facilities look down and up, to varying degrees.

There are numerous reasons why a fund would seek to obtain a NAV or hybrid facility. However, typically, they provide favourable liquidity for a fund after the end of its investment period or approaching the end of its lifecycle when the pool of uncalled investor capital commitments has been diminished such that they are unlikely to solely support a subscription credit facility or a fund's increased liquidity demands; or where the fund documents restrict the ability to call capital from investors to repay debt. Such fund finance products would allow funds to provide liquidity for portfolio companies in times of need or even potentially to facilitate an early return to investors.

2.3   Secondaries transactions

Figure 3. Secondary acquisition

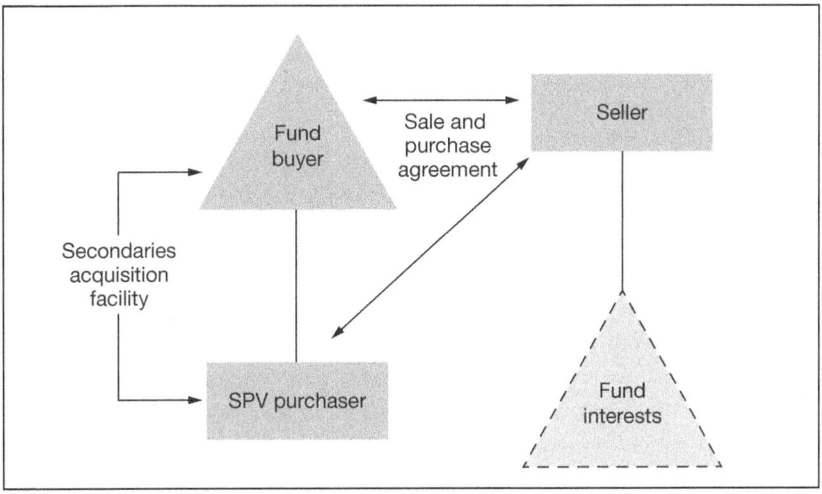

Innovative liquidity solutions are routinely made available to funds in the global secondaries market in line with the growth in the secondaries market generally. While the 'secondaries' market contains a multitude of different forms of transactions, for our purposes the focus is the investment by a fund in other fund interests, which can either be:

- the acquisition by a fund purchaser from a fund seller of a portfolio of fund interests (a 'secondary acquisition'); or
- the transfer by a sponsor of all or some of the assets from one of its managed funds into another continuation fund of which the fund purchaser becomes the majority equity holder (a 'GP-led' transaction).

Figure 4. GP-led

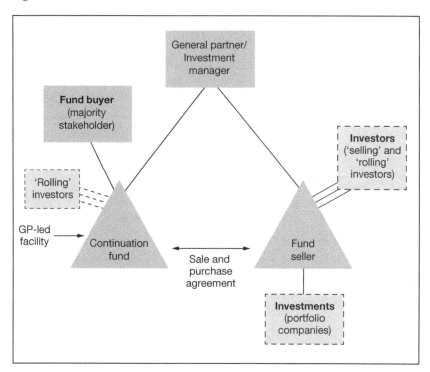

Funds pursue secondaries transactions for numerous reasons. In the case of secondaries acquisitions, these tend to be driven by secondaries-focused funds and thus these transactions are at the heart of the fund's investment strategy. Moreover, while GP-led transactions were initially viewed as a fund seller liquidating underperforming or overly matured assets, GP-led transactions are increasingly viewed as key parts of certain funds' strategies that can benefit both the fund and its existing investors where it offers existing investors the choice to 'cash out' on their interests in the fund or 'go long' on the fund (potentially on better terms). This also allows the fund to manage its assets for a longer period, thus hopefully enhancing asset value, with the opportunity to earn further management fees.

Structurally, the lender on a secondaries financing will either lend to the fund buyer directly (a single-tiered structure), or lend to an SPV purchaser incorporated below the fund buyer (a two-tiered structure). Consequently, the security package on a secondaries transaction will typically include:

- security over the equity in the fund buyer (in a single-tiered structure) or SPV purchaser (in a two-tiered structure); and
- bank account security over designated accounts into which investment proceeds will be paid.

In a two-tiered structure, security will also be expected to be granted over the movement of funds from the fund buyer to the SPV purchaser, which will typically be structured as security over the loan from the fund buyer to the SPV purchaser.

2.4   Management and/or co-investment facilities

The final types of downward-looking liquidity solutions we will focus on in this chapter are 'management' and 'co-investment' facilities. In respect of management facilities, these are typically provided to a sponsor management company for working capital purposes; whereas co-investment facilities are provided to a sponsor/'house' fund (usually referred to as a 'co-investment' vehicle) that often sits alongside the main fund, to finance its investments made jointly with the main fund or its investment directly into the main fund. Typically, the co-investment vehicle's investors will directly or indirectly be employees of the sponsor (both current and former), and represent the fund's 'skin in the game' (ie, that the sponsor and its employees are backing their investments with their own money) – such skin in the game being a condition to third-party investors making their commitment to a fund. Co-investment facilities commonly sit alongside the subscription credit facility (or other liquidity solution) provided to the main fund and, together with management facilities, are relationship-driven financings, offered by lenders to certain key sponsor clients only.

Management facilities are made available to sponsor management companies typically against their cash flows arising from carried interest/management fees paid to them by their managed funds. In respect of co-investment facilities, while these are not based on (or secured by) uncalled investor capital commitments (given that investors are individual members of the fund themselves rather than institutional investors), typically these facilities also look to be based on income from carried interest/management fees (structured usually by way of a guarantee of the co-investment facility from the relevant sponsor management company that receives such income), as well as the performance of its investments, including against distribution proceeds the co-investment vehicle receives. On this basis, the security package granted on these facilities will typically consist of:

- security over the general partner/manager's right to receive the carried interest/management fee/other cash flows (collectively, the 'management fee'); and

- bank account security into which the management fee and/or investment proceeds will be deposited.

It is also not uncommon for security to be granted by the co-investment vehicle itself; however, given that co-investment facilities are not structured on the uncalled investor capital commitments of the co-investment vehicle, such security tends to be downward-looking asset security granted by the co-investment vehicle (which in practice includes security over its bank account and potentially any investments made by it, together with any receivables therewith).

3.   Taking security for fund finance liquidity solutions
Considering the range of different fund finance liquidity solutions and the different structural and commercial considerations that each requires, the process of taking security in fund finance transactions can differ significantly depending on whether the transaction is upward or downward looking and, in the case of the latter, the type of transaction. These considerations are discussed in depth below.

3.1   Upward-looking financings

(a)   Due diligence
As mentioned above, the security package on a subscription credit financing typically consists of capital call security and account security, and the due diligence considerations differ based on each piece of security.

Capital call security: As discussed, the purpose of the capital call security is for the lenders to take security over the right of the fund to call, and enforce the payment of, uncalled investor capital commitments from the fund's investors in order for those amounts to be applied towards the repayment of amounts outstanding under the credit agreement. From an English law perspective, this amounts to an assignment[2] of:

- the general partner's or manager's right to issue capital call notices to investors;
- related rights in the fund documentation, such as the right arising in the fund's favour by virtue of each investor's commitment to provide capital;
- the right of the fund to receive capital and enforce the non-payment thereof; and

---

2   The specific term will vary based on the governing law of the security (eg, 'pledge', 'charge'). In this chapter we use the English law terms; however, the purpose of the security is the same across the various jurisdictions.

- the ability to exercise the LPA remedies in respect of defaulting investors (ie, investors which have failed to fund capital call notices at such times and in accordance with the process set out in the LPA).

It is not uncommon for the 'assigned rights' concept to be subject to particular scrutiny when negotiating capital call security, and a key part of the due diligence stage in the context of a subscription credit facility is establishing which rights belong to which entity.

The lender's due diligence of the fund documentation (and, in particular, the LPA) will be to establish:

- what the fund is permitted to do and what limitations (if any) are placed on it; and
- in what circumstances investors may refuse (permissibly or not) to honour capital call notices.

While each transaction and the related fund structure is unique, and notwithstanding that each LPA is a bespoke document (ie, unlike credit agreements, there is no 'standard form' of LPA), there are a few issues which lenders (and, typically, their legal counsel) will place particular emphasis on in the due diligence (this is by no means an exhaustive list):

- the capacity of the fund to borrow, grant security and give guarantees. Generally, the LPA will contain powers authorising the fund (and the general partner on its behalf) to do this and any limitations. For example, indebtedness – which may or may not include guarantees for this purpose – is typically capped at a certain amount (often expressed as a percentage of total investor commitments) that may be outstanding at any time. There is often a limitation on the period for which any particular borrowings may be outstanding (eg, that any piece of debt must be repaid (with the proceeds of such repayment not coming from other debt) within 12 months of having been incurred;
- how capital calls are made – that is:
  - who has the power to issue them (more on this below);
  - what time periods need to be complied with (eg, LPAs commonly provide that investors must be given at least 10 business days' notice before sums are due);
  - whether capital call notices need to be in a certain format; and
  - whether capital calls must be issued to all investors at the same time (referred to as a *'pro rata* call');
- what the process is for an investor to be considered to be a defaulting investor and what remedies are available to the general partner in such circumstances;
- what the process is for an investor to be 'excused' from an investment

(ie, the ability for an investor to choose not to honour a capital call without being considered to be in default);

- the ability for the general partner/fund to 'overcall' on its investors (ie, to make additional capital calls on investors to cover a shortfall caused by the default and/or excusal of one or more other investors in respect of a capital call notice); and
- the circumstances in which the fund's investment period is terminated and/or suspended – whether in the ordinary course or due to a specific event (eg, a 'key person' event) – and how such termination/suspension impacts the fund's ability to make capital calls to investors for the repayment of debt and other liabilities.

As the fund finance market – and in particular, the use of subscription credit facilities – continues to grow, an increasing number of institutional investors are becoming familiar with fund sponsors' use of these liquidity solutions. Accordingly, it is increasingly common for side letters (ie, agreements between an investor and the fund that seek to vary certain terms of the fund documentation (most commonly the LPA)) to contain provisions that have the potential to directly impact the credit agreement and related security package. Specifically, side letters may:

- prescribe that capital calls must follow a certain template (eg, the Institutional Limited Partners Association recommended form) which contains calculations that a lender may be unable to complete; or
- grant a particular investor the right to elect to be treated as an excused investor in respect of a certain type of investment, or (in respect of sovereign/governmental investors) to claim sovereign immunity or provide that claims against it must be brought in a particular jurisdiction.

These side letter issues are significant for lenders, for two principal reasons. First, the side letter provisions can be fundamentally important in the event that the lender seeks to enforce its security and, for example, bring a claim against an investor which has refused to fund a capital call notice issued by the lender if the capital call notice was not issued validly under the terms of the side letter. Issues such as these can also have a broader impact in circumstances (which are relatively standard) requiring a *pro rata* call, as other investors could seek to assert defences against their obligation to fund a capital call if they are aware that other investors have not been validly served with a capital call notice. Second, care must be taken to ensure whether side letter provisions granted in favour of one investor will actually apply *vis-à-vis* each investor – for example, through 'a most-favoured nation' provision, which allows certain investors to have the benefit of side letter terms granted to other investors.

One of the key structural questions to consider at the preliminary stages of a subscription credit facility is which fund parties will grant security; while it is accepted that the fund will grant security in favour of the lenders, a lender will consider a wider security net where necessary to obtain the collateral it expects. In circumstances where the fund is a limited partnership, security should also be granted by the relevant entities that own those assigned rights (discussed above), which often includes rights of the general partner of the fund. As such, the general partner will invariably be a party to the capital call security in its own capacity, in addition to the fund.[3]

Indeed, while the general position is that certain of the assigned rights (principally, the right to issue capital call notices to investors) are vested in the general partner, it is not uncommon for the general partner to have delegated its power to an investment manager. In those circumstances, it is critical to review carefully such contractual arrangements (ordinarily a management agreement or the LPA itself) to consider the scope of the general partner's delegation therein, to ensure that a lender is not fettered in enforcement of its capital call security. Where such a delegation has been made to the investment manager, such investment manager will also be a party to the credit agreement and capital call security, granting a security interest over its rights and powers under the fund documentation. However, sponsors will be very focused to ensure that the investment manager's obligations under the finance documents are limited, in order to avoid any cross-contamination in an enforcement scenario against that investment manager with any other funds it manages (where the lender has no recourse against such other funds).

Account security: The due diligence required in respect of the bank accounts that are being charged pursuant to the account security is relatively straightforward – certainly when compared to the considerations involved in the capital call security. Ultimately, the fund will provide details of the bank accounts that are to be subject to the account security, including the jurisdictional locations of such accounts; and the fund will typically be expected to deliver proof to the lender that the bank accounts are open and being maintained.

There are, however, a few key considerations to consider at the due diligence stage, including ascertaining whether side letters to fund documentation include provisions that capital call proceeds received by the fund must be deposited into a bank account in the name of the fund or into a specific account as identified in the investor's subscription agreement. Additionally, the account

---

3   This general principle may differ between jurisdictions. While this chapter does not focus on these particular jurisdictions, the security package should always be discussed with legal counsel in each relevant jurisdiction.

security must align with the lenders' expected control over such secured bank account; for example, security over 'operational' bank accounts, which the fund uses for its day-to-day operations, will likely require that 'control' over such bank accounts remain with the fund until the point at which the account security becomes enforceable. Such account security structure is the most common form of account security seen in upward-looking fund finance transactions, given that in the ordinary course, the fund is permitted to withdraw the proceeds of any capital calls paid into such a bank account for the purposes of making investments or repaying debt, with control from the point of enforcement being vested with the lenders. Comparatively, 'blocked accounts', with control being vested with the lenders from the start, can also feature in transactions. It is fundamental that the lenders ensure that the account security both reflects any due diligence considerations relating to the accounts and is structured in such a way as to correctly reflect the type of account that is being secured.

Compared to the capital call security, the question of who grants the account security is more straightforward: the account security is simply granted by each fund party that holds the bank accounts that are being secured, which is customarily the fund. Care should be taken to ensure that the ownership of each relevant bank account and any nuances in relation to the flow of funds through the account structure are correctly reflected; for instance, if the bank account is held by a custodian on behalf of the relevant fund party (eg, if legal and beneficial title to the relevant bank account is split), this should be reflected in the security.

(b) Perfection

A key part of taking any security is that any steps necessary to ensure that the security will have the appropriate ranking and priority, and be enforceable against third parties (including any insolvency practitioner) that the lender is expecting to be taken (typically referred to as 'perfection' of the security), is carried out in a timely manner. While perfection requirements vary depending on the relevant jurisdiction, there are key considerations with perfecting both capital call security and account security, as set out below. Registration of security (within appropriate time limits) in one or more jurisdictions may also be an important perfection step. The requirements as to registration will be highly dependent on the circumstances applicable to any given transaction; an analysis of specific registration regimes is outside the scope of this chapter and advice should always be taken from appropriate legal counsel.

From an English law perspective, the typical approach is to ensure that capital call security is first ranking in priority and is directly enforceable against the fund's investors. This requires that the capital call security be perfected by notifying the fund's investors of the existence of the capital call security, which is done by each fund party that has granted capital call security signing and delivering to each investor a 'security notice' (the form of which is typically appended to the capital call security). When negotiating capital call security, it is always useful to consider both the timing and the method of delivery of the security notices.

Specifically, while the fund will need to balance investor relations and administrative considerations, the lenders will want to ensure that the capital call security is perfected and that priority of security is achieved on signing, or as close to it as possible. Hence, while market convention (particularly in Europe) had traditionally been for the fund to include the security notice in the next quarterly investor report, in recent years, as many fund investors have become more familiar with capital call security – and in particular, more accustomed to receiving security notices – there has been a concerted shift whereby security notices are more commonly delivered to investors within a very short period of time from the grant of such capital call security (or, if later, the date on which an investor subscribes to the fund). Moreover, while funds are increasingly using electronic investor portals/datarooms to communicate with investors, any proposal to deliver security notices to investors via these platforms must always be analysed both against the notice provisions in the fund documentation and from the perspective of the jurisdiction whose laws govern the capital call security.

In terms of account security, lenders will usually also be looking for this to be first ranking in priority and directly enforceable against the account bank. This requires perfection by way of a signed notice (an 'account notice') delivered from each party which has granted the account security to the account bank or an account control agreement entered into with the account bank. The terms of the account notice and account control agreement will be significant insofar as the account bank is not a party to the account security itself. Therefore, the account notice and/or account control agreement puts the account bank on notice of the account security and will provide details of 'control' of such bank account – whether that be with the fund until the account security has become enforceable or determined by the instructions of the lenders (or a security trustee on behalf of the lenders). In connection with the account notice specifically (in addition to it being a perfection step), the account security will often impose an obligation on the fund to deliver to the lenders a signed acknowledgement of the account notice from the account bank – for example, in order to consent to the creation of the account security (which may be restricted under the terms and conditions applicable to the account), or to waive any prior ranking security interests or rights of set-off which the account bank may have over the account. However, legal counsel should always be consulted, as the acknowledgement may or may not be a perfection requirement in the relevant jurisdiction. Bank account providers are increasingly looking to standardise their procedures in relation to maintaining accounts which are subject to security in favour of other institutions – for example, by that account bank having its own form of account control agreement or account notice/acknowledgement and requiring that this form be used for all accounts held with that account bank. In such circumstances, it will be necessary to ensure that the requirements of the lender taking security and the account bank do not cut across one another (or, if they do, for an appropriately balanced position to be agreed).

As mentioned above, this chapter focuses specifically on the position under English law; but in certain jurisdictions (some of which are commonly seen in fund finance transactions), the requirement for notification of security to be given goes beyond mere perfection and is instead a crucial step required to be taken in order for any security to be valid at all. In those circumstances, the issues highlighted above will be even more important; legal counsel in the relevant jurisdiction(s) should always be consulted, given that this is obviously a key part of lenders' recourse packages.

3.2   Downward-looking financings

(a)   Due diligence

The due diligence exercise on downward-looking financings has certain commonalities with that undertaken on upward-looking financings, but there are key differences. Specifically, while the due diligence on the funds will be similar in any fund financing – for example, the fund documentation will need to be analysed to ensure that each fund party is permitted and able to enter into the particular transaction – downward-looking financings focus less on diligencing the fund's investors (subject to certain exceptions, as discussed below) and more on ensuring that the particular portfolio assets can be secured in the manner envisioned.

NAV and hybrid financings: As mentioned, NAV financings are typically secured by:

- security granted over the fund's interests held in underlying portfolio assets (and, depending on the structure, over a holding company that holds the portfolio assets); and
- receivables security over cash flows on investments and/or intra-group debts (ie, debts between the fund, portfolio and/or holding companies).

Where the portfolio assets held by the fund are equity interests in portfolio companies, as on any security over equity, the governing documents of the entity whose equity is being secured and any key contracts must be carefully reviewed:

- to ensure that there are no prohibitions on the security being granted in the first place (eg, no third-party consents required for the granting of such security, particularly where such entity may not be wholly owned by the fund); and
- to uncover any provisions which may complicate the lenders' enforcement (eg, directors' powers to refuse to register transfer of shares, pre-emption rights, change of control triggers).

A similar analysis is required in respect of receivables to be secured where the fund will be required to disclose to the lender all contractual arrangements or information evidencing the receivables owed either to the fund or by the entity whose equity is being secured. These arrangements will need to be carefully reviewed to ensure that any underlying obligations therein are not contravened, such as prohibitions on assignments or confidentiality/non-disclosure provisions. Where the portfolio assets held by the fund are interests in underlying debt instruments, the issues highlighted above in respect of general receivables which are to be secured would apply; but the lender may need to temper this against the fact that a fund could hold positions in a very large (and potentially fluctuating) pool of debt instruments. In such circumstances, lenders may need to take a commercial view as to whether detailed diligence on all underlying contracts (which may be governed by the laws of a variety of jurisdictions and be in differing languages) is appropriate; if not, it is often the case that the security is taken by way of a portfolio-wide floating charge, rather than being taken specifically over individual portfolio assets.

The security package on hybrid transactions can differ widely; these financings are by definition an amalgamation between subscription credit financings and NAV financings. As a general rule, lenders on a hybrid transaction will most likely start from the understanding that the fund will grant capital call security and account security (ie, the traditional upward-looking package on a subscription credit financing) and full downward-looking security (ie, equity security over underlying portfolio and/or holding companies and/or receivables security, in each case as discussed above). However, legal counsel should always be consulted for discussions on the appropriate security package on hybrid transactions.

Secondaries transactions: Most secondaries transactions (irrespective of whether they are secondaries acquisitions or GP-led transactions) will entail, directly or indirectly, security over fund interests. This security is typically structured such that the security is granted over the fund interests on the one hand, but also over a broader 'assigned rights' concept on the other (as with capital call security), such that the lenders also have recourse to the ancillary rights, title and powers that accompany the fund buyer's and/or SPV purchaser's interests, as well as all payments/receivables arising from such fund interests that it holds (eg, distributions owing to it). Therefore, such security will require significant due diligence of the underlying fund documentation.

The key due diligence aspect for the security package on a secondaries transaction is to discover and manage the third-party consents that may be required for both the granting of security over underlying fund interests held by the fund buyer or SPV purchaser and/or the enforcement of such security (which will ultimately entail a transfer of partnership interests). Invariably, such granting of security and enforcement will be prohibited by the underlying fund documentation unless consent of the underlying general partner has been obtained. Managing the consent process can be time consuming and burdensome, particularly as fund documentation generally provides general partners with full discretion on whether to provide such consent to granting such security and a subsequent transfer (directly and often indirectly) of investors' interests. Where the consent of a general partner is not provided, the security structure becomes significantly more complex in order to navigate around the failure to obtain consent, including potentially having such fund interests held through a different vehicle so the lender has a clean enforcement strategy.

A further item of diligence on secondaries transactions is in respect of confidentiality restrictions in underlying fund documentation, which on occasion may prevent the fund buyer or SPV purchaser from being able to identify the specific security issues as mentioned above. It will also be usual during any third-party consent process to ensure that, to the extent there are confidentiality restrictions, the relevant underlying general partner provides its consent to the disclosure of such information as may be necessary for the relevant lender to complete its due diligence and benefit from its expected security package.

Management and/or co-investment facilities: The distinguishing factor of the security package in connection with a management and/or co-investment facility is the security over the general partner/manager's right to receive the management fee. Consequently, the due diligence process on these facilities is focused on assessing how the general partner/manager's right to receive the management fee operates in the fund documentation (ie, the LPA and/or management agreement) of the funds it manages and how the management fee is structured over time (eg, if it is subject to a ratchet and/or whether it changes after the end of the investment period of the main fund), in order to ensure that this right can be effectively secured. Additional considerations are given to any direct or indirect security restrictions which could prohibit the grant of security, such as non-assignment provisions in the LPA or management agreement.

Provided that there are none, the management fee security will commonly take the form of security over such contractual rights to receive the management fees. An alternative structuring strategy to support such security is to ensure that the management fees are deposited into a bank account, which the lender can control following enforcement or earlier. Ultimately, the structure will be a commercial decision, which will largely be driven by whether the fund will be dependent on receiving management fees throughout the life of the facility to meet its ongoing expenses.

(b) *Perfection*

As security packages on downward-looking financings are so varied and oftentimes complex, it is not possible to summarise in this chapter the various perfection requirements. In such fund finance transactions, specific analysis should be undertaken by appropriate legal counsel.

4. Conclusion

While the concepts are often conflated, fund finance encompasses more than simply subscription credit facilities; rather, fund finance is a diverse product area which encompasses a wide array of liquidity solutions. This chapter has sought to discuss some of the most prevalent solutions and the typical structural and legal considerations associated with them, which will hopefully aid participants in their discussions with legal counsel and on a commercial level.

Islamic finance

Barry Cosgrave
Mayer Brown

1.   Introduction

While the term 'Sharia law' is used extensively within Islamic finance, *Sharia* law is not a codified system of law that is set out in statute. Instead, *Sharia* law as we refer to it is made up of three main components:

- the *Koran*;
- the sayings of the Prophet Muhammad, or *Hadith*; and
- the teachings of the Prophet Muhammad, or *Sunnah*.

It is from these three primary sources that individual *Sharia* scholars seek to extract the principles that underpin Islamic finance. Those scholars each have different interpretations of *Sharia* law that fall within different schools of Islamic jurisprudence, depending on which branch of Islam those scholars identify with. There are two main branches of Islam: *Sunni* and *Shia*. The majority of Muslims are *Sunni*; and within Sunnism there are several prominent schools of jurisprudence that have different interpretations of *Sharia*, which in turn influence the views of different scholars and how they apply those views to Islamic finance: *Hanafi*, *Hanbali*, *Sharfi'i* and *Maliki*. With the notable exception of Saudi Arabia (where the *Hanbali* school of thought is almost universal), it is very hard to state that *Sharia* is the 'law of the land', owing to the fact that many Muslim countries are happy to accommodate the various schools of thought that exist within Sunnism.

It goes without saying that applying the above to complex cross-border financing arrangements is no easy task, and working closely with scholars throughout the lifecycle of a transaction has been an extremely important factor in the development of Islamic finance over the past 20 years or so. The role of the scholar is a little like a hybrid of a law firm and a rating agency – on a given transaction, the scholar will:

- give initial clearance on the structure to be used;
- review the transaction documentation from a *Sharia* perspective and input with comments; and
- issue a *fatwa* at the time of signing of the transaction documents confirming that, in his or her opinion, the transaction documents and transaction structure comply with *Sharia*.

However, the importance of this being the opinion of that scholar only cannot be overstated. As we will discuss later in this chapter, challenges have been made to Islamic finance structures over the years on the basis of a failure to comply with *Sharia* notwithstanding the fact that a *fatwa* was issued. These challenges arise because of the pluralism that exists within Islam; but it is equally important to note that the *Sharia* compliance of financing structures is a matter for the conscience of the individual parties to that transaction, which are each responsible for satisfying themselves that a given transaction complies with their religious beliefs.

2. Principles of Islamic finance

While differences of opinion exist between scholars, there are certain core principles of Islamic finance on which all scholars agree. First, and most prominently, the charging of interest for the use of money (*riba*) is prohibited. 'Interest' is generally interpreted as any return that is pre-determined, guaranteed or calculated other than by reference to profits actually generated. Instead, wealth should be invested in productive enterprise so that the owner earns a return by sharing both in the profits generated and in the assumption of the risk of any losses. This is not to say that Islam forbids the making of profit through commercial activities; in fact, the opposite is true. The key is how that profit is generated, which *Sharia* directs should be on the basis of a cooperative approach to business as opposed to a typical conventional lending relationship.

Second, *Sharia* prohibits uncertainty (*gharar*) in contracts. The sale of items whose existence or characteristics are not certain is not permitted. And it is this requirement that has led to commodity *murabaha* transactions (*tawarruq*) using London Metals Exchange (LME) metals as the underlying assets. We will discuss commodity *murabaha* in more detail later in this chapter; but the LME has strict rules about the purity of levels of metals that allows them to be characterised accordingly – for example, Grade A copper must conform with at least one of three specific chemical compositions.[1]

Third, speculation or gambling (*mayseer*) is similarly prohibited, which imposes a number of restrictions on the ability to use derivatives in Islamic finance. Contracts that provide for options or dealings in futures must be closely examined to consider whether they are speculative. This is a process that will involve the scholars and care must be taken to ensure that each scholar is appropriately briefed on the nature of a contract so as to ensure that appropriate input is given. The scope and applicability of *gharar* and *mayseer* are open to interpretation, and the views of scholars can differ materially. However, continuing with derivatives as an example, there are key distinctions between

---

[1] The specific chemical compositions of LME-grade metals can be found on the LME website: www.LME.com.

derivative contracts that seek to manage actual risks, such as currency swaps, versus option contracts that seek to try to predict future movements in values and that are likely to be deemed by *Sharia* to be speculative in nature.

In addition to the broad prohibitions on the type and nature of contracts, there are certain business sectors that are prohibited for Muslims and for which an Islamic finance transaction would not work. While not an exhaustive list, key industry areas that are forbidden include:

- alcohol;
- gambling (casinos, book makers);
- arms manufacturing;
- tobacco manufacturing; and
- adult entertainment.

Many of those industries are typically included, for example, as part of a prohibited list for conventional asset managers and so the restrictions tend not to cause too many issues for the majority of people. Things become more complicated with prohibitions on cinemas, the music industry and pork products. This can become an issue when financing a destination shopping mall that may include a cinema complex and a supermarket that sells pork products. Specific exclusions to the permitted use of proceeds must be included in any *Sharia*-compliant facility and alternative finance must be sought for those specific aspects.

Islamic finance requires that any financing be provided on the basis of the trading of assets: Islamic finance is essentially asset-based finance. More detail on these structures is provided below; but this requirement for assets to underpin the finance to be provided is most clearly seen in commodity *murabaha* (sale of commodities on deferred payment terms) and *ijara* (sale and leaseback), which are the structures most commonly used in *Sharia*-compliant banking facilities. This is not to say that Islamic finance uses asset-backed structures as we might see in a securitisation. There have been *Sharia*-compliant securitisation transactions, and there are many *Sharia*-compliant structures that involve the taking of security to support the payment obligations of the counterparty; but it would be incorrect to assume (as many investors did in the fall-out from the 2008 financial crisis) that Islamic finance structures are the *Sharia* equivalent of a securitisation. Absent validly created security under applicable laws, a *Sharia*-compliant facility will be treated in the same manner as a conventional unsecured facility and its ranking in any bankruptcy will be *pari passu* with other unsecured creditors.

3.   Structures

In this section, we provide a brief overview of the most commonly used structures in Islamic banking: *murabaha* and *ijara*. There are multiple additional structures and techniques that are employed, both in isolation and in combination with the structures listed below. However, for the purposes of this chapter, we have sought to focus on these most commonly used structures.

3.1 *Murabaha*

Murabaha is the most commonly used structure within Islamic finance, accounting for approximately 60% of the Islamic finance world. *Murabaha* – or, more specifically, commodity *murabaha* and reverse commodity *murabaha* (*tawarruq*) – is used by Islamic financial institutions globally to provide funding to a wide range of corporates and other financial institutions, across the full spectrum of industries. *Murabaha*:

- is the basic building block for Islamic risk management tools;
- facilitates the trading of distressed *Sharia*-compliant finance facilities; and
- is employed in a wide range of other products, including real estate purchases in non-Muslim jurisdictions, investments into conventional funds and securitisation structures.

It is the most flexible and time and cost-effective structure that can be used in Islamic finance, which has fuelled its popularity. This is not to say that *murabaha* is accepted by all scholars: there is a body of Islamic jurisprudence that rejects *murabaha* as disguised lending, favouring structures such as *ijara* instead. However, for companies that do not have an inventory of assets that can be used as the basis for an *ijara* structure, commodity *murabaha* is usually the only real option for a *Sharia*-compliant facility. Rather than have a 'lender/borrower' relationship as would be seen in a conventional loan, a *murabaha* facility involves the bank acting as seller of commodities and the counterparty acting as purchaser. The basic structure of a *murabaha* is set out in Figure 1:

- Step 1: The purchaser issues a notice of request to purchase to the seller.
- Step 2: The seller purchases commodities from Broker 1 for an amount equal to the principal amount to be financed.
- Step 3: The seller issues a transaction confirmation and offer notice to the purchaser.
- Step 4: The purchaser issues an acceptance notice to the seller.
- Step 5: The seller sells the commodities to the purchaser on spot delivery but deferred payment terms.
- Step 6: The purchaser on-sells the commodities to Broker 2 on a spot basis, thus receiving cash in an amount equal to the principal amount of the finance to be provided.
- Step 7: The purchaser makes payment of the deferred purchase price.

Figure 1. Commodity *murabaha*

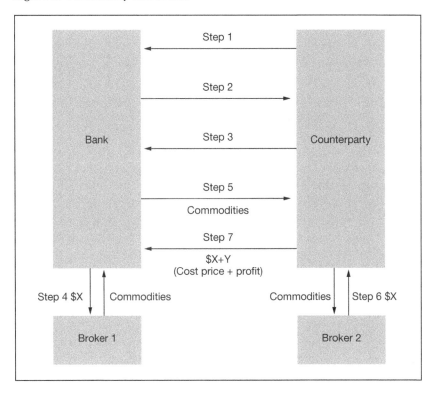

Islamic finance requires that there be a clear offer and acceptance between the seller and the purchaser. This can be somewhat formulaic, but it is necessary. While it is the seller that offers to sell, it is not typical banking practice for a bank to offer to advance funds to a counterparty absent a utilisation request. While structures are put in place that make a transaction compliant with *Sharia*, it is important that the economic conditions that apply to conventional finance are replicated within the Islamic banking sector. It is for this reason that the counterparty initiates the transaction by issuing a notice of request to purchase, which is the equivalent of a utilisation request.

It is also important that Step 2 occurs before Step 3 in order to avoid any risk of uncertainty (*gharar*) or speculation (*mayseer*) creeping in. The seller cannot offer to sell something that it does not own and so it therefore must first purchase the commodities from Broker 1. The seller takes comfort from the receipt of a notice of request to purchase that a transaction will be entered into with the purchaser. It is important to note that the buying and selling of commodities does not generally constitute the activity of commodity trading. Rather, the transaction involves the simple buying and selling of commodities as assets between two parties. It is also common for the bank to act as agent of the purchaser of the commodities to ensure that it completes the on-sale of the commodities to Broker 2. This is largely to ensure that the transaction is completed as envisaged, so that there are no doubts as to the obligation to make payment of the deferred purchase price arising.

The commodities themselves must be certain in nature and for that reason it is most common for LME metals to be used. These metals are stored in LME warehouses around the globe and are represented by warrants which are traded across the LME. Each of Stages 2, 5 and 6 must be recorded and this is done by way of ledger entry with the relevant brokers. Title to the commodities is transferred by way of those ledger entries and these records can be maintained to provide evidence to the *Sharia* scholars that the commodity trades did, in fact, take place. This is an important procedural point, as there have been instances where *murabaha* facilities have been entered into by parties, but the commodity trades were not effected. Islamic banks are audited by their *Sharia* supervisory boards on at least an annual basis and must be able to provide evidence that the trades have taken place. Absent this, the transaction will not be *Sharia* compliant and any profit earned on that transaction by the Islamic bank will have to be paid over to charity. (The calculation of profit is discussed further below.) Another important point about the commodities is that, in the case of LME metals, they must be base metals and must exclude gold, silver and platinum (other than platinum used in industrial facilities). The reason for this is that gold and silver are of intrinsic value and are therefore viewed as cash equivalent. This means that their trading for the purposes of a commodity *murabaha* would be the equivalent of a cash-for-cash transaction, resulting in *riba*.

3.2 *Ijara*

An *ijara* transaction involves the sale and leaseback of certain assets by a counterparty to an Islamic bank. As a general rule, *ijara* is viewed as the most *Sharia*-compliant structure, as it provides for the existence of 'hard' assets throughout the life of the transaction. There is less divergence between scholars on the efficacy of *ijara* as a result. *Ijara* transactions are particularly well suited to counterparties that have high-value assets – typically physical assets; although there are examples of non-tangible assets being used to underpin *ijara* contracts, provided that such assets are capable of being defined with sufficient certainty and of being appropriately valued – for example, the source code for proprietary software.

Sharia law, in contrast with the laws of many Muslim jurisdictions, recognises the concept of beneficial or equitable title as being distinct from legal title. Many of the jurisdictions of the Middle East, for example, are civil law jurisdictions which do not recognise the concept of beneficial title: the only title transfer that is legally enforceable is that of legal title. However, where the counterparty is using land as the asset to be sold and leased back, a transfer of legal title is not practicable, owing to the substantial transfer taxes that would become due on such transfer. One of the reasons that English law is a go-to law for Islamic finance is that it recognises the concept of beneficial ownership and the contractual framework therefore suits Islamic finance. Figure 1 is an example of an *ijara* transaction that uses land as the underlying asset.

Figure 2. An example of a *ijara* transaction

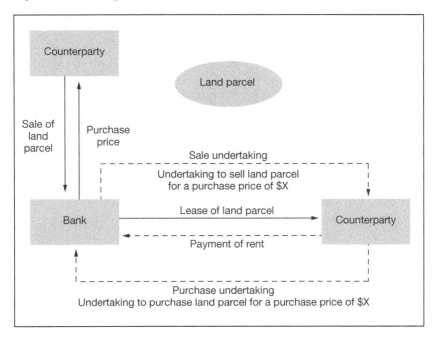

- Step 1: The counterparty sells the beneficial title in and to the land parcel to the financier pursuant to the terms of a sale and purchase agreement for a purchase price in an amount equal to the principal amount of the financing being sought.
- Step 2: The financier (as lessor) and the counterparty (as lessee) enter into a lease agreement (*ijara*) in respect of the land parcel, pursuant to which the lessee agrees to pay rent to the lessor for the period of the lease (eg, five years).
- Step 3: At the end of the lease period, the lessor has the right, pursuant to the terms of a purchase undertaking, to require the lessee to buy the land back from it at a pre-determined price which, for a bullet payment maturity, will be an amount equal to the principal amount of the finance, but will be a smaller amount for an amortising payment profile.
- Step 4: To provide comfort to the counterparty that it will get back the beneficial title to its land at the end of the lease period, the financier also

grants a sale undertaking to the counterparty enabling the counterparty to require the financier to sell the land to the counterparty at the same pre-determined price as for the purchase undertaking.

From the point of view of the financier, particular care must be taken in the drafting of the purchase undertaking, as it is structured a little like a conventional option and could be capable of expiry. It is therefore prudent to provide that the purchase undertaking has a long period post maturity for it to be exercised, rather than making it exercisable on a single day. This allows for any operational mishaps on the part of the financier to be addressed, as well as accounting for any negotiations in a distressed scenario to be undertaken.

Issues associated with variable profit rates in *murabaha* facilities are discussed in more detail later in this chapter, but *ijara* facilities are the most straightforward to structure when considering issues such as variable rates applicable to rent. However, *ijara* facilities are less popular than *murabaha* facilities, owing to the requirement that the counterparty have valuable assets that can be sold and leased back. There are also additional structural issues that come into play where special purpose vehicles must be established in order to hold the beneficial title to the asset being sold and leased back. *Sharia* scholars tend to prefer to use *ijara* facilities, but the practical obstacles that get in the way mean that the majority of bank finance transactions utilise *murabaha* facilities.

4.   Calculating profit and rent

While *Sharia* does not permit the charging of interest on moneys loaned, it does permit the earning of profit on compliant transactions. A commodity *murabaha* transaction between an Islamic bank (acting as seller) and a counterparty (acting as purchaser) sees the seller deliver the commodities to the purchaser on spot delivery terms, but with payment for those commodities to be made on a deferred basis. The seller is entitled to charge a profit on that purchase price to compensate it for that deferral. The 'deferred purchase price' (or similar term) comprises two components:

- the cost price – that is, the price paid by the seller to Broker 1 for the purchase of the commodities, equivalent to the principal amount of the finance to be provided; and
- the profit, which is calculated by multiplying the cost price by the profit rate. The profit rate can be either a fixed percentage or a floating or variable rate calculated by reference to a benchmark rate (eg, the Sterling Overnight Index Average[2] (SONIA)) plus a margin. Profit is calculated by

---

2   SONIA is based on actual transactions and reflects the average of the interest rates that banks pay to borrow sterling overnight from other financial institutions and other institutional investors. See Bank of England website: www.bankofengland.co.uk/markets/sonia-benchmark.

reference to a profit period which can be anywhere from one month to annual, although three-month profit periods are the most common.

Similarly, with an *ijara* facility, the periodic rent is determined by reference to a fixed or variable rate, with the variable rate capable of being benchmarked to a rate such as SONIA plus a margin. This amount is then paid at the end of each relevant period (typically quarterly) by the lessee.

Sharia does not permit the use of conventional interest rate calculations to be used; but it does allow those rates to be used as a benchmark for ascertaining what a profit rate or rental amount should be. It is therefore an important drafting point to state that a profit rate or rental amount is benchmarked to, for example, SONIA, as opposed to it being SONIA. The rationale for this benchmarking may be explained by analogy: if a person invents a new non-alcoholic drink that he or she wishes to take to market, it is okay for that person to use the price of a can of an alcoholic drink in order to ascertain the price that he or she will charge for a can of the new non-alcoholic drink. It is this rationale that explains why Islamic banks are permitted to benchmark the profit rates or rental amounts that they charge to the interest rates charged by conventional banks: absent that ability, Islamic banks would be charging rates that were not linked to, or appropriate for, the markets in which they operate.

5. AAOIFI Standard 59

The Accounting and Auditing Organisation for Islamic Financial Institutions (AAOIFI) is the *de facto* regulatory body for Islamic finance globally. In 2018 it formally issued Standard 59, which concerned commodity *murabaha* transactions and the sale of debt. The issue that AAOIFI was concerned with is the way in which a typical market-standard variable profit rate *murabaha* transaction is constructed. For a fixed-rate *murabaha*, the profit element of the deferred purchase price can be paid periodically (typically quarterly) and the cost price element can be paid either on a bullet basis at maturity or periodically on an amortising basis. This is because the profit element is fixed and thus there is no element of uncertainty (*gharar*) in the contract.

Where the profit element of the *murabaha* is variable (ie, calculated by reference to a benchmark rate), there is an element of uncertainty (*gharar*) owing to the fact that the profit element is only fixed at the beginning of the relevant profit period. The traditional approach that the market has taken to address this is to structure all *murabaha* facilities as revolving facilities even if they are intended to operate as term facilities – that is, the facility is comprised of a series of three-month duration commodity trades, with the deferred purchase price being payable in full at the end of that three-month period, but with the cost price element of such amount being used by the bank to enter into another three-month commodity trade on the same day for the same cost price as the previous one, with the new deferred purchase price being payable on the expiry of the next three-month period, and so on.

Standard 59 was concerned that this arrangement was too similar to conventional lending and has stated that the revolving nature of the market-standard *murabaha* facility will no longer be permitted. The UAE Central Bank has incorporated Standard 59 into UAE federal law and, as such, the previously standard structure for a *murabaha* facility has had to change. This creates a number of issues for both Islamic and conventional financial institutions in the United Arab Emirates, particularly where dual tranche conventional and *Sharia*-compliant facilities have been put in place. The simplest solution to this issue would be for Islamic financial institutions to simply apply a fixed profit rate to *murabaha* facilities, but this would prevent Islamic financial institutions from being aligned with their conventional equivalents in the banking market. One solution that has been landed upon is to bifurcate the cost price element of the deferred purchase price and the variable profit element. Assuming a case where a bullet payment profile is being used with quarterly payments of profit, this may be achieved by having a single, long-dated *murabaha* facility that carries a deferred purchase price that contemplates the cost price element plus a notional fixed profit rate (or amount) which is payable in full at maturity. The variable profit element is then captured via a series of short-term, three-month duration *murabaha* transactions that capture the profit rate only for that period. The 'profit *murabaha*' transactions rely on the principle of unilateral promise (*Wa'ad*), which obliges the counterparty, via a purchase undertaking, to enter into commodity transactions with the Islamic bank on a quarterly basis. If the counterparty fails to enter into a profit *murabaha* transaction, then the deferred purchase price payable pursuant to the terms of the long-dated *murabaha* transaction will become immediately due and payable.

6. Benchmark rates for Islamic finance

Islamic banks have traditionally taken a similar approach to their conventional counterparts in using the London Inter-Bank Offered Rate (LIBOR) as the rate to which they benchmark profit rates and rental amounts. However, as the banking world transitions away from LIBOR, it has been recommended that Islamic finance adopt term SONIA as its preferred rate to which to benchmark.

The move from IBOR-based rates to risk-free rates (RFRs) presents another challenge in the structuring of *murabaha* facilities. The main issue is that RFRs are backward-looking rates, such that the rate is only set at the end of a given period rather than at the beginning. This gives rise to concerns around uncertainty (*gharar*), as it is not possible to set the profit element of the deferred purchase price when it is required. In order to address the use of such rates, Islamic financial institutions are being encouraged to use term SONIA (in the same manner as for export credit facilities). If RFRs are to be used, Islamic financial institutions may need to take a more structured finance approach to what were previously simple corporate facilities by introducing purchase undertakings and/or the concept of *musawama* to the *murabaha* structure. A *musawama* contract is very similar to a *murabaha* contract, with the exception that where a *murabaha* contract involves spot delivery of the commodities, but with payment being made on a deferred basis, a *musawama* contract involves spot delivery versus spot payment. This means that the *musawama* purchase price can be any price agreed between the parties, rather than comprising a cost price plus incremental profit amount. It is therefore possible to use commodities with a low cost price, which can then be sold for a much higher *musawama* price.

7. Recourse in *Sharia*-compliant facilities

Sharia-compliant facility agreements contain all of the protections in the form of representations, warranties, covenants and events of default that one would expect to see in a conventional facility. Subject to local law issues that may impact on a particular counterparty, Islamic banks should have the same recourse opportunities that conventional banks enjoy. Maintenance and financial covenants are as important to Islamic banks as they are to conventional ones and, as such, counterparties should not expect to receive different treatment than would be expected from a conventional bank.

There are, however, two points of difference for a *Sharia*-compliant facility agreement. The first is that a representation and covenant is generally included where the counterparty will state that:

- it has satisfied itself as to the *Sharia* compliance of the transaction and structure; and
- it will not attempt to disclaim its contractual obligations on the grounds of non-compliance with *Sharia*.

The second is a complementary event of default which states that any attempt to disclaim a contract on the grounds of non-compliance with *Sharia* will constitute an event of default; and it is common for no grace period to apply to this event of default on the basis that it is entirely within the gift of the counterparty. This additional drafting originates from a number of cases where counterparties have tried to disclaim their obligations using an *ultra vires* argument. Some of these cases are discussed below in more detail, but the summary is that certain *Sharia*-compliant businesses have attempted to avoid certain of their obligations arising pursuant to *Sharia*-compliant contracts by submitting to the courts that the structure and documentation into which they entered were not compliant with *Sharia* and, as their constitutional documents permitted them to enter into *Sharia*-compliant transactions only, the transaction in question was *ultra vires* the counterparty. While these submissions have not been upheld or otherwise remain untested due to other factors, the market has sought to introduce protections that give Islamic banks recourse in the event that such claim is made. While the drafting may not be sufficient to defeat an *ultra vires* claim were it to be considered in full by a court, it provides a degree of comfort to an Islamic bank and also an element of evidence as to the counterparty's views as at the time of entering into the facility documentation.

8. Secondary market trading of *Sharia*-compliant facilities

The conventional practice of trading debt in the secondary market at a discount to its principal amount is not something that can be applied to Islamic finance in the same manner. The issue that arises is that it is not possible for an Islamic bank to sell or buy a debt other than at par. The reason for this is that it is not possible to buy a payment stream at a discount using cash, as this would give rise to what is classed as usurious interest (the intention is obviously to recover more on the debt than the amount paid for it and such enhanced recovery would be classed as *riba*). However, Islamic banks must be able to manage their portfolios in a similar manner to conventional banks in order for them not to be at a disadvantage to the market. It is therefore possible to replicate a conventional secondary market debt trade in Islamic finance by having the purchaser of the debt deliver commodities as consideration for the purchase of the debt rather than paying cash. It is essentially a *murabaha* contract where the payment of the deferred purchase price by the bank selling its debt is satisfied by way of the transfer (or assignment) of the debt to the buyer. Such *Sharia*-compliant secondary market trading is becoming more common in the Islamic finance world and is likely to continue to do so as Islamic financial institutions begin to address the issues that will arise as a result of the COVID-19 global pandemic.

9. *Sharia*-compliant securitisation structures

As noted above, the majority of *Sharia*-compliant transactions are asset-based structures, not asset backed. *Sharia*-compliant securitisations, factoring arrangements and similar asset-backed transactions have been undertaken in the market, but these are relatively few and far between. A *Sharia*-compliant securitisation uses the techniques described above for Islamic debt trading to effect the sale of income streams: the buyer of the income stream delivers commodities as consideration for the assignment or true sale of the underlying income streams. Such transactions can be structured as bank facilities or as notes (*sukuk*), and the economics of any such deal should be the same as for a conventional securitisation. It is also possible to have a *Sharia*-compliant securitisation sit alongside one or more conventional tranches, allowing for a lot of flexibility. As the Islamic finance market continues to grow in sophistication, it is likely that such structures will become more prevalent.

10.   Intercreditor issues in Islamic finance

It is common for dual tranche conventional and *Sharia*-compliant facilities to be entered into where conventional and Islamic banks co-finance a particular asset. This is particularly common in the project finance and asset finance spaces. However, there are certain matters that must be considered in relation to certain 'common terms' that apply to all financiers. One key one is that the Islamic bank will need to recuse itself from taking part in any vote to be made by the finance parties that would involve a non-compliant action by the finance parties. Were it not to do so, the Islamic bank would need to be able to vote against any such action, which could (depending on the percentage of the total facility held by the Islamic bank) prejudice the rights of the rest of the syndicate. The Islamic bank will also have to be able to give up certain other rights that it would otherwise have by operation of law, such as the right to receive default interest – but in a way that does not prejudice the rights of the conventional banks to make such claims. Careful drafting is needed in the facility agreement (or common terms agreement) to address these issues.

11.   Hedging and risk management

As a general rule, the use of derivative instruments is not permitted by *Sharia* on the grounds that such instruments are inherently uncertain (*gharar*) and may constitute gambling (*mayseer*). However, *Sharia* does permit the managing of risk that would otherwise be faced by an Islamic financial institution. Broadly, the permitted risk management tools cover profit rate swaps, foreign exchange swaps and supply (eg, fuel) hedging. The International Swaps and Derivatives Association (ISDA) and the International Islamic Financial Market (IIFM) have together developed the *Sharia*-compliant equivalent of the ISDA Master Agreement specifically to allow for *Sharia*-compliant risk management products to be made available: the IIFM/ISDA Master *Tahawwut* Agreement. A key diligence point for a scholar to permit the entry into of such risk management products is that there must be an identifiable risk to which the product relates – for example, a variable rate *murabaha* facility must be in place for a profit rate swap to be made available – and the scholar will likely request to see a copy of that facility agreement. While *Sharia*-compliant risk management products have been controversial at times, in light of the need to avoid uncertainty in *Sharia*-compliant products, it may reasonably be concluded that in a world of variable profit rates and foreign exchange implications, such risk management products are necessary as a means to promote Islamic finance.

12.   Case law

As with conventional finance transactions, a large majority of *Sharia*-compliant facility agreements are governed by English law. Part of the reason for this is that there is a small but growing body of case law in the English courts that deals with *Sharia*-compliant transactions. The approach that the English courts have generally taken is that they will consider English law governed documents that are put before them on the basis of the principles of English contract law, notwithstanding the fact that such documents also purport to be *Sharia* compliant. The courts will not consider whether such contracts comply with *Sharia*, because *Sharia* is a matter of conscience for the parties and not something on which an English court can adjudicate.[3] Some doubt was thrown on this in *Blom Bank v TID* in 2009, where the judge, in rejecting a claim for summary judgment, suggested that the claims made by TID that it had acted *ultra vires* (on the basis that, as a *Sharia*-compliant investment company, it claimed that it had entered into a contract that was not *Sharia* compliant) could be worthy of consideration at a full trial with the use of expert evidence.[4] It should be noted that this case was only considered at a hearing for summary judgment in which the judge concluded that the case was too complicated for summary judgment to be handed down and was better suited to a full hearing. As such, no precedent has been set and the relevant parties settled the issues out of court without a full trial occurring. However, the fact that *Sharia* might be considered as part of English law proceedings caused something of a stir within the Islamic finance community. The concerns that Blom Bank might have raised were somewhat alleviated by the approach taken in the High Court in *Dana Gas*, where English contract law principles were applied to a *Sharia*-compliant instrument.[5]

13.   Conclusion

The Islamic finance market has developed at a significant pace over the past two decades and has become ever more sophisticated. As this trend continues, we expect to see more sophisticated financing structures developed and it is inevitable that a greater body of case law will also come into existence. Islamic finance professionals will also need to find new and innovative ways to keep pace with regulatory changes that impact both the Islamic finance industry in isolation and the banking sector globally.

---

3   *Shamil Bank of Bahrain v Beximco Pharmaceuticals*, [2004] EWCA Civ 19 and *Islamic Investment Company of the Gulf (Bahamas) Ltd v Symphony Gems NV* [2014] EWHC 3777 (Comm).
4   *The Investment Dar Company KSCC v Blom Developments Bank SAL* (Rev 1), [2009] EWHC 3545 (CH).
5   *Dana Gaspjsc v Dana Gas Sukuk Ltd* [2018] EWHC 277 (comm).

Project finance

Meredith Campanale
Danuta de Vries
Shri Maski
Rachel Speight
Mayer Brown

1. Introduction

Security is extremely important in project finance transactions. Classic project finance transactions are secured financing transactions in which lenders commit and provide funding to a special purpose entity ('project company' or 'borrower') to finance the development and construction or the expansion, refurbishment or redevelopment of an asset ('project'). One of the most important and unique features of a project finance transaction is that the lenders can be repaid only from the revenues generated by the completed and operating project. While the project company will, in turn, be owned (directly or indirectly) by operating entities ('sponsors') with balance sheets and assets of their own, project finance by its nature is limited recourse or non-recourse – meaning that, generally speaking, these sponsors are not obligated to support the project company.[1] Therefore, the security package for project finance transactions tends to be extremely comprehensive in order to provide the lenders with reassurance when lending into such structures.

Section 2 examines general security considerations in project finance transactions in detail. As a typical project finance transaction is single asset and involves a defined group of secured lenders, a classic project finance security package will generally be 'all asset' security, extending even to the shares that the sponsors hold in the project company. However, in practice, a security package on a project finance transaction may vary from the classic model due to several factors, including:

- the cost of taking and perfecting such security;
- whether security over a particular asset is available in the jurisdiction in question; and
- market practice for a particular sector.

---

[1] The exception being during the construction period of many types of projects, where the sponsors often provide equity support covering cost overruns or the lenders' debt service in order to support completion of the construction of the project. There may also be limited sponsor support in respect of project-specific risks that the lenders are unwilling to have allocated to the project company, although this is less common and much more limited in nature.

The general rule is that lenders in a project finance transaction will want the most comprehensive security package available.

Section 3 applies some of the general concepts to a relatively new, but increasingly significant, asset class in project finance: offshore wind. According to statistics from the International Renewable Energy Agency, at the end of 2020, global installed offshore wind capacity was more than 34 gigawatts (GW) – an approximately elevenfold increase from 2010, when it was nearly 3 GW.[2] More than 70% of this installed capacity is in Europe, including in the United Kingdom (which, at the time of writing, boasts the world's largest offshore wind farm). However, other notable jurisdictions with significant actual or proposed offshore wind programmes include Taiwan, Japan, South Korea and the United States.

Offshore wind is of interest in the context of project finance security packages for various reasons. First, offshore wind financings are approached in markedly different ways across different jurisdictions, leading to differences in the security package on offer. Second, offshore wind installations may be beyond a country's 12 nautical mile territorial sea, leading to interesting questions about, among other things, the efficacy of the lenders' security package. Finally, new developments in offshore wind turbines mean that floating installations are now possible at a commercial scale, raising questions about how lenders could obtain security over such installations and the suitability of current legal frameworks for addressing such innovations. This chapter addresses some of these questions, comparing the security package for offshore wind financings in the United Kingdom, Taiwan and the United States, and looking at some considerations regarding security for floating offshore wind (FOW).

2. Security in project finance

2.1 General remarks and principles
Security plays an important role in structuring different types of financings, including project financings, as it alters the risk profile of the transaction and gives the lenders, as secured creditors, additional benefits, including:

- increased control over the project and its assets; and
- in case of insolvency of the project company, priority over unsecured creditors and the right to appoint a receiver or an administrator (or relevant insolvency official in the jurisdiction in question).

There are several characteristics of project finance transactions which increase the significance of security in those transactions:

---

2   International Renewable Energy Agency, "Offshore renewables: An action agenda for deployment" (2021), p11.

- Special purpose entity: The project company (or borrower) is usually a special purpose entity that is distinct from the sponsor(s) and is created with the sole purpose of developing, constructing and operating a particular project. As such, the lenders cannot rely on their borrower's historical financial record, creditworthiness or other assets when assessing the transaction risk in the same manner they would in other commercial lending transactions, and will therefore rely more heavily on security provided for the funding.

- All assets security: As project lenders will be repaid only from the revenues generated by the project, it is essential that they have the means of ensuring that, in case of the project company's default, they have access to all project assets and a direct contractual relationship with the key contractual counterparties in order to be able to have the project completed and operating (and generating revenue). Project lenders will therefore seek to take security over all of the project assets (including key commercial agreements) which, if the project company defaults, will enable them to sell the project as a going concern.

- Limited assets initially: In the case of a financing of the development and construction of a project (rather than a refurbishment, redevelopment or expansion), at the time the lenders commit and make available the loans, the project company may not have any significant tangible assets. At that point, its most significant assets are likely to be its contractual rights arising under the concession/licence, construction contracts, offtake/sales contracts, insurance contracts and other contracts then in place that are material to the project. Lenders to the project company are essentially funding a promise that the project will be built as planned and contracted for, and there will be no revenues to repay the loans until the project is constructed. Lenders will therefore want to ensure that, in case of the project company's failure to complete the project, the project company's contractual rights will be available and exercisable by them, so that upon enforcement they can exercise control over the arrangements necessary for the project to be built.

It is also important to reflect on the role of the sponsor in project finance transactions. The sponsor is the driving force behind the project, arranging financing for it and, in the process, building relationships and trust with the potential project lenders. The sponsor may also play other important roles in the project, such as providing key technology or operation and maintenance services or acting as an offtaker. The lenders want to ensure that the sponsor remains committed to the project. This is achieved by requiring the sponsor to provide one, or a combination, of:

- equity funding for an agreed portion of the construction/development costs (often required to be spent before any loan proceeds can be utilised);

- project completion support, which may take the form of equity support for cost overruns or an undertaking to contribute equity to pay the lenders' debt service;
- undertakings from the sponsor regarding share retention; and
- security over the sponsor's interest (direct or indirect) in the project company.

While, as its name suggests, project completion support falls away once the project is completed, share retention requirements often extend well beyond project completion,[3] depending on how integral to the success of the project the sponsors' tacit support and involvement is considered to be. In addition, the loan documents usually provide that failure of the sponsor to comply with any of its undertakings is an event of default. All these mechanisms are designed to ensure the sponsor's long-term commitment to the project.

2.2   Taking security – considerations

The parties will wish to bear in mind the following points when taking security in project finance transactions.

(a)   *International project finance transactions*

Many project finance transactions are cross-border transactions involving multiple jurisdictions. The following facts must be taken into consideration and will affect the structuring of the project finance transaction and the security package:

- the location of the project, the project company, the sponsor, the lenders, the contractors and the offtakers;
- the governing law of the project and finance documents; and
- the location of assets to be secured (eg, plant and equipment, bank accounts).

Due diligence must be undertaken (enlisting the help of local counsel) in order to determine, in relation to each relevant jurisdiction, among other things:

- the types of security available under local law;
- the way in which such security must be held (including whether the concept of a security trust is recognised);

---

3   Where there is more than one sponsor, share retention undertakings may apply only to the 'key' shareholder (eg, a shareholder providing technology or taking the project's product through an offtake arrangement or one whose reputation and involvement lends weight to the project). Also, sponsor share retention requirements may step down over time, meaning that initially all share transfers may be prohibited, but eventually the sponsor may be permitted to sell an agreed percentage of its ownership interest in the project company. This is the subject of negotiation on a case-by-case basis for each project.

- any drafting and execution formalities (eg, notarisations, translations);
- perfection steps for each type of security; and
- any registrations, filing and consents required under local law and enforcement rights and processes.

Most civil law jurisdictions do not recognise or have the concept of a security trust; in such jurisdictions, either a 'parallel debt' structure is utilised or security must be granted in favour of all the lenders. It is common in international project finance transactions to have 'onshore' security instruments governed by the laws of the location of the project and 'offshore' security instruments governed by other relevant laws (eg, providing security over the project company's bank accounts located abroad or its rights under project agreements or insurances governed by foreign law).

(b) Cost/benefit analysis

As mentioned above, as a matter of principle, project lenders typically seek to take security over all or substantially all of the assets of the project company. However, when structuring the required security package, a number of practical factors need to be considered, including:

- the ability as a matter of law to create security over a particular asset in the jurisdiction in question;
- the time and cost of creating and perfecting each security interest (eg, registration fees, notarisation costs, stamp duty);
- the nature of the security and its practicality (eg, a possessory security interest which requires a transfer of possession of the secured assets to the security holder is unlikely to be workable, as a high level of control over an asset might force the lenders to be involved in commercial decision-making processes);
- the effectiveness of each type of security (including whether it is registrable), and the complexity and timing of the applicable enforcement process; and
- market practice in the jurisdiction or sector in question.

On the basis of the above, the project lenders might conclude that a 'full security package' is not available, is not the best option or does not provide the best value to them. They may decide to forgo security over some project assets and, instead, request other assurances or risk mitigants from the project company and/or the sponsor (eg, increased fees or interest, sponsor support).

(c) Multiple assets lead to multiple security interests

Project financings by their nature are complex and involve many different assets. These include, most typically:

- the project site (including land, buildings and fixtures);
- various movable assets (eg, equipment, raw materials, any unsold production from the project);
- cash balances in bank accounts;
- the project company's contractual rights (eg, under the concession/ licence, construction contracts, feedstock supply agreements, sales contracts, consents and permits, insurance policies); and
- any IP rights relating to the project.

The type of asset involved will determine the type of security used. Under English law, the traditional debenture is a convenient, standalone instrument which allows lenders to create:

- a mortgage over land;
- fixed and floating charges over other assets; and
- security assignments over contractual rights and other choses in action.

In many other jurisdictions – particularly civil law jurisdictions – different types of assets require different types of security to be created and separate security agreements to be entered into with respect to different types of assets or the same type of assets but with different characteristics (eg, contractual rights involving different counterparties). Different perfection requirements apply to different types of security. Registration of security – in particular relating to international financings – frequently requires translations, notarisations and apostilles in relation to the security documents. For this reason, in international financings in jurisdictions where a solution akin to the English law debenture is not available, lenders often undertake a cost/benefit analysis (referred to above) in relation to structuring the security package.

2.3 Typical security package in project finance transactions

A typical security package in a project finance transaction covers the following key asset classes.

(a) *Shares in the project company (and, where applicable, its holding company) and rights attached to such shares*

Security over shares and the rights attached to such shares (eg, the right to receive dividends) is typically granted in many secured transactions and is not much different in the project finance context. The security is granted under the law of the jurisdiction of incorporation of the project company. Share security owes its popularity to the fact that, in theory, it is easier and quicker to enforce security over shares rather than individual assets, giving lenders immediate control over the management of the project company and its assets. It also serves a defensive purpose by deterring other potential creditors of the project company.

Additionally, share security is a way of ensuring the sponsor's commitment to the project as it prevents the sponsor from disposing of its interest in the project, whether held directly or indirectly through a holding company. However, in the context of a project finance transaction, there may be additional considerations that lenders need to consider. For example, the host government:

- may be heavily involved in regulating the sector in question due to its critical importance as a matter of national security;
- may actually own the resources that the project company is exploiting (eg, power, oil and gas, minerals); or
- may own the land on which the project is situated.

The transfer of shares in the project company may be restricted under the terms of the project concession/licence granted by the government or related laws or regulations and, as a result, the creation and/or enforcement of security over such shares often requires consent from or an arrangement with the governmental concession/licencing authority (see section 2.4(a)).

(b) **Land and immovable assets (eg, buildings (plant), fixtures)**
As in many other types of secured transactions, in project finance transactions, security is granted over the project site in which the project company has an ownership or other interest or rights and which is essential to the construction and operation of the project. In most jurisdictions, mortgages or comparable forms of security over land and other fixed assets require the most formal legal instruments and are subject to perfection by registration in the local land registry. In many countries, such registration must be completed at the land registry local to the project site, which might mean a difficult-to-reach destination in the case of remotely located projects.

(c) **Movable project assets (eg, equipment, supplies, unsold production)**
Although this is one of the most common asset classes to be secured, it often presents challenges in cross-border transactions, particularly where:

- under the applicable law, movable assets can be secured only by way of a possessory pledge or similar instrument;
- local law does not provide for floating charges or equivalent security arrangements; or
- security over after-acquired property cannot be taken at the outset of a transaction.

(d) **Bank accounts**
In project finance transactions, security over bank accounts – both onshore and offshore – is a critical part of the lenders' security package, as loan repayment is reliant on cash flows from the particular project in question. Account security

forms part of a broader regime of account controls imposed by the lenders. Lenders to a project finance transaction require full visibility regarding the cash flows of the project company and institute detailed restrictions over how and when loan proceeds and revenues generated by the project are utilised. While, in theory, the cash flows of a single-asset project company with a defined group of lenders should be fairly straightforward to delineate, because of the high degree of control required by the lenders, the project accounts structure is often extensive and complex – especially when offshore and onshore bank accounts and sub-accounts denominated in different currencies are involved. In project finance transactions, in addition to accounts often seen in a secured financing (eg, proceeds/revenues account, debt service reserve account, distribution account), additional project accounts might be opened such as:

- a loan disbursement account;
- an equity contribution account;
- an insurance and compensation proceeds account; and
- reserve accounts for significant lump-sum expenditures (eg, major maintenance, taxes).

The project company is usually prohibited from opening other bank accounts without the consent of the lenders and from granting security over any such new bank accounts. The account banks holding the project accounts are typically required to acknowledge the security interest of the lenders in the accounts and undertake to follow the lenders' instructions in case of the project company's default. It is common in project finance transactions to put in place account agreements between the lenders (represented by the facility agent and/or the security trustee), the project company and the account bank(s) to regulate the specific purpose and operation of each bank account. (An account bank typically does not agree to take any responsibility for ensuring that such restrictions are complied with, but will agree to cooperate with the facility agent or security trustee after the account bank is notified of a default or event of default under the financing).

(e)   *(Key) contractual rights*
The project company is party to a wide variety of contractual arrangements that project lenders will seek to have security over, particularly where those agreements are key agreements without which the project cannot be completed or are key to operation and revenue generation. The key agreements, often referred to as 'material project documents', typically include the following:

- the concession/licence agreement and any other key licences, consents and permits;
- construction contracts (including any contractor performance security or parent company guarantees);

- operating/management contracts (eg, performance guarantees, spare parts);
- feedstock and utility supply contracts (pre- and post-completion, including electricity, water, raw materials);
- offtake/sale contracts or tolling agreements;
- insurance and reinsurance contracts;
- intercompany or shareholder loan payment rights; and
- hedging contracts.

Security over the contractual rights of the project company under the above contracts generally follows the law governing the relevant contract. Depending on the applicable law, an assignment by way of security, cession, pledge or another type of charge is created over the contractual rights in favour of the lenders (represented, where possible, by a security trustee). Perfection requirements usually involve notification of the counterparty of the security interest. Figure 1 shows a simplified example of the contractual arrangements between the parties to a project finance transaction.

Figure 1. Project finance parties and contractual arrangements

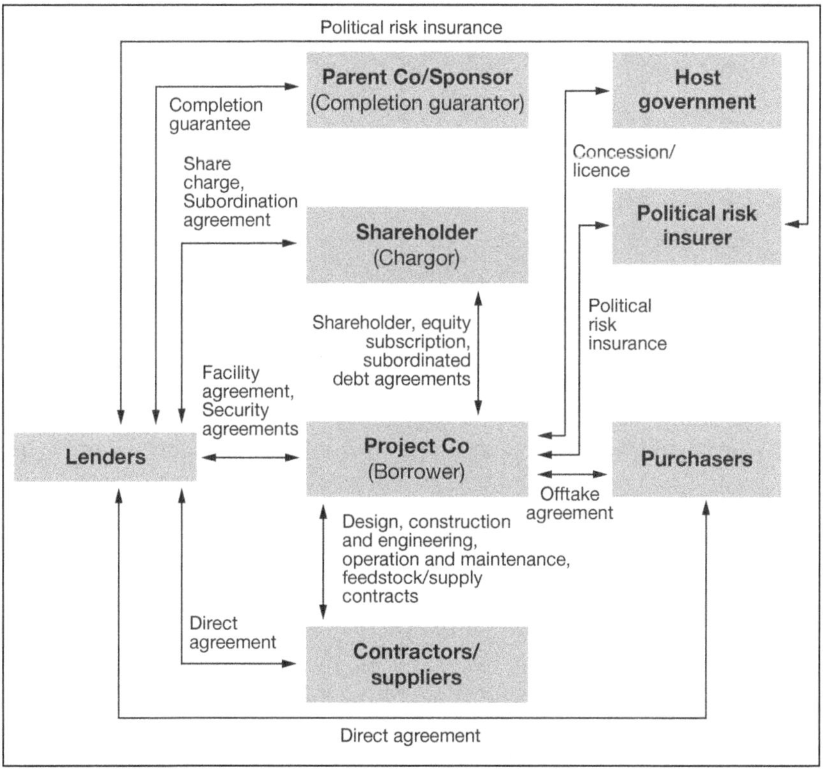

2.4   Special points of note in security for project finance transactions

Certain features of the security package for project finance transactions as described above merit further elaboration; as does the role of the so-called 'direct agreement' – quasi-security that is an important feature of project finance transactions and that is distinct from other categories of secured finance transactions.

(a)   Concession/licence and related agreement with the host government

Project lenders typically want to secure what is arguably the most important asset of the project company: the concession/licence rights. The rights and obligations of the project company under a concession/licence are set out in:

- an agreement with the host government;
- applicable host government laws and regulations; or
- occasionally, a specific legislative act where awarding a concession/licence requires the host government's parliamentary approval.

Local law and the terms of the concession/licence will determine whether security in favour of the lenders over the rights of the project company under the concession/licence can be granted. Accordingly, experienced or well-advised sponsors try to ensure, at the licence awarding stage, that the terms of the concession/licence expressly anticipate future project financings and the possibility of granting some form of security over the project company's rights to future project lenders. The government often reserves consent rights either in relation to the granting by the project company of security or in relation to the enforcement of such security by project lenders – in both cases with the intention of ensuring that the concession/licence rights, if transferred away from the project company, go to a qualified and eligible entity, capable of constructing and/or operating the project in accordance with the terms of the concession/licence and meeting all other obligations set out in the concession/licence.

Where obtaining a security interest is not possible, the lenders will look to obtain from the host government some other form of assurance that the project – even when transferred to a new owner – will continue to benefit from the concession/licence and associated government support. To achieve this, the lenders may ask the host government either to:

- enter into a tripartite agreement with the lenders and the project company; or
- issue an acknowledgement or a comfort letter confirming to the lenders that:
  - the concession/licence will not be terminated if the project company defaults or breaches the terms of the concession licence; and
  - the lenders will be given the opportunity to cure any breaches of the

project company before the government takes any action towards terminating the concession/licence or otherwise withdrawing its support for the project.

(b)   Assignment of reinsurances

Insurance policies are an important and mandatory element of every project finance transaction. It is in the interests of the sponsor and the project company to put in place adequate and robust insurance to cover any losses that the project company may suffer during the construction phase and the operating phase of the project. Additionally, lenders will not commit to the financing unless and until an adequate and robust insurance package has been arranged in relation to the project, and will expect this to be confirmed by a specialist insurance adviser as a condition precedent to disbursing any funds under any loan facilities. (The sponsor/project company's views and the lenders' views on the adequacy and robustness of the proposed cover often diverge, and so the insurance package is often the subject of lengthy negotiation, particularly given the potentially significant cost implications associated with such insurances.) Given the large insured amounts, the lenders will expect the insurances to be underwritten by reputable major international insurance companies. This is not always possible. In many jurisdictions, local law requires that domestic insurers provide insurance for local enterprises. In such circumstances, it is common for local insurances to be reinsured by reputable major international insurance companies.[4] When looking to take security over project insurances, project lenders must look to take security over the primary insurances as well as the reinsurances. While the rights under the primary insurances may be easily secured/assigned by the project company (the insured and the borrower) in favour of the lenders under a general or specific assignment or pledge of insurance rights, taking security over the rights under the reinsurances is more complicated, as the reinsured party entitled to the rights under the reinsurances is the insurer providing the primary insurances (rather than the project company), which is a third party as far as the project financing is concerned. There are at least two ways in which security over insurances and reinsurances may be taken:

- The primary insurer assigns it rights under the reinsurances to the lenders (either with or without the project company being a party to the assignment agreement) and, as a perfection measure, notifies the reinsurers of the assignment requesting their acknowledgment of the

---

4   Lenders do not wish to rely on the local insurances for these projects. The local insurance market in the jurisdiction in question may not have sufficient underwriting capacity to adequately insure a multimillion or even multibillion-dollar project. Additionally, local insurers may not have a recognised international rating (or be rated at all). For the lenders, this calls into question the value of the local insurances. For this reason, lenders usually insist on international reinsurances. (Often local insurers procure international reinsurances as well.)

same, including an undertaking to pay any reinsurance proceeds directly to the lenders after they are notified that a default has occurred under the project financing; or

- The primary insurer assigns its rights under the reinsurances to the project company, which then further assigns those rights to the lenders alongside the rights of the project company under the primary insurances. The reinsurers here are also notified and asked to acknowledge the assignment of the rights under the reinsurances.

Both structures described above have been used in project finance transactions. The second structure permits the parties to overcome any restrictions to which the primary insurer may be subject that prevent it from granting security over its own assets and rights to secure a third party's (ie, the project company's) debt obligations.

(c) *Direct agreements/tripartite agreements as quasi-security*
Given the importance of the contractual arrangements of the project company, in addition to security assignments of the project company's contractual rights, it is common for lenders in project finance transactions to enter into tripartite agreements with the project company (and occasionally the sponsor) and each counterparty to a project agreement. The purpose of these agreements is threefold:

- to stop the counterparty from terminating or suspending its obligations under the relevant project agreement in the event of a default or breach by the project company of its obligations towards the counterparty;
- to give the lenders notice of any default of the project company and the right to 'step in' and cure such default in its place in order to ensure the continuance of the contract performance by the counterparty (and subsequently to 'step out') or to permanently transfer the contract from the project company to a substitute; and
- to have the counterparty acknowledge and agree to the security granted by the project company to the lenders over the project company's rights under the relevant project agreement.

These are crucial arrangements for the lenders. As the lenders' repayment depends on the project being completed and operating, the lenders will be compelled to ensure that any termination or suspension event under the project agreements is avoided, and will take measures to ensure that any defaults on the project company's part that would trigger the termination or suspension of the project agreement are remedied. In many cases, the defaults will relate to non-payment, so should be relatively easy to remedy. There may, however, be instances where the project company must be replaced. Figure 2 shows an

Figure 2. Direct agreement mechanics

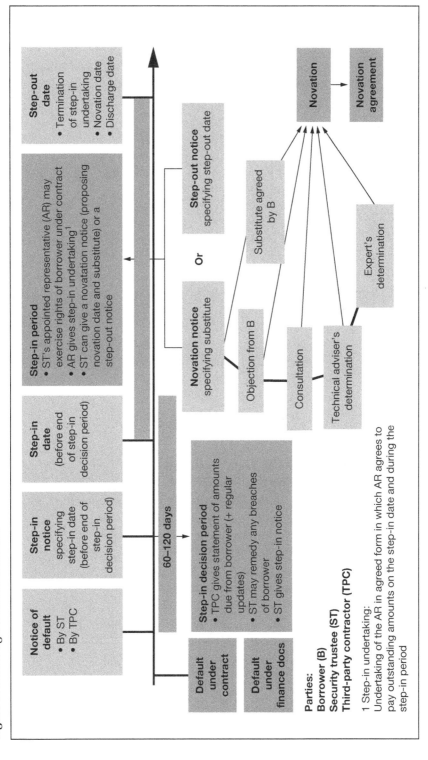

example of the mechanics of a direct agreement, although different types of underlying contracts might require different mechanics and a modified approach.

3. Security in offshore wind financings

This section looks at offshore wind and considers the security package commonly provided across three jurisdictions: the United Kingdom, Taiwan and the United States. As noted in the introduction to this chapter, offshore wind projects are a relatively new, but increasingly significant, asset class in project finance. The United Kingdom, Taiwan and the United States either have developed significant offshore wind programmes or are looking to do so. As noted above, even within a single project finance sector, the security package for a project finance transaction will differ depending on the jurisdiction in which the project is being constructed. A comparison of the offshore wind security package in these three jurisdictions illustrates this point.

3.1 Security in UK offshore wind financings

The UK offshore wind market has been active since the first demonstration project was commissioned in 2000 and the Crown Estate announced the Round 1 awards of the offshore wind development sites in 2001.[5] This market is actually several jurisdictions in one (England, Wales and Northern Ireland, managed by the Crown Estate; and Scotland, managed by the Crown Estate Scotland), although the security regimes for offshore wind project financings in these jurisdictions generally follow similar patterns.

This section examines the security package that is usually provided to the lenders in the limited recourse financing of an offshore wind project in the United Kingdom. A number of offshore wind projects in the United Kingdom have been financed on balance sheet (with full recourse) or are holdco financings (utilised where there are multiple sponsors and one sponsor does not wish to utilise project finance as a source of funding). This section discusses only project financings with debt at the project company level and security over project assets.

(a) Typical security package

Generally speaking, provided that the offshore wind assets are located within the United Kingdom's 12 nautical mile territorial sea, a classic project financing structure, with a classic project finance security package, is available in UK offshore wind financings. This consists of 'all asset' security provided under a debenture, including:

- a share charge;

---

5   Reuters, "Timeline: Development of UK offshore wind" (23 September 2010), www.reuters.com/article/us-britain-offshorewind-timeline-idUKTRE68M11L20100923.

- an assignment of key project agreements (including the various contracts forming the construction package, the power purchase agreement (PPA) and any related credit support, the contract for difference (CfD),[6] the operations and maintenance contract, the shareholders' agreement/joint venture agreement and any hedging agreements), licences and insurances;
- a mortgage over the lease with the Crown Estate or Crown Estate Scotland (as the case may be);
- a charge over bank accounts and investments;
- security over physical assets (noting that security over materials and equipment, including the turbines, will be by way of a floating charge only);
- an assignment of the project company's rights in respect of equity contributions and any subordinated loans;
- security over other assets such as intellectual property, book debts, intangibles and goodwill; and
- a floating charge over all its assets.

Security over any bilateral connection agreement with National Grid is available in theory, but may not be provided; and security in the UK offshore wind context is further complicated by the offshore transmission owner (OFTO) regime, described below.

There are some additional considerations in relation to UK offshore wind security packages. First, as noted above, a typical project finance security package is available only if the offshore wind farm is located within the United Kingdom's 12 nautical mile territorial sea. If the project is outside of these limits, then security may still be taken over project assets such as materials and equipment; however, such security will be by way of a floating charge only and is consequently unable to be registered and perfected. Lenders will also still be able to have security over 'onshore' assets such as bank accounts, contracts and insurances.

Second, as the UK market is relatively mature, many projects are structured on a 'merchant' basis, meaning that there is no long-term PPA. In that case, lenders will wish to have security over whatever instruments provide the project with its route to market – whether:
- a series of short-term PPAs;
- a trading services agreement with an energy trader which will sell the electricity produced by the project through derivatives instruments; or
- industry standard master trading agreements.

---

6   The CfD is the key government support mechanism potentially available to offshore wind projects in the United Kingdom. A CfD is a contract entered into between the generator and the Low Carbon Contracts Company (a state-owned company that manages such contracts on behalf of the government). The CfD essentially acts as a price hedge and the generator is still required to enter into arrangements to sell electricity generated.

Lenders will want security over any CfD arrangements as well.

Third, the UK OFTO regime, which governs the construction and ownership of offshore transmission assets, must be factored into the security structure. The OFTO regime has several different models;[7] in the 'generator build' model most frequently used, the developer of the applicable offshore wind generation project is responsible for carrying out the development, design, financing and construction of the relevant offshore transmission assets. Following construction, these assets are then sold by way of a competitive tender process to an unrelated entity, which operates, maintains and ultimately decommissions those assets. The transmission assets may form part of a general project financing of the project assets or be financed by the generator on balance sheet. If initially project financed, these assets will form part of the project security package provided by the project company to its lenders. However, appropriate provision will need to be made in the financing documentation for such assets to be released from the security upon their sale to the OFTO.

Overall, apart from the specific nuances described above, security in a project company-level project financing in the UK offshore wind sector is not dissimilar from security over a conventional independent power project. The decade of successful project financings in this sector – which shows no sign of abating – attests to the comfort of the lenders operating in this space.

3.2 Security in Taiwanese offshore wind financings

Although Asia is generally considered to lag behind Europe in including offshore wind in its energy mix, Taiwan stands out as a stellar exception. The Taiwanese government has an ambitious programme to harness Taiwan's offshore wind potential, with a target of 15GW of offshore wind energy generation by the end of 2035. The rapid expansion of the Taiwanese offshore wind market – combined with a more investor-friendly regulatory landscape compared to other Asian jurisdictions and the abundance of wind resource in the Taiwan Strait – has attracted a number of international developers,[8] financiers and export credit agencies.[9] However, financing structures for

---

7   The two permissible models provided for in the Electricity (Competitive Tenders for Offshore Transmission Licences) Regulations 2015 are:
   • the 'generator build' model, where the generator develops, designs, finances and constructs the offshore transmission assets, before selling them to the OFTO; and
   • the 'OFTO build' framework, where different tender options are permitted to enable the OFTO and generator to have greater or lesser degrees of control over the procurement, construction and management of the offshore transmission connection.
   The key underlying principle of the OFTO framework (whichever option is selected) is that the OFTO is responsible for constructing and financing the construction of the offshore transmission system.
8   Including Copenhagen Infrastructure Partners, JERA, Orsted, Swancor Renewables and wpd.
9   Atradius, Credendo, Eksport Credit Fonden (EKF), Euler Hermes, Eksfin – Export Finance Norway (formerly GIEK), Export-Import Bank of Korea (KEXIM), Korea Trade Insurance Corporation (K-Sure), KfW, Nippon Export and Investment Insurance (NEXI) and UK Export Finance (UKEF) have all provided financing (or financing cover) for Taiwanese offshore wind projects that are currently under development.

Taiwanese offshore wind projects are still evolving. Some of the earlier projects[10] were financed entirely through equity, but limited recourse financing is becoming increasingly common.[11]

This section examines the security package that is usually provided to the lenders in the limited recourse financing of an offshore wind project in Taiwan. Limited recourse financing structures for Taiwanese offshore wind farms tend to be fairly typical, consisting of a Taiwanese special purpose project vehicle – usually a company which is a wholly owned subsidiary of either an offshore holding company or a Taiwanese holding company. The project company:

- obtains all the permits and licences required to develop the wind farm;
- executes a PPA with Taipower; and
- enters into arrangements for constructing, operating and financing the project.

Like most civil law systems, Taiwanese law does not recognise the concept of a floating charge or lien.[12] Thus, the comprehensive 'all assets' security package which is usual in common law jurisdictions cannot be provided in Taiwanese offshore wind financings.[13] It is also not certain whether security over future property can be granted under Taiwanese law and, consequently, the assets sought to be secured will need to exist at the time the security is taken to avoid enforceability risk.[14] Consistent with the approach in other civil law jurisdictions, the project company will provide undertakings in the financing documents to periodically notify all newly acquired assets to the lenders or their security agent and execute all documents necessary for creating and perfecting security over those assets. The security available to the lenders in Taiwanese offshore wind financings is, therefore, much more limited compared to projects in common law jurisdictions and, as is typical in cross-border project financings, comprises onshore and offshore security.

(a) *Onshore security*

Secured assets: The onshore security package (governed by Taiwanese law) includes:

- pledges over the project company's (and holding company's)[15] shares and the project accounts;[16]

---

10   Phase 1 of the Formosa 1 offshore wind farm.
11   Formosa 2, Chang Fang and Xidao offshore wind farms.
12   Hsin-Lan Hsu, Lee and Li, Attorneys-at-Law, *Lending and Taking Security in Taiwan: Overview* (Practical Law).
13   Lee and Li Attorneys at Law, *The Lending and Secured Finance Review*, edition 5, "Credit support and subordination in Taiwan".
14   Hsu (n 12).
15   If it is a Taiwanese entity.
16   All the project accounts are typically onshore.

- assignment of the project company's (and holding company's) rights under the equity documents, the project agreements[17] and the project insurances;
- chattel mortgages over the project company's movable assets such as materials and equipment;
- mortgages over real property; and
- a security power of attorney.[18]

Lenders will usually consider a number of issues in relation to the onshore security package, including the following.

Hardening periods: All security governed by Taiwanese law is subject to a six-month hardening period.[19] As insolvency risk cannot be avoided, adequate mitigation will need to be included in the financing documentation, such as restrictions on transfers of assets or requiring appropriate representations, warranties and undertakings from the security providers.

Land mortgage: The land/seabed to which the turbines are attached is not typically subject to a mortgage in favour of the lenders, as the project company is only granted rights to install turbines, sea cables and other equipment on the seabed as part of the permitting process, but does not have a proprietary transferable interest in the land. This is similar to the position in offshore wind projects in other jurisdictions, but may differ from some of the UK nearshore wind farms,[20] where the Crown Estate's leases over the wind farm sites have been granted to the project companies. The project company will, however, have a proprietary interest in the land and buildings it will lease for onshore facilities, including onshore cabling, onshore substations and port facilities for both installation and maintenance. The project company's leasehold interests in these facilities can be mortgaged in favour of the lenders.

Security/step-in rights over certain project agreements: Taiwanese government entities have hitherto been reluctant to allow project companies to grant security or step-in rights to their lenders over certain project agreements to which such entities are a party, although Taipower has agreed to limited step-in rights with respect to the PPA in recent offshore wind farm projects.[21] The security power of

---

17   To the extent these are governed by Taiwanese law.
18   This is consistent with the approach in project financings in jurisdictions which do not enforce lender step-in rights.
19   Cheng-Chieh Huang (James), Maggie Huang and Andrea Chen, Lee and Li, Attorneys-at-Law, *Restructuring and Insolvency in Taiwan: Overview* (Practical Law).
20   For example, Dudgeon and Westermost Rough.
21   An interview with Lee and Li Attorneys at Law discussing project finance in Taiwan, Lexology, April 9, 2021.

attorney referred to above could mitigate some of the risk arising from the absence of comprehensive security and step-in rights over the project agreements with Taiwanese government entities. Pursuant to the security power of attorney, lenders would be able to act on behalf of the project company (including exercise its rights and perform its obligations under the relevant documents) in certain circumstances, such as where a default has occurred and is continuing.

Security over (and step-in rights with respect to) other Taiwanese law governed documentation to which Taiwanese government entities are not party can, of course, be granted.

Holding company share pledge: There is no uniform position on the pledge over the holding company's shares. Some offshore wind financings in Taiwan have featured security over shares of the holding company; others have not. This will ultimately depend on the corporate structure adopted by the sponsors; but it would be prudent for lenders to take security over the holding company's shares, especially if it is a party to any project agreements and particularly with any Taiwanese government entities. Lenders would be at risk if they did not have control of the holding company in circumstances in which they had enforced their pledge over the project company's shares and thus acquired control of the project company.

Enforcement: For the most part, Taiwanese law allows holders of security considerable flexibility to enforce their security. Thus, pledges (including pledges over shares or bank accounts), assignments and chattel mortgages governed by Taiwanese law may be enforced by both judicial and non-judicial means. In other words, self-help remedies will be available under Taiwanese law to enforce:
- the pledges over the project company's (and holding company's) shares;
- the pledges over the project accounts;
- the security assignments; and
- the chattel mortgages.

The only exception appears to be mortgages of land or immovable property, which can be enforced solely through a judicial process.[22]

(b) Offshore security package
The offshore security package is usually governed by the laws of a common law jurisdiction such as England, Hong Kong or Singapore (as may be relevant), and consists of:

---

22   Hsu (n 12).

- fixed security (by way of assignment and fixed charge) over:
  - the project reinsurances;
  - the project company's rights under the agreements which are not governed by Taiwanese law – such agreements would be expected to include:
    - the construction, supply and O&M arrangements, including any bonds, parent company guarantees or sureties provided thereunder;
    - the hedging arrangements entered into to manage interest rate, foreign currency or other economic risks;
    - the equity contribution and subordination arrangements; and
  - the holding company's shares, if it is an offshore entity; and
- floating security over all of the project company's present and future assets.

Taiwan is, and is expected to remain, perhaps the most attractive Asian market for offshore wind for the foreseeable future. Several offshore wind projects in Taiwan have already obtained limited recourse financing and are currently under construction. The security package described above should – in theory at least – provide the project lenders with comfort that they have both the ability and the flexibility to take enforcement action to protect their interests should they choose to. Taiwan, however, does not have an established track record of cross-border limited recourse financings; and although it has a well-developed judicial system, the ability of the Taiwanese courts to understand and enforce complex financing and security arrangements is largely untested.

3.3 Security in US offshore wind financings

The US offshore wind market is still nascent. At the time of writing, only one commercial-scale offshore wind farm – the Vineyard Wind project – has been approved and has reached financial close. Therefore, the market standard for security in US offshore wind financings is still to be established. Nevertheless, given current US energy policy, many more US offshore wind projects are expected to move ahead in the next few years, and the capital-intensive nature of such projects will bring with them large financings involving a significant security package.

(a) Tax equity financing

The security package that will be available to financiers and the mechanisms of its enforcement will be dictated by the nature of the financing provided. The US model for renewables financings typically involves so-called 'tax equity' financing – explained in more detail below – which brings with it an established security regime with parameters dictated to a significant extent by the US federal tax code. Absent major changes to the US federal tax code,[23] tax equity financing is expected to play a significant role in US offshore wind financings in the way that it does in US onshore renewables financings.

In its simplest terms, US tax equity financing is a form of holdco financing. Project sponsors use tax equity financing in cases where they do not have sufficient US taxable income to utilise the substantial tax benefits accruing to renewables projects under US tax law, including tax credits and accelerated depreciation. In the most common tax equity financing structure – the so-called 'partnership flip' model[24] – the project sponsor ('cash equity member') forms a partnership ('tax equity partnership') with a number of financiers ('tax equity investors'). The tax equity investors are generally large banks or insurance companies which can make use of the tax credits available to the project. Through the tax equity partnership, tax equity investors are seeking an agreed internal rate of return in exchange for the monetisation of their tax benefits. The tax equity partnership – generally a limited liability company or a limited liability partnership – is a holdco that owns the project company, which in turn owns the project assets. Debt to finance the project will generally consist of a construction loan at the project company level for the duration of the construction period, to be taken out by the tax equity investors' investment (along with cash equity) and often partial conversion into debt of the cash equity member (ie, of the project sponsor) that is structurally subordinated to the tax equity. (See Figure 3 on the next page.) In certain renewables financings, there may also be hedging debt at the project company level; however, we generally expect that US offshore wind projects, at least initially, will be financed on the basis of a long-term PPA with a creditworthy utility or offtaker and therefore will not have hedging debt. Generally speaking, tax equity will not accept being in a structurally subordinated position to debt, but exceptions are made for construction debt and hedging debt, subject to certain restrictions described below.

(b)   Typical tax equity security package

A typical security package in a US offshore wind tax equity financing will likely consist of the following:[25]

- during the construction period, liens in favour of the construction lenders over all assets of the project company; and
- after the construction period, liens in favour of the back-leverage lenders

---

23   See the discussion in section 3.3(c) below.
24   There are other tax equity financing structures, such as sale-leasebacks and inverted leases, but the partnership flip structure is the most common because the banks that do most tax equity investing are most comfortable with this structure.
25   Liens in favour of the hedging provider over project assets (the extent and ranking of which is subject to intense negotiation) are also a common feature of certain renewables financings in the US market. However, as noted above, we do not expect hedging debt at the project company level to be a feature of US offshore wind financings.

Figure 3. Tax equity 'partnership flip' structure

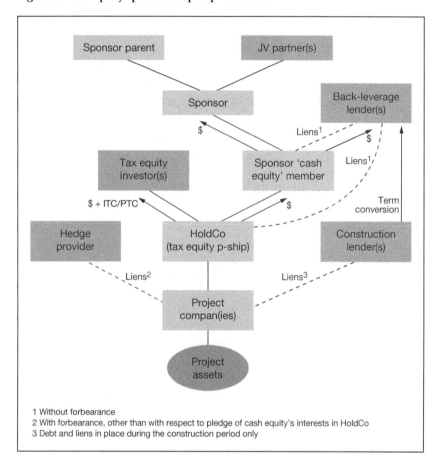

1 Without forbearance
2 With forbearance, other than with respect to pledge of cash equity's interests in HoldCo
3 Debt and liens in place during the construction period only

over all assets of the cash equity member, such assets primarily consisting of the cash equity member's interest in the tax equity partnership (including dividends and voting rights).

Under the US federal investment tax credit regime,[26] the US federal government can 'recapture' previously claimed but unvested tax credits if the taxpayer (ie, the cash equity or tax equity owner of the project) sells or

---

26   US offshore wind projects are eligible for two forms of US federal tax credits:
   • the investment tax credit (ITC) model, where the tax credits available in relation to the tax equity investment vest upfront; and
   • the production tax credit (PTC) model, where the tax credits available in relation to the tax equity investment vest as the project is placed into service and operates over time.
   Although potentially eligible for both kinds of credits, it is anticipated that, given the high capital expenditures necessary for the development and construction of such projects (as well as the phase-out of the PTC for wind projects starting construction after 2021), such projects will elect the ITC model. However, a full discussion of the ITC and PTC models is beyond the scope of this chapter.

otherwise disposes of the energy property or stops using it in a manner that qualifies for the tax credit within the five-year vesting period[27] (known as the 'recapture period'). This has led to a typical feature of tax equity deals called 'forbearance' whereby, following the construction period,[28] entities with liens on the project's assets or on the project company's membership or other company interests as collateral (commonly, only hedge providers)[29] agree for the duration of the recapture period not to enforce on the security except in certain limited and agreed circumstances. (It is often the case that such a lienholder will also have a pledge over the interests of the cash equity investor's interest in the tax equity partnership, and the lienholder may foreclose on those interests at any time without forbearance.) Upon the expiry of the recapture period, a lienholder is customarily free to exercise remedies with respect to any collateral, including by foreclosing on the project assets or on any holdco interests in the project company. In contrast, back-leverage debt is structurally subordinated and thus will not directly affect the assets being funded by the tax equity; therefore, the liens provided to the back-leverage lenders are not subject to forbearance.

(c)   *Non-tax equity security package*

The security regime will look different where tax equity financing is not utilised. Sponsor-developers may elect to forgo tax equity financing where their taxable income is sufficient to support the use of the tax benefits themselves or where they choose not to utilise such tax benefits.[30] Additionally, from time to time, draft US federal tax legislation is proposed[31] that calls for the adoption of a 'direct pay' system that would modify the current tax credit payment system. A direct pay system could be structured in various ways. However, in one variation, the tax credit would be treated like a deemed tax payment by the sponsor-developer, enabling that sponsor-developer to claim an overpayment or refund in the amount by which the deemed tax payment exceeds its tax liability (thereby enabling sponsor-developers with insufficient taxable income

---

27   While the ITC may be realised entirely in the first year of a project's commercial operation, it vests rateably over a period of five years.

28   During the construction period, securing forbearance by the construction lenders is not a significant concern, because the US federal tax credits arise at the time of substantial completion of the project (and therefore there is nothing to recapture until such time). Tax equity and construction lenders typically agree that, prior to substantial completion, construction lenders may enforce on the project security provided that tax equity investors' interests are bought out in connection with the enforcement process.

29   However, as noted in section 3.3(a) above, commodity hedging is unlikely to be relevant initially for offshore wind projects. Much more rarely, liens at the project asset or project company membership level may be granted to debt holders higher in the structure, although this is likely to be for deal-specific commercial reasons.

30   However, given the high levels of capital expenditure that will likely be necessary for US offshore wind projects and the very large tax credits that this would generate, sponsor-developers may feel that forgoing tax equity as a source of liquidity would be disadvantageous.

31   Most recently the Build Back Better Act (HR 5376), passed by the US House of Representatives in November 2021, but at the time of writing, stalled by political disagreement among Democrats in the US Senate.

to directly claim the credit rather than monetising it through tax equity financing).[32] In these cases, the absence of tax equity and its concerns about structural subordination and recapture means that a more classic project finance structure, with project company debt and a comprehensive 'all asset' security package over project assets, would likely be utilised.

Security in financings in the US offshore wind market where tax equity financing is employed will likely pose challenges for sponsors-developers and lenders alike. All indications are that non-US sponsor-developers and lenders will play a major role in the development of this market and the first generation of US offshore wind projects. The US tax equity financing and security structure will be new to these participants and contains some features that will require non-US lenders to rethink their customary security protections and potential enforcement routes. However, given the tremendous potential of the US market and capital's need for green investments, many non-US sponsors and lenders may eventually get comfortable with classic US tax equity terms.

3.4 Floating offshore wind – a fresh approach to security?

(a) A new frontier

It is not often that there are new developments in the context of taking security in project finance transactions. As explained above, the security structure in project finance transactions tends to follow a well-trodden path, refined over many years. However, the project financing of FOW, with its unique characteristics, may represent scope for novel developments.

Wind power is typically stronger and more consistent in offshore ocean areas than on land. Until recently, the development of offshore wind turbines was based on structures which are fixed to the seabed. This makes it difficult to harness wind power potential in ocean areas that have strong wind speeds but are too deep or otherwise have challenging seabed conditions (eg, a steep continental shelf or an uneven seabed). FOW technology enables wind turbines to be installed on floating platforms, which are stabilised by means of chains or cables (steel or synthetic) that are anchored to the seabed through various methods. Therefore, FOW offers huge potential to expand the current scale of renewable power sources.

The early FOW projects have been pre-commercial and largely on balance-sheet demonstration projects. However, in the last few years, several government tenders have been issued for commercial-scale floating offshore windfarms and more are on the way.[33] The number of FOW initiatives around the globe is increasing, in places such as the United Kingdom, Norway, France,

---

32 Even with a direct pay system, there may still be advantages to having tax equity financing in place to absorb other tax benefits generated by the project, such as depreciation.

33 See Aylin Ocak, "Floating offshore wind activity", inspiratia (5 January 2021), www.inspiratia.com/renewables/regions/eu-europe/region-insight/article/floating-offshore-wind-keeps-gaining-ground.

South Korea, Japan and the United States. The right FOW assets, with carefully structured financings, are likely to be of interest to:

- commercial banks;
- private equity investors;
- pension and infrastructure funds; and
- export credit agencies and development finance institutions.

(b)   Security over FOW assets

But how should lenders take security over FOW assets? Should these be treated in the same way as traditional ships? Perhaps not. But nor are these assets the same as fixed offshore wind turbines (as FOW assets have the potential to be redeployed). Perhaps instead, given that these FOW assets share certain characteristics with the mobile units utilised in the oil and gas industry, the financing and security structure for FOW could borrow from the oil and gas sector? In any event, different national approaches to the characterisation of FOW, and therefore the means of taking security over FOW assets, will lead to uncertainty among the lender community. This may discourage investment and financing right at a time when FOW is set to become an important source of renewable energy.

By their nature, disputes impacting FOW are likely to involve multiple legal systems. The ownership and/or security interests over the FOW assets may be registered in one state; the asset itself may be moored and operated in the territorial seas of a different state; and the FOW assets could become involved in an incident or accident with an entity involving yet another state. Commentators[34] caution that these disputes may not always benefit from existing international maritime conventions, which often either do not apply to unusual watercraft such as FOW assets or have ambiguous application. All these uncertainties have led to the suggestion[35] that it may be time to consider the introduction of a maritime convention to resolve the various international legal uncertainties as they relate to FOW.[36] This convention could be along the lines of the Cape Town Convention,[37] which provides for international recognition of international interests in aircraft, and is intended to override domestic law requirements, such as stamp duties or local registrations. A need to consider the special status of FOW assets has been echoed in various

---

34   Alexander Severance, "*Mare Incognitum*, Part I: Do we now need (to at least discuss) a Mobile Offshore Renewables Unit Convention?" *Tulane Maritime Law Journal*, Vol. 45:287.
35   *Ibid.*
36   Similar suggestions were made by Ole Böger in relation to the Cape Town Convention being extended to cover security over ships; Ole Böger (2016), "The Case for a New Protocol to the Cape Town Convention Covering Security over Ships" *Cape Town Convention Journal*, 5:1, 73-102, www.law.ox.ac.uk/sites/files/oxlaw/ole_boeger_-_the_case_for_a_new_protocol_to_the_cape_town_convention_covering_security.pdf.
37   The Convention on International Interests in Mobile Equipment and the related Protocol on Matters Specific to Aircraft Equipment.

countries. For example, the Petroleum Safety Authority in Norway – while acknowledging the similarities between floating turbines and other mobile offshore units – has confirmed that it will be looking to develop a more bespoke regulation for the FOW turbine sector in 2021.[38]

In the meantime, FOW assets will sit somewhat uneasily within the existing framework for shipping and offshore industries – requiring registration in a national ship registry where the domestic law considers these to be 'ships', but accepting that this may not be possible in all jurisdictions.[39] Registration in this way may enable lenders to obtain security in the form of a registerable and enforceable encumbrance over the asset in the form of a ship mortgage, the form of which will be determined by the state of registration.[40] Other security available for lenders will follow that described elsewhere in this chapter, including:

- bank account charges (to capture the cash flow generated by the FOW asset);
- share pledges;
- insurance; and
- assignment of key contractual rights.

What is clear is that local law analysis will be key.

FOW represents a technological innovation that has the potential to contribute in a very meaningful way to the global decarbonisation of energy provision. To meet the ambitious renewables targets set by governments, these FOW projects will need to be developed at scale, with large capital costs – characteristics that often point to the need for external project finance. External investment will necessitate a greater degree of certainty around the governing law applicable to, and the non-possessory security that can be granted over, these mobile FOW assets. Certainty could be achieved through international cooperation and the development of a novel maritime convention specifically addressing FOW assets, which could sit alongside the established project financing security structures discussed elsewhere in this chapter. Without this certainty, there is a danger that FOW may not meet its full potential.

---

38   Sigve Knudsen, director of legal and regulatory affairs at the Petroleum Safety Authority (PSA), "Wind powers in place", PSA website, "Technical and supervisory news", 21 August 2020; www.ptil.no/en/technical-competence/explore-technical-subjects/news/2020/wind-powers-in-place/.
39   For example, Section 313 of the English law Merchant Shipping Act 1995 states that "'ship' includes every description of vessel used in navigation", which arguably would preclude FOW assets.
40   However, as pointed out by Severance (n 34), even if a FOW asset is registered as a 'ship' in one jurisdiction, there is still the question of whether other jurisdictions touched by that FOW asset (eg, the jurisdiction in which it operates or passes through in transit) would recognise such registration or any security interest over such asset.

4.   Conclusion

Lenders to project finance transactions – like lenders to many other types of secured finance transactions – will look to the collateral package on offer as a very important factor in deciding whether to participate in a project financing. However, what distinguishes the classic project finance transaction from other kinds of secured finance transactions is the extensive nature of this collateral package, driven by:

- the sole purpose nature of the borrower;
- the defined creditor group; and
- the limited or non-recourse nature of the financing.

An 'all asset' security package remains the ideal and an English law debenture provides a simple means for a project company to furnish a comprehensive security package to its lenders. However, project finance transactions are located in a diverse array of jurisdictions globally, many of which do not offer the same degree of legal flexibility; assets of project companies located in these jurisdictions will need to be secured using the best means available, with exceptions based on legal, cost, commercial and market considerations. Offshore wind as an asset class illustrates the point about differences between jurisdictions. And FOW assets – which in the security space more closely resemble assets such as ships, aircraft and oil and gas units, rather than many fixed, immovable project finance assets – present new challenges for lenders.

Emerging markets – general features

Ashley McDermott
Mayer Brown

1. Introduction

Unlike the various products discussed in Part 2 of this book, such as acquisition finance, funds finance and real estate finance, emerging markets finance is not specific to a particular asset or product. In essence, it describes financings which involve parties located in particular locations and can therefore include a broad range of assets and financial products.

The past couple of decades have seen an increasingly diversified pool of creditors in emerging market loan financings, as well as incremental shifts towards more established legal, political and economic environments in some markets and disappointing deviations in these respects in others. This has resulted in greater depth and complexity in deal structures, and consequently in the legal documentation and security required.

In Part 3 of this book, we discuss some common difficulties encountered by secured lenders when structuring and enforcing secured loans in emerging markets. We focus on international, non-concessional loans rather than local, trade-related or concessional financing. We assume that the creditors are located outside of the primary jurisdiction of the debtors. We look at how it can be difficult for an international creditor to navigate the complexities of local law in relation to lending into, and taking security in, emerging market jurisdictions – both in terms of the initial negotiation, execution and perfection of security and with respect to enforcement. We first consider the general features of international loan financing in emerging markets. Subsequent chapters focus in turn on three particular regions: Africa, Central and Eastern Europe, and Latin America.

2. What is an 'emerging market'?

Although the term has been used in financial markets for over 40 years, there is no definitive criterion of what constitutes an 'emerging' market. Traditionally, the term was used to refer to countries whose economies were in an emerging growth phase; though this is not to say that the economies of emerging markets are always growing. Some argue that it is more appropriate to use terms such as 'developing', 'frontier' or 'growth' markets. These, however, are as overly simplistic and potentially misleading as the more common term 'emerging'.

The World Bank classifies countries into income groups on an annual basis depending on their gross national income (GNI) per capita. There are four categories: low, lower-middle, upper-middle and high.[1] Most financial market participants refer to low or lower-middle countries as 'emerging' markets. However, relying on this measure would exclude jurisdictions such as the United Arab Emirates, which is classified as an emerging market jurisdiction by many, including the widely referenced MSCI Emerging Markets Index.[2]

There may be few shared characteristics between some emerging market jurisdictions. For example, a country in Eastern Europe may have a very different economic, legal and political climate from a country in Latin America. Similarly, there are likely to be as many differences as there are similarities between two countries in sub-Saharan African which, although located in the same region geographically, might be very far apart from the perspective of a secured creditor.

For example, the legal regime in Angola is a civil law-based system heavily influenced by Portuguese law, with legislation being the primary source of law on which courts base their judgments. There is no concept of binding precedents, such as exists in many common law jurisdictions. In contrast, although it shares a border of over 1,000 kilometres with Angola, Zambia has a dual legal system made up of a constitution, statutes and court precedents, supplemented by local customary law. The general characteristics of a jurisdiction's legal regime (ie, civil law, common law or sometimes a mixture of both) are usually very useful indicators of the types of security likely to be possible in that jurisdiction and of how that security may need to be documented, perfected and enforced.

Perhaps the common denominator among such varied jurisdictions is that the economic, legal and political climates are less certain than in developed markets; although in recent years, even this rationale has carried less weight – partly due to certain unexpected economic and political events in various developed markets, but also because of improvements in many emerging market jurisdictions. For example:

- the Organisation for the Harmonisation of Business Law in Africa (OHADA) has adopted a uniform law to modernise the rules relating to the creation, perfection and enforcement over security in the OHADA region. This was

---

1   For the current 2022 fiscal year, the World Bank defines:
- low-income economies as those with a GNI per capita of $1,045 or less in 2020;
- lower middle-income economies as those with a GNI per capita of between $1,046 and $4,095;
- upper middle-income economies as those with a GNI per capita of between $4,096 and $12,695; and
- high-income economies as those with a GNI per capita of $12,696 or more.

See World Bank Country and Lending Groups, https://datahelpdesk.worldbank.org/knowledgebase/articles/906519-world-bank-country-and-lending-groups.

2   The MSCI Emerging Markets Index was launched in 1988, including 10 countries with a weight of about 0.9% in the MSCI All Country World Index (ACWI). Currently, it captures 26 countries across the globe and has a weight of 12% in the MSCI ACWI Index. In addition to the Emerging Markets Index, MSCI classifies 31 countries as frontier markets, 22 of which are included in the MSCI Frontier Markets Index. See www.msci.com.

certainly a step in the right direction and has allowed (for example) security to be held and enforced by a single security agent on behalf of a syndicate of lenders, as is the case in most common law jurisdictions;[3] and

- the United Arab Emirates recently passed a law addressing some of the previous limitations when taking security in that jurisdiction.[4] This new law should make it easier for a lender to take a registered security interest over movable assets (including future assets) in the United Arab Emirates (although note that security over certain immovable assets such as land will still need a local security agent and a parallel debt provision).

That said, there is undoubtedly less commercial, political and legal certainty in emerging markets when contrasted with developed markets. While emerging markets may offer better returns for investors and often experience faster economic growth than developed markets, few legal systems in emerging markets offer the same contractual certainty and flexibility as can be found in developed markets. The judiciaries in emerging markets are typically less experienced than, for example, the judiciary in England and Wales or New York. Judges may be politically influenced. The legal systems in emerging markets may be less accustomed to interpreting complex cross-border agreements; and the courts are often considered by international creditors as being less creditor friendly than the courts in the key international financial centres of the world such as London, Hong Kong, New York and Singapore.

3. Participants in emerging markets secured financings

During the past couple of decades, the creditors regularly lending into emerging markets have changed dramatically. The vast majority of those lending into emerging markets used to be official creditors from 'Western' jurisdictions; and the transactions largely consisted of sovereign lending and project finance. Now the participants and types of loan transactions involving emerging market borrowers are a lot more diverse. They include commercial banks and funds from all over the world, as well as a broader range of development banks and multilateral institutions.

Indeed, while banks such as the European Bank for Reconstruction and Development (EBRD) and the African Export-Import Bank (Afreximbank) have been lending into emerging markets for several decades, they have been joined by new international organisations such as the Asian Infrastructure Investment Bank (AIIB).[5] In addition, long-established development banks – such as the

---

3   For further reading, see Katherine Hensby, "OHADA: cementing the role of the security agent in Africa" (April 2015) 4 *Butterworths Journal of International Banking and Financial Law* 216. See more on OHADA in the "Africa" chapter.

4   Federal Law 4/2020 on Guaranteeing Rights Related to Movables (Mortgage Law).

5   AIIB began operations in 2016 with 57 founding members. By the end of 2020, it had 103 approved members and it expects to have funding needs of around $10 billion per annum by the mid-2020s.

Asian Development Bank, the African Development Bank, the Eastern and Southern African Trade and Development Bank and the US International Development Finance Corporation – have become more active in providing and facilitating the financing of private development projects in lower and middle-income countries, often working with other development banks, export credit agencies, commercial banks and funds in increasingly complex structures.

Over this period, China has become the largest official creditor – largely through policy banks such as the Export-Import Bank of China and the China Development Bank lending to borrowers in emerging markets. Although much of this debt is advanced to, or guaranteed by, sovereigns or parastatal entities (meaning that it is unlikely to be secured), Chinese banks also regularly participate in project financings and other loans with private debtors, and their influence on emerging markets financings more broadly is undeniable. For example, a recent study by the Peterson Institute for International Economics revealed that the documents governing many loans advanced by Chinese creditors contained unusual provisions that are much more onerous for borrowers than the terms of non-Chinese creditors. These include, in particular, terms relating to confidentiality, seniority of debt and lender discretion – especially with respect to contract termination and certain events of default.[6]

4.   Types of secured financing in emerging markets

The types of secured financings in an emerging market jurisdiction evolve as the country develops. We can describe this (admittedly in an overly simplistic and shorthand manner) as follows.

Initially the economic, political and legal regime of a jurisdiction is such that creditors (often, at this stage, development banks or commercial banks supported by export credit agencies) are only prepared to lend to the sovereign itself or to state-owned companies which are actually or tacitly guaranteed by the sovereign. Such loans are typically borrowed or guaranteed by the Ministry of Finance (or equivalent) of the relevant jurisdiction. We do not cover such loans in any detail in this book as they rarely, if ever, involve security. Loans to countries that borrow from the World Bank Group are likely to be subject to the World Bank negative pledge, which prevents such countries – and any private companies that they own – from easily granting security to other creditors.[7]

After a period of successfully servicing such debt, political stability and

---

6   For further reading, see Anna Gelpern, Sebastian Horn, Scott Morris, Brad Parks and Christoph Trebesch, "21-7 How China Lends: A Rare Look into 100 Debt Contracts with Foreign Governments" (May 2021), Peterson Institute For International Economics Working Paper, www.piie.com/sites/default/files/documents/wp21-7.pdf.

7   For an in-depth analysis of the World Bank's negative pledge clause and its implications for project financings in emerging markets, see Adam Cooper and Raj Bavishi, "The World Bank's negative pledge clause: implications for major energy and infrastructure project development and finance" (April 2015) 3 *Butterworths Journal of International Banking and Financial Law* 188B.

economic growth, a country's attractiveness to international creditors gradually improves. A broader range of creditors (including investors in fixed-income products) become willing investors, sometimes without sovereign support. Bond markets develop and project financings become bankable; and larger domestic companies can tap the international debt markets, often with credit support from international sponsors or parent companies. As well as private creditors, export credit agencies are more willing to underwrite larger ticket sizes, with increasing country limits.

The extraction and export of commodities are often of crucial importance to emerging market jurisdictions. As such, a large number of the secured financings involving emerging markets are commodity finance or project finance related.[8] Islamic finance has also become increasingly important.[9] In addition, there is an urgent need for new or improved energy and infrastructure projects across the emerging markets – for example, the construction and maintenance of airports, dams, roads, bridges and rail and bus rapid transit systems, as well as power stations (many of which are now powered by renewable energy, such as wind or solar), water supply and wastewater systems. The COVID-19 pandemic has also highlighted the need for improved healthcare facilities in many jurisdictions, with export credit agencies and development banks being particularly active in this space.[10]

As is the case in the rest of the world, there is now a significant focus on ensuring that projects in emerging markets being financed by international creditors are environmentally and socially responsible and sustainable. It is worth noting, in this respect, the fact that many commercial banks and international funds have been party to the Equator Principles for some time, and development banks such as the EBRD have required detailed environmental and social due diligence and related ongoing contractual protections in their loan agreements for many years. In this respect, it might be argued that this is an area where financings in developed markets lagged behind many of those in developing markets until the recent surge in green and sustainability-linked loans.

In most cases, emerging markets financings are denominated in US dollars, with some euro-denominated financings. Indebtedness in other currencies is sometimes seen in emerging markets where expedient for deal-specific reasons (eg, where amounts due to contractors or suppliers involved in a project in a borrower's jurisdiction are owed in a particular currency).

---

8   Project finance is covered in detail in Part 2, so is not discussed in detail in Part 3.
9   Islamic finance is covered in detail in Part 2, so is not discussed in detail in Part 3.
10   For example, Afreximbank disbursed more than $6.5 billion in 2020 to help member countries manage the adverse impact of the financial, economic and health shocks caused by the COVID-19 pandemic; see "Afreximbank recognised for role in Africa's fight against COVID-19", press release, 7 February 2021, www.afreximbank.com/afreximbank-recognised-for-role-in-africas-fight-against-covid-19/.

5.   Common legal issues in emerging markets

It is obviously important for lenders to know that they have robust legal means to ensure that funds advanced by them will be repaid, and that they will be paid interest accrued in the meantime. Security interests can allow lenders to use the proceeds of sale of particular assets to repay outstanding amounts and can also provide secured lenders with priority over other creditors of the debtor. However, even when security is granted, these benefits will materialise only where the relevant laws dictate and those laws can be enforced.

Secured creditors are relatively well protected under English law and New York law, which are the governing laws most commonly used for the main finance documents in international financings.[11] Nevertheless, it is usually necessary for security to be governed by the law of the jurisdiction in which the asset is located or to which it is subject (commonly referred to as the *lex situs* doctrine).

With regard to emerging markets financings, valuable assets may be located in the relevant emerging market, meaning that security documents must be governed by the laws of that jurisdiction. Such laws are often less well established and can often be less creditor friendly; and there may be currency controls in the relevant jurisdiction. Therefore, while a secured creditor may theoretically have a better position than an unsecured creditor of the same debtor, the practical value of security will depend on the ability of that secured creditor to enforce its rights and to convert, transmit and apply the proceeds of enforcement against the hard currency indebtedness.[12] We noted above that some emerging market jurisdictions have attempted to modernise laws and regulations relating to security in recent years. Even where that is the case, such laws and regulations are relatively young, and it is therefore hard to predict with certainty how they will be applied. This can make it difficult to structure a security package in a 'bankable' manner.

Where possible, one way of addressing the uncertainty of 'local law' governed security is to take security over assets located outside of the relevant jurisdiction. For example, pre-export financings in the structured trade and commodity finance sector are structured so that lenders obtain security 'offshore' as much as possible (ie, governed by laws other than those in the

---

11   Commercial banks and funds tend to use documentation based on a Loan Market Association (LMA) recommended form of facility agreement for use in developing markets transactions. The LMA has also published recommended forms of local law documentation aimed specifically at borrowers in South Africa; Kenya, Nigeria, Tanzania, Uganda and Zambia (KNTUZ Agreement); and Zimbabwe (Zimbabwean Agreement). Development banks and multilaterals tend to use their own form of loan agreement or general terms and conditions.

12   For example, if a loan to a Brazilian borrower is registered with the Central Bank of Brazil under the *Módulo de Registro de Operações Financeiras*, remittances of payments from the Brazilian borrower to foreign lenders relating to the enforcement of security under a properly created and perfected security interest, as well as related commissions, fees and expenses (up to a pre-determined amount), are permitted without further approvals. Other similar yet distinct rules and requirements exist in other jurisdictions with currency controls.

jurisdiction where the underlying obligor and valuable assets or project are located). Lenders advance hard currency funds to a commodity exporting borrower in an emerging market jurisdiction after having been granted security over offtake contracts (ie, sale and purchase agreements between the borrower as the seller of certain commodities and eligible offtakers as creditworthy purchasers of those commodities). These contracts are usually governed by English or New York law (or the law of some other developed market), as is the security over such contracts, rather than the laws of the jurisdiction where the borrower is located. Payments must be made by the offtakers in the same hard currency as the loan is denominated into a bank account outside of the jurisdiction of the borrower (eg, in London, New York, Singapore or Switzerland) over which the lenders have security. If the borrower continues to export, sufficient funds will be generated to repay the loan. To the extent this does not happen, lenders have security over assets that should be easier to enforce than security over assets located in the borrower's jurisdiction. Therefore, instead of credit risk and political risk, lenders are exposed only to performance risk.

Such structures also help to mitigate currency controls, which in some emerging market jurisdictions require the approval of the central bank or another public authority in order for a borrower to convert local currency amounts into the hard currency in which the secured obligations are denominated, or to transfer such amounts out of the country to pay such secured obligations.[13]

Where a borrower does not generate sufficient exports to eligible offtakers or have other assets located outside of the relevant jurisdiction, it may be necessary or desirable to obtain security over certain assets located in that jurisdiction. For example, the borrower or other debtors may have real estate or other immovable property or valuable equipment or inventory located in the relevant jurisdiction. There may be bank accounts into which material amounts are to be paid over the life of the transaction that need to be located in the relevant jurisdiction (eg, if the debtor's customers are in the jurisdiction and typically pay in local currency in that jurisdiction).

Such security will likely need to be governed by the laws of the relevant jurisdiction. Careful analysis must be undertaken and counsel obtained from that jurisdiction on whether and how such security can be granted, and what steps are required to perfect that security; and otherwise to ensure that, if required in the future, such security can be enforced. The following are some common issues that arise in such circumstances.

---

13   For more on pre-export finance and prepayment facilities, see Claude Brown, "Commodity finance" (February 2017), 2 *Butterworths Journal of International Banking and Financial Law* 89.

5.1 Types of security possible

English law allows a creditor to have the benefit of security over all assets of a company by means of an 'all assets' debenture. This typically includes fixed charges and assignments over specific assets, as well as a floating charge over other assets of the company from time to time. Many jurisdictions do not allow this, meaning that it is necessary to have a specific security document for each asset of a company. Furthermore, in some jurisdictions, it is not possible to pledge or secure future assets; or it is necessary to describe every secured asset in the security document. In such cases, for example, if a company opens a new bank account or acquires new equipment, inventory or contractual rights, it is necessary to enter into and perfect a new security document (or an amendment or supplement to the original security document) at that time in order to create security over such assets.

5.2 Legal restrictions and change of control provisions

As is the case in most jurisdictions, there are certain assets over which debtors may not grant security. In emerging market jurisdictions, this is often the case in relation to material licences – especially where the business conducted by the borrower is strategically important for the relevant country. Such licences can also contain 'change of control' provisions. Pursuant to these, even if creditors were to take security over the shares of an offshore holding company of the operating company in the relevant jurisdiction (something commonly considered to achieve a more robust security package, for similar reasons to those explained above in relation to pre-export financings), an enforcement over such shares could result in adverse consequences. The terms governing such matters in a material licence or other material agreement can sometimes be ambiguous, as they can be based on dated templates from the relevant agency or ministry in the relevant jurisdiction. Material licences and other material contracts should be carefully reviewed as early as possible when structuring a secured financing in an emerging market.

5.3 Security trustee, parallel debt and similar

In both developed and developing markets, the laws of some jurisdictions do not recognise the trust or agency concepts that are commonly used in common law jurisdictions to allow security to be shared by an ever-changing syndicate of lenders in a manner that is not administratively burdensome or overly costly. Brazil is a good example. While it is not contrary to Brazilian law for a security agent to enter into Brazilian law governed security documents on behalf of a syndicate of lenders, the security trustee is often appointed by the international lenders under a Brazilian law power of attorney, in addition to having been appointed as security agent generally under an English or a New York law governed facility agreement. This is done so that in an enforcement scenario, it will not be necessary to have that facility agreement translated into Portuguese and presented in a Brazilian court (together with an English or a New York law banking expert) to evidence that it has the necessary power and authority to enforce on behalf of the syndicate.

In some jurisdictions, lenders get comfortable using certain contractual structures to achieve a similar result. For example, in a parallel debt structure, each debtor contractually agrees that it owes an additional debt to the security agent which will exist simultaneously (or 'in parallel') with the debt owed by it to the lenders and in the same amount. Joint and several creditor structures are also sometimes seen, especially where there are doubts as to the enforceability of parallel debt structures. In Russia, a mixture of parallel debt, joint and several creditorship and conduit or fronting bank structures has historically been used. After changes to the Civil Code in 2014, it is now theoretically possible for an agent to hold security on behalf of a syndicate of lenders.

5.4 Local licensing

Taking or enforcing security governed by the laws of certain jurisdictions (as well as, in some cases, general lending in that jurisdiction) requires the secured party to be licensed in that jurisdiction. This can result in local banks or specialist agency firms acting as 'local' or 'onshore' security agent. In other cases, deals are structured so that loans are advanced to, and security is granted by, holding companies outside of the relevant jurisdiction, so that security can be taken outside of that jurisdiction without the local licensing requirements applying (although there are potential disadvantages with such structures that should be considered).

5.5 Language (of security document and underlying loan)

In order to enforce a security document governed by the law of some jurisdictions in the courts of that jurisdiction, it is sometimes either legally required or, at times, practically preferable for that security document to be drafted in the local language. As a result, in many international secured financings where this is the case, it is common to see bilingual security documents, with English text down the left-hand side of each page and the other relevant language down the right-hand side. Usually, the non-English language will prevail in the event of any inconsistency between the two. This can be somewhat uncomfortable for lenders unable to read the prevailing text, although the English translation can help to smooth this process.

5.6 Execution (eg, apostilling, notarisation)

In order to register or enforce security documents in many jurisdictions, it is necessary to have 'wet ink' originals. In addition, it is sometimes necessary for signatures to be apostilled or notarised – particularly when the relevant document is being executed by that signatory outside of the relevant jurisdiction. As a result, security documents in emerging market financings are rarely executed solely via email.

5.7 Enforcement

Consideration should be given at the outset to how security over certain assets in emerging markets can be enforced to the extent required. In some jurisdictions (eg, Egypt), extra-judicial enforcement over certain assets is not possible, even where the parties agree this at the outset. Even where extra-judicial enforcement is permitted, lengthy processes may sometimes need to be followed (eg, public auctions with numerous formalities and rounds being required over a long period). From a practical perspective, certain jurisdictions may have laws or regulations in relation to who can hold security over or own certain assets. For example, in Kenya, non-citizens or companies not wholly directly and indirectly owned by Kenyan citizens may not own freehold title over real estate. Finally, insolvency laws in the relevant jurisdiction can often result in automatic stays, which may prevent a speedy enforcement of security following the commencement of insolvency proceedings. This is the case, for example, in much of Central and Eastern Europe.

5.8 Stamp duty

In many jurisdictions, it is necessary to have documents stamped in order for them to have probative value in any court proceedings in that jurisdiction. Where applicable, stamp duty may be calculated as a percentage of the secured obligations on the initial or principal security document or as a percentage of the value of the secured asset (eg, 0.1%, with nominal stamp duty being levied on additional security documents relating to the same financing). In some cases, the ability to pay a reduced, nominal amount on subsequent security documents lasts only for a particular period of time after the date of the initial or principal security document (eg, 90 days).

In Nigeria, security documents are subject to the payment of *ad valorem* stamp duty. The applicable rate payable on a charging instrument is usually around 0.375% of the secured obligations. On most international loan facilities, this will result in a material amount. As such, for many years the practice of 'upstamping' has been a common compromise between lenders keen to avail themselves of the benefits of security and borrowers keen to ensure that the ensuing stamp duty costs are kept to a reasonable level. Nigerian law does not require that a security document securing a loan facility be stamped and registered in an amount based on the total amount of that facility. However, where a security document is stamped for an amount lower than the facility amount, a lender will be permitted to enforce the security only for up to the amount in respect of which it has stamped and registered the relevant security.

Upstamping sees the parties commercially agreeing to stamp the security documents for an initial amount and only subsequently upstamping them for an additional amount.

This does not work in all jurisdictions. Many require that stamp duty be paid within a relatively short period of time after a security document is signed. There are also potential risks associated with the approach in Nigeria. For example, it may result in priority issues where other creditors have purported to take security over the same assets and paid stamp duty on that security in the interim.

5.9   Registration

As is the case in developed markets, it is necessary for certain security to be registered to ensure (among other things) that third parties are made aware of its existence and to preserve the priority of the secured creditor(s). Registration processes in emerging markets can be time consuming and expensive – not least because local tax offices or registries can be inefficient. This has been exacerbated by the COVID-19 pandemic, with registries in many jurisdictions being unable to accept submissions electronically, but having to close physical registries. Well-intentioned attempts to modernise security registration regimes in some jurisdictions can also have unintended consequences. For example, in one particular jurisdiction, a law was passed to make it necessary for secured creditors to register security granted to them by any company in that jurisdiction over any immovable assets in order for that security to be enforceable against third parties as from a certain date set out in that new law. However, by the time that date arrived, the new registry office necessary to ensure that such security could be registered did not yet exist, resulting in a disconnect between statutory law and what was possible in practice.

5.10   Other perfection requirements

Where it is necessary to notify counterparties to contracts or account banks of the creation of security over contracts or bank accounts, in theory there is little difference between developed markets and emerging markets. However, the law governing how such notices must be delivered can vary widely; and at times, it includes formal delivery methods. With respect to physical assets, such as equipment or inventory, some jurisdictions require that the parties affix a plaque denoting the secured creditors' interests in order to perfect the security.

5.11   Preferred creditor status

In project or syndicated loan financings involving a multilateral development bank, the latter may insist on the inclusion of express contractual provisions to acknowledge that it must be given priority with respect to any enforcement proceeds in certain circumstances. This often contemplates a scenario in which security proceeds have been realised because of the status or standing of the multilateral development bank, which would not have been realised had the multilateral development bank not existed in the group of lenders.

5.12   Other factors to consider

There can also be additional issues to consider when creating or perfecting security governed by the laws of, or granted by a company in, an emerging market jurisdiction, to ensure that it is possible to enforce that security as quickly as possible. In some cases, it may seem unlikely that international creditors would ever be able to enforce that security. Nevertheless, it may still be worthwhile taking it for defensive purposes, to ensure that nobody else does and that the relevant assets cannot easily be sold to third parties.

6.   Conclusion

As different lending entities become accustomed to emerging markets financing, it becomes increasingly important for their legal advisers to gain and develop a broad understanding of the security landscape across different jurisdictions, as well as a close relationship with local counsel, to be able to address consistently and constructively their clients' concerns.

Africa

Ian Coles
Alban Dorin
Mayer Brown

1. Introduction

Africa is large: approximately 5,000 miles long north to south and, at its widest, approximately 4,600 miles wide east to west. Within its boundaries are 54 different countries, which vary significantly in all respects, including topography, climate, population density and economics. African countries also vary significantly with respect to their legal systems, meaning that it is not feasible to provide a single, homogenous review of the principles of taking security across the continent. This chapter identifies the main types of legal systems in Africa; summarises the basic principles applicable to the taking of security in those systems; and identifies some of the key legal and regulatory concepts in specific jurisdictions.

The great potential for economic growth in Africa is well documented; but in order for this potential to be realised, the availability of finance is crucial. This is particularly the case with regard to small and medium-sized enterprises (SMEs) in Africa, which have found it particularly difficult to access financing solutions in recent years. While commercial banks, development finance institutions and similar international financial institutions have financed the construction of large-scale projects such as ports, refineries and petrochemical plants for many years, unless this is complemented by financial solutions for smaller projects and businesses, economic growth will be inhibited.

Encouragingly, a combination of international banks, local banks and private credit funds have been doing more in this respect in recent years. Indeed, a comprehensive survey on African banking conducted by the European Investment Bank in 2020 indicated that most local banking groups intended to grow their loan books with a significant concentration on borrowers in the SME sector. While there are several barriers to achieving this aim – including a shortage of bankable projects, a lack of managerial capacity and a historically high default rate – the lack of effective collateral to secure loans was also listed as a very important factor; in fact, 37% of respondees cited a lack of adequate collateral as an impediment to further lending in the sector.[1] As such, it is clear

---

1   www.eib.org/attachments/efs/economic_report_banking_africa_2020_en.pdf.

that the continued development of legal systems which support a transparent and reliable set of laws and regulations for the taking and enforcement of security is essential to a country's development.

2. Overview

The various categories of legal systems in Africa are largely a product of colonial history. When European nations colonised Africa in the 19th century, they each brought their own judicial and legal practices and principles. The three most influential systems – chiefly a function of the number of countries they colonised – were those imported by England (Anglophone), France (Francophone) and Portugal (Lusophone). Many Francophone jurisdictions have adopted the OHADA Treaty,[2] which provides for the implementation of common legal principles in 17 countries, largely in West Africa. In Southern Africa, the position is not as linear. In countries such as South Africa, Botswana and Namibia, early settlers from the Netherlands brought with them a civil law construct based largely on principles of commercial Roman law. Subsequent colonial activity in a number of those jurisdictions (eg, Great Britain in South Africa and Germany in Namibia) did not lead to a comprehensive replacement of this Dutch heritage, but rather some lesser adjustments and additions, with the result that many have mixed approaches to the taking of security. In the Maghreb, there are a number of different approaches – again largely a function of colonial history. Morocco, Algeria and Tunisia have been largely influenced by the position in France – although there are also Islamic influences in Algeria. Libya has traces of influences from the Ottoman Empire, France, Italy and Egypt; but *Sharia* law is now more prevalent. The legal system in Egypt is based on a combination of the Napoleonic Code and Islamic law.

The above high-level summary of the primary legal systems across Africa illustrates that the continent is legally very diverse, and few countries have identical laws and regulations in relation to the creation, perfection or enforcement of security. This chapter looks at the laws and regulations in certain Anglophone, Francophone and Lusophone countries, as well as three countries (Ethiopia, Egypt and South Africa) which do not neatly fit into any of these three groupings.

3. Anglophone jurisdictions

Countries throughout Africa have historical links with the English common law tradition. This chapter looks at three of them by way of differing examples of how that tradition has survived and developed since the countries in question

---

2   OHADA is the French acronym for *'Organisation pour l'Harmonisation en Afrique du Droit des Affaires'*, which translates as 'Organisation for the Harmonisation of Business Law in Africa'. It was initially signed on 17 October 1993 in Port Louis and was amended on 17 October 2008 in Quebec.

gained independence and subsequently entered a stage of continued economic growth. These are Ghana, Kenya and Nigeria.

3.1   Ghana

Security can be taken over multiple assets in Ghana without too much formality or complication. Charges, pledges, assignments and mortgages are the most frequently used instruments. Floating charges – creating security over a class of assets, both present and future – are also available. It is possible for a company to grant security over all of its assets in a single security document. Ghanaian law also recognises security trusts and the ability of security trustees to hold security on behalf of a syndicate of lenders.

In general, the principles relating to security are similar to those under English law. In order to perfect a security assignment of a chose in action, the relevant contractual counterparty must be notified. In order to create a fixed charge over a bank account, the secured party must have sufficient control over the relevant bank account. However, there are important registration requirements in Ghana to be aware of, some of which are referenced below.

Ghanaian law governed security granted to secure loan obligations must usually be registered with the Collateral Registry within 28 days of the creation of the security.[3] Where such security is created by a Ghanaian company, the requirement to register at the Collateral Registry is in addition to the requirement to register such security with the registrar of companies, which must occur within 45 days of creation of the security.[4] Security that is not so registered will be void. Security over land must be registered with the Lands Commission, which can be a time-consuming process. The cost of such registrations is not usually material.

Before a security document can be registered, it must be stamped. Indeed, it is necessary to pay stamp duty on all security documents in order to ensure that they are enforceable in Ghana. The amount of stamp duty payable will depend primarily on how many security interests are created and of what type. Generally, the initial security interest is subject to stamp duty of 0.5% of the secured obligations, while each additional security interest created is subject to stamp duty of 0.25% of the secured obligations. For instance, where multiple security documents are entered into creating multiple security interests to secure the same secured obligations (or multiple security interests are created over different assets in a single security agreement), stamp duty of 0.5% of the secured obligations will be payable on the initial (primary) security interest. Any subsequent security interest covering those same secured obligations will incur further stamp duty of 0.25%.

---

3   Section 22(1) of the Borrowers and Lenders Act (1052/2020).
4   Section 110(1) of the Companies Act (992/2019).

Prior to enforcing Ghanaian law governed security, there are certain notification requirements. A secured creditor that intends to enforce its security must provide 30 days' prior written notice of such intention to the security provider.[5] The notice becomes effective 30 days after it is received by the security provider. A secured interest that is registered with the Collateral Registry may be realised without court action. Security interests may also be enforced through court action. Court proceedings may result in the sale of the secured assets or the appointment of a receiver over the relevant assets. During insolvency proceedings, the rights of a secured creditor (in respect of fixed charges) are subject to statutorily prescribed preferential claims (eg, tax liabilities and employee salaries accrued for the four-month period prior to the commencement of the winding-up proceedings).[6]

3.2 Kenya

Kenyan law is a mixture of statutory and common law, much of which is derived from English common law, as well as elements of customary and Islamic law. It is possible for security to be granted over most classes of assets without significant difficulty (including future assets and contingent rights). Kenyan companies may also grant debentures over all of their assets. Security can be taken over both movable and immovable property. There are no general restrictions on foreign lenders advancing loans to Kenyan borrowers or being granted the benefit of Kenyan law governed security. Agency and trust concepts are recognised under Kenyan law.

The Movable Property Security Rights Act 2017 (MPSRA) aims to enhance the ability of individuals and companies to access credit using movable assets as security. It also aims to promote consistency and certainty in secured financing over movable assets, as well as over receivables by way of outright transfer.

The distinctions between fixed and floating charges are similar to those under English law. Security over shares (other than shares which have been dematerialised) can also be taken through the deposit of share certificates with the relevant secured party. This should also include a signed memorandum of deposit and a share transfer form, which is undated. In the case of dematerialised shares which are listed on the Nairobi Stock Exchange, security must be registered as required by the Central Depositaries Act 2000.

Formal charges over immovable property must be in a prescribed form as set out in the Land Act and the Land Registration Act, which also stipulate certain execution formalities. A formal charge must be registered at the Lands Registry and, if created by a corporate entity, at the Companies Registry. Informal charges, which need not be in a prescribed form, can also be created, either by

---

5   Section 60(1) of the Borrowers and Lenders Act.
6   Section 107(3) of the Corporate Insolvency and Restructuring Act (1015/2020).

way of deposit of the title deeds with the creditor in question or through written undertakings between the creditor and borrower; but these are less common in international secured loans.

If a Kenyan company created security over most assets, it must register such security with the Companies Registry by the prescribed deadline (being 30 days from the creation of the security or, if the security was created outside of Kenya, 21 days from the day on which the security document would have been received in Kenya if dispatched with due diligence following execution).[7] An unregistered charge is (insofar as it purports to create security over the assets of a company) void against third parties such as liquidators, administrators or creditors of the company. However, it may be possible to enforce an unregistered charge against the chargor as an informal charge. The creditor must obtain court approval in order to enforce informal charges.

Security over ships and aircraft also require registration with the Kenya Maritime Authority and the Kenya Civil Aviation Authority, respectively. Perfection of security over third-party rights (eg, the debtor under a receivable) will require registration of a notice in the Collateral Registry.

Debentures and charges must be stamped with duty as assessed by the collector of stamp duty pursuant to the Stamp Duty Act (Chapter 480, Laws of Kenya). If the security is taken over movable property only, then stamp duty is not payable if the security is registrable under the MPSRA. As a matter of Kenyan law, 'movable property' means any tangible or intangible asset. 'Tangible assets' include "all types of goods and includes motor vehicles, crops, machineries and livestock". 'Intangible assets' include "receivables, choses in action, deposit accounts, electronic securities, and IP rights". 'Immovable property', in respect of which stamp duty is payable, includes any interest in land. The MPSRA expressly states that it does not apply to the creation, lease or transfer of an interest in land; although for the avoidance of doubt, security may be created under the MPSRA over tangible assets that are attachments to immovable property (an 'attachment to immovable property' is a tangible asset that, despite the fact that it is physically affixed to immovable property, is treated as movable property).

The requisite stamp duty must be paid within 30 days of execution of the security agreement in question (or within 30 days of the document being brought into Kenya if executed abroad). Stamp duty is assessable at the rate of 0.1% of the secured obligations initially. Stamp duty on subsequent security documents securing the same secured obligations may be charged at a nominal rate if the security is created by the same borrower. If the security provider is a third party, stamp duty is assessable as collateral security at the rate of 0.05%. Save as exempted under the MPSRA, security cannot be registered without

---

7   Section 878 of the Companies Act 2015.

stamp duty having been paid. Evidence of payment of stamp duty is a condition for registration. Furthermore, where an instrument that is required to be stamped is not stamped with the appropriate stamp duty, the document cannot be produced in evidence in a court of law in Kenya. These requirements mean that it is not usually possible to structure around stamp duty requirements on financings involving Kenyan law governed security using methods that may be possible in other jurisdictions.

Enforcement of security can take place in several ways. In the case of a fixed or floating charge, the security agreement will usually stipulate the procedure for enforcement and provide for the appointment of an administrator. In the case of security over immovable property, the process is somewhat extended, since the default leading to enforcement must have been continuing for at least one month, following which the chargor will have two months (three months in the case of a payment default) to cure the default before enforcement proceedings can commence. A forced sale of the secured land (by either auction or private sale) imposes further required notices and waiting periods.

Insolvency proceedings generally do not adversely impact the effectiveness of security; although if the company creating the security is subject to a moratorium (which applies if the company is in administration), then the secured party must obtain the prior approval of the court or the consent of the administrator to enforce. The holders of fixed charges will be entitled to receive the proceeds of security realisation in full in an insolvency scenario; but floating charge holders will rank after certain preferred creditors, such as:

- employees (with respect to unpaid wages);
- tax authorities; and
- those owed amounts as a result of the insolvency proceedings.

3.3   Nigeria

Along with Egypt and South Africa, Nigeria is one of the three largest economies in Africa. It was the largest in 2020 in terms of gross domestic product (GDP). However, the value of its currency and the state of its economy are heavily dependent on oil and gas prices, which can be volatile.

Security over most types of assets can be taken in Nigeria and security trusts and trustees/agents are generally recognised. Fixed charges over specified assets and floating charges over a class of assets (including all assets of a company) are possible. While the legal tradition in Nigeria is largely based on English law, there have been several recent legislative initiatives relating to secured financings. For example, Nigeria's Secured Transactions in Movable Assets Act (STMA) was enacted on 31 May 2017 to regulate the creation, perfection and realisation of security interests in movable assets and, to an extent, immovable assets. This new law was specifically designed to improve the ability of SMEs to access financing. The jury is still out as to how effective it has been in this respect, as it has (among other things) created potentially conflicting registration regimes, which has not necessarily led to greater certainty and confidence among secured creditors.

Legal and equitable mortgages can be granted over real estate. The scope of secured assets in connection with security over real estate extends to buildings and permanent fixtures attached to the land in question. A legal mortgage must be created by a deed. In order to create a legal mortgage, the consent of the governor of the state where the land is located must be obtained. In addition, stamp duty is payable and the legal mortgage must be registered at the local Lands Registry. An equitable mortgage can be created with minimal formality through the deposit of title deeds with the secured creditor. However, unlike with a legal mortgage, the beneficiary of an equitable mortgage is unable to enforce it without a court order. As such, legal mortgages are usually preferable. Both legal and equitable mortgages created by a Nigerian corporate entity must be registered with the Corporate Affairs Commission (CAC). Security over real estate can also be taken by way of fixed or floating charge. As with the legal mortgage, a fixed charge over land requires the prior consent of the relevant local governor and must be registered at the CAC.

The mortgage and charge can both be used to create security over tangible property such as equipment or inventory. Nigeria recognises both fixed and floating charges, with the distinction between the two being largely the degree of control exercised by the secured creditor over the assets in question. Security over such assets can also be created using a pledge which involves the deposit of the secured asset in question with the creditor. Under the Companies and Allied Matters Act 2020, mortgages and charges (whether fixed or floating) created by a company (other than legal mortgages and fixed charges over shares) must be registered with the CAC within 90 days of creation. Failure to register a registrable security document with the CAC will render the mortgage or charge void against a liquidator or any creditor of the relevant company. Companies are also required to maintain a register of security interests created by them at their registered office. Registration with the National Collateral Registry is also required (albeit that some charges created prior to the creation of the registry can be subject to different requirements). While the crucial aspect of a pledge is possession, such that registration of the security is not required, it is common for a creditor and a debtor to enter into a security agreement which documents some of the terms and conditions applicable to the pledge and its enforcement.

Different rules and regulations apply to certain categories of assets such as ships and aircraft. Specific rules also apply to the creation of security over shares and bonds. Legal mortgages over shares will require the creditor to be listed as the shareholder of record in connection with the shares in question. Security over dematerialised shares is effected by entry in the Central Securities Clearing

System (for shares) and the Scripless Securities Settlement System (for government securities). However, equitable mortgages are more frequently used for security over these types of assets. This will generally require the deposit of the relevant certificates with the creditor, along with (preferably) a memorandum of deposit detailing the rights of the secured creditor. There is no requirement to register security over shares with the CAC. A floating charge over shares, however, must be registered at the CAC. Shares in Nigeria are generally not issued as bearer shares, so pledges are uncommon.

Choses in action such as receivables and other debts are generally secured using either a floating or fixed charge or an assignment by way of security. Assignments by way of security must be in writing, but otherwise there is little by way of required formality. Notice of the assignment to the relevant counterparty is customarily given and is required in order to constitute a legal assignment. The assignment is subject to stamp tax and is registrable as a charge.

Stamp duty on a security agreement is required if that agreement is to be capable of being used as evidence in civil proceedings in Nigeria. Stamp duty is generally assessed at the rate of 0.375% of the secured obligations, although this is always required to be assessed by the stamp duties commissioner (the level for a legal assignment by way of security can be higher). Fees are also involved in connection with any required registration.

It is common to utilise the concept of 'upstamping' to mitigate what would otherwise be material stamp duty needing to be paid in respect of large secured loan financings. This involves secured lenders agreeing that the borrower may initially pay stamp duty on a portion of the secured obligations only, rather than on the entire secured amount. At the same time, the borrower is required to contractually agree that it will pay the balance of such stamp duty upon the occurrence of certain future events or circumstances (eg, a default). The practical reality is that, unless the lenders require funds to be set aside in a secured bank account to cover such future stamp duty, it is possible that the borrower may never 'upstamp' the security document. However, the lenders know that they have the option to do this if it makes commercial sense to do so in the future in order to enforce security in Nigeria. Until the upstamping occurs on the document, lenders will be protected only up to the amount of secured obligations on which stamp duty has been paid; hence, lenders may lose priority to any subsequent security granted over the secured assets during the period between the initial stamping and the full upstamping of the security document (although contractual restrictions such as a negative pledge can help to mitigate this risk). There are also concerns relating to hardening periods with upstamping structures.

The circumstances in which security can be challenged include financial assistance, preferences and deficient corporate benefit, although none of these are particularly common. In insolvency proceedings, the holders of fixed charges are entitled to receive the full value of the secured asset in question. The holders of floating charges are primed by certain categories of preferred creditors, such as:

- employees (with respect to unpaid wages);
- tax authorities; and
- those owed amounts as a result of the insolvency proceedings.

4. Francophone jurisdictions

4.1 OHADA Treaty

OHADA was established by the Treaty of 17 October 1993 signed in Port Louis (Mauritius) and is a harmonised system of business laws and implementing institutions adopted by 17 West and Central African nations. Most of the Francophone African jurisdictions are members of OHADA (Benin, Burkina Faso, Cameroon, Central African Republic, Chad, Côte d'Ivoire, Congo, Comoros, Democratic Republic of Congo, Gabon, Guinea, Guinea-Bissau, Equatorial Guinea, Mali, Niger, Senegal and Togo); but others are not and are therefore subject to their own security laws (eg, Algeria, Mauritania, Morocco and Tunisia).

For OHADA members, the OHADA legislation (in particular the 'uniform acts' adopted by members) applies immediately and uniformly, and prevails over local law. OHADA law covers most areas of business law, including the law relating to the taking of security.

(a) Taking security under OHADA

The general principle in Francophone African jurisdictions (as in other civil law jurisdictions) is that specific security must be granted by the debtor for each type of asset. There is no concept of a floating charge in Francophone African jurisdictions which would extend to the assets of a debtor generally. Security packages are therefore documented through several separate security documents for each secured asset.

The OHADA Uniform Act on Security dated 15 December 2010 sets out a detailed security regime for each asset relating to a debtor, such as shares and other securities, bank accounts, receivables, real estate assets, general business concerns, IP rights and movable assets/equipment. The provisions which apply to each relevant security closely reflect French security law and will look familiar to lawyers practising French law. Local courts sometimes continue to refer to French case law for the interpretation of certain OHADA security provisions.

Common legal principles apply to most OHADA security. For example, each grant of security must be evidenced in writing and must be granted by the debtor in respect of a payment obligation. Also, security can be enforced only upon a payment default by the relevant debtor. Each security agreement must also be subject to registration with a corporate registry (the *Registre du Commerce et du Crédit Mobilier* (RCCM)) for enforceability purposes, which may trigger significant registration costs, as further described below.

Each security is considered as an accessory to the underlying obligation (and therefore may be void if that underlying obligation disappears), and may secure existing, future or even conditional obligations. Any holder of security benefits from a preferential right over the relevant secured assets and the security follows the secured asset in whichever hands it may be owned. Guarantees are also addressed by the Uniform Act on Security, such as suretyship or independent guarantees.

The security package in Francophone jurisdictions which are not members of OHADA (eg, Mauritania and Morocco) is closer to the typical old-fashioned French law security package (ie, before the reform of French legislation relating to security adopted in 2006).

(b) **Parties**

Any security can be created, registered, managed or enforced by a security agent acting in its name on behalf of the secured parties. The security agent must be a foreign or national financial institution or credit institution; and the secured assets transferred to the security agent must be segregated from the other assets of the security agent by operation of law. The security can be granted either by the principal debtor or by a third party which guarantees the obligations of the principal debtor.

(c) **Enforcement and insolvency**

Three enforcement options are available to a secured creditor which benefits from OHADA security:
- public auction of the secured assets;
- transfer in court proceedings of the secured assets to, or at the direction of, the secured creditor; and
- an out-of-court enforcement procedure if agreed in the relevant security agreement.

The latter enforcement option is the most efficient, as it allows self-help remedies without going through a potentially lengthy and costly court enforcement process. While this enforcement option is widely included in security agreements in international financing transactions, it is seldom used in practice in local financings.

In the case of the insolvency of a security provider incorporated in an OHADA jurisdiction, a stay of enforcement may apply as from the date of the commencement of insolvency proceedings until the end of those proceedings. The security may also be void if entered into during the hardening period (usually, the period between the actual insolvency of the debtor and the date of commencement of the insolvency proceedings).

(d) *Priorities*

Some OHADA security entails an outright transfer of ownership of the relevant asset, such as the assignment of receivables by way of guarantee or the retention of title. This creates the most protective right for a creditor in case of an insolvency of the debtor and avoids competition with other creditors. However, it is sometimes not commercially acceptable or desirable.

The priorities relating to security over movable and immovable assets are specified in the Uniform Act on Security. The claims which generally rank ahead of OHADA secured claims include:

- certain employee claims; and
- claims relating to the costs of enforcement of security or preservation of the secured assets.

The ranking between competing secured creditors with security over the same assets is determined by the date of effectiveness of the security against third parties (which is generally the date of registration of the security with the RCCM – see below). Specific priorities may also apply in the case of an insolvency of the security provider.

(e) *Registration and costs*

Pursuant to the Uniform Act on Security (Article 51), all security over movables (which includes most security other than security over real estate assets) must be registered with the relevant commercial registry (ie, the RCCM) in order to be enforceable against third parties.

Stamp duties to register the security have not been harmonised by OHADA and range from nominal stamp duties (eg, in Mali) to 1% of the secured amount (in Burkina Faso), which can result in material additional costs in (for example) large project financings in a number of Francophone African jurisdictions. However, as a matter of practice, registration costs can be mitigated for jurisdictions where stamp duties are high by registering only a portion of the financed amount and focusing only on security over the most valuable or liquid assets, or over the shares in a holding company, which would allow the entire business or project to be sold as a going concern. Upstamping is also sometimes a possibility. In addition to stamp duty, notarial fees may need to be negotiated in order for the security documents to be executed in accordance with local law. These vary but can also be meaningful amounts, especially with respect to large financings.

(f) **Impact of exchange control regulations**

While not strictly related to the creation or perfection of security, exchange control regulations may create significant issues that need to be anticipated when structuring a financing transaction in Francophone Africa, including with respect to security enforcement. In Francophone Africa, most jurisdictions are members of economic unions such as the West African Economic and Monetary Union (for the West African jurisdictions) or the Economic and Financial Community for Central African States (for the Central African jurisdictions). As a very general overview, the main principles which apply and which must be taken into account in a secured financing are as follows:

- Loans to a local borrower must generally be made through a locally licensed bank;
- There is strict control of payments in foreign currencies (although special regimes exist in some jurisdictions in relation to the enforcement proceeds);
- Approvals are generally required for a local company to open accounts in foreign currencies and to open offshore accounts; and
- While funding does not generally require governmental or regulatory approval, a declaration to the Central Bank is often required.

5. Lusophone jurisdictions

Legislation in Lusophone African jurisdictions relating to the taking of security is largely inspired by the Portuguese civil law tradition and the types of security available will be very familiar to any practitioner versed in that tradition. On 25 November 1966, Portugal enacted Law-Decree 47,344, which approved the Portuguese Civil Code and extended its validity and effectiveness to all its colonies at the time. Although the Lusophone African countries have been independent for almost 40 years, the provisions of the Portuguese Civil Code remain largely unchanged in their respective domestic Civil Codes.

These Civil Codes provide for security instruments in the form of surety, pledge of assets and rights, mortgage, assignment of rights by way of security and floating charges. The principles used in connection with each of these instruments very much follow those seen in other countries with a Portuguese civil law tradition, such as Brazil. In general, any instrument creating a security interest must:

- be registered before the relevant registry body/office (depending on the nature of the secured asset in question – generally whether the same is an immovable or a movable asset); and
- contain each of the following:
  - the identification of each of the debtor, creditor and (if relevant) guarantor;

- the nature of the instrument evidencing the secured obligation;
- a description of the secured obligation and maximum amount (if applicable);
- a description of the asset, property or right to be the subject of the security;
- the term of the security;
- the date and place of execution of the instrument; and
- the signature of the debtor, creditor and (if relevant) guarantor.

5.1   Surety

Surety is a security that secures a payment obligation through a guarantee obligation. In order to execute a surety instrument, the guarantor must explicitly agree to issue the surety regarding a future or conditional obligation, either without or (if so agreed between the debtor and the guarantor) with the debtor's consent or knowledge. A 'sub-guarantor' may also secure the surety given by the principal guarantor. Following payment under the surety, a guarantor will be subrogated to the rights of any creditor discharged by the guarantor. The guarantor is also obliged to notify the debtor of any fulfilment of its obligations under the surety.

5.2   Pledge

The pledge is a type of security which vests the creditor with the right to satisfy the underlying payment obligation out of the value of the pledged assets in priority to other creditors of the debtor in question. The pledge can be granted by the debtor or by a third party over movable assets, credit rights and any rights not susceptible to security by way of mortgage.

The pledge will take effect once the pledged assets or a document reciting the pledge of the assets in question is delivered to the creditor or to a third party nominated by the creditor. The establishment of the pledge is subject to any form of documentation (eg, notices) and publicity which might be required for the transfer of the underlying pledged rights or assets themselves (eg, in the case of security over real estate, cars or aircraft, whether a transfer of the ownership of the secured asset would require registration). Where a right relating to a payment obligation is the object of the pledge (eg, a receivable), the pledge will become effective once the underlying debtor is notified. In other cases, where the pledge is subject to registration, it will become effective once it has been registered.

When the secured obligation becomes enforceable, the creditor may either sell, through a judicial sale, the pledged asset or resort to an extrajudicial sale if previously agreed to by the parties. The pledge will terminate if:

- the pledged asset or the document stating its availability is returned;
- the secured obligation is satisfied in full;

- the asset subject to the pledge ceases to exist; or
- the creditor waives its right to the pledge.

If the pledged asset ceases to exist, the creditor will have the right to demand substitution of an asset with equivalent value. Failure to do so will result in the underlying debt becoming due and payable.

5.3   Mortgage

The mortgage is a type of security which vests the creditor with the right to be paid through the sale of immovable and related assets owned by the debtor or by a third party in preference to other creditors.

In order to be valid as against other creditors, the mortgage must be duly registered before the Property Registry through a testament or public deed.

While the owner of a mortgaged asset cannot be prohibited from disposing of the same, if it does so, the mortgage will be considered terminated. If the creditor wishes to waive its right under a mortgage, the mortgage waiver must be in writing and signed by the creditor through an authenticated document subject to certification.

5.4   Assignment of rights

The assignment of rights by way of security is a broad form of available security, with the most frequently used example being income consignment. This security consists of the assignment of the income generated by a debtor's immovable or movable asset, subject to registration, in order to secure an underlying payment obligation (which can be a future or conditional obligation). Income consignment may be granted for a limited prescribed term or until full payment of the secured debt in question. If the object of the security is the income of immovable assets, the consignment must not exceed a 15-year term. The income consignment of movable assets must be granted through a written private instrument; while for immovable assets, it must be registered through a public deed or testament before the relevant registry office. The legal framework for the income consignment is very similar to that which applies to the mortgage.

The consignment will cease to be effective if:
- the main secured obligation is satisfied;
- the underlying asset ceases to exist; or
- the creditor waives the consignment.

As with the pledge, if the asset ceases to exist, the creditor will have the right to demand the replacement of the asset in question. If the debtor does not provide such a replacement, the creditor may demand the immediate payment of the secured debt obligation.

5.5   Floating charge

A floating charge (also referred to as a 'floating lien)' occurs when a debt is secured against assets defined by reference to a group rather than with individual specification (eg, raw materials, inventory). While such security is generally admissible in Lusophone jurisdictions, it is not covered in any great detail by current law.

5.6   Further considerations

As mentioned above, the laws and regulations applicable to security instruments are almost identical throughout the various Lusophone African countries. Typically, security instruments give effect to the security in question as between the relevant parties from the moment of their creation. However, in order to be considered valid as against third parties, the security must be made public. In addition, and in the case of a mortgage, the security must be formally registered in order to be effective as against third parties. A security instrument will be considered public when made available for public consultation at the property registry or securities registration centre, or when the secured asset or document proving its availability is handed to the creditor or a third party designated by the creditor. Security over vehicles, aircraft and ships and security over shares, bonds and similar not represented by negotiable instruments must be registered in order to be considered public. The creation of security over assets may require regulatory consent in certain sectors (depending on the nature of the asset but including, for example, mining rights and oil and gas extraction rights).

Default under the secured obligation will vest the secured creditor with the right to enforce the security. Typically, enforcement may be judicial or extrajudicial. Once enforcement has been initiated, the creditor may request the delivery of the secured asset. If the enforcement is pursued through judicial sale, the creditor will be required to prove its right to enforce under the relevant security agreement in order to have a judicial sale granted by the judge in charge of the proceedings. In either judicial or extrajudicial enforcement, other creditors of the debtor will need to be summoned in order to determine the priority between such creditors. The priority of multiple security interests over the same asset is determined by the date on which the various security interests became public. Registration made before a property registry or securities registration centre will prevail over any attempted registration or perfection by other means, even if any such attempt occurred prior to the official registration.

With regard to bankruptcy or judicial reorganisation, creditors with perfected security have preference over all other classes of creditors, except claims for employee wages and certain other customary categories. Furthermore, in the general creditors' meeting, creditors with perfected security vote in a specific class, where their vote is equivalent to the aggregate amount of their respective security. They will also vote in a class for unsecured creditors with the remaining amount of their credit, if any. Slightly differently, some countries – such as Cape Verde – have established that in bankruptcy or judicial reorganisation proceedings, creditors with real security (ie, the holders of mortgages or pledges, as well as certain creditors such as the state and employees) shall have preference over all other classes of creditors.

Recently, Angola approved Law 11/21, which established the movable securities legal regime. Law 11/21 came into force on 21 October 2021. It introduced several changes to movable assets registry proceedings and regulation in Angola, such as in relation to required forms of execution and credit collection priority rules. Under the latter, security over movable assets becomes effective as against third parties only:

- on the date it is made available for consultation on the website of the Central Movable Security Registry;
- by delivery of the tangible asset or the document that confirms the availability of the asset; or
- in the case of security over a bank account or a financial asset, by entering into a control agreement.

Law 11/21 has very similar provisions to legislation in other Lusophone African countries – for example, Law 19/2018 of Mozambique and Law-Decree 48/2020 of Cape Verde. In this sense, the new Angolan regime is closer to those which exist in other Lusophone African countries. However, at the time of writing, there is little certainty on how this new law will be implemented practically or interpreted by the courts. For example, the new electronic registry was not operational initially when the law became effective; hence, market participants anticipate having to register security over movable assets at the vehicle registry in order to attempt to comply with the new law, until the specific new registration regime is operational.

Guinea-Bissau is the only other country that has changed some of its Civil Code provisions on security. Guinea-Bissau intended to update the provisions relating to security with a view to bringing them further into line with OHADA principles. In that regard, types of security such as income consignment and mortgage on movable assets have been abolished. In addition, the guarantee and a new form of pledge have been included in the revised Civil Code. The new provisions applicable to the guarantee include:

- a requirement that the guarantor enter the maximum value of the guarantee in manuscript (both in words and in numbers);
- a requirement that the document evidencing the underlying guaranteed obligation be attached to the guarantee; and
- the need to add the underlying debtor to any litigation brought against the guarantor.

The new form of pledge introduced the concept that delivery of the pledged asset to the creditor will no longer be required.

6. **Ethiopia**

Notwithstanding recent political difficulties, Ethiopia is one of the great success stories of African growth and for several years has had one of the fastest-growing economies on the continent. Measured by GDP, it was the seventh-largest economy in Africa in 2020; and it is also home to the largest airline in Africa. As a result of this growth, financial activity has increased and international financial institutions are looking at significant project-related transactions in the country. However, legal obstacles to implementing financings provided by offshore banks remain, including with respect to foreign exchange and related issues.

With respect to the taking of security, the government has moved forward with an attempt to place the legal system in a position which gives adequate comfort to lenders. Originally based on French Civil Code principles, the law on the granting of security in relation to movable property – first implemented in 1960 – has been comprehensively updated and amended in a manner which is similar to Article 9 of the Uniform Commercial Code in the United States, as well as the UNCITRAL Model Law on Secured Transactions. The new legislation on the taking of security over movable property was intended to create a legal environment which would enable SMEs to access credit more easily (the previous law was deemed to present a significant obstacle to the availability of credit).

The amendments (which came into force in 2020) in large part mitigate the earlier requirement of the possession of movable assets in order to perfect any security interest. 'Movable property' for this purpose is given a very broad meaning, extending to both tangible and intangible assets and the right to use land (although as land itself is vested in the state, security over the same is not possible). At the same time, a Collateral Registry was also established. The registry is exclusively operated on an electronic basis – something which has attracted criticism from some commentators, on the grounds that relatively few Ethiopians can access it. This seems somewhat of a quibble – the creation of a collateral registry must be viewed as a positive development. In addition, the new law removed a distinction between bank and non-bank creditors. The new law does not, however, deal with security over ships, aircraft or exchange-traded securities. Security over ships and aircraft is generally taken by way of mortgage.

The new law recognises three methods of perfecting security interests – registration, possession and control – depending on the nature of the asset which is the subject of the security interest. Perfection by possession is used in connection with negotiable instruments, certificated securities and cash. Control is relevant in connection with moneys in a deposit account or electronic securities. Registration applies to all other assets covered by the new legislation. The nature of the required registration has also been amended to remove the requirement that the entire security agreement be registered – now only notice of the nature of the security is required. The new registry, operated by the National Bank of Ethiopia, ensures full transparency by being available for public review. In the case of security perfected by registration, multiple security interests over the same asset can be created, with priority between those interests being dictated by the timing of registration.

Given the country's civil law background, the concepts of security trusts and security trustees are generally not recognised in Ethiopia, although there is no reason why multiple parties cannot by private contract agree that a third party is to be appointed agent to enforce security and apply the proceeds of the same.

In connection with the enforcement of security over movables, the secured party and borrower can agree on the scope of available remedies in the relevant security document. In the absence of such agreement, the secured party is generally free to realise value from the secured asset through whatever process and at such time as it might select (although 10 business days' prior notice of the planned enforcement is required). There is no requirement for a court-administered process in connection with the enforcement of any such security. However, it is deemed unlikely that an offshore creditor would be able to exercise remedies in this way, as authorisation from the National Bank of Ethiopia is required for the remission of currency offshore.

Bankruptcy proceedings will not generally adversely impact on the rights of secured creditors.

7.   Egypt

We now turn to Egypt, one of the three largest economies in Africa (the second largest in 2020 measured by GDP). Secured financing principles have been used in Egypt for many years, both in large international project finance transactions in the oil and gas and petrochemicals industries and in smaller domestic transactions. As described earlier in this chapter, the historical background to the legal and judicial system in Egypt is a mixed heritage of English, French and other influences. *Sharia* principles have more recently been woven into this background.

Egypt has an established commercial establishment mortgage (CEM) concept, which can extend to all of a company's tangible and intangible assets, other than land and other real property. The CEM requires a list of the relevant charged assets and must be signed by both mortgagor and mortgagee before a notary before being registered in the relevant commercial registry office. Registration must occur within 15 days of the date of signature of the CEM. Registration is valid for five years, but can be renewed for continuous periods of five years (continuation does not impact on priority in any way). Unlike an

English floating charge, the secured assets must be listed with some specificity, so this may involve periodic updating if the assets covered by the CEM change from time to time.

The latest legislation in Egypt – the Movables Pledge Security promulgated by Law 115/2015 and its Executive Regulations (MPS) – provides for an electronic centralised registration system supervised by the Financial Regulatory Authority. This register is intended to create priority as against third-party creditors. The MPS also improved manual registration and perfection procedures, which under the CEM had an impact on timelines and hindered perfection processes. The MPS also extends to pledge of future assets or bank accounts, which were not at first captured by the CEM. However, the legislation relating to the registry is relatively new and there is some uncertainty as to whether the new regime completely supersedes and replaces the pre-existing registration process applicable to CEMs.

As such, some Egyptian lawyers recommend following both registration options for the time being, where both the MPS and the CEM are uploaded to the relevant electronic register, until enforcement of the MPS is tested.

Real estate in Egypt can be secured using a real estate mortgage (REM). An REM will also include any annex or improvements which are associated with the underlying property. To be effective in priority against third parties, an REM must be notarised and registered at the office of a notary public. Registration can be a very lengthy process; but once the REM has been registered, its priority is backdated to the date of delivery of the REM for registration. Registrations must be renewed every 10 years in order to ensure continuing priority.

Other types of security – such as assignments of contractual rights, including insurance proceeds, receivables or bank accounts, as well as pledges of shares – are also recognised under Egyptian law. However, a share pledge does not, in and of itself, entitle the pledgee to vote the underlying shares. Such a right, if agreed to by the pledgor, must be expressly stated in the relevant pledge agreement and be supported by a power of attorney granting that voting right. The process for perfecting the share pledge will depend on whether the shares in question are deposited with the Misr for Central Clearing, Depositary and Registry (MCDR). If the shares are so deposited, perfection can be accomplished by being reflected on the register. If they are not so deposited, the pledge must be recorded on the certificates, which will need to be deposited with the pledgee or its agent, with the pledge being annotated on the relevant company's shareholder register.

While Egyptian law does not recognise the concept of a trust or trustee, security agents are frequently appointed – particularly in international project finance transactions – with their duties and obligations being regulated by negotiated contractual terms and conditions.

Self-help remedies in connection with the enforcement of security are generally not available; enforcement invariably requires a court application and an auction process. Security remains enforceable in bankruptcy subject to the rights of certain preferred creditors as well as, among other things, laws relating to preferences. According to Article 51(3) of Law 93/2000, in the event of enforcement of security over dematerialised shares (eg, shares deposited with MCDR), upon the occurrence of an event of default that is continuing, enforcement can take place after five days of service of a notice by way of court bailiff. This may take the form of an acquisition of such shares or the sale thereof. The valuation formula in enforcement must be referred to in the pledge of shares agreement.

8. South Africa

As mentioned earlier in this chapter, the legal and judicial system in South Africa (as well as several other jurisdictions in Southern Africa) has evolved under a number of different influences, starting with Dutch and Napoleonic influences and continuing through to the English colonial period. As a consequence, there exist a variety of legal principles which would be familiar to civil and common lawyers, but with deviations which might not be so familiar.

As a general proposition, however, it is a relatively straightforward matter to take security over most assets in South Africa. Trusts are recognised, but the concept of a security trustee is not – rather, security in a syndicated lending environment is commonly granted to a security agent under a parallel debt type structure. Alternative structures involving a special purpose vehicle (SPV) for the purpose of taking security for the benefit of multiple lenders are also common. In such a structure, the SPV grants a guarantee of the borrower's obligation to the lenders. The borrower then counter-indemnifies the SPV in respect of the guarantee and secures that counter-indemnity with the relevant secured assets. The SPV may be owned by an independent owner through a trust (or similar). On occasion, the shares in the SPV may also be charged to the lenders. A third option might be to grant security to the lenders on a joint and several basis; but that is not common and it is unclear whether it would survive judicial scrutiny.

South Africa does not recognise the English-style floating charge. Rather, in determining the appropriate security instrument, it draws a distinction between real estate and movable assets and, in connection with the latter, between tangible and intangible assets (although certain intangible assets relating to immovable property – for example, a mining licence – might be classified as intangibles).

Security over 'real estate' – defined in South Africa as immovable property, including buildings – is accomplished using a mortgage bond which, to be perfected, requires registration under the Deeds Registries Act 1937 in the same registry where the relevant immovable property is registered. Security over other tangible assets also requires a mortgage; in this case, in the form of a special or general notarial bond. The former covers specific identified (and identifiable) assets. Perfection is achieved through registration at the deeds registry, which must occur within three months of execution. The general bond covers all tangible assets other than real estate, but requires a judicial order to take possession of an asset covered by the bond in order for the security to be properly constituted. Registration must also be made within three months of execution.

Fees are payable in connection with both mortgage bonds and notarial bonds, and can be substantial. These are payable to conveyancers and public notaries, respectively, and are paid on a sliding scale ranging from 0.8% to 1.9% of the amount secured. Fortunately, however, the level of fees can be negotiated.

Security over bank accounts is taken pursuant to an instrument known as a 'cession'. This also applies to other contractual rights such as receivables. Notice to the relevant counterparty (eg, the account bank or the debtor) is not required to perfect the security; but, as is common elsewhere, in the absence of notification, payment by the bank or the relevant contractual counterparty to the provider of the cession will discharge the underlying obligation. Cessions can take one of two forms. In the first, title to the property in question remains with the chargor (so similar to a pledge). In the second, title is transferred to the chargee, subject to the right to have title transferred back once the debt in question is discharged. The cession, along with a pledge, is also commonly utilised to take security over shares. The secured creditor usually takes possession of the certificated shares. Perfection over security relating to uncertificated shares which are deposited with South Africa's central securities depositary takes place by the relevant securities account being annotated with the details of the security in accordance with the Financial Markets Act 2012.

Self-help remedies in enforcement are available for certain types of security, but not in connection with a mortgage bond or a general notarial bond. In the case of these bonds, a court order must be obtained which directs a court officer to attach the asset in question and therefore enables the holder of the security to perfect the security by possession.

9. Some concluding thoughts

The serendipitous manner in which African history, and in particular its colonial history, has influenced the development of legal systems in its various constituent countries explains in large part the variation in the laws applicable to secured financings in those countries. This, of course, is no bad thing. There is no reason why Africa as a whole should have a homogeneous approach to secured finance, any more than the various systems seem across Europe and Asia. Various countries at different levels of economic development and with different political outlooks and traditions require tailormade solutions. However, as is also the case elsewhere, a tendency towards certain fundamental principles which encourage secured lending should not be ignored.

Secured financing is without doubt a prime driver of economic growth – particularly in the case of SMEs. It is also clear that accessing credit is more difficult across Africa than in other regions of the world (in the World Bank Doing Business Rankings, both sub-Saharan Africa and the Middle East/North Africa rank below other geographical areas in connection with the parameter labelled "Getting Credit"). Reform of the law relating to secured financings is a dynamic observed in multiple jurisdictions. Initiatives such as the UNCITRAL Model Law of Secured Transactions serve to provide focus for change. Encouragingly, some of the changes implemented in African countries have also inspired changes elsewhere. For example, the implementation of a collateral registry in Ghana led others to consider such an approach.

While there have been many positive developments in connection with the overarching principles of security – such as types of security and formalities for the creation of the same – this, in and of itself, is insufficient. Continuing the trend of establishing security registries is obviously to be encouraged; but in addition to the mere establishment of a registry, infrastructure for the efficient operation of the same is equally important. Open access to the registry is also a key requirement.

In addition, provision for effective and efficient remedies to realise the value of security is critical. In many African jurisdictions, remedies – particularly in the nature of sale – must be effected through court-monitored proceedings, which can be slow, costly and uncertain. Effective self-help remedies should be encouraged and provided for. Finally, the robustness of security in insolvency proceedings – particularly in relation to both priority (other than with respect to customary preferred creditors such as unpaid employees and tax authorities) and realisation of value – must be ensured. The piecemeal implementation of legislative change across each of these areas of concern is potentially problematic in this respect; but a truly comprehensive approach to the reform may be some time away.

The authors would like to acknowledge the assistance of the following firms in the preparation of this chapter: Al Kamel Law Firm (Egypt); Anjarwalla & Khanna LLP (Kenya); Bentsi – Enchill Letsa & Ankomah (Ghana); Mesfin Tafesse & Associates (Ethiopia); Udo Udoma & Belo-Osagie (Nigeria); and (Mayer Brown) Tauil & Chequer Advogados (Brazil).

Central and Eastern Europe

Claudia Chiper
Robert David
Przemek Kozdój
Katerina Kraeva
Wolf Theiss

1. Introduction

Central and Eastern Europe (CEE) has seen dynamic political and economic change in recent decades, with most of the region leaving behind the communist regime and turning towards an economy based on capitalist principles. While not all countries have evolved at the same pace, it is fair to say that all of them have taken tremendous steps in the development of their legal frameworks. Furthermore, accession to the European Union has led to a level playing field in certain areas of law and ensured stability, predictability and a friendly environment for investors.

While many countries worldwide are still struggling with the effects of the COVID-19 pandemic, there has been a revival of investment in the region, which is partially also the driver of the financing market. Alongside local financing transactions, cross-border financing at the group level has become the norm, both in the context of acquisition financing and simply as a means of leveraging equity and freeing up capital for other investments.

In this chapter, when referring to 'the CEE' as a region, we are referring to a narrower region consisting of Bulgaria, the Czech Republic, Croatia, Hungary, Poland, Romania and Slovakia.

The concepts discussed are not country specific, but rather refer to the structuring of cross-border transactions with elements and a nexus in the CEE. This chapter aims to provide an illustrative overview of the most commonly encountered issues. We utilise examples from each of the above countries in order to highlight certain points.

2. Taking security

The most common forms of security interest are pledges and mortgages over immovable and movable assets. In Bulgaria, Croatia, Hungary[1] and Poland, the concept of a floating charge is recognised in various legal forms. In the Czech

---

1   In Hungary, a floating charge may be established over assets, but this ownership interest is not recorded in any authentic registry. Therefore, assets such as real estate, quotas (membership interests in limited liability companies), intellectual property, aircraft and ships cannot be the subject of a floating charge.

Republic and Slovakia, the floating charge concept is not recognised; but the same effects may be achieved by establishing a pledge over an enterprise or part thereof. However, the prevailing market practice is to create security over each category of individual assets. In Romania, the concept of a floating charge is also not recognised, but a similar result may be achieved by establishing security over classes of assets.

Taking a standard security package consisting of pledges over movable assets and mortgages over real estate generally involves the conclusion of agreements under private signature or as a notarial deed; or, under Czech law, as agreements with notarised signatures.

Unlike in most other countries, in Slovakia, the creation of a pledge over most asset classes (including, without limitation, real estate) does not require a notarised signature; but for certain classes of assets, such as shares in limited liability companies, the type of legal form which is most commonly used in cross-border transactions requires notarisation.

In Hungary, a notarial deed is not required for any security document to be validly established, but is required in order to make such documents directly enforceable. This means in practice that the beneficiary of the collateral need not initiate a lawsuit against the debtor to determine the outstanding claims of the borrower towards the beneficiary prior to the enforcement procedure.

Generally, security agreements may be concluded in English or any other foreign language, or in a bilingual format where a notarial deed is required; while in certain cases, a translation into the local language is required for registration purposes.

For example, in Hungary, by virtue of law, notarial deeds cannot be bilingual. Security documents may be executed in English or in any other foreign language, provided that the acting notary has a licence to prepare notarial deeds in that language. In contrast, in some countries – including Poland, Croatia and Slovakia – notarial deeds may only be executed in the official local languages. In the Czech Republic, Hungary and Slovakia, a translation is required for registration purposes.

Security interests over real estate must be registered for the purposes of public information and ranking. However, in Bulgaria, the Czech Republic[2] (only for certain asset classes), Croatia, Poland and Hungary, mortgages and pledges are validly established upon their registration in the respective registries. For instance, in the Czech Republic, pledges over receivables can be executed in the form of a notarial deed and registered in the Register of Pledges; and a registered pledge ranks ahead of a non-registered pledge. However, given

---

2   In the Czech Republic, a pledge or mortgage over certain types of assets (eg, ownership interests in limited liability companies or real estate) must be registered in the public register in order to be validly created. On the other hand, a pledge over other types of assets (eg, receivables) is validly created upon execution of a pledge agreement.

that the registration costs are relatively high, the prevailing practice is to register only negative pledges.[3] Once a negative pledge has been duly registered, no third party may perform any registration and the creditor's ranking is therefore protected.

As in Poland,[4] in Slovakia, a security package is sometimes supplemented by a notarial deed of enforcement, which is a type of notarial deed under which the debtor acknowledges the existence of the debt and agrees to direct enforcement of the claims secured by the notarial deed without requiring a final judgment or arbitral award. This notarial deed is considered an enforcement title for the purpose of in-court enforcement and allows the creditor, among other things, to request that a court-appointed bailiff enforce the secured claims. Experience shows that courts tend to scrutinise such notarial deeds of enforceability in great detail, which sometimes results in courts declining to allow enforcement on that basis. Nevertheless, this form of security is still often used as supplementary security in conjunction with more traditional security instruments.

Costs are attached to taking security, especially if notarisation is required. For instance, in Romania, the establishment of an immovable mortgage requires an immovable mortgage agreement in the form of a notarial deed, and notarial and registration fees proportionate to the secured amount apply. These fees are approximately 0.2% of the secured amount.[5] In Slovakia, the notarial fees for drawing up a notarial deed of enforceability range between 0.05% and 1% of the secured amount. The fees for perfection of a pledge over securities (eg, shares in joint stock companies) are also linked to the value of the secured receivable and are generally higher than the notarial fees for most other types of security.

In Poland, a notarial deed creating a mortgage costs around €1,000 and the court registration fee ranges up to 0.1% of the value of the secured receivable. In Hungary, if the security documents are incorporated in a notarial deed, notarial fees apply, the amount of which depends mainly on:

- the value of the underlying transaction;
- the number of notarial deeds issued by the notary; and
- the number of pages of each notarial deed.

If the notarial deed is concluded in a foreign language, the fees double. Notaries must issue an electronic certified copy of the notarial deed, and court enforcement is conducted on the basis of this electronic certified copy of the notarial deed. Notarial fees in a typical cross-border transaction where notarial

---

3   The notarial fees associated with the registration of a negative pledge do not exceed €100.
4   Where a submission to enforcement is generally concluded.
5   The fees are calculated by applying the following formulae:
       Notary fees = [(Secured amount in RON – RON 500,000) × 0.07% + RON 1,285] + value added tax (19%); and
       Land registration fees = secured Amount in RON × 0.1% + RON 140 per land register.

deeds are concluded in a foreign language may range between €7,500 and €15,000.

In Croatia, notarial fees for establishing an immovable mortgage or pledge over movable assets or rights depend on the secured amount, but may not exceed HRK 20,000 (approximately €2,700) plus value added tax.

Typically, in a cross-border financing where a company is established in the CEE, the company may be party to the finance documentation either as a borrower (together with other subsidiaries and their holding company) or as a guarantor offering security for the obligations undertaken by the holding company or the borrower. From a corporate law perspective, corporate members of a group of companies are viewed as separate legal entities and, therefore, when acting *vis-à-vis* other members of the group – including in a group financing scenario – they should do so at arm's length. Therefore, structuring a transaction and the relevant security package in a group financing usually presents several issues that must be addressed. We discuss the most common legal issues in this chapter.

3. Structuring limitations

3.1 Secured receivables

English law based concepts of trust commonly used in syndicated facilities are often not recognised by local courts in the CEE. Instead, the concept of parallel debt is used.

Although the Polish Supreme Court has recognised foreign law governed parallel debt as grounds for a valid claim, it is not possible to set up a parallel debt structure governed by Polish law. For transactions governed by Polish law, the concepts of mortgage administrator and registered pledge administrator are often applied. The security that the administrator holds for the benefit of creditors is, by law, separated from its estate and therefore the creditors are ringfenced against the insolvency of such administrator.

In Slovakia, the valid creation of a pledge requires the existence of the pledgee's claim against the relevant debtor. This conceptual problem is typically resolved through the concept of parallel debt or joint and several creditorship of the lenders. Even though the parallel debt concept is not specifically recognised by Slovak law, it is often used in practice in secured lending transactions, where the facility agreement and intercreditor agreement are typically governed by law other than Slovak law.

In Hungary, the Civil Code – in force as of 2014 – introduced a very similar concept to the English law concept of security agency/security trustee. In brief, the lenders may appoint a person (from either the lender group or an unrelated third party) to act as their security agent in connection with the Hungarian security documents. This appointment allows the security agent to sign the

Hungarian security documents. As a result, the security agent will be registered in the relevant registries and is entitled to enforce the security. By using the Hungarian law security agent concept, there is no need to rely on the English law security agent/trust concept or the parallel debt approach. This is helpful because the enforceability of such concepts in the Hungarian courts is rather ambiguous. When a Hungarian security provider is involved in the transaction, in practice, the facility agreement or the intercreditor agreement, as applicable, is supplemented with the Hungarian law provisions on the appointment of such security agent in relation to the security instruments governed by Hungarian law.

Romanian law also does not recognise the concept of trust, although it does regulate the concept of *'fiducia'*, which has similarities to the concept of trust. However, Romanian law does recognise the concept of the security agent, but only in relation to pledges over movable assets; immovable mortgages are left outside its scope of application. In cross-border transactions, parties generally prefer to supplement the facility agreement in order to introduce the concept of joint and several creditorship. Alternatively, the concept of parallel debt may be used. However, this concept has not been tested in court and therefore its use may trigger a qualification in the local counsel's legal opinion.

Similar to Romania and Slovakia, Croatia does not recognise the concept of the security agent. The valid creation of security in Croatia requires the existence of a creditor's claim against the relevant debtor. In the case of syndicated transactions governed by foreign law which provide for a security agent, the problem in relation to taking security in Croatia is typically solved by including language which establishes joint and several creditorship on the part of the lenders. While this practical aspect has not yet been tested in court, it is widely used.

3.2 Cross-stream and upstream security or guarantees
Group financing usually warrants, from a commercial perspective, that corporate members of a group guarantee the debt of their corporate affiliates – parent (upstream), siblings (cross-stream) or direct or indirect subsidiaries (downstream); or a combination thereof. This may take various legal forms, including:

- corporate guarantees;
- joint and several liability;
- *in rem* security interests or quasi-security; and
- indemnities.

Downstream security or guarantees established by a parent for the benefit of its subsidiaries constitute permissible aid, due to the implied corporate benefit that parents are supposed to obtain from their subsidiaries as a result of a successful business (eg, dividends, increase in share value). Therefore, it is less likely that downstream security may be challenged, as long as the subsidiary is not a resource drain on the parent company.

The provision of upstream or cross-stream security interests is possible, subject to the strict limitations of mandatory capital maintenance rules.

For example, Romanian law provides that a company may only undertake obligations and perform actions with a view to deriving a gain (a lucrative purpose). Lack of adequate corporate benefit may be challenged both in and outside of insolvency by shareholders and creditors. A successful challenge may render the security ineffective either entirely or in part, depending on how disproportionate such security is by reference to the actual benefit that the security provider is deemed to receive in exchange for establishing the security. If challenged in court, the security may be rendered ineffective. Further, if the security is enforced and value is transferred to the secured parties, this transfer may be reversed and the proceeds may be clawed back from the secured parties, together with any applicable statutory interest.

Under Romanian law, a lack of corporate benefit may also be challenged as a criminal offence for misuse in bad faith of the company's credit or property. Criminal liability lies with the company's directors, general managers, executive managers, founders and – arguably – shareholders.[6] There are several exceptions pertaining to treasury arrangements, such as cash pooling and borrowing or receiving guarantees by a founder from its subsidiary or from a direct or indirect parent. Some practitioners argue that there is a risk that the secured parties may be viewed as accessories or accomplices to a criminal offence, as they generally require the companies to provide security in order to make funds available. However, there is no case law to support this view and most practitioners view this as a rather remote theoretical risk.

Several options are used in practice to mitigate the above risk. The first option is to identify a corporate benefit. As a rule, the corporate bodies of the Romanian company will be required to assess this aspect based on the factual economic grounds and attest to it in their decision approving the entry into the relevant security documents. Unanimity regarding the approval of the entry into the envisaged finance documents is generally required in order to avoid potential

---

6   Under the Romanian Companies Law (31/1990), the founder, director, manager or legal representative of a Romanian company ('relevant person') is criminally liable (potentially also independently of a breach of capital maintenance rules and the existence of corporate benefit) if he or she:
- uses in bad faith the company's assets, credit or standing for purposes that run against the company's interests or for his or her own benefit, or for the benefit of a company that he or she is directly or indirectly interested in; or
- causes a Romanian company to grant a guarantee or a security or to undertake any similar obligation to cover/secure the own liabilities of such relevant person, provided that such company is:
  - an entity that the relevant person administers;
  - an entity which is controlled by the entity administered by the relevant person; or
  - an entity which controls the entity administered by the restricted person (in all situations subject to a €5,000 de minimis threshold).

Any act or agreement which is sanctioned as a criminal offence may be declared null and void for illicit cause.

challenges to the decision by the other shareholders or directors. For instance, if the Romanian subsidiary will itself receive part of the proceeds of the loan, one may argue that there is sufficient benefit for it to grant security. However, in such a scenario, it may be argued that the security granted by the Romanian subsidiary will be limited to the actual benefit it has received. In other cases, it may be that no funds reach the Romanian subsidiary, but a more general corporate benefit may be identified based on the factual economic relationships between the group companies. For example, the Romanian company achieves income by servicing one of its sister companies or parent company which is contracting the financing in order to finance its working capital needs.

The second option is for the Romanian company to receive consideration from the relevant entity which benefits from the funds under the financing. This consideration should be established on an arm's-length basis. In practice, a fee similar to that received by banks for the issue of letters of guarantee is taken into account.

The third option is to include a limitation clause in the finance documents whereby the security provider limits the scope of the security to that permitted by the law. This option creates difficulties for the finance parties, because it makes the assessment of the value of the security problematic. Further, its effectiveness has not been proved in court; and some finance parties would argue that such language points to an issue which is rather theoretical and remote, because there have been successful enforcement cases in similar structures.

The choice from among the above options depends on the circumstances of each transaction and the value that the secured parties place on the security to be granted by the Romanian company.

Bulgarian law does not explicitly require the existence of a corporate benefit upon granting security for a third-party/parent debt. However, certain legal provisions of a general nature might be applicable in this regard, as follows:

- The managers of Bulgarian guarantors must perform their duties and exercise their powers in the interests of the company and its shareholder(s). A breach of this requirement will not affect the validity of the transaction, but may result in the personal liability of the managers; and
- Granting security without benefit or obvious rationale for the security provider may be interpreted as an act with a detrimental effect and may thus be subject to certain avoidance claims, such as:
  - an *Actio Pauliana*[7] in or outside of insolvency; or
  - insolvency avoidance claims.

---

7   Under Bulgarian law, a creditor is entitled to make a claim in court requiring that certain acts or deeds performed by its debtor to the detriment of its interest be declared void. This procedure allows creditors to protect their rights from fraudulent legal transactions intended to reduce in bad faith a debtor's estate by transfers to third parties.

Furthermore, in respect of the capital maintenance rules, there is a general principle that shareholders may not directly or indirectly reclaim their contributions and are entitled only to dividends and other payments following:

- profit;
- a reduction in share capital;
- termination of participation;
- liquidation; or
- corporate restructuring.

For limited liability companies, there is no relevant case law that sheds light on whether this capital maintenance principle constitutes a restriction on upstream guarantees or security interests. Therefore, limited liability companies are preferred in cross-border financings. Stricter requirements exist in relation to joint stock companies, which make them inappropriate for acquisition structures with external funding.

Polish law does not require the testing of the corporate benefit upon the grant security for a third-party debt. However, such testing may be helpful from a transfer pricing perspective. The Polish limitations of upstream and cross-stream guarantees refer to the protection of the share capital of companies and unjust distributions to shareholders; and further to the balance-sheet insolvency test.

Under Czech law, according to newly implemented provisions, a company is prohibited from granting benefits to a shareholder or its affiliates free of consideration. This rule is primarily problematic when it comes to group financing. A Czech entity usually accedes to a facility agreement as a guarantor or provides *in rem* security as a pledgee, and does not always directly benefit from the loan provided to the other entities within the group. It is not entirely clear as to how broadly this restriction will be interpreted by the Czech courts or legal experts. Some commentators suggest that establishing benefits free of charge can lead to the invalidity of such instruments.

In order to comply with these new rules, a Czech company must be provided with consideration (a benefit) at market value in exchange for providing a guarantee/security for a loan utilised by its parent company or other member of its group or any other consideration that the Czech company provides to its shareholder. The consideration can be of either a monetary or non-monetary nature.

Another option to deal with this prohibition is to establish an official business group – that is, a structure where a dominant entity exerts influence over the activities of a dependent entity aimed at the coordination and conceptual management of at least one of the important components or tasks within the holding's business activities, in order to ensure the long-term promotion of the concern's interests under the holding's single policy. Subject to other conditions, the provision of benefits without direct consideration within this structure is permitted by Czech law.

Lastly, under Czech law, a resolution of the general meeting of a Czech joint stock company or limited liability company is required where security is granted over assets that, if enforced, would materially change the company's actual scope of business activities. The relevant corporate documents – such as the articles of association, memorandum of association or deed of foundation – may contain additional requirements for corporate approvals (eg, board approval) when it comes to establishing security over the assets of a company.

As from 1 January 2016, Slovakia implemented provisions which have made the grant of upstream security in the form of a guarantee or other type of security problematic. Any such upstream security must be granted in exchange for adequate consideration for the security provider. Although this law has now been in place for five years, there is no case law setting a precedent on the consequences of the absence of such adequate consideration. However, the prevailing market view is that the grant of such security will likely be considered null and void. To overcome this issue, in practice, it is required that the Slovak security provider receive adequate consideration and, to this end, that intra-group documentation capturing the arrangement be concluded in writing. An external expert, such as an auditor or tax adviser, must issue an opinion confirming whether the consideration is adequate.

As in Bulgaria and Poland, Hungary does not require the testing of the corporate benefit upon granting security for the benefit of a third-party debt. Although general legal provisions might be applicable,[8] their breach does not lead to the invalidity of the security.

Similarly to the situation in Slovakia, in Croatia, based on the concept of 'adequate consideration', business transactions between shareholders and their company (eg, the sale of an asset) must be concluded at arm's length. This implies that the relation between the received funds and benefit and the provided collateral or assumed liability should be proportionate.

The question of whether disproportionate consideration may nonetheless be legal if the management of the company acts with the duty of care of a prudent businessperson is still untested in Croatia. In other words, it is unclear whether a company can take certain actions that have no apparent corporate benefit for the company itself if such actions are properly approved by its management, acting with due care and diligence.

Thus, certain economic benefits should be assessed based on the circumstances of the relevant transaction. However, the risk that, if challenged, such a benefit could be deemed inadequate by a court remains. One possible

---

8   One of the basic legal requirements is that the directors of a Hungarian entity perform their duties and exercise their powers in the interests of the company and its shareholders/members.

way to determine the corporate benefit is to assess its amount or value versus the value of the secured assets.

3.3 Financial assistance

Financial assistance is most likely encountered in acquisition finance scenarios where a leveraged buy-out is employed. All countries in the CEE regulate this concept. In the Czech Republic, the concept applies to both limited liability companies and joint stock companies. In Hungary, it applies only to listed joint stock companies; while in the rest of the CEE (ie, Croatia, Poland, Romania, Slovakia and Bulgaria), it applies only to joint stock companies. As a rule, no whitewash procedure is available, except in the Czech Republic and Hungary.

Financial assistance is prohibited under Romanian law based on the theory that the company would be using its credit or assets for the benefit of a potential shareholder to the detriment of the other (existing) shareholders and creditors. The concept is rather narrow under Romanian law,[9] in the sense that it prohibits a Romanian company from advancing funds, granting loans or creating guarantees/security interests in view of the acquisition of its own shares by third parties. There are exceptions for transactions concluded by credit institutions and other financial institutions in the normal course of their business and acquisitions of shares by employees, provided that the net assets are not reduced below the subscribed share capital and those reserves which cannot be distributed pursuant to the provisions of law and of the company bylaws.

While most legal scholars take the view that limited liability companies should not be subject to the same restrictions as joint stock companies unless expressly provided by law, in some decisions the Romanian courts have applied rules specific to joint stock companies to limited liability companies based on similarity grounds (ie, the existence of the same rationale behind a legal provision). There is therefore some degree of uncertainty as to the application of the prohibition on financial assistance to limited liability companies. However, the prevailing view is that such provisions should not apply to limited liability companies.

Although the law does not expressly stipulate any sanctions for breach of the financial assistance rules, practitioners have formed the view that loans granted in breach of the financial assistance prohibition are invalid and must be repaid on the grounds of unjustified enrichment; and that any security interests or guarantees granted in breach of such prohibition may also be declared invalid.

However, a minority opinion exists according to which breach of the

---

9   The provisions in the Romanian Companies Law are similar to those set out in Article 23 of the Second Company Law Directive (77/91), in its old form.

financial assistance restrictions may trigger the potential criminal law liability of the directors of the company that provided the security interests. However, the provision in Romanian law that governs this sanction is poorly drafted; and in the absence of any case law in this respect, the prudent approach would be to consider that the breach of financial assistance rules may fall under such provisions and may thus entail the criminal liability of the company directors.

The most common method of dealing with the prohibition on financial assistance is the upstream merger of the target and the acquirer. From a practical perspective, once the target has been merged into the acquirer, the assets become the estate of the latter and can therefore be encumbered in favour of the financing parties.

Another method is to structure the acquisition facility agreement to include various financing tranches with different purposes. In this scenario, the Romanian company may secure only those tranches which do not refer to the acquisition of its own shares.

Although widely applied in practice, none of the above methods has been tested in court and therefore a degree of risk exists.

While the exemptions from the financial assistance restrictions for joint stock companies in Bulgaria are similar to those in Romania, analysis must be conducted on a case-by-case basis, considering that the consequences of breach of such rules may lead to the invalidation of the transaction.

Croatian law contains several provisions reflecting the principle of protection and maintenance of a company's registered share capital. One of the key provisions reflecting this principle is a general prohibition on a Croatian company making any payment to its shareholders if it would result in the return of what was paid to the company by way of contribution to its share capital. Therefore, if the net asset value of the company's assets would fall below its registered share capital as a result of the grant of security for the benefit of another company, it may validly grant such security only against receipt of certain consideration.[10] Any benefit received by a shareholder in violation of these provisions may be clawed back and returned to the company.

Under Polish law, a joint stock company may finance the purchase of its shares by granting a loan, pre-payment or security only where the following procedural and financial requirements are met:
- The financing must be made at arm's length; and
- The management board of the company granting the financial assistance must prepare a report setting out:
    - the purpose of providing the financing;

---

10   At the time of writing, there is no case law providing guidance on whether, to what extent and in which circumstances the grant of security by a company for the benefit of its shareholders would comply with the Croatian capital maintenance rules.

- the company's benefit in providing the financing;
- the terms of the financing, including protection of the company's interests;
- the impact of the financing on the liquidity and solvency of the company; and
- the purchase price, with an explanation of why this is recognised as a fair price.

The report must be published and filed with the registration court. The final decision on providing financing is made by the general shareholders' meeting. Typically, companies support their decision on granting security with the opinion of a reputable expert confirming that the security was granted at arm's length and that the shareholders can rely on the management board's report.

In the Czech Republic, financial assistance rules may apply if a loan is granted in order to finance the acquisition of shares in a Czech joint stock company or limited liability company, and/or its direct or indirect parent. Under these rules, the target may grant a guarantee or security only subject to certain conditions, including the following:

- The transaction is made at fair market conditions; and
- The provisions of security or financing do not cause the target to become insolvent.

Furthermore, similar to the requirements in Poland, the statutory body of the target must draw up a written report stating, for example:

- the reasons for the provision of financial assistance;
- the benefits and risks;
- the conditions under which the financial assistance will be provided; and
- the reasons why the financial assistance does not conflict with the interests of the target (ie, a whitewash procedure).

The provision of financial assistance must be approved by the shareholders' meeting of the target. The requirements applicable to joint stock companies are onerous and therefore such companies are usually unable to provide financial assistance.

In Slovakia, financial assistance rules expressly apply only to joint stock companies. Although some observers hold the view that the limitation should also apply to limited liability companies, the prevailing market practice does not support such an opinion.

In Hungary, financial assistance rules apply only to listed joint stock companies. A listed joint stock company may provide financial assistance for the acquisition of its shares only if:

- the transaction is entered into under market conditions;
- the source of such financial assistance is its assets available for the payment of dividends; and
- the general meeting approves the decision by at least a three-quarters majority upon recommendation by the management board.

The recommendation of the management board must set out:
- the reasons for the financial assistance;
- the risks involved;
- the commercial terms;
- the price of the shares; and
- the advantages that the company is likely to gain by providing such financial assistance.

The management board must submit the recommendation to the court of registration.

3.4   Common directors

In Bulgaria, Poland, Hungary, Croatia and the Czech Republic, having common directors is not an issue. However, in Romania and Slovakia, certain restrictions apply when joint stock companies are involved in a transaction.

Under Romanian law, two or more joint stock companies sharing common directors may not extend security interests including guarantees to each other. This is based on the assumption that the relevant directors find themselves with a conflict of interests and may influence the decision-making process regarding the extension of the security or the guarantee at the level of a relevant security provider.

The security or guarantees established in the context of a common directorship situation concerning two or more joint stock companies may be challenged as null and void. The consequence of a successful challenge is that such security of guarantees will be rendered invalid. Further, if the security or guarantees have been called upon, the assets transferred may be repossessed and the proceeds may be clawed back from the secured parties, together with any applicable statutory interest. Furthermore, breach of common directorship rules may trigger the criminal liability of the directors.

In practice, having a common director for various subsidiaries in the same group is rather common. To mitigate this issue, in practice, it is recommended that shareholders unanimously approve the entry in the relevant finance documents, and that directors be removed. If removal of the director is not possible, the company should be converted into a limited liability company. If this is also not possible for practical reasons (eg, where special licences require that the company be organised as a joint stock company), the common directors (or their relevant relatives) should be ring-fenced by abstaining from participating in any negotiations, board or shareholders' meetings, and from the execution and implementation of the relevant finance documents. If their abstention creates quorum or voting hurdles, additional directors may be appointed – at least on a temporary basis – in order to meet such quorum or voting prerequisites.

In Slovakia, a similar restriction applies with respect to joint stock companies, and this is thus a common red flag in secured lending transactions where a Slovak joint stock company acts as a security provider. Where a Slovak joint stock company grants security for the purpose of securing the debt of another company with overlapping directors or persons otherwise authorised to act on behalf of the company, this requires the prior approval of the supervisory board and the transaction must be concluded on an arm's-length basis. Breach of this requirement results in the security being considered null and void.

Although similar restrictions do not apply in the Czech Republic and Croatia, the law in both countries requires that a director or a member of a statutory body, as applicable, notify the supervisory body of the company or its general shareholders' meeting if the director becomes aware of a conflict that may arise between his or her interest and the interests of the company. The supervisory board or, as applicable, the general shareholders' meeting may suspend the execution powers of that director for a certain period.

In addition, in all countries discussed above, directors and members of the statutory body of a company are generally required to act with due managerial care in the interests of the company, and have fiduciary duties. Before entering into a security agreement, the members of the relevant statutory body should thus make an informed assessment as to whether entering into the agreement would be detrimental to the company. Failure to observe such duties triggers the liability of the directors or members of the statutory bodies, especially where the company becomes insolvent as a result thereof.

Latin America[1]

---

1. Overview

Maria Alevras-Chen
Douglas A Doetsch
Mayer Brown

The legal codes in most Latin American countries are based on Roman law principles, which were imported to the region by Portuguese and Spanish colonisers. Since the colonial period, these Latin American countries have slowly and fitfully adapted their codes – including those governing secured transactions – through various reforms to civil and commercial law. In recent years, these reforms have included borrowings from common law countries, such as the electronically searchable registries of security interests now in place in Mexico and Colombia, as well as updated insolvency codes in a number of jurisdictions. Despite these innovations, the creation and enforcement of creditors' rights under security agreements often remain cumbersome, formalistic and time consuming – particularly in comparison to many common law security instruments.

Perhaps the most important development in secured transaction practice in Latin America in the last 20 years is the increasing use of trust agreements or fiduciary assignments to govern assets serving as collateral security. Mexico and Brazil – the two largest jurisdictions in the region – have been pioneers in the use of these fiduciary instruments to give additional certainty to secured creditors. For example, in Mexico, the assignment of collateral to a trust (by way of a trust agreement with a Mexican financial institution acting as trustee) removes the assigned assets from the bankruptcy estate of the debtor – meaning that in order to enforce, there is (at least in theory) no need to go to court, because the assets are already owned by the trust. A similar result obtains in Brazil, through a fiduciary assignment of collateral assets to the creditor. In both

---

1   The compilation of this chapter was coordinated by Douglas A Doetsch of Mayer Brown LLP. The names of the authors of each section in this chapter, and their firms, are given at the start of their respective contributions.

jurisdictions – again, at least in theory – the assets thus assigned are not subject to the debtor's insolvency proceedings, because the assets were transferred at the time the secured credit transaction was executed.

The common law jurisdictions of the English-speaking Caribbean are the great exceptions to the collateral security regimes described below in the largest Latin American countries. For Jamaica, Barbados and other former English colonies, the common law rules borrowed from England prescribe that collateral security continues to be created and enforced by way of documentation similar to that in the United Kingdom.

The sections below summarise the creation and enforcement of collateral security in the most active Latin American jurisdictions for secured transactions: Brazil, Mexico, Colombia, Peru, Argentina and Chile – with special emphasis on the two largest countries, Brazil and Mexico.

2.   Brazil

Luis Otero Montes
Tauil & Chequer Advogados

2.1   Historical basis for secured transactions

Brazil's legal system follows in the tradition of the continental European civil law system, which is grounded in classical Roman law. The Federal Constitution establishes fundamental principles of the Brazilian legal system, which all other laws and judicial decisions must follow.

Business law is set out in many different Brazilian legal statutes. However, two of them merit special mention:

- the Law of Introduction to the Norms of Brazilian Law (Decree Law 4,657 of 4 September 1942), which establishes general rules of legal interpretation; and
- the Civil Code (Law 10,406 of 10 January 10 2002, as amended), which unifies in a single code the rules on personal/civil rights and obligations and commercial transactions.

During most of the colonial period (1500-1822), internal commercial activities and local credit transactions in Brazil were very limited (indeed, almost non-existent), because all of the country's economic activities were strictly regulated by the king of Portugal. For around 300 years, credit lines associated with extractive and productive activities were granted directly by the Portuguese crown to nobles and members of the Portuguese government; and subsequently to members of the Portuguese bourgeoisie holding concession rights to undertake certain activities in the Brazilian territory (eg, the economic cycles of *Pau Brasil* wood extraction and sugar, cotton, gold and diamond production).

In the context of the Napoleonic Wars in Europe, the Brazilian legal system took its first step towards modernisation in 1808, when the adoption of Portuguese governance opened up Brazilian ports to international commerce (mainly with England), leading to the development of an internal market for imported goods and the incorporation of the first Brazilian financial institution.

The modernisation of Brazil at the outset of the 19th century – when Brazil was a member of (and the headquarters of) the United Kingdom of Portugal, Brazil and Algarve (with the royal capital located in Rio de Janeiro) – inspired the country's independence and the development of a national legal system independent from Portuguese and European laws.[2]

As banking and industrial activities experienced significant growth due to investments by local entrepreneurs during the second half of the 19th century, secured transactions became more common in order to finance the acquisition of lands, raw materials and production. Traditional types of security were granted in the form of:

- pledges of movable assets, goods, bonds of public debts, shares and other credit titles; and
- mortgages over immovable assets.

Both types were regulated by the Commercial Code of 1850 (Law 556 of 25 June 1850), which was inspired by the French Napoleonic Commercial Code (1808), the Spanish Commercial Code (1829) and the Portuguese Commercial Code (1833).

During the twentieth century, secured credit transactions were largely used in Brazil for financing different types of assets (especially cars and machinery), as well as real estate.

The Civil Code of 2002 – which unified civil and commercial laws in a single piece of legislation – was enacted following the success of the Real Plan during a time of unprecedented political and economic stability in Brazil. Accordingly, this legislation contributed to the development of a more sophisticated finance and secured transactions regime in line with Western international standards.

2.2 Types of security interests

In rem collateral security creates liens over specified assets as collateral, so the ownership of the assets is directly associated with the grantor's satisfaction of its secured obligation. In other words, collateral security and *in rem* security agreements grant the secured creditor priority over the assets granted as security for satisfaction of the creditor's loan, while also protecting the assets and the creditor's right against other creditors of the original owner.

---

2   In addition to Portuguese law, Spanish and French laws were used in Brazil for commercial transactions, as the Portuguese legal system in force at that time contained a general principle called 'good right law', under which the laws of illuminated Christian nations could be used to cover gaps in Portuguese law.

Under Brazilian law, security (*in rem* collateral security) varies depending on the type of collateral securing an obligation (normally the full and punctual repayment of a debt).

The most common types of *in rem* collateral security used in secured transactions in Brazil are as follows:

- pledges, which are used for movable assets and rights (including credit rights such as receivables and rights over bank accounts);
- mortgages, which are used for immovable assets (eg, real estate), ships and aircraft; and
- fiduciary security, comprised of:
  - fiduciary assignment, which is used for movable assets and rights (including credit rights such as receivables and rights over bank accounts); and
  - fiduciary transference of property, which is used for immovable assets and shares of corporations.

A traditional pledge and a mortgage result in the creation of a pure lien over the assets or rights granted as security. By contrast, the fiduciary security instrument transfers the ownership of the assets subject to the security interest and a right to indirect possession of the asset (fiduciary property) to the creditor, while the security provider retains possession and the right to use the assets. Because of this formal transfer of ownership, the assets transferred are removed from the bankruptcy estate of the debtor at the time the fiduciary security instrument is entered into (like a trust agreement used as a collateral security instrument in Mexico and elsewhere in Latin America). As a result, the trend is for Brazilian creditors to prefer such security instruments.

2.3 Creation of a security interest

The creation of a security interest under Brazilian law (also known as an *in rem* guarantee) is a very formal procedure. For the validity and enforceability of a security agreement in Brazil:

- the obligation giving rise to the security (and the transaction to which it relates) must be considered legal, valid and binding under the relevant applicable laws;
- the security agreement must contain a complete description of the secured obligations and of the assets or rights given as security;
- if applicable, the instrument must follow the required legal form; and
- the parties to the security agreement must perform all formal perfection requirements.

In order to create a valid security interest in Brazil:

- the collateral must be sufficiently specified and described in the relevant security agreement, rendering the concept of the floating charge unavailable in almost all circumstances;[3] and

- a creditor of a secured obligation may not take possession of an asset granted as security in exchange for an accord and satisfaction or similar settlement agreement.

In Brazil, a creditor must always implement the judicial or extrajudicial sale of its collateral, apply the resulting proceeds to repay its debt and return any amounts in excess of the outstanding securing obligations to the borrower/security provider.

Private instruments (for pledge and fiduciary security) and public deeds (for mortgages) must:

- be in writing and, in the case of public deeds, be prepared by a notary public;
- be executed by both the creditor and debtor and witnessed by two signatories in order to be enforceable;
- describe the principal terms and conditions of the secured obligation, and at least the total secured amount, tenor and payment conditions, interest rate and other applicable costs and charges; and
- contain a detailed description of the assets or rights that are subject to the security interest.

Brazilian security instruments must be registered with either:

- the Registry of Deeds and Documents; or
- the Real Estate Registry.

Mortgages and fiduciary transfers of real property, and some specific types of pledges, are registered with the Brazilian Real Estate Registry; while all other types of collateral are registered with the Brazilian Register of Deeds and Documents. Other registrations may be required depending on the type of assets being granted as security, such as shares that require the annotation of the existence of the security in the share registry book or in the system of the depositary of the shares.

The fees for registering a security interest are charged by the Brazilian Real Estate Registry or the Brazilian Registry of Deeds and Documents based on a

---

3   As an exception to the general rule, the Corporation Law (6,404/76) expressly authorises the creation of a floating charge by Brazilian companies in connection with the issuance of debentures. In this case, a floating charge ensures the debenture holders a general privilege over the assets of the company in case of liquidation, but does not prevent the sale of such asset by the company. For other types of transactions, certain contractual structures may be used to create a security similar to a floating charge – for example, if a company intends to grant as collateral all its future receivables derived from commercial agreements or new equipment, it is possible to establish in the security agreement periodic amendments related to the section that individualises the assets.

percentage of the secured obligations, limited to a cap which is reviewed and adjusted annually by state public authorities. The fees for registering a security over real estate are also based on a state fee table and are calculated based on the higher of:

- the secured obligation; and
- the reference value of the real estate used for real estate tax purposes.

It is a condition for registration of any agreement creating a security interest in Brazil, and also for its admissibility in evidence before any local court, that the agreement be drafted in the Portuguese language and signed in Brazil. Documents drafted in foreign languages must be translated into Portuguese by official sworn translators; and in case of execution abroad, the signatures of all parties that have signed the document outside Brazil must be notarised by a licensed notary public at the place where the agreement was signed, and then apostilled in accordance with the Hague Apostille Convention of 5 October 1961.

In the context of the COVID-19 pandemic and the different lockdown measures adopted in the country, electronic certified signatures and electronic channels for filing documents for registration before the competent Brazilian Real Estate Registry or Registry of Deeds and Documents began to be widely used.

2.4 Security normally granted in connection with credit transactions

Brazilian security packages associated with credit transactions are normally tailored according to:

- the type of loan being granted;
- the nature of the borrower's business;
- the availability of unencumbered assets to be granted as security; and
- the formalities associated with the creation of the security interest (ie, not only the legal formalities mentioned above, but also the need for prior approval from public authorities or third parties to create or enforce the security).

For example, although normal asset finance transactions are secured by the asset subject to financing alone (normally new, free and clear of other liens), depending on the credit analysis of the borrower's financial condition and the potential depreciation of the asset during the tenor of the loan, other security or payment guarantees may be required by lenders.

Official credit programmes of the Brazilian government – such as the *Sistema Financeiro da Habitação* housing financing programme and the Brazilian Development Bank's FINAME programme for financing the acquisition of new machinery and equipment manufactured in Brazil – are secured by fiduciary transfer of the real estate or equipment being financed.

In project finance transactions in Brazil, the security package normally includes security over:

- the shares of the borrower (usually a newly incorporated special purpose company);
- all revenues and other credit rights related to the project;
- rights related to the main project agreements, including:
  - the engineering, procurement and construction agreement;
  - the operation and maintenance (O&M) agreement;
  - insurance; and
  - emerging rights from concession agreements, if applicable;
- project accounts, such as:
  - the collection account through which revenues from the project are to pass; and
  - in certain cases, reserve accounts in which minimum balances for covering debt service and/or O&M expenses will be retained; and
- project assets – although assets to be transferred back to the government at the end of the concession term may not be subject to security.

As mentioned above, creditors normally prefer to formalise the security instruments in the form of fiduciary assignments or fiduciary transfers, as enforcement of such security will still be possible if the debtor files for judicial recovery and the relevant assets or rights will be removed from the bankruptcy estate.

2.5   Enforcement of security interests in Brazil

(a)   *Enforcement outside of insolvency*
As mentioned above, in Brazil, creditors cannot exercise self-help in order to take possession and ownership (automatic adjudication or payment in kind) of an asset subject to a security interest and satisfy the outstanding obligations. Brazilian law mandates that the collateral be sold in the context of enforcing security; only the proceeds resulting from such sale may be applied to repay the outstanding debt.

A security agreement in Brazil is enforced either before the Brazilian courts or by means of a private sale of the assets granted as security – in this case provided that the relevant security agreement authorises the creditor to do so (which is the common market practice in structured banking and capital markets transactions, including the grant of an irrevocable power of attorney for the benefit of the creditor empowering it to amicably sell the asset upon the occurrence of an event of default or acceleration of the debt, as the case may be).

Extrajudicial sale is also called 'amicable sale' and may be provided for in the terms and conditions agreed by the borrower and creditor under the security agreement. Normally, this path allows the creditor to freely sell the asset in the form it deems appropriate; but it is also common to include rules on:

- a mandatory prior valuation process conducted by specialised third parties;
- the definition of minimum values; or
- pricing criteria.

If the agreement contains no rules on valuation or pricing, the Brazilian courts may cancel transactions challenged by a former owner of the asset if it is proven that the sale involved fraud or an excessively low price considering the asset's market value (an irrelevant amount, locally called '*preço vil*', which is not defined by law).

In case of extrajudicial enforcement of fiduciary security over real estate, Law 9,514/1997 provides for the methods and requirements for out-of-court procedures, as follows:

- If the debt is due and totally or partially unpaid, the ownership of the real estate is formally registered in the name of the creditor.
- At the request of the creditor, the borrower will be summoned by the officer of the relevant real estate registry where the property is registered to pay the pending obligations within 15 days, as well as those that fall due up to the date of payment, including:
  - conventional interest;
  - penalties and other contractual charges; and
  - legal charges, including taxes, condominium contributions attributable to the property and collection and summons charges.
- Once the ownership has been considered on its behalf, the creditor, within 30 days of the date of registration, will promote a public auction for the sale of the real estate.
- After the transfer of the fiduciary property to the fiduciary creditor's books and until the date of the second auction, the debtor is assured the pre-emptive right to acquire the property at a price corresponding to the outstanding amount of the secured debt, together with all applicable interest, charges and expenses under the credit agreement, if any, including costs and emoluments; the creditor will then deliver the remaining amount, if any, to the debtor. If the real estate is sold, the creditor will discharge the debtor of any remaining amount.

For judicial sales, creditors holding mortgages, pledges or fiduciary security may make use of a general collection lawsuit to enforce collateral and/or guarantees whenever their claims are based on an instrument for a certain, liquid and payable obligation. Following the filing of such a lawsuit by a creditor, the court will order the attachment and valuation of the borrower's assets or rights that are subject to the security. At that point, the borrower may file a defence which, in general, does not have the effect of staying the enforcement proceeding. However, if the parties do not agree on the value of the property, the judge will appoint an expert to determine it.

After the valuation of the asset, the Civil Procedure Code (Law 13,105 of 16 March 2015) authorises the creditor to request:

- a public auction sale;
- the transfer of the property in its favour for satisfaction of the debt; or
- a private sale.

(b) Treatment of secured creditors in case of insolvency

On 9 June 2005, Law 11,101, replaced Federal Decree-Law 7,661/1945 as the Bankruptcy Law. This law aims to facilitate the reorganisation of viable enterprises and the efficient liquidation of enterprises which are not economically or financially viable. The Bankruptcy Law contemplates three different proceedings:

- judicial reorganisation;
- out-of-court reorganisation; and
- bankruptcy or liquidation.

If a company complies with the legal requirements for judicial reorganisation and the judge authorises the commencement of judicial reorganisation proceedings, an immediate stay will apply for a 180-day period from the relevant judicial order. Under Article 49 of the Bankruptcy Law, all claims existing on the date of filing are subject to the effects of the judicial reorganisation proceedings, even if not yet due. In this regard, a lender's right to enforce its loan and/or any security during the stay period is suspended.

However, as briefly mentioned above, creditors secured by fiduciary security are not subject to the effects of judicial reorganisation or the other proceedings above. Article 49, paragraph 3 of the Bankruptcy Law mentions real estate and movable assets; but the Brazilian Superior Court of Justice understands that the fiduciary assignment of credit rights are also encompassed by this exception.[4] The same applies in a liquidation scenario, so any assets of the debtor that were given as security under a fiduciary security will not be considered part of the liquidation estate (ie, the creditor may enforce its rights over the collateral and request restitution of the asset).

With regard to the other types of security (pledge and mortgage), the stay

---

4   Notwithstanding the fact that this exception was created by law and the favourable position of the Brazilian Superior Court of Justice, there are certain court decisions in which part of the credit was not covered by the fiduciary security (considering the value of the asset vis-à-vis the value of the credit), and the court decided that this part should be classified as an unsecured credit and, thus, should be subject to the judicial reorganisation proceeding. In addition, during the stay period, creditors cannot sell or remove from the debtor's establishment any capital goods that are essential to the debtor's business.

period will apply and the relevant creditor will be unable to enforce them within this period.

2.6 Conclusion

Brazil has a very dynamic financial market, with a sophisticated banking system and growing capital markets. Although financing transactions are normally governed by Brazilian law and denominated in reais (due to the mandatory use of Brazilian reais for public tariffs and private transactions in Brazil), and local security must be governed by Brazilian law, market practice in Brazil follows best international practices with respect to structured credit transactions.

Brazil continues to provide a favourable environment for investment and the expansion of credit transactions – especially for infrastructure investment involving a combination of foreign loans, capital markets and different sources of funds from different types of lenders (eg, banks, institutional investors, export credit agencies). These developments are beneficial to the Brazilian economy, as they create a more stable and mature credit market.

3. Mexico

Jan R Boker
Ariel Ramos
Mayer Brown

3.1 Historical basis for secured transactions in Mexico

Most civil law codes around the world are rooted in classical Roman law. Due to colonialism, the civil law was exported from core countries such as Spain to Mexico. However, commercial law[5] in independent Mexico was consolidated with the entry into force on 1 January 1890 of the current Commercial Code,[6] which was largely inspired by the Spanish Commercial Code (1885), the Italian code of 1882 and, to some extent, the French Commercial Code.[7] Since then, the Commercial Code has undergone several reforms, with entire chapters deleted to be replaced by statutes addressing more specialised commercial law topics, such as:

- the General Law of Negotiable Instruments and Credit Transactions, first enacted on 27 August 1932, regulating the main security devices in the secured finance space;

---

5   Mexican law distinguishes between 'commercial law' and 'civil law'. Mexican civil law includes the obvious examples such as family law and inheritance law, but also includes general principles of contract law, property law and collateral devices in the context of civil law such as mortgages, civil law pledges and personal guarantees. 'Commercial law' encompasses negotiable instruments and contracts between individuals and entities dedicated to business and commercial activities, banking, bankruptcy, insurance and secured transactions.

6   Felipe de J Tena, *Derecho Mercantil Mexicano* (16th edition, Porrúa, 1996), p47.

7   Roberto L Mantilla Molina, *Derecho Mercantil* (29th edition, Porrúa, 1998), p18.

- the Banking Institutions Law, enacted on 18 July 1990, which replaced the former banking laws; and
- the Bankruptcy Law, enacted on 12 May 2000, which replaced the former Law on Bankruptcy and Suspension of Payments, originally enacted on 20 April 1943.

One of the primary goals of the North American Free Trade Agreement, launched in January 1994, was to increase investment opportunities between the United States, Canada and Mexico. To achieve these objectives, Mexico opened up access to foreign investment in its banking industry. This led to reforms to Mexican collateral instruments such as the commercial pledge, the non-possessory pledge and the guaranty trust in the following years. The amendments aimed to modernise the secured transactions framework in Mexico by establishing a single registry of security interests over personal property (the *Registro Único de Garantías Mobiliarias* (RUG)), which was similar to other registries of this kind (including the Uniform Commercial Code registries in the United States). The RUG was launched in 2010, alerting creditors to previously filed security interests over personal property and assignments of receivables, and making such filed security interests and assignments opposable *vis-à-vis* third parties, both in bankruptcy scenarios and when creditors claim an interest in the same assets. These reforms have made loans against personal property such as equipment, inventory and accounts receivable held in Mexico more attractive to lenders.

3.2 Types of security interests in Mexico
One reform that has not gained traction in Mexico is the implementation of a single concept of 'security interest'. For that reason, a variety of security mechanisms are established in various statutes and laws.

(a) Security interests over real property/real estate
In Mexico, real estate falls roughly into three categories:
- public property – that is, real estate that belongs to the Mexican federal state or to one of the 32 states of the union;
- communal land or parcels, which belong to a particular community and are protected under the Federal Agrarian Law; and
- private property real estate, which belongs to the owner registered as such in the corresponding local public registry of property.

Security interests over real estate in the context of secured finance are always over private property real estate and require certain formalities in addition to filing with the relevant public registry of property (eg, formalisation of the contract creating the mortgage before a notary public).
The two main security interest devices over private real estate are:

- the mortgage, which is regulated under civil law contained in each of the 32 Civil Law Codes of the Mexican states (depending on where the real estate is located); and
- the guaranty trust, which is regulated under the General Law of Negotiable Instruments and Credit Transactions and falls within the body of federal commercial laws (the location of the real estate is relevant only for the purposes of registration with the local public registry of property).

Mortgage: In the context of secured finance, a 'mortgage' is a contract pursuant to which a lien (*in rem* right) over the private property real estate is created by the owner to secure the obligations of a borrower for the benefit of the lender. The Civil Codes of each of the 32 Mexican states regulate the mortgage in a very similar way (the main differences are the costs of filing with the public registry of property). The mortgaged real estate will always be specifically described and will usually include all assets affixed to the real estate.

If expressly agreed, mortgages may include the products of an industrial process. However, neither the raw materials nor the work in progress will be considered part of the mortgage.

If the borrower is found by a court to be bankrupt, the lender will be deemed to be a 'secured creditor', which gives the lender certain rights, including the right:

- to foreclose on the mortgaged real estate under the supervision of the bankruptcy court; and
- to payment priority as against unsecured and subordinated creditors.

The foregoing assumes formalisation before a notary public and due filing of the mortgage with the relevant public registry of property.

Foreclosure of the mortgage is a judicial proceeding before the competent local courts at the location of the property. Upon enforcement and transfer of the property, taxes will apply.

Guaranty trust: The guaranty trust is regulated under Articles 395 and 407 of the General Law of Negotiable Instruments and Credit Transactions as a contract pursuant to which the borrower or a third party, as settler, transfers to a trustee institution[8] the ownership of the real estate that will be used as

---

8   Duly authorised Mexican financial institutions may act as trustees, which may include the following:
- credit institutions;
- insurance institutions;
- bond institutions;
- brokerage houses;
- multi-purpose financial corporations;
- authorised warehouses; and
- credit unions.

collateral to secure certain obligations in favour of the lender, which acts as beneficiary in first place (as beneficiary, the lender may have the right to provide instructions to the trustee or benefit from the trust, as set forth in the trust agreement).

For contract and bankruptcy purposes, the trustee is considered to be the title holder of the assets and rights subject to the trust estate.[9] The real estate must be assigned to the trustee before a notary public and registered with the relevant public registry of property.

Foreclosure under the guaranty trust may be judicial (before a federal court) or extrajudicial (out of court), following the procedure expressly agreed between the parties to the trust agreement. However, for the beneficiary or the trustee to enforce the trust agreement out of court, the borrower must deliver the pledged assets for sale and must not challenge the amount of the debt or claim violations of its constitutional rights to due process of law. It is not uncommon that out-of-court procedures become judicial procedures at some point. Nevertheless, upon an event of default that is notified to the trustee, the trustee must act pursuant to the terms of the trust and the instructions of the beneficiaries as provided therein.[10]

Finally, a guaranty trust may include personal property as collateral assets (both tangible and intangible); if that is the case, an additional filing with the RUG is necessary for the security interest to be opposable before third parties.

(b)   Security interests over personal property (movable assets)

The *prenda* or pledge takes many forms under Mexican law. In the context of secured transactions, Mexican law distinguishes between:

- pledges where the grantor of the pledge remains in possession of the pledged asset; and
- pledges where possession is temporarily transferred to the lender (or to the collateral agent).

Pledges where possession is transferred to the lender or to a third party: The main types of such pledges are as follows:

- a commercial pledge;
- a pledge over money;
- a pledge over securities; and
- a *bono de prenda*.

---

9   The Bankruptcy Law provides that the trust assets may be separated by their beneficiaries (ie, the lender) from the assets of the bankrupt (ie, the borrower or guarantor).
10   The trust agreement may include immediate actions even before the foreclosure mechanism is initiated, such as interim relief and judicial actions to protect the assets that are subject to the trust agreement.

Commercial pledge: The commercial pledge (to be distinguished from the civil law local pledge) is an agreement regulated under Articles 334 and 345 of the General Law of Negotiable Instruments and Credit Transactions between the pledgor (the owner of the asset and grantor of the pledge) and the pledgee (usually the lender or the collateral agent), whereby the pledgor creates a security interest over tangible movable property – generally by delivery or endorsement of the pledged assets to the pledgee. The pledgee remains in possession of the pledged assets until satisfaction of the secured obligations.

Regarding the registration of this pledge, the Mexican legal system considers that the transfer of possession of the pledged asset is sufficient for publicity purposes; and only in specific cases – such as a pledge over company shares – is registration in the corporate books of the company issuing such pledged shares necessary for perfection.

Pledge over money: Article 336*bis* of the General Law of Negotiable Instruments and Credit Transactions provides for a pledge over money. In this case, ownership over the money is deemed to be transferred to the pledgee. Therefore, when there is a breach of the guaranteed obligations, the pledgee may keep the cash, up to the amount of the secured obligations, without the need for an enforcement or judicial resolution procedure.

The novelty of this device, enacted in 2014, is that it will be understood that the transfer of ownership of the cash was carried out with the consent of the parties as a 'form of payment' of the debtor's obligations and not as a foreclosure of the pledge.

Pledge over listed securities: A pledge over listed securities is a contract that creates a pledge over listed securities regulated in Article 204 of the Securities Law. For its perfection, the lender must submit a request to the Institution for the Deposit of Listed Securities to open an account in which such securities are deposited as collateral. The parties may agree on a extrajudicial foreclosure process (similar to a guaranty trust). This type of pledge also allows the parties to agree to the transfer of ownership of the listed shares as a 'form of payment' of the debtor's obligations (similar to the pledge over money described above).

***Bono de prenda*:** In the context of raw materials, commodities and all types of goods that may be deposited with an authorised warehouse, Articles 229 to 251 of the General Law of Negotiable Instruments and Credit Transactions provide for a specific type of pledge known as a '*bono de prenda*'. The goods are deposited with the warehouse, which issues a certificate of deposit that constitutes ownership of the deposited assets. The warehouse may also be requested to issue a pledge bond, which is initially attached to the relevant certificate of deposit. Upon execution of the credit transaction between the borrower (the holder of the *bono de prenda*), the *bono de prenda* is filled in with the credit transaction's main terms and delivered in favour of the lender, perfecting a pledge on the assets indicated in the certificate of deposit to which it relates. By law, only the holder of the certificate of deposit together with the *bono de prenda* is entitled to possession of the warehoused assets, thus establishing the secured party's superior rights in the collateral to secure its loan. However, warehousing relates only to specific property, thereby precluding the application of the concept of a floating lien.

Pledges where the assets remain with the grantor: The main types of pledges where the assets remain with the grantor are as follows.

Non-possessory pledge: This type of pledge is a contract regulated under Articles 346 to 380 of the General Law of Negotiable Instruments and Credit Transactions pursuant to which a lien (*in rem* right) over movable assets and rights – existing or future, specific or universal – may be created.

Possession and operation or exercise of the assets remain with the pledgor until an event of default has occurred and the pledgee has instructed the pledgor to deliver possession to the pledgee or a third party.

Like the other security devices, this pledge must be in writing; and if the amount of the secured obligation is equal to or greater than 250,000 Investment Units (approximately $85,625), the parties must ratify their signatures before a (local) notary public or a (federal) public broker. The ratification fees are subject to the amount of the transaction – usually a percentage, depending on the complexity of the deal.

Registration before the RUG is necessary for this pledge to be opposable *vis-à-vis* third parties. If the pledge is created over assets such as aircraft, copyright or ships, special registrations with special registries are required.

The pledgor, unless otherwise agreed, will have the right to:
- use the pledged assets;
- collect and keep any gains/proceeds generated from/by the pledged assets; and
- dispose of the assets in the ordinary course of business.

Any assets or rights that the debtor receives or is entitled to receive as payment for the transfer are subject to the pledge. Notwithstanding the foregoing, the parties may agree on the destination of the pledged assets.

Foreclosure of this pledge can be either:
- judicial (performed through the federal courts); or
- extrajudicial (out of court).

Extrajudicial foreclosure may be challenged before the courts on the grounds of violation to the constitutional rights of due process of law and hearing rights. As a result, in practice, it is customary for pledges to be subject to judicial process provided under law.

Purchase money security interest (PMSI): Article 358 of the General Law of Negotiable Instruments and Credit Transactions recognises a PMSI-type concept in specifically described collateral which may be covered by a pre-existing non-possessory pledge. This means that a new creditor can obtain a security interest in purchase money collateral even when a previous security interest exists over 'all' movable goods that the debtor uses in the realisation of its preponderant activities. The PMSI must be filed with the RUG and specifically describe the assets that it covers.

(c)   *Security over accounts receivable*
Traditionally, Mexican law did not specifically address the use of accounts receivable as a collateral device. Borrowers and lenders worked around this gap by relying on the general provisions of the Civil Code dealing with the assignment of contract rights. The use of this method required the borrower to notify all of its account debtors of its assignment of the receivables. However, currently, the non-possessory pledge, the guaranty trust and the industrial mortgage allow accounts receivable to be included as a part of the collateral for these types of security devices.

Special mention goes to the assignment of accounts receivable in the context of securitisations:[11] further to the 2014 reforms to the Commercial Code, the assignment of receivables must now be filed with the RUG (Article 390 of the code) in order to achieve the following effects:

- Purchasers of receivables can check whether the receivables that they intend to purchase are free and clear of any previous liens or assignments; and
- Such purchases enjoy priority over third-party creditors which have not registered their acquisition with the RUG.

3.3   Treatment in insolvency of debtor
The Bankruptcy Law governs business reorganisation and liquidation procedures of Mexican commercial entities. A business reorganisation procedure aims to:

- preserve the existence and operation of the commercial enterprise of the bankrupt entity; and

---

11   However, under Mexican law, the assignment of receivables in a securitisation or factoring does not create a security interest over the purchased receivables, but rather a sale between seller and purchaser that requires filing with the RUG for the purposes of making the assignment opposable *vis-à-vis* third parties set forth above.

- prevent a generalised default of payment obligations by the bankrupt entity and its counterparties (ie, prevent systemic risk).

The Bankruptcy Law provides for one sole bankruptcy proceeding, encompassing two successive phases: reorganisation and liquidation. The reorganisation stage is designed to be completed in 185 days; although one 90-day extension may be granted if requested by the bankruptcy trustee or creditors representing 50% of the recognised claims. An additional 90-day extension may be granted if requested by the debtor, together with creditors representing 75% of the recognised claims.

Only federal courts sitting in the domicile of the debtor have jurisdiction over bankruptcy proceedings. Special federal district courts will be set up to hear bankruptcy cases. Administrative matters within the proceedings are entrusted to bankruptcy experts: that is, auditors or examiners, conciliators (mediators between creditors and the debtor) and receivers.

In the case of liquidation, a creditor from a lower-priority class cannot be paid until all creditors in higher-priority classes have been paid in full. The priority of claims, in descending order, is as follows:
- privileged labour claims – that is, labour claims for the last year's salary, benefits and severance payments;
- administrative claims and post-commencement financing;
- claims incurred as a result of payments for regular expenses in connection with the security, repair, conservation and management of the estate assets;
- claims for judicial or extrajudicial procedures for the benefit of the estate;
- burial expenses (individual debtors only);
- terminal illness expenses (individual debtors only);
- secured claims (ie, secured by either a pledge or a mortgage);
- labour claims (other than privileged labour claims);
- unsecured tax claims;
- priority claims, which are those from creditors with a privilege or a retention right;
- unsecured claims (including consumer claims);
- subordinated claims; and
- claims against unlimited partners of the debtor, if they arose after the partner became an unlimited partner.

With respect to the guaranty trust, the assets transferred to it retain independence and separation from the borrower's assets. With this, the assets held in such trust are protected from the rest of the borrower's creditors and are destined to satisfy the secured obligations in favour of the lender that is appointed as beneficiary under the guaranty trust.

3.4 Conclusion

There is no doubt that since 2000, Mexico has made significant progress to strengthen the secured finance system. Despite the complexities that still exist due to the lack of a single security interest and the fragmented nature of the legislation, the implementation of a centralised, transparent and free registry of security interests (eg, the RUG) has greatly alleviated the main concerns of lenders, including the need to search multiple local public records and the absence of a single electronic search engine that allows creditors and purchasers to find security interests that have been granted by an entity in favour of its creditors.

In practice, the guaranty trust continues to be the mechanism of choice in large and complex transactions involving several different types of assets – especially because the assets leave the debtor's estate and enter the trustee's estate; and because its foreclosure occurs before the federal courts. This gives the creditor protection in the event of bankruptcy and greater ease in asserting rights to the collateral.

4. Colombia

Juan Pablo Moreno[12]
Mayer Brown

4.1 Historical basis for secured transactions in Colombia

As in other civil law jurisdictions, the creation, attachment and perfection of security interests in Colombia are codified in a variety of statutes that have been subject to various modifications and amendments over the years, aimed at reducing the time, costs and steps required to perfect and enforce a security interest.

Currently, most matters related to the creation, attachment and perfection of security interests in real estate assets are governed by the Civil Code, enacted in 1873. Conversely, most matters relating to the creation, attachment and perfection of security interests in movable assets are governed by Law 1676/2013, commonly known as the Movable Assets Security Law, which replaced the regulations on creation, perfection and enforceability of security interests over movable assets set forth in the Civil Code and in the Code of Commerce. The purpose of Law 1676/2013 was to increase access to financial products for medium and small-sized companies[13] by:

- reducing the time, procedures and cost needed to perfect and enforce security interests; and
- expanding the types of assets that can be subject to a security interest.[14]

---

12 The author acknowledges the collaboration of Felipe Alarcón Siera and Jorge Alberto Padilla Sanchez from Brigard & Urrutia Abogados in Colombia.
13 Pursuant to Law 590/2000, entities that have no more than 200 employees and assets with a value not exceeding $5 million.

The most significant changes introduced by the law were:

- an expansion of the types of assets that may be subject to a security interest;
- the creation of a new centralised system where filing and searches of security interests may be conducted;
- new types of publicity of security interests against third parties; and
- new methods to enforce security interests against debtors/guarantors.

4.2   Types of security interests

(a)   Security over real estate assets

Pursuant to Article 2434 of the Civil Code, a security agreement over real estate assets (ie, a mortgage) must be executed by means of a public deed and registered with the Registry of Public Instruments at the place where the real property is located. Failure to comply with such requirements will result in the mortgage being declared void and unenforceable.

The issuance of the notarised public deed and the filing of the mortgage with the Registry of Public Instruments for the purposes of perfecting the security interest are subject to certain notarisation and registration fees/taxes.

(b)   Security over movable assets

Pursuant to Article 14 of Law 1676/2013, a security interest over movable assets in Colombia is created by means of a security agreement providing at least each of the following:

- a proper identification of the debtor/grantor and the secured party(ies);
- a complete description of the collateral;
- a description of the secured obligations; and
- the maximum amount to be secured by the collateral.

Law 1676/2013 expanded the types of assets that may be subject to a security interest by, among other things, establishing that the proceeds derived from the transformation, sale or substitution of collateral may be subject to a security interest.[15] This new feature is a significant departure from the

---

14   In 2014, the Doing Business rankings published by the World Bank ranked Colombia as one of the worst countries in the world when it comes to enforcing a contract, placing it 155th out of 189 countries ranked. The ranking was based on:
- the length of time that it takes to enforce a contract (1,288 days);
- the amount of procedures and steps involved (34); and
- the costs *vis-à-vis* the debt value of the contract (nearly 45%).

The ranking also placed Colombia 25th out of the 32 countries ranked in Latin America when it comes to enforcing a contract. These results (and the ranking results from previous years – 157th in 2013, 149th in 2012 and 150th in 2011) were the reason why the Colombian government enacted a new law to facilitate the enforcement of security interests over movable assets.

15   Article 13 of Law 1676/2013.

traditional concept of security interest under Colombian law (and civil law generally), which only covers the specific asset named in the security agreement and follows the pattern of more dynamic laws, including the Uniform Commercial Code and the guidelines promoted by UNCITRAL. The new system also eliminated the obligation for creditors and debtors to create, perfect and register a security interest each time an asset is sold, transformed or substituted. Law 1676/2013 also introduced the concept of a PMSI.[16] Pursuant to the law, a PMSI is a security interest in goods that secures the repayment of the debt owed in connection with the purchase price of such goods. Under this law, once the PMSI has been duly filed, it is awarded super-priority treatment *vis-à-vis* other security interests created over the goods sold.

As a general rule, a security interest over a movable asset is perfected once a registration statement has been filed before the national public registry[17] (*Registro Nacional de Garantías Mobiliarias* (RNGM)) managed by the National Association of Chambers of Commerce.[18] In some cases, a security interest may be enforceable against third parties through possession of the collateral by the creditor, even if a registration statement is not filed.[19] A security interest over deposits in bank accounts is enforceable against third parties if the creditor (or an entity acting on behalf of the creditor) exercises control[20] over the deposits subject to the guarantee. Nonetheless, a security interest registered with the national public registry has priority over a security interest that was not so filed. If no security interest was filed (and the security interest is not a security interest that can be enforced against third parties through possession or control), priority will be determined based on the execution date of the underlying security agreement.

In addition, depending on the underlying collateral, additional perfection requirements may apply. For example:

- security over shares of stock must be registered in the issuing company's stock ledger;
- security over IP rights must be registered with the relevant IP registry; and
- security interests on automobiles must be registered with the National Vehicle Registry.

Law 1676/2013 also simplifies the process of publicising a security interest

---

16   Article 22 of Law 1676/2013.
17   Pursuant to Article 22 of Law 1676/2013, a PMSI is enforceable against third parties only when a registration statement has been properly filed.
18   Article 39 of Law 1676/2013.
19   For example, a 'pledge with possession' does not require the filing of a registration statement in order for it to be enforceable third parties.
20   Law 1676/2013 defines 'control' as an agreement or understanding between the depositary, the debtor/guarantor and the creditor whereby the depositary agrees to comply with the instructions of the creditor with respect to any amounts deposited in the secured accounts.

against third parties through the creation of the RNGM.[21] Pursuant to the new law, all security interest filings may be made, modified, extended, cancelled, transferred and searched in the new national centralised system.

Another important feature of Law 1676/2013 is that it allows anyone to:

- access online the centralised registry to search for assets that are subject to a security interest;
- determine the value of the secured obligation; and
- confirm the status of the underlying assets.[22]

It also allows anyone to request physical copies of any given registration statement.[23]

Law 1676/2013 also provides for a variety of safeguard mechanisms for both debtors and creditors to monitor the assets that are subject to a security interest. For example, Law 1676/2013 provides that:

- creditors must be authorised by debtors in order to file, modify or extend a security interest; and
- creditors may authorise a third party to conduct such filing or modification on their behalf.[24]

Law 1676/2013 also establishes that a registration statement is valid only for the period set forth in the registration statement, which may be extended for periods of three years.[25] If the registration statement is silent as to the period for which it will be valid, the law specifies that the registration statement is valid for five years.[26]

4.3   Enforcement of security interests

(a)   Security over real estate assets
Pursuant to Articles 467 and 468 of the General Procedural Code of Colombia, the secured party named in the mortgage may request the adjudication of the mortgaged property for the total or partial payment of a secured obligation by means of a judicial allocation proceeding or a mortgage foreclosure proceeding. The enforcement of a mortgage is a lengthy procedure carried out through the civil courts. The procedural rules are deemed by Colombian law as public order laws and may not be waived or changed between the parties in order to expedite the procedure.

---

21   Article 38 of Law 1676/2013.
22   *Ibid*, Article 46.
23   *Ibid*, Article 46.
24   *Ibid*, Article 40.
25   *Ibid*, Article 38.
26   *Ibid*.

(b) Security over movable assets

Law 1676/2013 established a variety of mechanisms to enforce a security interest. Depending on the agreement between the parties in the security agreement, a creditor can enforce a security interest against the debtor:

- through a civil court (as set forth under the General Procedural Code of Colombia);[27] or
- through two new mechanisms introduced by the law:
  - extrajudicial enforceability;[28] and
  - direct payment.[29]

Law 1676/2013 allows a creditor and a debtor to agree on the extrajudicial process that a creditor must follow in order to enforce a security interest. If the parties have not agreed on the process that must be followed in order to enforce a security interest, the debtor and the creditor must follow the process set forth under Law 1676/2013, which requires the creditor to file an enforceability statement before the national public registry and to instruct a Chamber of Commerce or a notary public to notify the debtor of such filing.[30] The notification of the enforceability statement limits the debtor's ability to sell or transform the asset subject to the security interest. The debtor will be responsible for any damages caused to the creditor if the assets are transformed or sold after the date on which the enforceability statement was filed.[31]

A creditor may also enforce a security interest against a debtor through so-called 'direct payment', if agreed by the parties in the security agreement or if the creditor is in possession of the collateral.[32] Under this mechanism, a creditor may directly sell the collateral for its appraised value as set by the Superintendence of Companies, in order to release the debtor's outstanding debt through the proceeds of the sale. No judicial process need be followed. Nonetheless, if a debtor is in possession of the collateral and fails to relinquish it to the creditor, the creditor may initiate a summary proceeding against the debtor to force the debtor/guarantor to relinquish the collateral.[33]

4.4 Commercial trusts

Many secured transactions in Colombia – particularly those involving project finance and structured financed transactions – are carried out through commercial trusts. These are most commonly used to ring-fence the assets transferred to the trust from the risk of the debtor's insolvency, because once the

---

27   *Ibid*, Article 61.
28   *Ibid*, Article 62.
29   *Ibid*, Article 60.
30   *Ibid*, Article 62.
31   *Ibid*.
32   *Ibid*, Article 60.
33   *Ibid*.

assets are transferred to a trust, they cease (subject to certain exceptions relating to future receivables) to be part of the estate of the settlor.

Pursuant to the Code of Commerce, commercial trusts are created pursuant to a written agreement whereby a grantor (the settlor of the trust) transfers to a trust company (ie, a financial entity regulated under Colombian law) one or various assets to be managed by the trust company in accordance with the specific instructions of the settlor set forth in the trust agreement.[34]

A trust agreement typically includes the following parties:

- an entity or person (the settlor) that transfers property in trust via a trust agreement, and that confers the administration of such property to a trust company (the trustee) for the benefit of the beneficiary and/or itself;
- the trust company (the trustee), which is the person that manages the trust – and therefore the assets that were transferred to it by the settlor – in accordance with the rules established in the trust agreement. Trust companies are financial entities subject to the supervision of the Financial Superintendence of Colombia; and
- the beneficiary or secured creditor, which is the person in whose favour the trust is constituted and that will receive the benefits of the trust according to the terms of the trust agreement. The beneficiary or secured creditor need not be a party to the trust contract. The beneficiary is not required to sign the trust agreement, but it must be registered with the trust company in that capacity.

Under Colombian law, commercial trusts may be created for various purposes and as such, depending on the underlying purpose of the trust, the trust agreement must meet certain requirements established under Colombian law. For instance, trust contracts may have investment purposes, construction purposes, guarantee purposes, administration purposes and payment purposes, among others.

Similarly to a mortgage, the transfer of real estate property to a trust must be documented by means of a public deed which must be registered with the Registry of Public Instruments. Conversely, for the transfer of movable assets to a security trust, a public deed is not required. In any case, for any type of security trust agreement (whether over real estate or movable assets), in order to be enforceable against third parties, a security trust agreement must be registered with the Centralised Registry in accordance with Law 1676/2013.

---

34 See Article 2.5.2.1.1 of Decree 2555/2010 and Official Letter 220-196115 of 14 October 2016 issued by the Financial Superintendence of Colombia.

5. Peru

Luis Schrader
Mayer Brown

5.1 General framework

Security interests in Peru (and their corresponding regulation) can be separated into two broad groups:

- security interests over real estate assets; and
- security interests over movable assets.

Regarding the former, the creation and perfection of security interests over such assets are governed by the Civil Code (Legislative Decree 295), which was enacted in 1984 and has since been extensively amended. Regarding the latter, the creation and perfection of security interests are governed by the Movable Assets Security Law (28677/2006).

The Peruvian legal system for the creation and perfection of security interests over movable assets is currently being revised. The enactment of Legislative Decree 1400/2018, which replaced the Movable Assets Security Law in its entirety, created a new system for the creation and perfection of security interests over movable assets – mainly through the reduction of several formalities and the creation of the Movable Assets Security Informational System (SIGM) which, once implemented, will constitute an easily accessible online system that will include the information of all security interests created. However, such legislative decree is currently not yet in force, as the condition for its entry into force is the implementation of the SIGM, which has not yet been created as of this date.

In addition to the aforementioned security interests, the use of trusts has grown in popularity in recent years as a means of securing obligations. There are two main types of trusts in Peru:

- securitisation trusts; and
- banking trusts.

Securitisation trusts are generally used as an investment vehicle to issue notes or securities backed by underlying assets which serve as the collateral for the repayment of such securities. Conversely, banking trusts are generally used as collateral for financing transactions, as they provide a swift and cost-efficient way of creating and enforcing collateral. Banking trusts in Peru are regulated by the Banking Law (26702/1996).

5.2 Security interests over real estate assets

As mentioned in section 5.1, security interests over real estate are regulated by the Civil Code, which primarily addresses the creation and perfection of mortgages. Mortgages are the most common security interest over real estate and there are several formal and procedural requirements for their creation and perfection.

Pursuant to Article 1097 of the Civil Code, a 'mortgage' is defined as the creation of a security interest over real estate in order to serve as collateral for compliance with an obligation – whether personal or that of a third party. In addition, Article 1098 of the Civil Code requires that a mortgage be executed through a notarised public deed.

In addition to the requirement to have the mortgage executed through a notarised public deed, Article 1099 of the Civil Code establishes the following requirements that must be met for a mortgage to be valid:

- The person that creates the mortgage must have good title over the real estate;
- The mortgage must secure a determined or determinable obligation; and
- The value of the mortgage must be determined or determinable and be registered in the Real Estate Property Registry of the Peruvian Public Registry.

The creation and perfection of mortgages in Peru involve several formal and procedural steps. The actors involved include:

- the mortgagee;
- the secured creditor;
- a notary public; and
- public officials at the Peruvian Public Registry.

Due to these formal requirements, the creation and perfection of mortgages involve the payment of fees to a notary public as well as registration fees to the Peruvian Public Registry.

5.3   Security interests over movable assets

As mentioned in section 5.1, security interests over movable assets are regulated by the Movable Assets Security Law. The law provides that a security interest over movable assets consists of the creation of a security interest over a movable asset in order to secure the performance of an obligation.[35] According to Article 4 of the law, a security interest can be granted over:

- one or more specific movable assets;
- a generic category of assets (eg, equipment of the grantor); or
- all movable assets of the grantor, both existing and future.

Pursuant to Article 17 of the law, the creation of a security interest over

---

35   Article 3 of the Movable Assets Security Law.

movable assets requires the execution of a security agreement which includes the following, among other things:

- identification of the parties, including their addresses;
- due execution of the security agreement by at least the grantor;
- in case of non-registered movable assets, a sworn statement from the grantor stating that it has good title over the movable assets and, in the case of registered assets (eg, vehicles), the corresponding registration details;
- the value of the movable assets and the amount of the security interest;
- identification of the movable assets;
- a description of the secured obligation;
- the 'certain date' of the security agreement; and
- the term of the security interest.

While the Movable Assets Security Law does not require that the security agreement be in the form of a notarised public deed, Article 17 provides that it must be executed in a form that affords certainty as to the creation of the security interest. For this reason, in practice, most transactions involving the grant of security interests over movable assets are notarised. In addition, in order to perfect a security interest over movable assets, the law includes a registration form which allows the secured creditor to file for registration with the Peruvian Public Registry directly.

The perfection of security interests over movable assets depends on the class of movable asset that is being granted as collateral. There are two broad classes of movable assets:

- non-registered movable assets (eg, equipment, inventory); and
- registered assets (eg, vehicles).

Registered assets have their own identification in the Peruvian Public Registry, which serves as a specific registration system through which secured creditors can register and perfect their security interests. For non-registered assets, the Movable Assets Security Law created a specific registry called the Movable Registry of Agreements – an integrated system administered by the Peruvian Public Registry that allows secured creditors to register their security interests over non-registered assets and facilitates easily accessible electronic certification of the creation and perfection of their security interest.

As mentioned in section 5.1, the Movable Assets Security Law is currently in the process of being replaced by Legislative Decree 1400/2018, which will introduce significant changes to how security interests over movable assets are created and perfected in Peru. Once in force, the legislative decree is expected to establish a less burdensome and less formalistic method to grant security interests.

5.4   Banking trust agreements

As mentioned in section 5.1, the creation of banking trusts in Peru is regulated by the Banking Law. This is because trust companies are regulated financial entities in Peru (ie, banks or specialised trust administrators). Banking trusts are not a security interest *per se*, as according to Article 241 of the Banking Law they involve the transfer of ownership (in lieu of the creation of a security interest) of an asset from a grantor to a regulated trust company for the creation of a trust in order to serve a specific purpose for the benefit of the grantor or a third party.

The creation of a banking trust requires the execution of a banking trust agreement, which:

- requires the participation of the grantor and the trust company; and
- must follow the legal formalities for the transfer of ownership of the underlying assets comprising the banking trust (ie, if the assets being transferred are real estate assets, the banking trust agreement must be in the form of a public deed).

Participation of the beneficiaries is not required.

Once the ownership of the assets has been transferred to the banking trust, the trust company will be responsible for the administration of such assets, in accordance with the rules set forth in the banking trust agreement and for the term indicated therein, which generally cannot exceed the legal term of 30 years.[36] Banking trust agreements are also recorded in the corresponding public registry for the type of asset being transferred.

Since the creation of banking trusts involves the participation of an additional party (the trustee) and has associated structuring and administration costs (which are charged by the trust company, usually on a monthly or yearly basis), banking trusts in Peru are most commonly used for project finance and structured finance transactions. Nonetheless, banking trust agreements are sometimes also used for real estate transactions involving the construction and development of new projects.

5.5   Enforcement of security interests

(a)   Enforcement of mortgages

Article 1097 of the Civil Code recognises the right to the judicial sale of the mortgaged real estate asset as one of the rights of a secured creditor. This means that the sole method of enforcing a mortgage is through a judicial sale of the real estate asset.

The rules for a judicial sale are set out in the Civil Procedural Code and the proceedings are generally carried out by the civil courts at the place where the

---

36   Article 251 of the Banking Law.

real estate asset is located. These proceedings are generally highly formalistic and can be lengthy and time consuming, as they usually involve appraisal and public sale proceedings. The requirement for a judicial sale cannot be replaced or waived by the mortgagor and the mortgagee.

(b)   Enforcement of security interests over moveable assets

The Movable Assets Security Law allows the parties to decide how to foreclose a security interest over movable assets. To this end, the parties can choose between an extrajudicial or judicial sale of the assets.

An extrajudicial sale – which is the most common foreclosure proceeding – requires the grant of an irrevocable power of attorney at the time of execution of the security agreement, which allows a third party (which cannot be the secured creditor) to enforce the transfer of the movable assets in case of foreclosure. The procedure is very straightforward and usually involves the delivery of a notice (through a notary public) by the secured creditor to the grantor and the holder of the irrevocable power of attorney, in which the secured creditor notifies the commencement of the foreclosure procedure; this can start three business days after receipt of the letter by the grantor.[37] The Movable Assets Security Law also provides that if 60 days (which term may be modified by the parties) have elapsed since delivery of the notice by the secured creditor and the sale of the movable assets has not occurred, the secured creditor may commence a judicial sale.

(c)   Enforcement of banking trust agreements

In contrast to security interests where ownership is retained by the grantor, the creation of banking trusts involves the transfer of ownership to the trust company, which makes any foreclosure proceeding very smooth. The trust company, in compliance with the rules set forth in the banking trust agreement, usually proceeds directly with the sale of the asset (which may be a direct sale, a direct adjudication to the beneficiary or a public sale), and quickly liquidates the secured obligation with the proceeds of the sale. This is one of the most attractive features of banking trusts over other types of security interests as collateral for secured obligations.

---

37   Article 47.3 of the Movable Assets Security Law.

6.   Argentina

Pablo Gayol
Cecilia Mairal
Marval, O'Farrell & Mairal
Gabriela Sakamoto
Mayer Brown

6.1   Overview

Under Argentine law, security interests may be created through:

- mortgages;
- pledges (including registered and floating pledges);
- credit assignments; and
- trusts.

Security may be taken over a wide variety of property, such as:

- personal and real property;
- securities;
- trademarks;
- shares;
- cash; and
- receivables.

However, certain assets that are subject to immunity may not be used as security interests.

Under Argentine law, it is not possible to grant a global security interest in all assets of an entity through a general security agreement. Rather, security interests are granted through different types of instruments, the scope, nature, formalities and requirements for perfection of which vary depending on the instrument.

6.2   Main types of collateral instruments

(a)   Mortgages

Under Argentine law, a mortgage may be established over real estate, ships and aircraft. A mortgage will generally secure the principal amount (even if adjusted), accrued interest and other related expenses owed by the debtor to the creditor. To satisfy the 'specialty or singularity' principle established by the Civil and Commercial Code, the secured obligation must be properly and specifically identified. The maximum principal amount of the secured obligation must be determined in monetary terms. The specialty principle is satisfied in connection with undetermined credits if:

- the maximum amount guaranteed, for all concepts, is stated in the mortgage deed; and
- the term of the guaranty does not exceed 10 years.

All mortgages must be registered in the relevant registry to become effective *vis-à-vis* third parties. Mortgaged property may remain in the possession of the mortgagor (ie, its owner).

Mortgages over real estate may be created only by a notarial deed signed before a notary public. The mortgage deed then must be filed for registration with the Public Real Estate Registry at the place where the property is located. Under Argentine law, mortgages grant the registered mortgagee a first priority right over the underlying real estate as from the date on which the mortgage is signed before a notary public, provided that the filing for registration is submitted within 45 days of its execution. A mortgage is foreclosed through a special summary proceeding that allows the property to be sold at a public auction. However, foreclosure may be also conducted through out-of-court proceedings under certain conditions. Foreclosure of a mortgage (or a pledge) is subject to special rules if the debtor is subject to bankruptcy proceedings.

Mortgages over ships or aircraft may be created by a notarial deed or an authenticated private instrument and then registered in the relevant registry. Under Argentine conflict of law rules, mortgages over ships and aircraft are governed by the law of the relevant vessel's flag. Argentina will recognise mortgages on ships and vessels established outside Argentina to the extent that the foreign state recognises mortgages established in Argentina.

(b) **Pledges**

As a general rule, to perfect a pledge on a non-registrable movable asset or document of credit, the pledged asset should be delivered to the creditor or placed in the custody of a third party. The Civil and Commercial Code states that a pledge must be executed through a public deed or a private instrument, in which case it will be effective *vis-à-vis* third parties only if there is evidence of the effective date of its execution. Additionally, as with mortgages, the 'specialty or singularity' principle established by the Civil and Commercial Code must be satisfied.

The Civil and Commercial Code provides that in the event of default on the secured debt, the creditor may sell the pledged assets through a court auction. In principle, the creditor may not obtain ownership of the asset unless the parties expressly agree that the value of the asset will be assessed at the time of the enforcement. However, a creditor which has a pledge on an asset has a priority right to the proceeds from an asset sale. Unless the debtor and creditor agree on a special sales proceeding, the pledged asset must be sold by public auction and duly announced in the *Official Gazette*.

Registered pledges: Under Argentine law, it is possible to create pledges on assets that remain in the possession of the pledgor. These pledges are known as 'registered pledges' and include both fixed and floating pledges. Fixed pledges affect only the relevant registered assets, while floating pledges affect the original pledged assets and subsequent assets derived from the transformation or replacement of the original pledged assets. The amount of the pledge is limited to the amount of the secured obligation, including, without limitation, interest and other ancillary amounts.

Registered pledges do not require a public deed. They may be established through an authenticated private instrument using forms provided by and filed with the Registry of Pledges. Fixed pledges fall under the jurisdiction of the Registry of Pledges at the place where the assets are located; while floating pledges fall under the jurisdiction of the Registry of Pledges at the place where the debtor is domiciled. The pledge becomes effective *vis-à-vis* third parties only upon filing.

Pledge certificates, which are delivered by the relevant public registry, grant the right to initiate summary enforcement proceedings. Claims may be filed, at the option of the creditor, in the jurisdiction where payment was agreed, where the goods are located or where the debtor is domiciled, unless the debtor is considered a consumer. In that case, it is mandatory to file the claim in the jurisdiction where the debtor is domiciled. The proceeds of the enforcement of a pledge must be applied first to pay all taxes and expenses incurred to protect the assets and second to pay principal and interest of the debt secured by the pledge.

Pledges of shares: Pledges of shares are governed by the Civil and Commercial Code and the General Companies Law (19,550). Under Argentine law, shares must be issued in non-endorsable registered form or book-entry form. Pledges over shares must be reported to the issuing company or the registrar (if any), and must be recorded in the issuing company's or registrar's books. The pledge takes effect *vis-à-vis* the issuing company and third parties from the date on which it is registered in the company's or registrar's books.

A pledge of shares grants the creditor a priority right over the proceeds of the sale of the shares. For shares or other securities traded on stock markets, those held as collateral may be sold through a stockbroker as soon as the pledgor fails to comply with its obligations under the pledge.

(c)   *Security assignments and trusts*
Security may also be obtained through credit assignments and trusts. Assets may be placed in trust with a receiver which holds them as a separate estate that, according to the Civil and Commercial Code, is not subject to insolvency proceedings of the settlor, receiver or beneficiaries, unless:

- creditors can provide evidence that their claims were established fraudulently; or
- the trust is declared null and void in an insolvency proceeding.

Alternatively, credits may be assigned as a security in favour of creditors. One of the main differences between a security assignment and a trust is that in a security assignment, the assigned assets are typically limited to rights or credits, including receivables. With trusts, however, there is no such limitation and they may be used as vehicles for taking security over most forms of movable and real estate assets.

As a general rule, Argentine law requires that a debtor be given notice of assignment for the assignment to be effective *vis-à-vis* the debtor. Such notice must be given to the debtor by public instrument, typically through a notary public; or by private instrument that must have a certain date in order to be enforceable *vis-à-vis* third parties. Additionally, in case of guaranty assignments (whether or trust or otherwise) over present and/or future credits, the notice to the debtor must be replaced by publication by the assignor of its jurisdiction in the *Official Gazette* and in one of the major circulation newspapers at a national level notifying the assignment.

According to the Civil and Commercial Code, the rules on pledges of credits also apply to the assignment of credits as security.

6.3 Security agent and assignment of security interests

The Civil and Commercial Code restricts the assignment and transfer of *in rem* security rights and establishes that such security interests may not be transferred without the corresponding transfer of the secured obligations. However, notwithstanding this restriction, Argentine law provides that in financings with two or more creditors, a security agent may be appointed. Thus, security interests may be granted in favour of the security agent, which will act for the benefit and according to the instructions of the secured creditors. The secured obligations may be transferred to third parties, which will benefit from the security interests granted in support of such obligations on the same terms as the original creditors.

7. Chile

Loreto Ribera
Carey y Cía
Gabriela Sakamoto
Mayer Brown

7.1 Overview

The Civil Code states that all assets or property located in Chile are subject to Chilean law. This means that any security interest granted over any asset or property located in Chile, including equity interests in Chilean companies, must be granted pursuant to Chilean law.

Under Chilean law, it is not possible to grant a global security interest in all assets of an entity through a general security agreement; instead, they are granted through several types of security documents regulated under different bodies of law. The scope, nature, formalities and requirements for the perfection of each type of security interest under Chilean law are specifically provided for in the relevant statute and vary from one type of security to another.

7.2   Main types of collateral instruments
Securities can be classified into two main groups:
- security granted over assets or rights *in rem*; and
- personal guarantees or *in personam* rights.

(a)   Forms of securities over assets
The main security over movable assets (including inventory) and non-movable assets (ie, real estate, mining concessions, water rights, vessels and aircraft) in Chile are described below.

Civil pledge: This type of pledge can secure all kinds of obligations and can apply to all kinds of movable property, including all kinds of personal rights and credits. A civil pledge is perfected by the delivery of the pledged asset to the pledgee, without requiring any kind of registration. If the pledge is granted over a credit, the creditor must also notify the debtor, prohibiting it from making any payment under the pledged credit to anyone other than the creditor. This type of pledge is not commonly used in practice, as the pledgor must deliver the pledged asset itself, and therefore the ability to use and enjoy the asset is substantially lost.

Commercial pledge: This type of pledge secures commercial obligations and, like the civil pledge, may apply to all kinds of movable property, personal rights and credits. It is not certain whether a commercial pledge can secure future obligations, as the amount of the secured obligation must be determined in the pledge agreement at the time of its execution. Under the Commercial Code, the following formalities must be met to perfect a security interest created under a commercial pledge and make it enforceable against third parties:
- It must be executed by means of a public deed or by a private instrument entered in the register of a Chilean notary public;
- The amount of the secured obligation and a description of the pledged assets must be specified in the pledge agreement; and
- In the case of a commercial pledge over a credit right or receivables, the debtor must be notified in writing of the pledge and be instructed to make all payments to the pledgee.

Pledge over securities in favour of banks: This pledge may secure all current and/or future obligations of the pledgor to the pledgee, but is limited in terms of the kinds of assets that may be pledged. Only bearer instruments, credits 'payable to the order' (ie, not in bearer form) and shares may be subject to this type of pledge. This kind of pledge can be used only to secure the pledgor's own obligations, and not third-party obligations. The formalities depend on the kind of asset that is being pledged. Bearer instruments require only that the instrument be handed over by the pledgor to the pledgee, unless the parties expressly provide otherwise (eg, an instrument handed for collection). Credits payable to the order must be endorsed as a guaranty to the pledgee. Finally, shares must be pledged by means of a public deed or private instrument, which must be notified to the company that issued the shares by a Chilean notary public. Like civil and commercial pledges, this type of pledge does not permit the pledgor to remain in material possession of the pledged assets. On 1 September 2015, the Constitutional Court of Chile ruled in one case that Article 6 of Law 4,287, which regulates execution of this type of pledge, was inapplicable. The court stated that this summary execution proceeding violated constitutional rights to due process and effective judicial protection. Although the court's ruling was limited to the specific case and does not have general applicability, it has raised concerns about the possibility of future challenges.

Pledge without conveyance: This pledge can be granted over all kinds of existing or future tangible or intangible assets to secure the pledgor's or third party's obligations, both present and future, irrespective of whether such obligations are determined or undetermined at the time the pledge is entered into. A pledge without conveyance must be executed by means of a public deed or by a private instrument entered in the registry of a Chilean notary public. In addition, the agreement evidencing this pledge must expressly set forth the following:
- the identities of the parties;
- the existing secured obligations, or that the pledge secures present and future obligations;
- the assets being pledged; and
- the amount (whether determined or undetermined) that is being pledged and whether the pledge secures several obligations.

A pledge without conveyance must be registered in a special registry specific to these kinds of pledges; and upon registration, a pledge without conveyance will be enforceable against third parties.

Pledge over deposited securities: This type of pledge was created in 2016 in order to simplify the pledging of securities held by custody companies incorporated under Law 18,876. This type of pledge requires the depositary to enter into a master agreement with all depositors. The pledge is granted, amended and released through electronic communications delivered to the custody company.

Mortgage: Mortgages in Chile are granted by means of a public deed. A mortgage may secure both existing and future obligations. Mortgages are perfected through registration of the mortgage deed in the Mortgage Lien Registry and in the Prohibitions Registry (commonly, the mortgage deed will also include a prohibition against transferring, conveying or entering into acts or contracts with respect to the mortgaged property). The relevant registrar will be the registrar at the place where the property is located.

(b)   *Personal guarantees*

The most common personal guarantees in Chile are sureties and joint and several guarantees. In the case of sureties, one or more third parties are compelled to pay the debtor's obligation if the debtor fails to do so. In the case of joint and several guarantees, the liability for default is enforceable directly against the debtor and guarantors as a group or against any one of them as an individual, at the choice of the enforcing creditor.

The main characteristic of joint and several guarantees is that the guarantors become equally liable to the creditor as the primary debtor. Therefore, they are not entitled to request that:

*   the debt be claimed first from the debtor and be collected from them only if the debtor does not pay; or
*   the debt be divided equally or proportionally among the various guarantors.

Under Chilean law, personal guarantees are accessory to the main obligations and cannot exceed the amount of such obligations. This is expressly regulated for sureties, which cannot exceed the main obligation being guaranteed and cannot be granted under terms that are more onerous than those of the main obligor; although they can be granted under terms that are more effective (eg, securing its obligations as guarantor through a mortgage).

The Civil Code does not require that any formalities be met to grant sureties; but if the obligation intended to be secured is a commercial obligation, the surety must be granted in writing.

7.3   Enforcement

Collateral security located in Chile must be enforced in Chile and – other than in the case of a pledge over deposited securities, where no judicial procedure is required – must be done pursuant to a judicial proceeding before the competent Chilean court in accordance with the rules set out in the Code of Civil

Procedure or in other applicable laws. In general, the enforcement procedure involves a brief discussion stage in which the defendant may submit limited defences, followed by the liquidation and public auction of assets by court-appointed auctioneers. If the pledged asset is a claim for an amount of money, the creditor will collect this claim upon its maturity, on the understanding that the creditor is the legal representative of the claim's owner for this purpose.

Personal guarantees are enforced pursuant to the ordinary proceeding regulated by the Code of Civil Procedure. However, if the guarantee agreement is contained in a public deed and the obligation secured by such guarantee agreement is also contained in a document with executory force, the guarantee will constitute an executive title and will entitle the creditor to commence a summary proceeding to collect the principal and interest set forth in such executive title.

Under the Insolvency Law, for a period of 30 days (which may be extended for up to 90 additional days) from the issue of a notice of reorganisation by the competent court, secured creditors may not commence foreclosure proceedings.

8. Conclusion

As is clear from this discussion of collateral security mechanisms in the largest Latin American countries, there are numerous commonalities among the various collateral instruments and enforcement mechanisms in these jurisdictions, due to their common heritage of Spanish and Portuguese law based on Roman law principles. These common features include:

- different instruments for personal property and real property, as well as for various kinds of personal property; and
- various types of creditor roles in respect of collateral (eg, possessory or non-possessory).

However, the specific types of collateral documents vary substantially between countries; for example, the Portuguese law-based Brazilian requirements are distinct from the Spanish law-based requirements in Mexico and other former Spanish colonies. And even among the Spanish-speaking jurisdictions, there are significant differences between civil and commercial codes, forms of collateral documentation and enforcement procedures. The lesson for prospective creditors approaching each of these jurisdictions is clear: engage experienced specialist local counsel from the relevant jurisdiction.

Security trustees

Gary Silverman
Mayer Brown

1. **Introduction**

In this chapter, we briefly survey the nature of the security trustee role; consider the security trustee's liability for breach of trust and breach of duty; look at the extent to which the security trustee has fiduciary duties; examine the security trustee's ability to exclude liability; note the duties that lie at the heart of the security trustee role; and question whether exclusion of liability has gone too far.

2. **The security trustee and enforcement**

2.1 **What is a security trustee?**

An important feature of a syndicated loan transaction is the role of the security trustee, also known as the 'security agent' or 'collateral agent'. In this chapter, we will use the term 'security trustee', because it more accurately describes the role from an English law perspective. As the name suggests, the security trustee is a corporate entity which holds security on trust for the benefit of others. The trust beneficiaries are called the 'secured parties' or 'secured creditors', and typically comprise:

- the security trustee itself;
- the lenders;
- any hedge counterparty;
- the facility agent;
- any delegate appointed by the security agent; and
- any receiver.

In a secured bond context, the secured parties will include the investors and various agents of the issuer.

The trust property in the context of an English law security trust is the security trustee's interest (the 'chose in action') in the underlying security instrument (eg, a mortgage over real estate, a charge over a bank account or a combination of other types of security for the performance of obligations owed by the obligor(s) to the secured parties under the finance documents); it is not usually understood to be the underlying security assets themselves (eg, the property secured by that fixed charge or assignment). Also, the security trustee does not normally hold the underlying security assets for safekeeping. By contrast, that is the role of a custodian.

2.2 Enforcement action

The security trustee will:

- hold the security for as long as the secured obligations remain outstanding;
- release the security once those secured obligations have been satisfied and discharged; or
- enforce the security where an enforcement event has been triggered and distribute the proceeds of enforcement to those entitled.

The nature of action that a security trustee may take will often vary depending on the enforcement and recovery strategy of the secured parties, and could variously include the following:

- seeking summary judgment in an English court;
- initiating insolvency proceedings in the relevant jurisdiction;
- appointing insolvency officials such as receivers, liquidators and administrators; and
- enforcing the security.

While the security trustee facilitates the enforcement of security (and, where necessary, appoints administrators to take control of the debtor in order to return as much value to the secured parties), having a security trustee does not guarantee that the value of the enforced assets will cover the debtor's financial obligation to the secured parties.

2.3 Remuneration

The security trustee will usually charge an annual fee during the life of the deal and sometimes also an upfront acceptance fee. If all goes well with the transaction, the security trustee should have little if anything to do. Its annual fee is effectively a retainer to keep the security trustee in the deal, not to remunerate it should it need to take enforcement action. If the security trustee is required to enforce security or otherwise perform exceptional tasks, it will normally expect to charge additional remuneration not covered by its annual fee. Such additional remuneration will often be calculated on the basis of actual time spent and based on hourly rates. The security trustee typically enjoys a senior claim in respect of its unpaid fees and expenses in priority of other secured parties. The security trustee's fees and expenses are generally paid free of taxes; and if any withholding or deduction is required, such payment is expected to be grossed up.

2.4 No legal requirement

It is not a legal requirement for a security trustee to be appointed on a loan transaction, but a security trustee will feature on a loan transaction if the composition of the group of lenders is likely to change over time. In this situation, a security trustee appointment obviates the cost and inconvenience of transferring the underlying security each time that a new lender is added or an existing lender transfers its interest. Similarly, in an issuance of secured international capital market instruments, it is generally not practicable to grant security to each individual bondholder. The benefit of having a security trustee is that only one security interest over the whole pool of assets need be granted to one person: the security trustee.

Also, when trading loans, the typical method of transfer is novation, which allows the transferring lender to transfer both the benefit and the burden of the loan; but novation will effectively cause the original finance documents to be cancelled and retaken, and the hardening period associated with the security to start afresh. To avoid the concerns that incoming lenders may have with new hardening periods, the security trustee enters into the relevant security documents on behalf of all lenders from time to time, ensuring that the security continues unaffected and the hardening periods do not start over.

2.5 Independence

Often (but not always), an independent trust company will be appointed as security trustee to demonstrate independence from the commercial parties associated with the transaction (independent of the debtor group and independent of any individual creditor), ensuring that where security needs to be enforced, the security trustee acts dispassionately in taking the necessary steps to enforce the security and distribute the proceeds of enforcement to those entitled.

2.6 No specific regulations

Security trustees are not specifically regulated in England and Wales, and accordingly there is broad flexibility (subject to operational constraints and requirements, depending on the type of loan or bond transaction involved) on the types of entities that can operate in this space. In the United Kingdom, there are no statutory requirements for an organisation to act as security trustee for loan financings or bond issuances. However, it is standard in the English law bond market for a security trustee to be a 'trust corporation' authorised to provide corporate trustee services.

2.7 No action clause

Where a security trustee features, the loan documentation (and, in relation to debt securities, the bond documentation) will include a 'no action' clause, which permits only the security trustee to take enforcement against the obligor and restricts the ability of lenders (or bondholders) from taking independent action (in the case of debt securities, unless the trustee fails to take action in accordance with the contractual provisions). The purpose of this provision is to prevent a multiplicity of actions by creditors, and it constitutes important protection for debtors and creditors alike. The no action clause prevents a race by creditors to be the quickest off the mark to get paid. In the context of debt securities, the English Court of Appeal recognised in *Elektrim SA v Vivendi Holdings 1 Corp* [2008] that the trustee structure would be ineffective were secured creditors able to pursue claims individually.

3. Is the role proactive?

The security trustee is not generally viewed as a proactive role. Various provisions of the loan documentation (and, in relation to debt securities, the bond documentation) underscore this. Among them, three key provisions may be worth briefly focusing on:

- The security trustee does not actively monitor performance;
- The security trustee acts on instructions and not on its own initiative; and
- The security trustee need not act on instructions unless indemnified to its satisfaction.

3.1 No monitoring; entitlement to rely on certificates

Finance documentation does not envisage the security trustee actively monitoring compliance by the debtor with its obligations. Loan documentation (and, in relation to debt securities, bond documentation) expressly excludes the security trustee from having to enquire whether any default has occurred, and allows the security trustee to assume (unless it has received written notice to the contrary in its capacity as security trustee for the secured parties) that no default has occurred. Hand in glove with it not having to actively monitor, the security trustee is entitled to call for and accept certificates from the obligor and other transaction parties as sufficient evidence of any fact or matter or the expediency of any transaction or thing which is *prima facie* within the knowledge of such party; and the security trustee will not be bound in any such case to call for further evidence or be responsible for any liability that may be occasioned by it acting on such certificate. A prudent security trustee will review the certificate, but need take no independent action to investigate.

3.2 Instructions and residual discretion

In both loan and bond transactions alike, investors are not willing to delegate meaningful discretion to the security trustee. In the syndicated loan market, the security trustee's role is described as solely mechanical and administrative in nature; and the security trustee is entitled (indeed, expected) to request instructions – or clarification of any instruction – from the agreed threshold of lenders as to whether and how it should exercise or refrain from exercising any right, power, authority or discretion. The security trustee is entitled to refrain from acting unless and until it receives any such instructions or clarification that it has requested.

In the bond context, although the security trustee is described by the trust deed as having "absolute and uncontrolled discretion" as to the exercise of any discretions conferred on it by the trust deed (which may, at law, oblige the security trustee to at least consider whether to exercise such discretion), the security trustee is not bound to take any step or other action or proceedings unless instructed by the bond trustee or other instructing party; and does not have the right to act if, in its opinion (or in the opinion of the bond trustee), to do so would be materially prejudicial to the interests of the bondholders/ secured parties.

In a syndicated loan context, where a security trustee would expect to be instructed in almost all circumstances, security trustees differ in approach regarding the level of residual discretion that they will accept in the absence of instructions. One approach (perhaps the most prevalent) is for the security trustee to have the right to act (or refrain from acting) as it considers to be in the best interests of the secured parties absent instructions. However, this may prompt legal counsel for the security trustee to clarify exactly whose interest the security trustee considers when such interests may diverge; and the security trustee cannot act in the best interests of all secured parties, which may not be easy to determine.

Two alternative approaches seek to address this potential concern. The first is to entitle the security trustee to act (or refrain from acting) "as it sees fit" in the absence of instructions, and to delete any express reference to the security trustee acting (or refraining from acting) as it sees fit "having regard to the interests of the secured parties". The second is to remove almost all discretion. In this situation, the lenders would retain complete control over the actions of the security trustee (subject to security trustee protections), with the deletion of any and all provisions stating that in the absence of instructions, the security trustee may act (or refrain from acting) as it sees fit. However, as the intention is not to hamper the transaction working from an operational perspective, a narrower discretion to do administrative tasks should be retained. Such narrow discretion would be couched in the following terms: "The Security Trustee may carry out what it considers in its absolute discretion to be administrative acts, or acts which are incidental to any instruction, without any instructions (though not contrary to any such instruction)."

3.3 Indemnification

Even if instructed, the security trustee is not bound to act unless provided with satisfactory indemnification. The primary financial protection for the security trustee is to be indemnified to its satisfaction and this is a right that the security trustee has at law, as confirmed in *Concord Trust v Law Debenture Trust plc* [2005] HL. In that seminal case, Lord Scott of Foscote noted that the trustee could ask for an indemnity in a "worst case scenario", as long as the risk is "more than a merely fanciful one".

As a practical matter, therefore, the security trustee would be entitled to evaluate the size of the indemnity and/or security that it requires by assessing the risk in the given circumstances on a worst-case scenario basis, taking into account, among other things:

- the potential costs of defending or commencing legal proceedings; and
- the risk (even if remote) of any award of damages being awarded against it.

It may require that such indemnity or security be given on a joint and several basis, supported by evidence satisfactory to it as to the financial standing and creditworthiness of the parties providing the indemnification and/or as to the value of the security.

(a) Indemnity at law and trustee lien

Because the security trustee administers the trust property for the benefit of the secured parties, it is the secured parties (as the beneficiaries of the trust) that bear the liabilities which the security trustee incurs in performing its duties. Therefore, the security trustee (like other trustees) may indemnify itself from the trust assets to satisfy debts properly incurred by it in performing the trust. This indemnity has two aspects:

- Where the trustee expends its own funds for trust expenses, it is entitled to be reimbursed from trust assets (the right of recoupment); and
- The trustee may pay trust liabilities directly out of the trust assets (the right of exoneration).

This right of indemnity is well established at common law and in statute, and is supported by an equitable lien. A typical provision in loan documentation would read:

The Security Trustee and every Receiver and Delegate may, in priority to any payment to the Secured Parties, indemnify itself out of the Security Assets in respect of, and pay and retain, all sums necessary to give effect to the indemnity in this Clause and shall have a lien on the Transaction Security and the proceeds of the enforcement of the Transaction Security for all moneys payable to it.

(b) Express indemnities

However, a security trustee will expect the loan documentation (and, in relation to debt securities, the bond documentation) to include express indemnities. Moreover, the security trustee will not expect to be bound to act on instructions unless (at that point) it is indemnified and/or secured and/or pre-funded to its satisfaction. This means that the security trustee may require indemnification that is greater in extent than what has been expressly set out in the loan documentation (and, in relation to debt securities, the bond documentation). A security trustee would expect to see the following key provisions in loan documentation (with similar provisions expected in bond documentation):

(A) *The Security Trustee may refrain from acting in accordance with any instructions of any Secured Party/Parties until it has received any indemnification and/or security and/or pre-funding that it may in its discretion require (which may be greater in extent than that contained in the Finance Documents and which may include payment in advance) for any cost, loss or liability (together with any applicable VAT) which it may incur in complying with those instructions.*

(B) *Notwithstanding any provision of any other Finance Document to the contrary, the Security Trustee is not obliged to expend or risk its own funds or otherwise incur any financial liability in the performance of its duties, obligations or responsibilities or the exercise of any right, power, authority or discretion if it has grounds for believing the repayment of such funds or adequate indemnity against, or security for, such risk or liability is not reasonably assured to it.*

In practice, if there is no enforcement action, the security trustee will not generally exercise its right to claim indemnity, but will rely on the provisions relating to compensation (including additional compensation) and expenses. Also, depending on the circumstances, a security trustee may be willing to rely on the express indemnities set out in the underlying documentation without more. This may be more likely on a loan transaction than a bond issue. On a loan transaction, the identity of the lenders will be known and they will be able to provide upfront indemnities 'hardwired' into the loan documentation. On a bond issue, on the other hand, the identities of the bondholders may not be known, and consequently it is rare to draft upfront indemnities into bond documentation. Therefore, a security trustee may be more likely to seek an indemnity, security and/or pre-funding from the instructing bondholders (often also accompanied by some upfront cash fighting fund), to reflect the fact that the issuer's indemnity may no longer be sufficient to guarantee payment to the security trustee of its fees, expenses and liabilities, without which the security trustee is not obliged to take any action. The markets recognise that the security trustee's right to effective indemnification reflects an understanding that the security trustee should not be taking economic risk on the transaction.

4.   Liability for breach of trust

The security trustee is liable for breach of trust. A 'breach of trust' is a breach of obligation imposed on the trustee expressly by the trust deed or impliedly by law. In *Armitage v Nurse* [1998] Ch 241, Lord Justice Millet described breach of trust as follows:

> *Breaches of trust are of many different kinds. A breach of trust may be deliberate or inadvertent; it may consist of an actual misappropriation or misapplication of the trust property or merely of an investment or other dealing which is outside the trustees' powers; it may consist of a failure to carry out a positive obligation of the trustees or merely of a want of skill and care on their part in the management of the trust property; it may be injurious to the interests of the beneficiaries or be actually to their benefit.*

The most common breach of trust is what Lord Justice Millet describes in the passage just quoted as 'want of skill and care' – the trustee breaches its duty to act with care and skill in the administration of the trust, resulting in a loss to the trust fund. This duty of care may be imposed by statute or by common law. The leading formulation of the common law duty of care and skill required of a professional trustee is that of Justice Brightman in *Bartlett v Barclays Bank Trust Co Ltd* [1980] 1 All ER 139 at 152:

> *Just as, under the law of contract, a professional person possessed of a particular skill is liable for breach of contract if he neglects to use the skill and experience which he professes, so I think that a professional corporate trustee is liable for breach of trust if loss is caused to the trust fund because it neglects to exercise the special care and skill which it professes to have… [trust corporations] hold themselves out as possessing a superior ability for the conduct of trust business, and in any event I would take judicial notice of that fact.*

A statutory duty of care was introduced by the Trustee Act 2000. Section 1 of the act requires the trustee to:

> *exercise care and skill as is reasonable in the circumstances, having regard in particular—(a) to any special knowledge or experience that he has or holds himself out as having, and (b) if he acts as trustee in the course of a business or profession, to any special knowledge or experience that it is reasonable to expect of a person acting in the course of that kind of business or profession.*

Security trustees and their advisers argue that the precise scope of the statutory duty (though similar to the common law duty) is uncertain, and profess to be better acquainted with the scope and requirements of the common law duty of care. Consequently, it is typical for the statutory duty of care under the Trustee Act 2000 to be excluded or restricted in loan documentation (and, as the case may be, bond documentation). A typical clause provides: "Section 1 of the Trustee Act 2000 shall not apply to the duties of the Security Trustee in relation to the trusts constituted by this Agreement."

Liability for breach of trust is not limited to acts or omissions which can be characterised as negligent. Where trustees act *ultra vires* – that is, outside the powers conferred upon them – it is not necessary for a beneficiary to prove negligence.

5.   Fiduciary duty

Traditionally, trust and agency are fiduciary relationships. Fiduciary duties are duties specifically imposed on fiduciaries which have an obligation of loyalty. The fiduciary obligation of loyalty is expressed by four duties which the fiduciary must observe:

- It must act in good faith;
- It must not make an unauthorised profit;
- It must not place itself in a position where its duties and interests conflict; and
- It must not act for its own benefit or for the benefit of a third party without the informed consent of the beneficiaries.

The duty to act with care and skill is not a fiduciary duty.

One important distinction between the role of facility agent and security trustee is that while it may be debated whether a facility agent is or is not a fiduciary, there is little debate in respect of the security trustee: the security trustee is a fiduciary. This distinction is reflected in typical facility agreement provisions. Those provisions relating to the facility agent seek to wholly exclude any application of the concept of the facility agent being a fiduciary with the words "nothing in this agreement constitutes the facility agent as a trustee or fiduciary of any other person"; whereas those provisions relating to the security trustee seek only to contain the application of the security trustee as fiduciary to the lenders/secured parties with the words "nothing in this agreement constitutes the security agent as an agent or trustee of any transaction obligor".

This is not to say that the security trustee is a fiduciary in all respects. In *Saltri III Ltd v MD Mezzanine SA Sicar* [2012] EWHC 3025, the court considered the liability of a security trustee in enforcing security as part of a non-consensual restructuring of a leveraged finance transaction. The court noted that a person can act as a fiduciary in certain respects, and not in others; and that where sophisticated parties have entered into commercial contracts to govern their rights and obligations, the nature and the scope of those rights and obligations will be defined by those commercial contracts and the court will be reluctant to import into that relationship wide-ranging duties on the basis of implied terms or broader fiduciary concepts. The conclusion is that if parties want to impose specific duties on the security trustee, they will need to set out those duties expressly in the commercial contracts governing the relationship.

In all transactions, the role and responsibilities of the security trustee should be clearly delineated and the practitioner representing the security trustee should ensure that ambiguities and uncertainties which could impact on the security trustee's role are avoided. In loan documentation, it is common to exclude all implied duties with a provision that reads: "The Security Trustee shall have only those duties, obligations and responsibilities expressly specified in the Finance Documents to which it is expressed to be a party (and no others shall be implied)."

Conflicts – or at least, the potential for conflicts – can be a live issue for security trustees which are part of large and diversified financial institutions. This issue is commonly addressed, at least in part, by the security trustee role being performed through a dedicated team that does not operate under common day-to-day control with groups engaging in other commercial activities. The dedicated trustee team is often split out as a different business line within the bank, often grouped within the transaction banking arm of such financial institution, being separate from the group's origination, structuring and trading businesses, with appropriate controls in place to restrict the flow of non-public information across product lines. The use of a segregated and/or independent trust entity, in markets where this is applicable, allows for greater independence of the actions of the security trustee.

Properly drafted loan (or, as applicable, bond) documentation will contain language that expressly allows the security trustee to have other related business interests. A typical clause would read: "The Security Trustee may accept deposits from, lend money to and generally engage in any kind of banking or other business with any Obligor." This will help to avoid conflicts. However, should a conflict of interest arise, properly drafted loan (or, as applicable, bond) documentation should entitle the security trustee to appoint a co-trustee or to delegate all or part of its role to another party to escape the conflict situation.

6. Exemption clauses and core duties

A 'trustee exemption clause' (also known as a 'trustee exclusion clause', 'trustee exoneration clause' or 'trustee exculpation clause') is a clause in a trust deed that seeks to limit the trustee's liability by:

- restricting or excluding the trustee's liability for failure to carry out the duties imposed upon it by the trust deed or by law;
- reducing the scope of the trustee's duties; or
- extending the trustee's powers.

Exemption clauses are a prerequisite for the use of trusts in loan and bond transactions between sophisticated counterparties, and provide security trustees with protection in an increasingly uncertain and hostile climate. The suite of exemption clauses is commensurate with:

- the relatively low fees that a security trustee charges (insufficient to warrant extensive liability);

- the security trustee's reactive function; and
- the fact that a security trustee does not have a commercial stake in the transaction in the same way as a debtor or creditor party.

English law recognises that a security trustee can validly restrict liability for damage or loss which results from its own negligence, and even from its own gross negligence, but cannot restrict liability for damage or loss which is caused by its own fraud or dishonesty.

The leading case in relation to trustee duties is *Armitage v Nurse* [1998] Ch 241, in which Lord Justice Millet identified an 'irreducible core' of trustee duties:

there is an irreducible core of obligations owed by the trustees to the beneficiaries and enforceable by them which is fundamental to the concept of a trust. If the beneficiaries have no rights enforceable against the trustees there are no trusts. But I do not accept the further submission that these core obligations include the duties of skill and care, prudence and diligence. The duty of the trustees to perform the trusts honestly and in good faith for the benefit of the beneficiaries is the minimum necessary to give substance to the trusts, but in my opinion it is sufficient.

The result of the decision in *Armitage* is that trustee exemption clauses can validly exempt trustees from all breaches of trust, except where such breaches are fraudulent or dishonest; and attempts to reduce the common law standard of care may be void if they go too far.

In international bond issues, it is normal practice for wording similar to the following to feature in trust deeds:

Nothing in this Deed will in any case in which the Security Trustee has failed to show the degree of care and diligence required of it as trustee having regard to the provisions of this Deed and the other Transaction Documents conferring on it any trusts, powers, authorities or discretions exempt the Security Trustee from or indemnify it against any liability for breach of trust or any liability which by virtue of any rule of law would otherwise attach to it in respect of any gross negligence, wilful default or fraud of which it may be guilty in relation to its duties under this Deed.

This is to reflect Section 750(1) of the Companies Act 2006, which states:

Any provision contained in – (a) a trust deed for securing an issue of debentures, or (b) any contract with the holders of debentures secured by a trust deed, is void in so far as it would have the effect of exempting a trustee of the deed from, or indemnifying him against, liability for breach of trust where he fails to show the degree of care and diligence required of him as trustee, having regard to the provisions of the trust deed conferring on him any powers, authorities or discretions.

The formulation is softened for the trustee by the final words "having regard to the provisions of the trust deed conferring on him any powers, authorities or discretions". This allows the exemption clause to be judged in the context of other provisions of the trust deed, including those which seek to reduce the scope of the trustee's duties or extend the trustee's rights and powers, such as the trustee's entitlement to rely on professional or other expert advice and certificates from directors of the obligor. Although Section 750(1) applies only in respect of note issues by UK companies, it is normal to find a liability formulation reflecting it no matter where the issuer is incorporated.

In any event, security trustees involved with syndicated loan financings and international capital market transactions have recognised that they should not, as a general rule, absolve themselves from liability for their own fraud, wilful misconduct/wilful default or gross negligence. These liability standards have become the industry accepted standard. A typical liability provision in a syndicated loan would read:

> *Neither the Security Trustee nor any Receiver or Delegate will be liable for any damages, costs or losses to any person, any diminution in value, or any liability whatsoever arising as a result of taking or not taking any action under or in connection with any Finance Document or the Security Property, unless directly caused by its gross negligence or wilful misconduct.*

That said, security trustees do exempt themselves from indirect or consequential loss or damage unless the claim for loss or damage is made in respect of fraud on the part of the security trustee. To accept this type of liability would be out of all proportion to the size and nature of the role of the security trustee in the transaction, and from a risk perspective, is not something that security trustees would accept.

7. Have we gone too far?

Debate has raged for many years over whether and to what extent security trustee protections and exclusions of liability are excessive and how active or passive the security trustee role should be. Since the financial crisis, activist investors have voiced concerns. In their view, the security trustee's role is too passive and security trustees should police the deal for the investors.

Such arguments are not, to my mind, particularly compelling. Security trustees receive relatively low fees and institutional investors – including activist investors – are highly sophisticated and have the ability to monitor complex investments. In 2006, the Law Commission published a report on trustee exemption clauses. One of the conclusions was that exemption clauses operate to control risk and to keep costs down, thereby encouraging a sufficient number of trustees to operate in the market. It also concluded that there is no clear alternative protection available to trustees, and that trustee indemnity insurance is not capable of filling the gap.

The security trustee's risk appetite differs from institution to institution, with professional corporate trustee houses having different requirements from a security trustee which also acts as lender. Some professional corporate trustee houses put active enforcement at the centre of their business; while for others, pre-default work is central – all of which informs the objectives and levels of comfort that may be required.

8.   Conclusion

We have seen that the security trustee is an important feature of loan (and bond) transactions where the composition of the investor group is wide and/or likely to change over time, and facilitates orderly enforcement of security. We have noted that while the security trustee is an important facilitation mechanism, it is not a commercial party to the transaction in the same way that the debtors or creditors are – it has no real financial stake in the transaction and should not be expected to take economic risk on the deal. We have also observed that the security trustee role is not a proactive role; investors are not willing to delegate meaningful discretion to the security trustee and will expect it to seek instructions before taking any material steps.

In addition, the security trustee has wide protections. English law recognises that the security trustee need not take any action unless indemnified to its satisfaction, and that it may validly restrict liability through exemption clauses. The courts are also reluctant to overlay fiduciary and other duties over and above those set out expressly in the commercial contract governing the relationship between sophisticated financial counterparties. Debate will continue to ensue over whether and to what extent security trustee protections and exclusions of liability have been set at the appropriate level, and whether and to what extent the security trustee should have a more active policing-type role.

Rescue financing: a US and UK comparison

Trevor Borthwick
Matt Wargin
Mayer Brown

1. Introduction

1.1 What is rescue financing?

Arguably no type of finance is defined more by the context in which it is provided than by any specific attribute or characteristic of the finance provided than what is commonly referred to as 'rescue financing'. There are certainly variations on what may be considered rescue financing. For the purposes of the discussion in this chapter, 'rescue financing' can be thought of as that area of lending which falls outside of healthy, business-as-usual lending and is often provided by a lender (or lenders) 'of last resort' – that is, lenders that will, or must, provide the required finance when no other lender will.

In certain situations involving 'emergency' financing (in contrast to rescue financing), the borrower may not otherwise be stressed – for example, where an unexpected accounting restatement results in existing committed finance facilities being unavailable to an otherwise viable and healthy business. In these types of situations, there might be a choice of lenders which will provide the emergency finance (albeit at a price). Rescue financing, on the other hand, is most commonly provided by a lender or lender group that already has exposure to the stressed or distressed company or group of companies in question. As a result, a provider of rescue finance is not likely to be providing finance (in the first instance at least) to earn fees or interest. Instead, under the circumstances, a key purpose of the financing will be to prevent an uncontrolled collapse of the borrower and avoid significant losses on the pre-existing exposure.

However, there is a growing class of lenders willing to provide rescue finance where they have no prior exposure, exemplified by lenders willing to provide so-called 'debtor in possession' (DIP) financing in insolvency cases where borrowers have filed for protection under Chapter 11 of the US Bankruptcy Code. These lenders are willing to take on significant risks involved in rescue finance in return for pricing that, in their view, reflects the potential losses they are prepared to accept (risks that may be mitigated in part by common, court-approved protections in the borrower's bankruptcy proceedings). No discussion of rescue finance can ignore finance provided by these lenders.

The type of facility provided by the lender in a rescue situation will also be driven by the circumstances. Often, the immediate need is for additional liquidity, but the stressed or distressed borrower may well need other facilities too: for instance, distressed oil and gas exploration companies might have almost as much need for letters of credit (to cover decommissioning and other permitting or licensing obligations) and hedging (against commodity price fluctuations) as for cash. Construction companies may need bonding facilities to allow them to win new contracts; and importers and exporters may need trade finance facilities such as documentary letters of credit to allow them to continue to trade. It is the need for such 'non-cash' facilities which often dictates that at least some of the providers of many rescue financings must be banks.

Given the stressed or distressed situation of the borrower in rescue financing, it is inevitable that one of the first requirements of any lender increasing its credit exposure will be security. The security package available will inevitably vary from borrower to borrower and will be dictated by a number of factors, including:

- the nature of the borrower's assets;
- the extent to which those assets are already given in security to existing lenders or other third parties; and
- the extent to which existing contracts inhibit the granting of new security to the rescue financier.

In formal processes, such as Chapter 11 or the new UK restructuring plan, provision may exist, or can be created, for a rescue financier to receive an acceptable first priority security package even absent the consent of such existing secured parties. However, given the friction costs and other downsides that formal insolvency proceedings may present, many rescue financings are – at least initially – negotiated on a consensual basis outside of a court proceeding.

It is sometimes possible to use existing contractual rights of the borrower (eg, negotiated exceptions to its negative pledge) to assemble a security package that a rescue financier can accept. However, reliance on such existing rights will often only allow the grant of limited additional security, so the consent of existing lenders may need to be sought to allow the rescue financier both the security it needs and the first priority (or so-called 'super priority') claim that will usually be the rescue financier's initial requirement. Consent requests to existing debtholders can be the starting point for extensive intercreditor discussion as the parties debate the relative merits of 'new' money being given the ability to control timing of any enforcement of security. The permutations of these debates are as variable as the borrowers seeking finance, and we will seek to highlight here some of the key issues that might arise.

In leveraged and other structured financings, where an existing security package and intercreditor matrix already exists, it may be possible to insert additional super senior debt into the structure. However, the most senior debt in the structure may be a working capital facility which is not at risk of loss in a collapse because it benefits from the highest priority claim to the existing security. If the consent of the working capital provider is required for a grant of security in priority to its own claim (as is often the case), the rescue financier may have to accept parity with the existing working capital facility. The working capital provider(s) have no incentive to agree to a prior claim.

1.2   Unique approach

As highlighted above, rescue finance is often not provided willingly by new money lenders. Even where it is, the lenders are not in the position of lenders in most other kinds of financing, in that their motivation to provide finance is not driven by any kind of customer relationship. Traditional rescue finance provided by banks was – and often still is – provided on the basis that the balance of probability suggests that lending additional funds to the borrower is more likely to result in the recovery of money already advanced than refusing to provide new money.

Where third-party lenders provide rescue finance, their motivation can vary from the aim simply to make an attractive return from the specific facility to a more complex 'loan to own' strategy, where the option to acquire the borrower or certain of the borrower's assets in certain circumstances may be a consideration.

In either case, the lender is providing the finance purely for its own commercial purposes, with very limited concern for the wider relationship between the lending organisation and the borrower. This means that the approach of lenders to rescue finance is very different from that often seen in other financing arrangements. This can be an unwelcome surprise to the management of borrowers in distress.

One key feature of European rescue finance is the level of diligence undertaken by lenders on the borrower's business. The independent business review (IBR) remains a common feature of European rescue finance and is essentially a detailed critique of the borrower's business by third-party financial advisers upon which lenders may base their analysis of whether the decision to provide new funding passes the critical test that makes recovery of existing lending more likely.

While lenders in rescue finance will also conduct other due diligence (eg, title investigation of security assets and reviews of contract terms), unless this due diligence affects the conclusions reached from the IBR, it is unlikely to affect the decision to lend. Minor defects in the title to security assets, for example, are likely to be tolerated without remedial action being required before funding, on the basis that any security is better than none. For example, where security is taken on property and there are restrictions on the title that do not prevent security being taken, lenders may accept that no attempt needs to be made to remove such restrictions. Again, security on contracts (excluding certain key contracts) may be taken whether or not a specific contract admits security being taken over it; although the security document may purport to release the relevant contract again if it would be terminable because of the grant of security or if consent to secure is sought from the counterparty after the security is executed, but cannot be obtained.

The IBR will also inform the contractual protections that lenders require. These protections are often common to the terms of the rescue financing and to the amended terms of any pre-existing finance. Typically, the terms will address the operation of the borrower's business in greater detail than is usually seen in most other financing arrangements and are likely to control aspects of the governance of the business, the management of cash and relationships with key stakeholders which most other financings would not address. The financial reporting requirements and financial covenant regime will also be more comprehensive and will often include forward-looking cash flow or liquidity testing. Rescue financiers will often also require the borrower to engage third-party financial advisers to provide enhanced transparency into the borrower's operation and greater lender comfort around the accuracy of the borrower's financial reporting and projections. The board may also be encouraged to appoint a chief restructuring officer (CRO) – someone with deep experience of rescue and turnaround situations – to help navigate the special challenges of this kind of situation; challenges which will be foreign to many boards of directors.

1.3   Relationship with other stakeholders

The common requirement of providers of rescue finance that they have priority over other creditors, coupled with the detailed and extensive contractual protections referred to above, means that rescue finance will inevitably impact on many other stakeholders in the business concerned. Management may find that their incentive plans are no longer relevant in the context of a rescue financing – particularly if the incentive plan targets or responds to the share price of the business, which may become increasingly 'out of the money' or diluted by the rescue financing. Shareholders are unlikely to receive dividends while any rescue finance is in place. If the providers of rescue finance take the view that they are covering a risk that should be borne by shareholders, shareholders may find that the rescue financing includes mechanisms such as warrants or convertible debt features to ensure that any equity 'upside' is shared with or redirected to the providers of the rescue financing.

Inevitably, though, the priority of rescue finance will mean that detailed and often extensive intercreditor discussions are required, unless the financing is part of a court sanctioned process. These discussions are not confined to the existing financial creditors; but where the business operates a final salary pension scheme, they will include the trustees of the pension fund and may also involve regulators such as the Pensions Regulator in the United Kingdom and other interested parties including (again in the United Kingdom) the Pension Protection Fund. While priority of the rescue financing is commonly accepted, the question of who controls the timing of enforcement can often lead to a complex debate. Key questions will include whether and to what extent contributions to the pension fund should continue while rescue funding is in place. In the United Kingdom, in recent years the regulators have encouraged pension trustees to be significantly more assertive – in some cases putting the availability of the rescue financing itself in doubt. It remains to be decided whether, in the longer term, it is appropriate that the rights of past employees of a business, represented by the pension trustees, should outweigh the rights of current employees, whose best interests will normally be served not so much by protection of the pension fund as by greater availability of rescue financing.

Providers of 'new money' in a distressed situation may feel that control should rest in their hands; but creditors whose consent is required before the new money can be secured, or even incurred, may view things differently. This is particularly the case where the amount of rescue financing required is small in comparison to the amount of pre-existing debt. In these cases, traditional models of creditor democracy (in terms of levels and composition of voting majorities) are often completely disregarded or are remodelled to fit the circumstances of the particular transaction.

Generally, the stakeholders in any business that have least interaction with any rescue financing are the customers and suppliers of that business. The underlying rationale for providing rescue finance is often the belief that the business can recover from whatever factors have created the situation of distress that it finds itself in. The rescue financing should be a bridge to that recovery; but the recovery itself relies on the confidence of customers and suppliers to continue trading with the business. Anything that might lead a customer or supplier to question its continued working relationship with the business is likely to be unwelcome to the providers of rescue finance and great care is often taken to maintain the confidence of these stakeholders in the future of the business.

1.4 Highly bespoke financing
It can be seen from the above that any rescue financing arrangement is likely to be highly bespoke to the situation of the particular borrower. The precise terms and mechanics of, and the security packages for, rescue financings are as varied

as the companies that require the financing. Similarities exist, however, in the processes by which rescue finance is obtained and provided – whether by agreement between the relevant interested parties or through a court-supervised process.

2.   Consensual arrangements

Regardless of the source of the capital employed in any given rescue finance arrangement, lenders providing rescue financing will have to navigate a variety of challenges to preserve and maximise their investments and to mitigate any downside risk. The principal goal of any lender providing rescue financing will be to preserve and maximise the return on its investment. This includes the obvious goal of ensuring repayment of the rescue capital infusion itself; but will often also include the long-term goal of maintaining the health and stability of the borrower as a going concern to protect the lender's pre-existing investment (which may be either debt or equity).

2.1   Collateral priority

One of the first questions for a provider of rescue finance is the basis on which its funding will be provided to the borrower. Even more so than any other type of lending, a first-priority collateral position will likely be a key requirement for the provision of rescue finance. However, in many scenarios – particularly where the rescue finance lender is not the existing senior secured lender – this will be an uphill battle, because the borrower's existing loan documents will make it difficult to provide a capital infusion other than as common equity or subordinated (or, in investment grade financing, *pari passu*) debt (in particular if the infusion is coming from the existing equity owners). The most straightforward source of collateral would be any existing unencumbered assets of the borrower. Where material unencumbered assets exist, they may nonetheless be subject to a negative pledge prohibiting the borrower from granting the rescue finance lender a security interest in the assets. It may be possible to advance additional financing (from existing or even new lenders) under the borrower's existing credit documents, at least on an equal priority basis with the existing facility. In leveraged financings, however, the ability to lend via this type of 'incremental facility' is typically limited to a set dollar threshold that may be insufficient to meet the borrower's liquidity needs.

2.2   Restrictions in existing debt documents

In addition to finding available collateral, the ability to obtain rescue finance may be constrained by other restrictions in a borrower's existing loan documentation, such as maintenance-based financial covenants – which are basically 'stress tests' that generally measure the borrower's financial condition – and incurrence covenants, which require the borrower to meet a specified financial metric whenever some particular corporate action occurs (eg, the borrower incurs debt). For example, the borrower may be required to satisfy an applicable 'leverage ratio', which may be difficult in a distressed situation where the borrower has significant debt and is likely underperforming in terms of earnings before interest, taxes, depreciation and amortisation (or another applicable earnings metric). The borrower's failure to maintain compliance with these types of financial covenants could result in default and trigger cross-defaults to other credit agreements (including those governing new money facilities).

The consent or cooperation of the existing lender group is thus likely to be necessary in order for the rescue financing to be put in place. The terms of any rescue financing will in many instances be determined by:

- the relative bargaining power of the new money and the old;
- how the existing lenders view their chances of recovery without an additional capital infusion; and
- the extent to which the rescue finance provider has its own interests to protect beyond its new money investment (eg, the extent of any pre-existing debt or equity investment).

The extent of the challenges posed by existing debt instruments will vary depending on the market norms for the type of financing and the relevant jurisdiction. Importantly, while amendments to or consents under existing documents can often be agreed by some level of majority of the existing lender group, there will always be certain rights – sometimes referred to as 'sacred' rights – which can only be amended or waived with the consent of all existing lenders. These 'sacred' rights may create blocking positions which an individual lender or group may wish to exploit – either as a ransom position in the hope that others will be willing to pay it out completely to allow the rescue financing to proceed or in order to protect its continuing position in the financing. Identification of any 'sacred rights' of existing lenders which might inhibit a rescue financing is thus a key part of any preparatory analysis for a rescue financier.

2.3 Control over enforcement

Another important issue in rescue finance is the question of who controls the course and timing of any exercise of remedies. The rescue finance provider will often want more restrictive covenants, and potentially a standstill with existing lenders, to ensure that it has control over the exercise of remedies and that the borrower's continued operations are not cut short by a default under its pre-existing debt obligations. However, the extent to which a rescue financier can obtain these rights will often depend on what the existing debt documents permit, as discussed above. In some cases, control of security enforcement may even rest with the pre-existing lender group where the amount of rescue finance is small compared to the pre-existing debt; or may be shared in some way between the rescue finance and the pre-existing debt.

Where control of enforcement is granted to or shared with the existing lender group, the argument to justify the position is often that the rescue financier should not be able to enforce security to recover a relatively small debt to the detriment of much larger claims, just because of a temporary downturn in the borrower's business. The rescue financier's view will be that the providers of any pre-existing debt should either provide the rescue finance themselves so that they retain control or accept that the provider of the rescue finance has control. Reaching a resolution of this debate is often a protracted process in rescue financings and one on which the borrower has limited visibility.

2.4 'Creative' rescue finance solutions: trapdoor and up-tier transactions

In recent years, creative providers of rescue finance in the United States have used so-called 'trapdoor' and 'uptier' transactions to structure infusions of debt capital on a priority basis, defying expectations around what many lenders considered to be 'sacred rights'-type provisions while maintaining compliance with the strict letter of the underlying agreements.

In broad terms, in a trapdoor transaction (synonymous with clothing brand J Crew, which executed a financing using this approach in 2016), the borrower exploits the fact that its existing loan documents permit 'investments' in subsidiaries to transfer valuable assets to an 'unrestricted' subsidiary (eg, a subsidiary that is not required to guarantee existing loan obligations and that also may not be subject to covenant restrictions in debt documents). This investment removes the asset from the existing lenders' collateral package, allowing it to serve as priority collateral for new financing arranged by and provided to the unrestricted subsidiary and affiliates.

In an uptier transaction, a group of existing lenders constituting 'required lenders' (typically a majority in dollar amount of commitments) under the existing loan documents leverages the ability of such 'required lenders' to amend most provisions of loan documents in order to allow the borrower to enter into a new financing with priority over the borrower's existing secured debt. Because subordination of security and claims of existing lenders are often not traditionally delineated as 'sacred rights' in recent vintage US leverage finance loans, such transactions have become increasingly common as a form of rescue finance; although in a number of cases non-participating lenders have chosen to litigate whether the transactions are legally permissible. In addition to permitting new indebtedness, an uptier transaction may include amendments that strip away affirmative and negative covenants from the existing loan documents to ensure that control over defaults resides with the new 'super priority' facility.

Trapdoor transactions are rare in European leveraged financing, the only example at the time of writing being Olympic Entertainment. The typical European covenant protections differ from the US protections, so uptiering as described above may be unlikely; but equivalent flexibility can be extracted from the increasingly loose protections in European leveraged loans, so variations of both types of structures may become prevalent in rescue finance in the European leveraged market in the near future.

2.5   Operational issues and lender liability

Given the 'make or break' stakes of rescue financing, lenders providing rescue financing generally seek greater visibility and understanding of the borrower's day-to-day operations. A number of methods may be employed to obtain an increased level of insight. Some methods are indirect, taking the form of tighter 'guardrails' such as performance-based covenants, regularly updated cash-flow projections and frequent reconciliations against actual performance. Others are more direct and may include a requirement for the borrower to engage third-party financial advisers and the appointment of an independent director or CRO.

In the leveraged market, lenders may also seek board observation rights to permit their designated representative to attend board meetings and receive copies of board minutes and other documents. However, rescue finance providers will want to exercise caution regarding the extent to which they influence or control the borrower's day-to-day operations – in particular in the United States, where there is a risk of 'lender liability' claims if the lender is found to have exercised undue influence or control over the borrower. In the United Kingdom, shadow directorship is a risk that lenders will wish to avoid; but in very general terms, the courts will not usually regard the conditions that a lender says must be met in order for it to provide or continue to maintain finance as being a sufficient influence on a borrower's day-to-day operations to justify imposing shadow directorship on a lender. In most cases, imposing a condition that the borrower appoint additional directors or a CRO or afford the lender board observer rights should not give rise to shadow directorship concerns; but lenders imposing these conditions will want to take specific advice on the issue in the context of the situation they face.

3.   Court-supervised processes

3.1   United States – DIP financing

When a distressed company files for bankruptcy relief under the US Bankruptcy Code, the company likely will no longer have access to its pre-existing financing sources. Further, notwithstanding contractual arrangements to the contrary, existing lenders cannot be required to fund and honour pre-petition credit facilities, absent a court order. Therefore, assuming that the company does not have sufficient cash flow to fund post-petition operations, the company will require new post-petition financing in order to survive. Bankruptcy financing, known as 'DIP financing', is court-approved financing that generally entitles participating lenders to significant legal protections and priority over other creditors, while providing the debtor with the capital needed to continue its operations post-filing. Typically, financing providers often prefer the certainty of a DIP financing over the riskier out-of-court rescue financing option due to the legal protections and priority afforded under a court-supervised process.

(a)   *Statutory overview: requisite court approval*

DIP financing can take a variety of different forms; and while the rights of the DIP lender depend on the type of credit granted, post-petition financing is generally authorised under Section 364 of the US Bankruptcy Code. First, Section 364 permits the debtor to obtain unsecured credit either:

- in the ordinary course, which does not require court approval (11 USC § 364(a)); or
- not in the ordinary course of business after notice and a hearing before the bankruptcy court (11 USC § 364(b)).

In both instances, the unsecured lender will receive a first priority administrative claim under Section 503(b)(1) of the US Bankruptcy Code, which provides priority over unsecured claims and must be paid in full, in cash, upon the debtor's emergence from bankruptcy.

Second, the court may authorise the debtor to obtain credit under Section 364(c) – with priority over any and all other administrative expenses – that is secured on the debtor's unencumbered assets or by junior security on previously encumbered assets.

Third, assuming that the debtor is otherwise unable to obtain secured credit under Section 364(c), the bankruptcy court may authorise the debtor to obtain credit secured senior or equal to security on already encumbered assets of the estate (commonly referred to as a 'priming lien'). As discussed below, the approval of such priming liens is subject to certain restrictions set forth in the US Bankruptcy Code and enforced by the bankruptcy court.

(b)   *DIP financing lender benefits*

Defensive DIP financing: Existing lenders are incentivised to provide DIP financing for many reasons. First, DIP financing provides existing lenders with an opportunity to preserve any pre-petition value and investment. As a threshold matter, DIP financing allows the debtor to continue its operations and to satisfy near-term obligations, including debt service, payroll, rent and other operating expenses. Without the requisite DIP financing, the debtor may be forced to liquidate and the existing lenders' recovery on pre-petition investments will be subject to significant risk.

Second, existing lenders have an interest in protecting their pre-petition collateral position. Here, existing lenders often seek to fund DIP financing arrangements as a means to mitigate the risk that third parties provide DIP financing on a basis that is senior or *pari passu* with the existing lenders' pre-petition security.

Third, existing lenders may be able to improve their collateral position *vis-à-vis* 'cross-collateralisation' – by pledging assets that serve as collateral for a pre-petition loan as collateral for the DIP financing loan.

Fourth, in the same vein as cross-collateralisation, existing lenders can seek to improve their priority position by securing their pre-petition claims with 'after-acquired' assets (ie, assets acquired by the debtor post-petition).

Lastly, given the existing lender's familiarity with the debtor's business, past financial performance and existing loan documentation, existing lenders often reduce the need for costly and time-intensive due diligence.

Offensive DIP financing: Lenders with no or minimal pre-petition lending relationships with the debtor may also seek to provide DIP finance. Similar to existing lenders, third-party lenders are motivated by a variety of incentives. First, new money providers are attracted by the financial benefits tied to the underlying DIP loan, such as increasingly high fees and interest rates.

Second, new money funders seek to gain collateral positions in the debtor's capital structure by obtaining liens on unencumbered collateral and/or encumbered collateral. With respect to previously encumbered collateral, it has become common practice for new money financing providers to lend on the basis that the new money loans will be secured by senior equal security on encumbered estate assets – commonly referred to as a 'priming lien' – pursuant to Section 364(d) of the US Bankruptcy Code. While the specifics are arguably beyond the scope of this chapter, to the extent that a lender is seeking to prime existing security with new post-petition security, the debtor must first obtain the consent of the existing lienholders or prove that the creditors' interests are adequately protected.

Third, new money funders often seek DIP financing arrangements as potential ownership opportunities in the post-bankruptcy or 'reorganised' company – commonly referred to as 'loan to own' strategies. Typically, loan to own strategies are pursued by one of two means:

- The funder provides DIP financing in exchange for an equity stake in the company; or
- The funder consents to an alternative treatment of its priority DIP claims, such as conversion to equity.

3.2   United Kingdom

Until 2020, no statutory process existed in the United Kingdom under which a distressed company could arrange rescue finance against the wishes of all or a class of its creditors. This was seen as a longstanding deficiency of the UK regime and a number of attempts, in various cases, were made to rely on a nexus with the US courts to import a Chapter 11 process into a UK restructuring – some of which were successful. The restructuring plan introduced in 2020 (see below) is very different from Chapter 11 – not least because simply commencing the process of implementing a restructuring plan does not provide any protection from the actions of creditors in the way that petitioning for bankruptcy relief does; but, crucially, it does provide a mechanism under which rescue financing can be imposed, subject to certain safeguards.

Before 2020, schemes of arrangement under the Companies Act 2006 were frequently used to implement rescue financing; but they depended on the majority support of all classes of the relevant company's creditors and, therefore, were only a mechanism to bring a deal that had widespread creditor support into being. The voting mechanism was complex and any class of creditors (including a class that was likely to make no recovery in the most likely alternative outcome to implementation of the relevant scheme (usually liquidation or administration)) could prevent the scheme from becoming effective. If rescue finance could not be arranged by agreement between creditors, therefore, there was a high probability that the debtor would have to enter some form of insolvency process.

The Corporate Insolvency and Governance Act 2020, which came into force in June 2020, introduced the long-awaited concept of a restructuring plan into UK company law by inserting the new Part 26A into the Companies Act.

The restructuring plan is not designed specifically to permit rescue financing. Rather, if a company is in financial difficulty, the new Part 26A allows an 'arrangement' to be proposed between a company and its creditors to "eliminate, reduce or prevent or mitigate the effect of" those financial difficulties.[1] Such an arrangement may or may not include provision for rescue finance; and to date, relatively few of the plans that have been proposed have included specific rescue financing arrangements. However, it is the clear intention of the legislation that rescue financing could be imposed using the restructuring plan; and in the case of the restructuring plan for Pizza Express,[2] existing financing terms were amended (against the wishes of the beneficiaries of those terms) to allow for rescue finance to be introduced at a later date. This is the only plan to date where such an amendment was made and it must be

---

[1]   Section 901(A) of the Companies Act 2006 as amended by the Corporate Insolvency and Governance Act.

[2]   [2020] EWHC 2873 (Ch).

noted that no rescue finance was actually introduced as a result of the plan; but it is unlikely to be long before another plan takes that extra step.

The requirements of the Companies Act in respect of a restructuring plan are similar to those for the scheme of arrangement (a tool that remains available both for rescue finance and for other purposes), in that creditors and shareholders must vote in classes to approve the restructuring plan. The approval of the court is required at the commencement of the process, to convene the relevant meetings of creditors and at the end, to sanction the relevant plan; but the court's discretion on whether to sanction the plan looks only at whether the requirements of the Companies Act have been complied with and whether the plan is reasonable. If the court considers that the plan that has achieved the approval of the necessary majority of creditors is reasonable, there is no scope to argue before the court that another plan, or a variation of the plan that was voted on, would produce a better outcome.

The majority required in each class is a simple 75% by value,[3] rather than the more complex majorities by value and by number required in the case of a scheme. If the court is satisfied that no member of a particular class has a "genuine economic interest in the company"[4] concerned, that class need not be allowed a vote.

While all classes that have an economic interest in the company are afforded a vote on the plan, the fact that one or more classes may vote against the plan does not mean that it will fail. Provided that one class with an economic interest votes in favour of the plan and it can be shown that none of the members of any dissenting class would be any worse off under the plan than they would be under any relevant alternative,[5] the court should exercise its discretion to sanction the plan. For these purposes, the 'relevant alternative' is "whatever the court considers would be most likely to occur in relation to the company"[6] if the plan were not approved. This 'no worse off' test is similar to the requirement in DIP financing that existing lienholders interests are protected.

The English courts have already demonstrated that if it can be shown that shareholders might be worse off under the plan than they would be in the relevant alternative, the plan should not be sanctioned.[7] In that particular case, the 'relevant alternative' was not necessarily an insolvency; but it seems likely that a principle that has been applied to protect shareholders can equally apply to creditors which might be prejudiced by a proposed restructuring plan. Equally, as in the *Pizza Express* case, where the 'no worse off' test is satisfied, it

3   Section 901F of the Companies Act.
4   *Ibid*, Section 901C(4).
5   *Ibid*, Section 901G.
6   *Ibid*, Section 901G(4).
7   [2021] EWHC 1759 (Ch).

is clear that so-called 'cross-class cram-down' is now available in the United Kingdom to permit rescue finance to be introduced over the objections of a 'blocking' creditor group.

4.   Conclusion

Rescue finance is a complex and multi-faceted type of secured financing. It is driven by necessity and, as discussed, is very specific to the context in which it is provided. At the time of writing, in the third quarter of 2021, the vast government stimulus packages that have been injected into Western economies in response to the COVID-19 pandemic have temporarily reduced demand for rescue finance to historically low levels; but as the stimulus packages are withdrawn, it should be expected that rescue financing will increasingly be sought by companies that have been unable to overcome the challenges of the pandemic.

Intercreditor arrangements

Andrew Crotty
Danister de Silva
Mayer Brown

1. Introduction

Where a finance transaction is structured to include different classes of secured and/or unsecured debt, an agreement is generally required between the various classes of creditor, the borrowers and any entities providing guarantees or security to regulate their rights and obligations in relation to that debt. These types of agreements can be broadly divided into three categories – subordination agreements, deeds of priority and intercreditor agreements – with the nature of the financing structure determining which type of agreement is most appropriate and the rights and obligations it needs to regulate:

- Subordination agreements are used to regulate the interaction of debt claims in relatively simple structures where the relevant creditors do not have competing security interests in respect of such claims. The subordination agreement will provide that the junior debt is subordinated in right and priority of payment to the senior debt by limiting the circumstances in which the junior creditors can be repaid or enforce their rights against a debtor, while also regulating their ability to amend the terms of the junior debt.

- Deeds of priority are used when two or more secured creditors have competing security interests over the same assets, with one secured creditor agreeing with another secured creditor to vary or confirm the legal priority of those security interests. They are used to provide certainty over which secured creditor controls the enforcement process and how the proceeds of enforcement are to be distributed between the secured creditors; and, depending upon the nature of the transaction, they may also include the provisions typically covered in a subordination agreement.

- Intercreditor agreements are the most complicated of the three categories, and are typically used on a structured deal where the amount of debt incurred by the borrowers is tightly controlled and arranged into various layers, each having a different priority. They are agreements between different classes of secured and unsecured creditors which regulate, among other things:

- the ranking of claims against debtors;
- the enforcement of rights against debtors; and
- the enforcement of a common security package and/or competing security interests.

Their primary purposes are:

- to ensure that each class of debt ranks in accordance with the agreed order of priority; and
- to set out an agreement between the creditors regarding how certain aspects of any restructuring or enforcement process should be conducted should the borrowing group run into financial difficulties.

In the London market, the starting point for the vast majority of intercreditor agreements is one of the precedents prepared by the Loan Market Association (LMA), which include forms to be used for:

- senior/mezzanine leveraged acquisition finance transactions;
- super senior/senior leveraged acquisition finance transactions (ie, unitranche transactions); and
- senior/mezzanine real estate finance transactions.

This chapter will explain the key issues which are covered by intercreditor agreements by reference to those LMA precedents.

2.   Parties and regulated debt

All creditors and all members of the borrowing group whose debt is to be ranked and regulated as part of the transaction's capital structure should be party to the intercreditor agreement. The parties will vary depending on the capital structure, but may include all or any of the following:

- Facility creditors: The senior lenders and super senior lenders or mezzanine lenders under any relevant facility agreements.
- Hedge counterparties: The providers of any interest rate swaps or foreign exchange hedging transactions which are permitted to benefit from the transaction security by the terms of the facility agreements and the intercreditor agreement.[1]
- Subordinated creditors: Including investors or any holding company sitting outside of the banking structure (to the extent they are a creditor in respect of any financial indebtedness of the borrowing group) and, in the case of a leveraged acquisition, the vendor of the relevant target

---

1   Since hedging which is provided by way of an interest rate cap just involves the payment of an upfront premium by the borrowing group and the borrowing group does not have any ongoing payment obligations in relation to such transactions, hedging provided by way of an interest rate cap will not benefit from the transaction security and the relevant hedge counterparties need not be party to the intercreditor agreement.

group, to the extent it is owed any amounts by members of the borrowing group (eg, vendor loan notes) following completion of the acquisition.

- Intra-group lenders: Any members of the borrowing group which have or may in the future provide intra-groups loans to other members of the borrowing group in an amount exceeding a *de minimis* threshold.[2]
- Debtors: Any member of the borrowing group which is a borrower, debtor, guarantor or security provider in relation to any of the debt which is to be regulated by the intercreditor agreement.

An English law intercreditor agreement will also include a declaration by the security agent (sometimes also referred to as the 'security trustee') that it holds all of the transaction security on trust for the secured creditors on the terms set out in the intercreditor agreement and the security agent will therefore be party to the intercreditor agreement in order to accept its appointment and its obligations to the other parties as security agent. The facility agent will also be a party in order to accept its administrative obligations with respect to decision making and notifications.

3.   Ranking of debt and security

The ranking and priority of the classes of debt which are regulated by the intercreditor agreement and any associated transaction security reflect the level of risk and return that each creditor class has agreed to accept in the capital structure and that the intercreditor agreement sets out, and reinforce this commercially agreed ranking by broadly attempting to ensure that senior debt is always repaid in priority to junior debt.

This underlying purpose runs throughout the intercreditor agreement, but is particularly relevant in the provisions with the following headings in the LMA precedents:

- ranking and priority;
- application of proceeds; and
- turnover of receipts.

In a senior/mezzanine structure, the liabilities owed to the senior lenders and the hedge counterparties rank first on a *pari passu* basis in terms of priority of payment and in relation to the transaction security; and the liabilities owed to the mezzanine lenders rank second. In a super senior/senior structure, however, the liabilities owed to the senior lenders, the super senior lenders and

---

2   The LMA precedent intercreditor agreement for use in relation to real estate finance transactions does not include provisions relating to subordinated creditors or intra-groups lenders so these parties would typically sign up to a standalone subordination agreement rather than the intercreditor agreement.

the hedge counterparties rank on a *pari passu* basis in terms of priority of payment and in relation to the transaction security, with the agreed ranking being implemented through the application of proceeds provision. Unsecured liabilities are postponed and subordinated to the liabilities owed to the secured creditors, but are not ranked as between themselves.

'Liabilities' are defined to include all present and future liabilities and obligations at any time of any member of the borrowing group to any creditor under the debt documents which are regulated by the intercreditor agreement. They may be both actual or contingent, and incurred solely or jointly by an individual debtor as principal or in any other capacity.

The provision entitled "Application of Proceeds" is also commonly known as 'the waterfall'. It is referred to as the waterfall because payments start at the top and flow downwards, with those first in line being paid first and any residue falling to those at the next level below; so the further down the waterfall a creditor is, the more likely that it may not receive all amounts owing to it following the realisation or enforcement of the transaction security. The order of priority of payment from proceeds received by the security agent from an enforcement can be summarised as follows:

- First, the agent and the security agent will be repaid all sums to cover their costs and expenses;
- Second, the secured creditors will be repaid all costs and expenses in connection with the enforcement of the transaction security;
- Third, in a super senior/senior structure, the super senior facility liabilities and any super senior hedging liabilities will be repaid on a *pro rata* basis between themselves;
- Fourth, the senior facility liabilities and any other secured hedging liabilities will be repaid on a *pro rata* basis between themselves;
- Fifth, in a senior/mezzanine structure, the mezzanine facility liabilities will be repaid on a *pro rata* basis between themselves;
- Sixth, payments or distributions will be made to any person to which payment is required to be made by law; and
- Seventh, the balance will be paid to any relevant members of the borrowing group.

The provision entitled "Turnover of Receipts" reinforces the commercially agreed ranking and order of priority by requiring that any creditors turn over any amounts received or recovered by them in respect of the liabilities owed to them (including any amounts received by way of set-off) to the security agent for distribution in accordance with the waterfall in any of the following circumstances:

- The receipt of such payment by the relevant creditor is not a permitted payment under the intercreditor agreement;

- Any of the facility liabilities have been accelerated or any of the transaction security has been enforced;
- The payment arose from litigation taken against a member of the borrowing group;
- The amount received constitutes the proceeds of enforcement of the transaction security; or
- The payment from any member of the borrowing group arose as a result of an insolvency event in relation to that member of the borrowing group.

The intercreditor agreement stipulates that any amounts received or recovered by a creditor which are required to be turned over to the security agent must be held on trust (ie, a turnover trust) for the security agent until they are paid over to the security agent, in an attempt to keep them outside of the bankruptcy estate of the relevant creditor.[3]

4.   Amendments to debt documents

Intercreditor agreements restrict the transaction parties from making certain amendments to the underlying documents which govern the terms of their respective debt.

In a senior/mezzanine structure, the senior lenders are permitted to amend the senior finance documents unless the intercreditor agreement prohibits such amendments without the consent of two-thirds of the mezzanine lenders by value, with such prohibitions typically preventing the senior lenders from increasing the size of the senior facility, the senior margin or the amount of fees payable to the senior lenders without the consent of the mezzanine lenders.

On one hand, the mezzanine lenders want to control the amount of senior debt that ranks ahead of the mezzanine debt and the amount of cash leakage to the senior lenders, because any increase in the amount of senior debt and/or senior leakage may increase the risk of a senior default, and may also reduce the amount of surplus enforcement proceeds available to repay the mezzanine debt in an enforcement scenario once the senior debt has been discharged. On the other hand, the senior lenders and the borrowing group want to retain the flexibility for additional funding to be advanced on a senior basis to allow additional financing for acquisitions or expansionary capex initiatives, or to ease cash-flow issues if the group experiences financial difficulties. To bridge this tension, the intercreditor agreement may include senior headroom concepts which allow the senior lenders to increase the amount of senior debt,

---

3   In the case of creditors which are not incorporated in England and Wales, such trusts may not be recognised by the courts of the jurisdiction in which they are incorporated in all cases resulting in the security agent only having a contractual claim to the relevant amounts.

the senior margin and/or the amount of fees payable to the senior lenders by agreed percentages or amounts without requiring mezzanine lender consent.

In a super senior/senior leveraged acquisition finance transaction, the relationship between the super senior and senior lenders in respect of amendments to the facility agreement under which the super senior and senior debt is provided will be governed by the facility agreement itself. The only restriction in the intercreditor agreement on the ability of the super senior and senior lenders to amend the facility agreement will be on amendments that concern the terms or coverage of the guarantees provided under the facility agreements, with such amendments requiring the consent of any hedge counterparties, since they also benefit from such guarantees.

In a senior/mezzanine structure, the senior lenders want to control the size and shape of the transaction's capital structure because any increase in principal or interest payments in relation to the mezzanine debt may impact the group's ability to repay or refinance the senior debt. Therefore, the intercreditor agreement for a transaction involving both senior and mezzanine lenders will typically prohibit the following without the consent of two-thirds of the senior lenders by value:

- any increase in the amount of the mezzanine debt;
- any amendment to the repayment schedule or any provision requiring mandatory pre-payments;
- any increase in the mezzanine margin or the amount of fees payable to the mezzanine lenders; and
- any amendment involving the inclusion of more onerous representations, undertakings, financial covenants or events of default, unless equivalent amendments have also been made to the senior debt documents.

The intercreditor agreement includes a general prohibition on amendments of the hedging agreements, unless the amendment does not breach the terms of the intercreditor agreement or the terms of any relevant facility agreement (including any hedging strategy letter, to the extent that one exists).

Amendments to any intra-group loan documents are generally not restricted and will simply be subject to the terms of the relevant facility agreements; while amendments to the documents relating to the subordinated debt owed by the borrowing group to a sponsor, group holding company or under any vendor loan notes are typically restricted unless the amendment is minor and administrative, and not prejudicial to the secured creditors.

Secured creditors are also prohibited from taking the benefit of any additional guarantee or security unless the same is also provided to the other secured creditors; and unsecured creditors are prohibited from taking the benefit of any security or guarantee.

5.   Permitted payments

Intercreditor agreements regulate the extent to which creditors are permitted to receive payments of principal, interest, fees and other amounts due under the relevant debt documents which are subject to the intercreditor agreement.

In a senior/mezzanine structure, payments of the senior facility liabilities may be received and retained by the senior lenders at any time in accordance with the terms of the senior finance documents. However, in a super senior/senior structure, payments of the super senior facility liabilities and the senior facility liabilities may be received and retained by the super senior facility lenders and the senior lenders at any time in accordance with the terms of the senior facility agreement.

The ability of the super senior lenders to place restrictions on payments of the senior debt in the senior facility agreement will largely depend on the commercially negotiated position and the amount and nature of the super senior debt in the structure, with some super senior lenders, for example, seeking to require that voluntary pre-payments or mandatory pre-payments of proceeds from disposals or insurance claims be applied in pre-payment of the super senior debt first in certain circumstances (eg, if there is a super senior event of default continuing or if there is super senior term debt in the structure).

In a senior/mezzanine structure, payments of the mezzanine facility liabilities are restricted while any senior liabilities remain outstanding, unless they are expressly permitted by the intercreditor agreement reinforcing the commercially agreed ranking and the principle that the senior liabilities should always be repaid in priority to the mezzanine liabilities. Payments in respect of the mezzanine liabilities (other than principal repayments or payments of capitalised interest) are generally permitted in the ordinary course, unless there are certain types of senior event of default continuing, which may include any senior event of default or only material events of default, depending on the commercial agreement of the parties.

The block on any mezzanine payments will be automatic in the case of a senior event of default relating to the payment of the senior liabilities, or will occur with notice from the senior lenders to the security agent (and then to the mezzanine agent) following the occurrence of any other senior event of default or material event of default, as applicable. Following the delivery of such a notice, all payments of mezzanine liabilities will be restricted for an agreed period (eg, 120 days); or if an enforcement standstill period has commenced (as explained in section 6), payments will be restricted until the end of that period.

To prevent the senior lenders from abusing this mezzanine payment stop regime in a leveraged acquisition structure, restrictions will usually be included in relation to:

- how much time can elapse between the senior event of default and the serving of the mezzanine payment stop notice;

- the number of mezzanine payment stop notices that may be served in relation to the same event of default; and
- the number of mezzanine payment stop notices that may be served in any 12-month period.

These protections (together with the enforcement standstill regime explained in section 6) encourage the senior lenders to react proactively to events of default rather than suspending mezzanine payments indefinitely without requiring a remedy, waiving the relevant default or implementing a restructuring/enforcing.

In a senior/mezzanine real estate finance structure, the mezzanine payment stop typically applies automatically following a senior event of default or material event of default, as applicable, and is generally not subject to any restrictions in terms of duration or frequency of the payments stop referred to above.

Repayments of mezzanine principal are generally not permitted without the consent of two-thirds of the senior creditors by value prior to the senior liabilities being discharged in full, unless:

- such repayments:
  - are specifically permitted by the senior facility agreement (eg, in a real estate finance transaction following the disposal of a property or using surplus rental income);
  - are required as a result of it becoming illegal for a mezzanine lender to maintain its participation in the mezzanine debt; or
  - arise as a result of the borrower of the mezzanine debt exercising its right of repayment as a result of the tax or increased costs provisions in the mezzanine facility agreement; and
- in each case there is no mezzanine payment stop continuing at the time of the repayment.

In a senior/mezzanine or super senior/senior leveraged acquisition finance transaction, payments in respect of the hedging liabilities are restricted unless expressly permitted by the intercreditor agreement. Examples of permitted hedging payments include:

- scheduled payments;
- payments in respect of tax gross-ups;
- non-credit-related close-outs;
- credit-related close-outs, provided that no senior event of default has occurred;
- hedging counterparty insolvency;
- hedging *force majeure*; and
- any payment made with the consent of two-thirds of the senior creditors by value.

A 'close-out payment' is a payment which is due when a hedging transaction is closed out and a payment is due to the hedging counterparty (ie, because the transaction is 'out of the money' from the perspective of the member of the borrowing group which entered into the hedge). For details of non-credit-related close-outs and credit-related close-outs, see section 6.

Payments to hedge counterparties in the ordinary course in a senior/mezzanine real estate finance transactions are regulated by the senior facility agreement rather than the intercreditor agreement.

The relevant debtors are not released from their payment obligations in respect of the mezzanine liabilities or the hedging liabilities as a result of the application of any restriction on the making of such payment in the intercreditor agreement.

In respect of other creditors of a group member, payments of intra-group liabilities are generally permitted unless the facilities have been accelerated or any of the transaction security has been enforced, as cash must be allowed to move around the borrowing group in the normal course, provided that such movement does not represent leakage from the creditors' security net. Payments of subordinated liabilities, however, are restricted unless expressly permitted by the senior and mezzanine facility agreements (if applicable).

6.   Enforcement

'Enforcement action' is widely defined in intercreditor agreements to cover all types of enforcement action, including:

- accelerating payment;
- putting loans 'on demand';
- calling on a guarantee;
- exercising set-off or netting rights;
- suing to recover unpaid amounts;
- closing out transactions;
- enforcing security; and
- initiating insolvency proceedings.

In super senior/senior and senior/mezzanine leveraged acquisition finance transactions, there are generally no restrictions on the senior lenders taking enforcement action in accordance with the terms of the senior finance documents (although obligations to notify or consult with the other secured creditors prior to taking enforcement action may sometimes be included). In senior/mezzanine real estate finance transactions, the ability of the senior lenders to take enforcement action will also be unrestricted, subject to a short standstill period during which the mezzanine lenders may exercise:

- their own enforcement rights if there is mezzanine-only security;
- any cure rights in respect of the relevant senior event of default; or
- their right to acquire the senior liabilities at par.

In super senior and senior/mezzanine transactions, the super senior lenders or, as applicable, the mezzanine lenders are prohibited from taking any enforcement action unless:

- the senior lenders have taken enforcement action (in which case the super senior lenders or mezzanine lenders are permitted to take the same enforcement action as the senior lenders);
- the senior lenders have given their consent to the taking of that enforcement action; or
- a super senior or mezzanine event of default has occurred and is continuing and the relevant standstill period which is applicable to that event of default has expired.

The length of the standstill period will vary depending on the seriousness of the event of default. For example, in the current London market, the standstill period is often:

- between 60 and 90 days following the occurrence of a non-payment event of default;
- between 90 and 150 days in relation to a financial covenant default; and
- between 120 and 180 days for any other event of default.

The standstill period gives the senior creditors and the borrowing group a pre-agreed period during which they can negotiate a potential solution to whatever issue has caused the super senior or mezzanine event of default; or, if a solution is not possible, during which the senior creditors may run an orderly and efficient enforcement process. The ability of the super senior or mezzanine lenders to enforce at the end of such period incentivises the senior creditors and the borrowing group to agree a solution or to take appropriate enforcement action before the standstill period expires or risk losing control of the process.

In senior/mezzanine real estate finance transactions where the mezzanine debt is structurally subordinated to the senior debt (ie, the mezzanine borrower sits above the senior borrower in the group structure), the mezzanine lenders will often have the benefit of mezzanine-only security in respect of the shares in the mezzanine borrower, with the mezzanine lender being permitted to enforce this mezzanine-only security during the standstill period referred to above by effecting the sale of the shares to an approved investor (as defined in the intercreditor agreement). However, if the mezzanine lender has this mezzanine-only security and an independent enforcement right, it is often the case that the mezzanine lender will be unable to enforce the common transaction security which has been granted in respect of both the senior and mezzanine debt; and its ability to take enforcement action against the senior borrowers or senior guarantors will be limited to taking the same enforcement action already taken by the senior lenders.

Intercreditor agreements generally prohibit hedge counterparties from taking enforcement action, but close-outs are permitted in the following circumstances:

- Non-credit-related close-outs:
  - if the minimum hedging required in the other finance documents will remain satisfied following the close-out, as a result of a hedging *force majeure* event (ie, illegality or a tax event); or
  - if there is excess hedging (ie, if the hedged amount exceeds the amount of the term debt in the structure).
- Credit-related close-outs:
  - if the senior or mezzanine lenders have accelerated their debt or enforced their security;
  - if a counterparty under a hedging agreement is insolvent (but only in respect of the relevant hedging agreement), with the consent of two-thirds of the senior creditors by value; or
  - if there is a non-payment event under a hedging agreement (but only in respect of the relevant hedging agreement).

Hedge counterparties must also close out any hedging transactions at the request of the security agent if the senior lenders have accelerated their debt or the transaction security is being enforced.

The taking of enforcement action in relation to intra-group debt and subordinated debt owed by the borrowing group to a sponsor, group holding company or under any vendor loan notes is generally restricted.

The secured creditors have no independent power to enforce the transaction security, except through the security agent; and the security agent will enforce the transaction security only upon the instructions of two-thirds of the senior creditors by value or, at the end of the standstill periods referred to above, on the instructions of two-thirds of the super senior or mezzanine lenders by value. The proceeds of enforcement of the transactions security are always applied in accordance with the agreed waterfall, regardless of which creditor group instructs or controls enforcement.

The timing and manner of enforcement action can often give rise to disputes between different classes of creditors, which will have different interests and enforcement strategies depending on their view of where value breaks in the structure (ie, which creditors will not be paid out in full and how much of a loss they expect to incur following completion of enforcement).

In a case known as *Saltri III* (*Saltri III Ltd v MD Mezzanine SA Sicar* [2012] EWHC 3025), the English High Court in London was asked to decide whether the action by a group of senior lenders to enforce their rights under an intercreditor agreement by a sale to a special purpose vehicle and a release of the 'underwater' mezzanine debt was valid (ie, owing to the deteriorating financial position of the company, the expected amount of the proceeds of security enforcement would be less than the amount of the senior secured debt and therefore the mezzanine debt would not receive any distribution in respect of such recoveries). The mezzanine lenders argued that the security agent was a fiduciary of the secured creditors in relation to the enforcement of the transaction security and was therefore obliged to act in the best interests of all of the secured creditors, even though the mezzanine lenders were not part of the instructing group under the terms of the intercreditor agreement. The court held that, as a matter of contract, the security agent could enforce the transaction security only in accordance with the instruction of the senior creditors; and that the senior creditors had the right to control the timing and the manner of enforcement, even if the timing and manner were detrimental to the interests of the mezzanine lenders. The security agent duties to the mezzanine lenders were therefore equivalent to the duty owed by a mortgagee to a mortgagor.

Following the occurrence of an insolvency event in relation to a member of the borrowing group:

- unless otherwise directed by the security agent, the intercreditor agreement permits all creditors to accelerate, demand under any guarantee, exercise rights of set-off or claim or prove in any insolvency process; and the security agent is also authorised to take any such action on any creditor's behalf; and
- the intercreditor agreement requires that all creditors and debtors direct that distributions out of the assets of that member of the borrowing group be made directly to the security agent for application in accordance with the agreed waterfall, with any receipts and recoveries received directly by the creditors being subject to the turnover obligations referred to above.

Such enforcement is permitted following an insolvency event to maximise the recovery proceeds which are available for distribution in accordance with the agreed waterfall.

7. Distress disposals and appropriation

Rather than enforcing security over individual assets on a piecemeal basis, greater value may often be realised by the secured creditors in an enforcement scenario by disposing of the borrowing group as a whole or certain members of the borrowing group as going concerns by way of share sale and free of all liabilities under the debt documents which are regulated by the intercreditor agreement. Many enforcement processes therefore involve the enforcement of a share charge whereby the shares in a holding company of the borrowing group are sold to a third-party purchaser or a newco controlled by one or more class of secured creditor free of any liabilities which, should they remain in the borrowing group following such a sale, would reduce the value of the borrowing group (and therefore the proceeds of enforcement from the sale) on a pound-for-pound basis.

The provisions of the intercreditor agreement in the clause headed "Distressed Disposals and Appropriation" in the LMA precedents are consequently extremely important in an enforcement context, as they give the security agent express powers to release the transaction security and the members of the borrowing group from their liabilities to the creditors in connection with an enforcement of the transaction security, thereby allowing the security agent to dispose of the borrowing group for its actual value on a debt-free basis, with the undiscounted sale proceeds then being applied in accordance with the waterfall.

While all creditors have a common interest in maximising the amount of enforcement proceeds that are realised, the different classes of creditors may often disagree about the timing or method of enforcement (ie, the senior lenders may prefer a quick sale with a limited marketing process in circumstances where they expect to be paid out in full in any case; whereas the mezzanine lenders may prefer a more fulsome marketing process if the value of the group may not extend to the full amount of the mezzanine debt and there is a possibility that this might increase the amount that the mezzanine lenders recover). Consequently, junior secured creditors often seek contractual protections in the intercreditor agreement to prevent the disposal of assets by the senior secured creditors pursuant to an enforcement process at too low a price. This protection typically takes the form of an obligation on the security agent to take reasonable care to obtain a fair market price or value having regard to the prevailing market conditions, which broadly mirrors the common law obligations of a mortgagee in possession while also confirming that the security agent is not obliged to postpone any enforcement in order to achieve a higher price or value.

In order to provide greater certainty for the security agent and reduce the risk of litigation by junior creditors, the LMA precedents include the following suggested list of safe harbours pursuant to which the security agent may satisfy the fair value obligation:

- an enforcement made pursuant to any process approved or supervised by a court of law;
- an enforcement at the direction or under the control of certain types of insolvency practitioners;
- an enforcement pursuant to a competitive sales process; and
- an enforcement in respect of which a fairness opinion has been provided.

The nature of these safe harbours will be hotly negotiated by any junior secured creditors, with a particular focus on:

- the circumstances in which the security agent is entitled to enforce pursuant to a private process on the basis of a fairness opinion rather than pursuant to a public auction;
- how a competitive sales process is defined (eg, how it is conducted and whether senior and/or junior secured creditors can participate); and
- any requirements for cash consideration/whether the secured creditors are allowed to credit bid.

The extent to which junior secured creditors have information or consultation rights prior to any enforcement action being taken will also be keenly contested.

Reform

Sarah Walters
Mayer Brown

The easy availability of credit is often considered to be one of the cornerstones of a modern market economy. Conventional wisdom suggests that the possibility of securing credit promotes the availability of credit. 'Security' may be defined broadly as a right over property to ensure the payment of money or the performance of some other obligation. Security is said to encourage lenders to make loans that they would not otherwise make, to lower the cost of credit and to serve as fair exchange for the credit. Creditors often wish to take security to give them priority over other creditors in the event of the debtor becoming insolvent, and also to provide them with a measure of control over the secured assets and more generally over the debtor's business. A debtor is perhaps more likely to pay a secured creditor because otherwise it would risk losing assets that may be crucial to the carrying on of its business. Moreover, the taking of security opens up the possibility of the creditor exercising self-help remedies; and it may also shorten a credit inquiry, in that a creditor might focus its investigations on the value of the secured assets.

It is also conventional wisdom – particularly among international financial institutions – that a modern law of secured credit should embody certain fundamental principles, including the principle that the law should provide for the granting of security in the widest possible range of circumstances. In other words, it should be possible to take security over all sorts of property to secure all sorts of credits. Moreover, all types of debtor should be free to grant security, and in favour of all types of creditor. Another fundamental principle is that security rights over property should be effectively publicised.

This chapter focuses primarily on the 'publicity' aspects of security and examines the issue of personal property security law reform in the common law developed world, particularly in England.

1. The English publicity system for company security interests and certain points of comparison

Since April 2013, the company charge registration regime for England (set out in Part 25 of the Companies Act 2006) has, on its face, been a voluntary one, whereby UK-registered companies[1] which have granted a charge, or any charge holder, can register details of the charge with Companies House. In reality, the consequences of non-registration of a charge are serious for both the company and the charge holder. For a charge holder, failure to register will mean the charge is void (insofar as any security is conferred by it) against a liquidator, administrator or creditor of the company. At the same time, the charge being void due to non-registration is also an issue for the charge holder, because as soon as that occurs, the money secured by it immediately becomes payable.

The registration obligation in Part 25 of the Companies Act 2006 applies to charges created by a company which do not fall within the list of exemptions set out in Section 859A(6) of the Companies Act 2006; it does not cover 'quasi-security'. The latter encompasses functionally equivalent legal devices such as finance leases, retention of title clauses in sale of goods contracts or factoring arrangements (ie, the absolute assignment of receivables). 'Quasi-security' may involve many of the same economic consequences as a charge, but has different legal characteristics and effects. At the same time, it should be borne in mind that the registration requirement is not limited to interests labelled as 'charges'. So mortgages, including assignments intended to operate as security interests, would qualify; as would a security interest labelled as a 'lien' or 'pledge' (which would generally be expected to fall outside the registration regime), but which has the characteristics of a charge. Hence, under the current regime there are grey areas concerning whether some types of charges should be registered under Part 25 of the Companies Act 2006; and in some more complex transactions, the question may arise whether an arrangement which purports not to be a charge is a security interest in disguise and should be recharacterised as one.

The company charge registration system does not apply to security agreements executed by individuals, but there is a parallel system in place: the Bills of Sale Acts. Basically, this legislation requires that chattel mortgages and other similar security agreements created by individuals be in a particular statutory form and be registered in court offices. Failure to comply with the statutory requirements results in the invalidity of the security. In fact, the requirements are so cumbersome and difficult to comply with that the Bills of Sale Acts are effectively bypassed in practice. Consumer purchases in England are often funded through hire purchase agreements which, technically speaking, are an agreement for the hire of goods coupled with an option to purchase the goods at the end of the hire period.

The Bills of Sale Acts have a consumer protection aspect to them, albeit one which is imperfectly and inappropriately realised. However, the company charge registration system has a different orientation. Its main rationale is the provision of information for persons such as credit reference agencies and

---

1   This charge registration regime also applies to UK-registered limited liability partnerships (LLPs).

prospective charge holders that wish to assess the creditworthiness of the company. For instance, prospective charge holders can ascertain from the register whether security has already been created over the assets of the company. In consequence, they are better informed about making a lending decision and structuring the terms of any loan.

The English system is essentially a transaction-based system of registration and should be contrasted with the notice filing system under Article 9 of the US Uniform Commercial Code and the Canadian and New Zealand Personal Property Security Acts:

> The most characteristic difference between notice filing and traditional systems of registration is that notice filing is parties-specific rather than transaction-specific. What is filed are not the details of a particular security but notice that certain parties have entered into, or may in future enter into, a secured transaction in relation to specified property. This approach has certain implications. A notice may be filed in advance of the transaction and the proposed transaction may never take place. The same notice may serve a series of connected transactions. And the information given on the register is necessarily rather general in character, being an invitation to further inquiry rather than a full account of the right in security.[2]

Article 9-style regimes also apply to all security interests, regardless of whether the security provider is an individual or a business entity. The main points of comparison between the English system and Article 9/Personal Property Security Act regimes are outlined in the following table.

Features	English-style registration	US-style notice filing
What is registrable/ fileable?	• Most categories of charge, but not 'quasi-security'. • Grantor – companies and LLPs.	• Transactions that are security in a functional sense (save certain excepted ones). • Grantor – not limited to companies.

continued on next page

---

2 Scottish Law Commission discussion paper, "Registration of Rights in Security by Companies" (October 2002), p8.

Features	English-style registration	US-style notice filing
Obligation	No longer an obligation on the grantor of the charge (the criminal sanction has been removed for failure to register), but serious consequences for them and the charge holder for failure to register.	Not an obligation, but an available means of perfection.
Priorities	Strictly no, but failure to register means charge holder loses priority.	Date of filing is reference point for settling order of priorities.
Non-registration	• Void against liquidator, adminstrator and other creditors. • Money secured immediately becomes payable.	• May lose priority. • Can also be avoided by a company's trustee in bankruptcy (equivalent to an English liquidator).
Timing	• Prescribed time to register. • After creation of charge. • Extension by court.	• No prescribed time. • May be filed in advance of transaction.

continued on next page

Features	English-style registration	US-style notice filing
Particulars filed	• Particulars such as: date of creation of charge; any specific land, intellectual property, ships or aircraft charged; whether fixed and/or floating charges and a negative pledge are included; names of charge holders. • Certified copy of instrument of charge (which is available on public register).	• Financing statement with name of debtor and secured party and indication of collateral. • May cover a series of connected transactions. • Security agreement not filed.
Certificate of due registration	• Issued by registrar. • Conclusive evidence that required documents have been delivered.	• None – filing office does not check accuracy of information.

While, unlike Article 9, the English system does not require the registration of quasi-security, in some respects it is more comprehensive. In the main, Article 9 and systems based on it do not apply to security over land or to security over certain types of property that may be registrable in specialist property registers (eg, security over IP rights and ship and aircraft mortgages). These exclusions are difficult to justify rationally. Pressure group politics and lobbying by vested interest groups undoubtedly have a part to play as well. They are perhaps explicable on the basis in particular that land tends to have its own distinctive legal regime. Also, in federal jurisdictions, land law is often considered to be a matter within the exclusive competence of the state or provincial legislature, as distinct from chattel mortgage law, which has a more cross-territorial reach.

2. More details on the English registration system

While there have been variations in procedure, the essential features of the registration scheme has remained the same for over 100 years.[3] To be registrable, a security interest must constitute a 'charge' which does not fall within one of the limited statutory exceptions set out in Section 859A(6) of the Companies Act 2006 and must be created by a UK-registered company or LLP. There is no longer a statutory list setting out what will constitute a 'charge' for these purposes, unlike in the earlier English company charge legislation. If the security interest does not meet these criteria, it is not registrable.

In England, the company charge registration regime was first introduced by Section 14 of the Companies Act 1900[4] and applied to four categories of charge:

- a charge for the purpose of securing any issue of debentures;
- a charge on uncalled capital of the company;
- a charge created or evidenced by an instrument which, if executed by an individual, would require registration as a bill of sale; and
- a floating charge on the undertaking or property of the company.

The categories have been extended over the years. Charges on land and charges on book debts became registrable in 1907.[5] In 1928 the list was extended to charges on unpaid calls, ship mortgages and charges on goodwill, patents, trademarks and copyright.[6] Charges on aircraft were added by the Mortgaging of Aircraft Order 1972.

Certain particulars of the charge – such as the date of creation, whether fixed and/or floating charges and a negative pledge are included and persons entitled thereto – together with a certified copy of the instrument of charge must be delivered to the companies registrar within 21 days of the date of creation of the charge. The registrar will compare the instrument of charge with the filed particulars and, once satisfied that everything is in order, will upload the certified copy charge to the public register and issue a certificate of due registration, which is stated by statute to be conclusive evidence that the required documents were delivered to the registrar. There is a procedure whereby a charge may be registered out of time, but this requires a court application.

An unregistered but registrable charge becomes void against a certain stated class of persons – namely a liquidator, administrator or creditor of the company. This provision has been interpreted as meaning that an unregistered charge becomes void only against unsecured creditors in a liquidation or administration. According to Lord Hoffmann in *Smith v Bridgend County Borough Council*: "The plain intention of the legislature was that property subject to a registrable but unregistered charge should be available to the general body of

---

3   For a detailed historical account of the development of the company charge registration provisions, see De Lacy, "Reflections on the Ambit and Reform of the Part 12 of the Companies Act 1985 and the Doctrine of Constructive Notice" in De Lacy (ed), *The Reform of UK Company Law* (Cavendish, 2002).

4   This followed the recommendations of the 1895 Davey Committee on Company Law Amendment. Chapter 25 of the Companies Act 2006 replaced Part 12 of the Companies Act 1985.

5   Section 10 of the Companies Act 1907.

6   Section 43 of the Companies Act 1928.

creditors (or a secured creditor ranking after the unregistered charge) as if no such charge existed."[7]

However, an unregistered charge is still valid towards the company and, outside liquidation or administration, the charge holder can exercise all remedies conferred by the charge by exercising a power of sale over assets covered by the charge or similar. The charge, though, is invalid against another person with property rights in these assets (eg, a secured creditor), and therefore the unregistered charge holder would have to hand over the proceeds of sale of the assets to such a person. While registration is not *per se* a reference point for determining priorities, the holder of an unregistered but registrable charge is reduced to the rank of an unsecured creditor in the event that the company which created the charge enters liquidation or administration.

Many common law countries still follow the broad outlines of the English approach towards registration of company charges, including Ireland, Singapore and Hong Kong. However, there are some differences in detail. For instance, in Singapore, there is no obligation to submit the instrument of charge along with the prescribed particulars to the registrar of companies. Because of the absence of the instrument of charge itself, the registrar does not, as a matter of course, check whether the particulars are a full and accurate description of the charge. Nevertheless, interestingly enough, the registrar is still required to issue a certificate of due registration.

3.   Article 9-style notice filing

Under Article 9, the security agreement itself is not filed but rather a simple record – a financing statement – that provides a limited amount of information.[8] The financing statement may be filed either before or after the security agreement is drawn up. The filed notice merely indicates that a person may have a security interest in the collateral (property) concerned; but to ascertain the complete state of affairs, it is necessary to make further inquiry of the parties. There is a statutory procedure under Section 9-210 of the Uniform Commercial Code (UCC) whereby a secured party, at the debtor's request, may be required to make disclosure. In many cases, however, the debtor or another prospective financier may be able to obtain the requisite information without the need to invoke the compulsory features of Section 9-210 of the UCC.

Notice filing under an Article 9 regime removes the need to make a number of repeat filings where there is a series of transactions between the parties.[9] The financing statement is effective to cover transactions under a security agreement that was not in existence and not even contemplated by the parties

---

7   [2002] 1 AC 336 at para 68.
8   Section 9-502 of the UCC, Official Comment.
9   See generally *ibid*.

at the time that the financing statement was filed, provided that the indication of collateral in the financing statement is sufficiently broad to cover the collateral concerned. Similarly, a financing statement is effective to cover after-acquired property of the type indicated and to perfect future advances under security agreements, irrespective of whether after-acquired property or future advances are mentioned in the financing statement, and even though they may not have been contemplated by the parties at the time that the financing statement was drawn up.[10]

In simple terms, a financing statement may cover the entire credit relationship of the parties. Therefore, a seller which is contemplating the supply of goods to a buyer over an extended period of time may take a security interest in all the supplies by filing a simple financing statement instead of having to register each contract of sale separately, which would be the case if a retention of title clause were held to constitute a registrable charge under present English law.[11] The creditor may state simply that it is taking security in certain collateral to cover advances made to the debtor, including future advances, irrespective of whether there is any commitment on the part of the creditor to make the advance.[12]

There are simple formal requirements for an effective financing statement:

- the debtor's name;
- the name of a secured party or representative of the secured party; and
- an indication of the collateral.

A financing statement must reasonably identify the collateral; alternatively, it is permissible to state that the financing statement covers all assets or all personal property.[13] However, a broad statement of this kind (eg, "all the debtor's personal property") would not be a sufficient description for the purposes of a security agreement.[14] Article 9, in fact, lays down fairly strict requirements for the description of collateral in the security agreement. These requirements are stricter than for the description of property in an English-style floating charge.

Section 9-506 of the UCC provides that a financing statement substantially satisfying the formal requirements is effective even if it has minor errors or omissions, unless the errors or omissions make the financing statement seriously misleading.[15] Records filed in the filing office do not require signatures

---

10   *Ibid*, Section 9-204.
11   See generally *Clough Mill Ltd v Martin* [1985] 1 WLR 111.
12   See Section 9-323 of the UCC.
13   *Ibid*, Section 9-504.
14   *Ibid*, Official Comment.
15   *Ibid*, Section 9-506(c). In an English-style registration system, the certificate of due registration issued by the registrar means that the registration can be accepted as valid even though the particulars registered were not an accurate description of the charge.

for their effectiveness, although there is a requirement that the debtor authorise the filing in an authenticated record.[16] A person that files an unauthorised record against a debtor is liable for damages.[17] Section 9-516 of the UCC provides that communication of a complying record to a filing office and tender of the filing fee or acceptance of the record by the filing office constitute filing.

In the United States, the complete divorce between security agreement and financing statement means that there is no scope for a conclusive evidence certificate issued by the filing office. A financing statement may be filed long before a security agreement is executed; moreover, the financing statement may be intended to cover more than one security agreement. In the United States, the filing office performs a purely ministerial function. It is not the function of the filing office to check the accuracy of the information provided:[18] "A filing office may not reject … an initial financing statement indicating that the debtor is a State A corporation and providing a three-digit organizational identification number, even if all State A organizational identification numbers contain at least five digits and two letters." Section 9-516 of the UCC provides an exhaustive list of grounds upon which the filing office may reject a record. Some of these are grounds that have the effect of rendering the financing statement itself ineffective; but some are not grounds that would have this effect. The latter include the failure to provide a mailing address for the debtor or the secured party of record. If the filing office improperly rejects a financing statement that complies with all requirements of Article 9, the financing statement is still regarded as effective,[19] except as against a purchaser of the collateral which gives value in reasonable reliance upon the absence of the record from the files.

4. The general features of Article 9

Apart from notice filing, there are many other significant differences between Article 9 and the current law relating to security interests in England. Article 9, for example, contains a comprehensive set of priority rules and makes quasi-securities registrable. The Canadian and New Zealand Personal Property Security Acts follow Article 9 in this regard. Article 9 abandons the old distinctions that are still prevalent in English law between the creation of security over an asset and the use of absolute title to achieve the same economic objective. Article 9 adopts the universal, generic concept of a security interest. All the old

---

16   *Ibid*, Section 9-509.
17   *Ibid*, Section 9-625.
18   *Ibid*, Section 9-516, Official Comment.
19   *Ibid*, Section 9-516(d). The effect is somewhat similar in an English-style registration system, although in the latter there is no protection for purchasers that acquire property in the reasonable but mistaken belief that the property is unsecured. The crucial issue is whether the particulars have been delivered to the registrar of companies within the prescribed period, and not whether the particulars appear on the register during that period or even at all.

terminology of the law still found in England – such as 'pledge', 'mortgage', 'conditional sale' and 'trust receipt' – has been replaced by the unitary concept of a 'security interest'. Article 9 makes no distinction between legal and equitable security interests or between fixed and floating security interests.

Section 9-109 of the UCC applies Article 9 to any transaction, regardless of form, that creates a contractual security interest in personal property and to a sale of accounts, chattel paper, payment intangibles or promissory notes.[20] 'Security interest' is defined in Article 1-201(b)(35) as meaning an interest in personal property or fixtures that secures either payment or the performance of an obligation. The term also includes any interest of a buyer of accounts, chattel paper, payment intangibles or promissory notes. The special property interest of a buyer of goods on identification of those goods to a contract for sale[21] is not characterised as a 'security interest'; but a seller may also acquire a security interest by complying with Article 9. In other words, even a 'simple' retention of title clause is transformed by statutory language into the taking of a security interest.[22] Article 9 applies irrespective of whether title to the collateral is with the secured party or the debtor; though there are special rules, for example, for the sale of accounts.[23]

4.1 Attachment and perfection of a security interest

The central concepts of Article 9 are 'attachment' and 'perfection'. A security interest is said to attach when it becomes enforceable between creditor and debtor (ie, it creates an obligation).[24] Section 9-203 of the UCC provides that a security agreement attaches if:

- value has been given;
- the debtor has rights in the collateral or the power to transfer rights in the collateral to a secured party; and
- one of a number of other alternative conditions are fulfilled, including that the debtor has authenticated a security agreement which provides a description of the collateral.

However, the parties may agree to postpone the time for attachment, in

---

20   However, Article 9 does not apply to a sale of accounts, chattel paper, payment intangibles or promissory notes as part of a sale of the business out of which they arose or to an assignment of the same which is for the purpose of collection only. Neither does it apply to an assignment of a right to payment under a contract to an assignee that is also obligated to perform under the contract; or to an assignment of a single account, payment intangible or promissory note to an assignee in full or partial satisfaction of a pre-existing indebtedness.

21   See Section 2-401 of the UCC.

22   For a description of the different forms of retention of title clause, see G McCormack, *Reservation of Title* (Sweet & Maxwell, 2nd ed, 1995), p2.

23   A 'payment intangible' is defined in Section 9-102(a)(61) of the UCC as meaning a general intangible under which the account debtor's principal obligation is a monetary obligation. General intangibles are the residual category of personal property.

24   Sections 9-203 and 9-315 of the UCC.

which case the security interest attaches at the agreed time. Section 9-204 of the UCC specifically states that a security agreement may cover after-acquired property, but the security agreement will not attach unless and until the debtor has rights in the collateral. The concept of 'rights in the collateral' is not free from controversy, although it clearly connotes something less than full ownership.

'Perfection', on the other hand, refers to the process whereby the security interest becomes effective against third parties.[25] Perfection generally occurs through filing and the date of filing is the reference point for settling the order of priorities between competing security interests in the same collateral. Section 9-308 of the UCC states that a security interest is perfected:

- when it has attached; and
- when all steps required for its perfection have been complied with.

A security interest is perfected when it attaches, if the applicable requirements for perfection are satisfied before the security interest attaches.[26] Although filing a financing statement is the standard way of perfecting a security interest, other methods of perfection are permissible or required in certain circumstances.[27] For example, security over investment property may be perfected by the secured party taking 'control' of the collateral. In the case of intermediated securities, this will occur if the securities intermediary agrees to follow instructions from the secured party, without further consent from the debtor. Moreover, certain security interests are perfected automatically upon attachment.[28]

4.2   Treatment of the floating charge

One of the fundamental features of Article 9 systems is to assimilate the treatment of fixed and floating charges. In other words, the fixed/floating charge distinction is abolished and replaced by the single unitary notion of a 'security interest'. In fact, pre-Article 9 US law did not recognise the equivalent of the floating charge. The leading authority is *Benedict v Ratner*,[29] where the US Supreme Court had to decide on the legal implications of a purported assignment of account receivables under which the assignor went on collecting the receivables from the debtors, which had not been notified of the assignment. The assignor continued to use the proceeds in the ordinary course of business without accounting in any way to the assignee. In England, an arrangement of this kind would be categorised as a floating charge and upheld

---

25   See generally *ibid*, Section 9-308.
26   *Ibid*, Section 9-308(a).
27   *Ibid*, Section 9-310.
28   *Ibid*, Section 9-309. These exceptions appear to be essentially pragmatic; based on industry need or lobbying by pressure groups.
29   (1925) 268 US 353.

on this basis; but the US Supreme Court held that the transaction was void against the assignor's trustee in bankruptcy as a fraudulent conveyance under the state law of New York. The court said: "Under the law of New York a transfer of property as security which reserves to the transferor the right to dispose of the same, or to apply the proceeds thereof, for his own uses is, as to creditors, fraudulent in law and void."[30]

It is perhaps unsurprising that lawyers in a country as legally sophisticated and commercially pragmatic as the United States sought to get around the limitations of the decision and a sophisticated avoidance industry developed.[31] As a result of pre-Article 9 legislative developments in the United States, most types of personal property – whether tangible or intangible – became available as collateral to secure loans.[32] Often change came as the result of particular legislation passed at the behest of finance companies. Special interest groups might plead for a particular legislative initiative and the result was a mismatch of complex and interlocking statutes, with intricate registration requirements, which lacked overall coherence and uniformity: "half a dozen filing systems covering chattel security devices might be maintained within a state, some on a county basis, others on a state-wide basis, each of which had to be separately checked to determine a debtor's status".[33]

Article 9 brought rationality and coherence, and one of the ways it did this was by recognising the functional equivalent of the floating charge.[34] Legal subterfuge was rendered unnecessary by a provision allowing for the creation of a 'floating' security interest on shifting collateral.[35]

4.3   Priorities

Section 9-322 of the UCC determines priorities among conflicting security interests in the same collateral and applies a basic principle that the first secured party to file a financing statement should have priority over competing security interests in the same collateral. The revised version of Article 9, which came into force in 2001, introduced additional variants on the basic priority position. This was done most notably by permitting perfection by control and providing this method of perfection with a status superior to that of perfection by filing.

Under the primary rule, priority dates from the earliest time that a security

---

30   (1925) 268 US 353.
31   See generally Gilmore, *Security Interests in Personal Property* (Little Brown, 1965) vol 1, Chapters 1-8.
32   Article 9 has been described as "an anthological collection of the most celebrated security law controversies of the preceding forty years" in Gilmore, "Security Law, Formalism and Article 9" (1968) 47 *Nebraska Law Review* 659 at 671.
33   See the official comment attached to the 1972 version of Section 9-101 of the UCC.
34   Grant Gilmore has said in "Security Law, Formalism and Article 9" (1968) 47 *Nebraska Law Review* 659 at 672: "Article 9 draftsmen argued from the premise that, under existing security law, a lender could take an enforceable interest in all of a debtor's present and future personal property to the conclusion that the new statute should provide for the accomplishment of this result in the simplest possible fashion."
35   Section 9-204 of the UCC.

interest is first perfected, provided that the security interest does not become unperfected at any stage thereafter. A perfected security interest has priority over a competing unperfected security interest.[36] The first security interest to attach has priority if competing security interests are unperfected.[37] However, Article 9 does not preclude a secured party from voluntarily giving up priority.[38]

The central importance of the 'first to file or perfect' priority rule should be emphasised. The secured party that first registers a financing statement obtains priority even though it is not the first in terms of executing a security agreement with a debtor or indeed acquiring an attached security interest in the collateral. Consequently:[39]

> *Once a financing statement is registered any person who is planning to deal with someone named as debtor in the financing statement has the ability to determine whether or not the interest he intends to acquire will be subject to a security interest having a prior status. If such a person goes ahead and acquires an interest in the personal property described in the financing statement without making some accommodation with a registering party or without obtaining a discharge of the financing statement, there is no reason to give his interest priority over a subsequent security interest acquired by the registered party.*

There is an exception to the general priority rule in the case of purchase money security interests (PMSIs)[40] involving goods and related software, which will rank ahead of a prior security interest containing an after-acquired property clause. The PMSI favours creditors that extend credit on the understanding that the debtor will use it to acquire collateral[41] and there is a complex definition in Section 9-103 of the UCC which requires a close nexus between the acquisition of the collateral and the security interest. What is required is the giving of value that enables the debtor to acquire rights in, or the use of, the collateral if the value is in fact so used.

Article 9 distinguishes between PMSIs and general security interests, awarding the PMSI a kind of super priority status that has traditionally been enjoyed by retention of title claimants. The possibility of enjoying super priority status has been extended to other financiers in certain circumstances. If a debtor has granted an all-assets security interest that extends over future

---

36   *Ibid*, Section 9-322(a)(2).
37   *Ibid*, Section 9-322(a)(3).
38   *Ibid*, Section 9-339. The official comment makes it clear that a person's rights cannot be adversely affected by an agreement to which the person is not a party. On debt subordination agreements under English law, see *Re SSSL Realisations* [2006] EWCA Civ 7; *Re Maxwell Communications Corp* (No 2) [1993] 1 WLR 1402; *Re British & Commonwealth Holdings plc* (No 3) [1992] 1 WLR 672.
39   See R Cuming and R Wood, "Compatibility of Federal and Provincial Personal Property Security Law" (1986) 65 *Canadian Bar Review* 267 at 285.
40   *Ibid*, Section 9-324 deals with the priority of PMSIs.
41   One of the justifications given for recognising PMSIs is that whereas a general financier takes account of average risk, the PMSI lender may have particular skills and can lend on particularly advantageous terms because of its special knowledge of the collateral – see generally A Schwartz, "The Continuing Puzzle of Secured Debt" (1984) 37 *Vanderbilt Law Review* 1051.

property, then notwithstanding the general 'first to perfect' priority rule, a creditor whose advances funded the acquisition of 'new property' in the debtor's hands outranks the earlier financier in respect of that property.[42]

PMSI super priority may be justified on the basis that the release of funds by the creditor increases the debtor's total pool of assets. The debtor is enabled to acquire new assets as distinct from merely rolling over existing debt, with the debt representing the purchase price of the assets being offset by the additional property. If the new property helps the debtor's business to earn extra profits, it may even improve the position of existing creditors by increasing the pool of assets subject to their security interest. Further, if an earlier creditor could rely on an after-acquired property clause to the detriment of a PMSI holder, the earlier creditor would obtain an unjustified windfall at the expense of the PMSI holder whose advance facilitated the acquisition of the property.[43] On the other hand, according super priority privileges to the PMSI makes the assumption that the provision of funds which is tied to the acquisition of 'new' assets is more beneficial in a business sense than more general loans which can be used to pay the wages of employees.[44] One advance may not necessarily carry any greater social benefit than the other.

However, it is necessary to comply with special requirements to obtain super priority status. Section 9-324 of the UCC, for instance, distinguishes between inventory and other goods; and a claim to PMSI status in inventory is more difficult to establish. 'Inventory' is defined as goods that:

- are held by a person for sale or lease;
- have been leased;
- are to be furnished or have been furnished under a contract of service; or
- are raw materials, work in process or materials used or consumed in a business.

Before a security interest in inventory can qualify as a PMSI:
- the PMSI must be perfected when the debtor receives possession of the inventory; and

---

42   Under Section 9-324(g) of the UCC, the holder of a PMSI that secures the unpaid purchase price of collateral will prevail over the holder of a conflicting PMSI that enables the collateral to be acquired. This means that a retention of title seller has priority over a lender that makes an enabling loan. This is somewhat different from Section 9-328 of the UCC, which deals with investment property. Priority in investment property is given to the secured party which has control. Section 9-328(2) of the UCC provides that if two or more secured parties have control, priority is determined by which obtained control first.
43   For a law and economics perspective on this view, see H Kanda and S Levmore, "Explaining Creditor Priorities" (1994) 80 *Vanderbilt Law Review* 2103 at 2138-2141.
44   See the comments in WJ Gough, Company Charges (Butterworths, 2nd ed 1996) at p436:
      It assumes that financial accommodation for the purpose of, for example, paying wages and salaries through cheques drawn on an overdrawn account is less important than for the purchase of stocks or plant and equipment. This is not a real world distinction. Credit, as a matter of business need, is indivisible in the sense that all business inputs, including wages, overheads, equipment and supplies are all vital to an ongoing business.

- the secured party must, before the debtor receives possession of the inventory, give notice in writing to every other secured party which has already registered a financing statement over the same collateral. The notice must state that the person has acquired, or expects to acquire, a PMSI in inventory of the debtor and describe the inventory.[45]

In the case of capital equipment rather than inventory, the qualifications necessary for obtaining PMSI status are somewhat less demanding. Automatic super priority over prior secured lenders is gained if the PMSI is registered within 20 days of the debtor acquiring possession of the collateral.[46] "The rules intimate that the acquisition of new inventory and its associated debt is more threatening to earlier creditors than the debt-financing of new equipment but that debt tied to new inventory is still less threatening than new money unlinked to particular assets."[47]

5. Reform proposals in England

In England, there have been consistent calls for reform of the law relating to secured finance transactions for over half a century, and various reports and consultations. The Law Commission has published consultation papers and reports suggesting replacing the existing transaction-based system of company charge registration with a notice filing system[48] in keeping with the North American and New Zealand models. The decision to recommend overseas legislation as a guide was taken partly because of time constraints; but also because the Law Commission saw "no need to re-invent the wheel"[49] and recognised that "the fact that Article 9 and the PPSAs have been so successful means that they deserve very careful consideration".[50]

The Law Commission suggested that the notice filing system could be applied to a broader range of security interests and also include 'quasi-security' – such as the assignment of receivables (factoring) and retention of title clauses in sale of goods contracts. There might be a comprehensive restatement of the law of security interests and, in time, the scheme could be extended to non-corporate legal actors. In the first instance, however, it was suggested that the

---

45   The official comment to Section 9-324 of the UCC explains the purpose of the notification requirement as being to protect a non-purchase money inventory secured party which, under an arrangement with the debtor, is typically required to make periodic advances against incoming inventory or periodic releases of old inventory as new inventory is received. If the inventory secured party receives notice, it may not make an advance. While the notification requirement is not the same as imposing a consent requirement before a PMSI over inventory can take priority, through the mechanism of an inventory secured party exerting pressure on the debtor it may function in roughly the same way.
46   Section 9-324(a) of the UCC.
47   See Kanda and Levmore (n 43) at 2139.
48   See generally Law Commission Consultative Report 176, "Company Security Interests" (2004) at para 2.46 and Law Commission Report 296, "Company Security Interests" (2005) at para 1.27.
49   Law Commission Consultative Report 176, para 1.20.
50   *Ibid*, para 1.5.

reform would involve the introduction of notice filing for an amended list of company charges and possibly also for 'quasi-interests', as well as rules on attachment, perfection and priorities of security interests.

The Law Commission suggested that its recommendations provided:

significant improvements and cost-savings in secured finance for companies. The use of technology can made the registration of company charges much easier, cheaper and quicker. The low cost of registration makes it feasible to provide lenders with a wide range of useful information about a company's property. The law on the priority of competing interests and the remedies available in the case of default can be made simpler, clearer and better suited to the needs of modern business finance.[51]

However, in the Law Commission's Final Report on Company Security Interests the original reform agenda was watered down considerably.[52] The general thrust of the notice filing proposals was preserved from the original consultation documents, but there were very considerable variations in detail.

The Companies Act 2006 included a power to amend the company charge registration regime, and the amending regulations[53] that came into force in April 2013 (and which remain in force today) gave effect to some of the Law Commission's recommendations concerning company charge registration – but by no means all. Some of the key amendments introduced by the regulations in April 2013 and reflective of the Law Commissions proposals were as follows:

- The electronic filing of company charge registrations was introduced;
- All charges created by companies became registrable, unless included in the limited list of exceptions;
- The requirement to deliver the original charge document(s) to Companies House was removed; but a certified copy must be filed and is made available on the public register; and
- The summary information required to be provided in the statement of particulars was changed and now includes, among other things, a notification for negative pledge clauses.

Nevertheless, many of the broader proposals – including the notice filing reforms and those relating to changes to priority and the sale of receivables – were not implemented in the amendments introduced in April 2013.

The Law Commission is not the only entity that has been working towards possible reform of the law of secured transactions in recent years. In particular,

---

51   Law Commission press release, "Law Commission consults on Provisional Recommendations on Company Security Interests", 16 August 2004.
52   For a synopsis of the revised proposals, see Law Commission, "Company Security Interests: Developing a Final Scheme" (May 2005), www.lawcom.gov.uk/. The final report was published at the end of August 2005 – Law Commission Report 296, "Company Security Interests".
53   The Companies Act 2006 (Amendment of Part 25) Regulations 2013.

the City of London Law Society Financial Law Committee (CLLS)[54] and the Secured Transactions Law Reform Project (STLRP)[55] have both been putting together proposals for reform of the law of security in England. Despite the changes introduced in April 2013 by the amendments to Part 25 of the Companies Act 2006, both the CLLS and the STLRP have highlighted deficiencies that remain in English secured transactions law and have been developing proposals for reform.

Many of the apparent issues in English security law as it stands can be traced back to the fact that it has developed over centuries and is scattered across an array of legislation and case law, and as such is complicated and at times inaccessible. Both the CLLS and STLRP proposals aim to adapt the existing law to improve clarity by offering a simplified and codified law of secured finance transactions. The CLLS has produced its draft *Secured Transactions Code and Commentary* and the STLRP has published policy documents and discussion papers; both have also held events encouraging discussion of their proposals by market participants, legal academics and others with an interest in secured finance transactions.

5.1   Bills of sale

In September 2014, the Law Commission was asked to review the Victorian-era Bills of Sale Acts by the government. In 2016, the Law Commission published a report recommending that the Bills of Sale Acts be repealed and replaced with legislation designed to reduce the burdens on lenders and to provide greater protection for borrowers. Draft legislation was published in September 2017: the Goods Mortgages Bill. However, following a consultation conducted by Her Majesty's Treasury, the government announced in May 2018 that it would not be introducing the new legislation; so for now, we remain tied to the antiquated Bills of Sale Act system.

5.2   Reactions

These discussions demonstrate that this is an extremely knotty problem – and one that is unlikely to go away anytime soon. There remains room for improvement and, in any event, English security law will need to continue to develop as market practices move on. There has been a considerable amount of practitioner resistance to some of the reform proposals and there is a body of thought that, as a general rule, the existing law works in practice.

In considering moving to an Article 9-style notice filing system, one criticism that has been levelled is that supporters of its introduction may have

---

54   See the CLLS website for more detail: www.citysolicitors.org.uk/clls/committees/financial-law/.
55   See the Secured Transactions Law Reform Project website for more detail: https://securedtransactionslawreformproject.org/.

overegged the pudding somewhat in playing up the advantages. While notice filing may be more convenient and flexible than transaction filing, it is also easy to overestimate these advantages. For example, after-acquired property clauses, future advances clauses and 'floating' security interests are fully recognised by English substantive law; and although registration must relate to a particular instrument of charge rather than the entire credit relationship of the parties, the registered particulars can capture the full flexibility of the legal provisions. Critics have suggested that divorcing registration from the actual conclusion of a security agreement opens up the possibility that the register may become a less reliable source of information about the state of a company's secured borrowings. A notice on the register may relate not to an actual transaction, but to one of a multitude of possible transactions that never ultimately materialise. Also, proposals to extend registration to interests that are not included in the current regime – including to sales of receivables – have been met with concern by many market participants, including those in the receivables finance, structured finance and securitisation markets.

On the other hand, a notice filing system such as that under Article 9 of the UCC and the Canadian and New Zealand Personal Property Security Acts does offer advantages; and with those regimes already in place, it is tried and tested. A notice filing system allows filing/registration in advance of the conclusion of a security agreement, which offers significant practical advantages in particular cases. For example, if multiple parties are involved in the security agreement, advance registration avoids any delays stemming from difficulties in arranging execution of the agreement by all the relevant parties. It also allows a secured party to confirm that registration has occurred correctly before advancing any funds under the secured loan. Another important issue in English security law as it stands is that the priority rules are extremely complicated – there are many exceptions to the 'first in time' rule and numerous possible permutations when considering the priority of two competing creditors' interests. A notice filing system, with a rule at its core that priority as between secured interests is by date of registration, would simplify this area.

6. Conclusion

While it seems almost an article of faith among some that Article 9 or a personal property security law is the only way forward, Article 9 itself is not beyond criticism. Article 9 is now more than 50 years old and is showing signs of middle-age spread in terms of size and complexity. The language and concepts of Article 9 often appear obscure compared with the facility and comprehensiveness of the floating charge. Also, with the greater ease of internet registration, there seems less justification for comparatively sparse details appearing on the register, as is the case with Article 9-style notice filing.

A central issue that presents itself whenever reform proposals in this area are raised is the fact that the legal issues cannot be dissociated from commercial realities, and some of these commercial practices have developed to become established over many years as a direct result of the law as it stands. Moreover, a full-blown reform along the lines of Article 9 would involve rewriting English insolvency legislation in terms of assimilating and accommodating the floating charge. Doing so risks reopening a hornets' nest of vested interests and these issues are not to be disregarded lightly.

Even a betting person would hesitate before laying any money on the wager that England will see personal property security law reform in the near future. In fact, the reforms to English security law introduced by the amendments to Part 25 of the Companies Act 2006 in April 2013 may have exhausted what was already a weak appetite for change – at least for some time to come. Nevertheless, personal property security acts have been introduced successfully in several jurisdictions now, and it is hard to deny that the codification and simplification of the English law of security would make a lot of sense. With the CLLS and STLRP proposals on the table, perhaps some elements of one or both of them will spur debate sufficiently to gain traction over the coming years.

The author would like to thank her colleagues Kevin C McDonald and Angelia Chia of Mayer Brown for their insights on the aspects relating to the UCC and Singapore respectively.

The publisher acknowledges the contribution of Gerard McCormack to this chapter in the previous edition.

About the authors

Maria Alevras-Chen

Counsel, Mayer Brown LLP

malevras-chen@mayerbrown.com

Maria Alevras-Chen is a counsel in Mayer Brown's Chicago banking and finance practice, and a member of the Latin America and securitisation groups. She has deep experience advising commercial banks, fund investors and issuers on structuring and executing securitisations, supply chain and trade finance facilities, advance payment structures and other complex financing arrangements, as well as other innovative cross-border debt and equity transactions across a multitude of asset classes and industries in Latin America. While Maria's experience includes transactions in 12 countries in the region, she has significant experience structuring and executing transactions in Argentina, Brazil, Chile, Colombia, Mexico and Peru in the fintech, infrastructure, mining, trade receivable and commodity sectors, among others.

Bill Amos

Partner, Mayer Brown

bill.amos@mayerbrown.com

Bill Amos is a partner with Mayer Brown, having qualified as a solicitor in England and Wales (1991) and Hong Kong (1995), and as a notary public (2006). He is the author of chapters in *Chitty on Contracts: Hong Kong Specific Contracts*, the *Maritime Law Handbook* and *Arbitration in Hong Kong: A Practical Guide*. A fellow and former council member of the Hong Kong Institute of Arbitrators, Bill has been appointed as arbitrator in numerous *ad hoc* and administered arbitrations.

Bill advises banks, insurers and trading companies on matters concerning asset finance, trade finance and international sale of goods. He has represented clients in a wide variety of high-profile cases covering an extensive range of commercial disputes. A leading individual in the Shipping (International Firms): China rankings of *Chambers Asia-Pacific* (2021), Bill is described as having "super detailed knowledge of shipping law and case history" and the "ability to find solutions in a prompt and expeditious manner".

Spyridon V Bazinas

Lecturer, author and consultant

spiros.bazinas@gmail.com

Spyridon V Bazinas is a law lecturer, author and independent consultant who advises states and national and international organisations on trade law reform matters. He was the secretary of the UNCITRAL Working Group VI (Security Interests) from 2003 to 2017, when it prepared a number of texts on security interests, including the Guide to Enactment of the UNCITRAL Model Law on Secured Transactions (2017) and the UNCITRAL Model Law on Secured Transactions (2016). He was also involved in UNCITRAL's work on insolvency, bank guarantees, procurement and electronic commerce. He has also provided technical assistance to states and lectured all over the world on a variety of international trade law topics. For a number of years, he has been teaching a course on secured finance (including insolvency and private international law) at the Law School of the University of Vienna, Austria and other law schools around the world. Spyridon has co-authored more than 10 books and published more than 50 articles on various topics and, in particular, on secured financing and insolvency.

Jan R Boker
Senior counsel, Mayer Brown LLP
jboker@mayerbrown.com

Jan R Boker has been senior counsel at Mayer Brown in Mexico since 2018. He advises US, Mexican, European and Asian financial institutions and clients on cross-border lending transactions, including structured finance, trade receivables and supply chain finance and securitisations. From 2009 to 2012 he served as general director at the Ministry of Economy, where he designed and implemented the Sole Registry of Movable Guarantees known as 'RUG'. From 2012 to 2015 he worked at the Ministry of Finance and Public Credit coordinating and supervising development banks, and actively participated in the 2014 financial reform. In 2015, he was appointed general counsel of *Financiera Nacional de Desarrollo Agropecuario*, where he restructured a large number of loans and improved the bank's origination and collection processes. Jan also advises on banking and financial services regulation to several financial institutions, including fintechs. He speaks Spanish, English and German.

Trevor Borthwick
Partner, Mayer Brown International LLP
tborthwick@mayerbrown.com

Trevor Borthwick is a partner in the finance and restructuring departments of Mayer Brown in London. He is widely regarded as one of the leading lawyers in the London investment grade finance market. He has more than 30 years of experience advising on restructuring and rescue finance and investment grade lending in the London market. Before joining Mayer Brown, he was a partner in another major international firm for more than 20 years.

Trevor has led teams on some of the largest restructurings in the London market in recent years, advising the coordinating committees on the provision of rescue finance and the terms of the restructured senior debt and security. Recent examples include leading the restructurings of Interserve plc and Debenhams plc, and advising the brokerage facility lenders in the restructuring of ED&F Man.

Trevor advises lenders (both banks and funds) and borrowers on a variety of restructuring matters and on 'business as usual' financings.

Stuart Brinkworth
Partner, Mayer Brown International LLP
sbrinkworth@mayerbrown.com

Stuart Brinkworth is the European head of leveraged finance and a banking and finance partner in Mayer Brown's London office. He has extensive experience spanning over 200 mid-market deals and advising across all elements of the debt capital structure, having been a partner in the City since 2006. He advises UK and international lenders (including credit and debt funds), private equity sponsors and sponsor-backed portfolio companies on a variety of UK, European and cross-border leveraged finance transactions, including private equity-backed leveraged buy-outs, public bids, recapitalisations, rescue-style financings and restructurings. Prior to joining Mayer Brown in 2018, he led the London finance practice of another large international firm.

Stuart attended Lancaster University for his LLB and completed the LPC at The College of Law.

Meredith Campanale

Partner, Mayer Brown International LLP
mcampanale@mayerbrown.com

Meredith Campanale is a partner in the banking and finance and global projects and infrastructure practices of Mayer Brown's London office. She advises on project financings across various sectors, including oil and gas, power, mining and metals and infrastructure. She has extensive experience representing sponsors and lenders – particularly development finance institutions, export credit agencies and multilateral agencies – on complex and innovative financings.

Meredith has advised on projects in Europe, the Middle East, Africa and the Americas.

She is qualified to practise in both New York and England and Wales.

Maggie Cheung

Partner, Mayer Brown
maggie.cheung@mayerbrown.com

Maggie Cheung is a partner at Mayer Brown. She advises banks and other financial institutions on various ship finance and leasing transactions, preparing cross-border bilateral and syndicated loan documentation and advising on finance structures. She also advises on other shipping industry matters, including registrations, charterparties and insurances. She acts for shipowners in various vessels construction and sale and purchase transactions.

Maggie has been recognised as a Leading Individual in Asset Finance (Hong Kong) by *The Legal 500 Asia Pacific* (2020–2022); as a Band 1 individual in Ship Finance (International Firms): China by *Chambers Greater China Region Guide* (2022); and a Leading Individual in Ship Finance (International Firms): China by *Chambers Asia Pacific* (2013–2021). Clients praise her as "exceptional, professional and friendly", "commercial and responsive", "experienced in PRC-related transactions" and "able to execute time-constrained transactions with efficiency".

Claudia Chiper

Partner, Wolf Theiss
claudia.chiper@wolftheiss.com

Claudia Chiper heads the capital markets and banking and finance teams in the Bucharest office of Wolf Theiss and has practised in these fields for almost 15 years. Claudia has extensive experience in dealing with and coordinating finance transactions, as well as advising international and domestic credit institutions, financial companies and corporations in relation to regulatory aspects of Romanian law, capital markets law and financial services. She is a specialist in payment services and has advised credit institutions, non-banking financial institutions, e-money issuers and other payment service providers on licensing issues, the launch and structuring of products on the Romanian market and consumer protection aspects.

Ian Coles

Partner, Mayer Brown International LLP
icoles@mayerbrown.com

Ian Coles heads Mayer Brown's Africa and mining practices and co-heads the global projects practice. He concentrates his practice on all aspects of bank and debt finance, ranging from projects and other structured finance to commodities financing and restructuring. He represents banks and other financial institutions, sponsors and other participants in finance transactions throughout the world.

Ian has led on a number of leading transactions in project finance across Africa and has led the practice to a Band 1 ranking for Africa in Mining (*Chambers Africa*). Continually recommended by the legal directories, he is listed as an Africa Specialist in the *Legal 500*; a Band 1 Lawyer in *Chambers UK*; a Hall of Fame member in the *Legal 500 UK*; and a Global Elite Thought Leader in *Who's Who Legal*.

Ian joined Mayer Brown in 1981, becoming a partner in 1987, and is the author of numerous articles in connection with Africa, mining and project finance.

Barry Cosgrave
Partner, Mayer Brown International LLP
bcosgrave@mayerbrown.com

Barry Cosgrave is a partner in the London and Dubai offices of Mayer Brown and head of its Islamic finance practice. He has worked on Islamic finance transactions for over 15 years in the Middle East, the United States, Europe and Southeast Asia. Barry covers all aspects of Islamic finance across multiple practice areas, including fund formation and investment management; structured finance; *Sukuk*; Islamic derivatives; and structured products, finance and project finance. Barry also has a particular expertise in *Sharia*-compliant special situations and restructuring, including *Sharia*-compliant debt trading.

Barry spent six years living and working in the Middle East and advises a wide variety of clients on the full range of Islamic finance matters. He is a regular speaker at industry events and regularly authors articles on Islamic finance. He has been listed as a leading expert in the *Who's*

Who of Capital Markets Lawyers (Islamic Finance) since 2013.

Andrew Crotty
Partner, Mayer Brown International LLP
acrotty@mayerbrown.com

Andrew Crotty is a partner in the banking and finance practice of Mayer Brown in London. His practice focuses primarily on the leveraged and real estate finance markets, in which he has broad experience advising private equity sponsors, corporates, banks, credit funds, pension trustees and other financial institutions on a wide variety of cross-border and domestic financing transactions, acquisitions, restructurings, loan-on-loan financings and general banking matters.

Andrew has extensive experience advising clients on complex capital structures, security and intercreditor issues. He advises clients at all levels of the capital structure, with deal experience covering a variety of sectors including aviation, financial institutions, mining and metals, residential and commercial real estate, retail, biotech and life sciences.

Robert David
Partner, Wolf Theiss
robert.david@wolftheiss.com

Robert David heads the local banking and finance team in Prague and specialises in acquisition finance, real estate finance, export finance, project finance, refinancing and recapitalisation, as well as general lending. He also has extensive experience in capital markets transactions (bond and Eurobond issues, initial public offerings and documenting derivatives transactions). Robert has advised a large number of clients – including financing banks, corporate clients and investors – on a wide range of high-profile cross-border and domestic banking and finance transactions. Prior to joining Wolf Theiss, Robert worked for renowned international law firms in Prague and London for over 20 years.

Alex Dell
Partner, Mayer Brown International LLP
adell@mayerbrown.com

Alex Dell is head of the banking and finance group of the London office, as well as co-chair of the firm's asset-based lending (ABL) practice.

He is focused on multi-jurisdictional receivables financing programmes and ABL transactions. Alex advises on a range of true sale issues, as well as borrowing base techniques, from both a lender and borrower perspective. He also has in-depth knowledge of off-balance-sheet considerations, payables finance, fintech platforms, bill discounting and floor planning. Alex represents banks, credit funds, sponsors and corporates, including some of the world's largest financial institutions and companies. He is widely recognised as a leading ABL and receivables financing lawyer in the United Kingdom.

Danister de Silva
Senior associate, Mayer Brown International LLP
ddesilva@mayerbrown.com

Danister de Silva is a senior associate in the banking and finance practice of the London office of Mayer Brown International LLP.

Danister represents debt funds, bank lenders, private equity sponsors and corporate borrowers in connection with domestic and international acquisition/leveraged financings, refinancings and restructurings. He also has experience in bank/ bond financings, securitisations and margin lending.

Before joining Mayer Brown, Danister practised in Sydney, Frankfurt and with a major international firm in London.

Danuta de Vries
Counsel, Mayer Brown International LLP
ddevries@mayerbrown.com

Danuta de Vries is counsel in the banking and finance practice of the London office and the global projects and infrastructure group. She has extensive experience acting for banks, development finance institutions, export credit agencies, development finance institutions and other financial institutions, as well as a variety of borrowing entities, on a broad range of domestic and international finance transactions. Her project finance work focuses on the mining and minerals sector. She frequently advises on export credit finance transactions on both the lending and borrowing sides. Danuta has vast experience working in emerging market jurisdictions, including in Africa, Asia and Eastern Europe. Danuta is recognised as a Next Generation Partner in Emerging Markets in *Legal 500 UK*.

Danuta joined Mayer Brown in 2007. While at Mayer Brown, she has completed client secondments at Fortis Bank (currently BNP Paribas), JPMorgan and HSBC Bank plc.

Douglas A Doetsch
Partner, Mayer Brown LLP
ddoetsch@mayerbrown.com

Douglas A Doetsch is a partner with Mayer Brown LLP, where he serves as head of the firm's Latin America/Caribbean practice and is a member of the banking and finance practice. He advises clients on infrastructure financings in the port, airport and road sectors; acquisition and other leveraged lending transactions; and structured credit transactions. He is also a leader in cross-border securitisation transactions, especially future cash-flow securitisations.

In his cross-border work, Doug also regularly advises on emerging market debt restructuring and debt exchange offers. In addition, his transactional work involves asset and stock acquisitions, real estate investments and cross-border joint ventures.

Chambers USA 2021 describes him as: "Simply amazing. He has seen practically every transaction in Latin America and has much experience in the region." Doug was also selected by Latinvex as one of Latin America's top 100 lawyers in 2021.

Alban Dorin

Partner, Mayer Brown LLP

adorin@mayerbrown.com

Admitted to the Paris Bar, Alban Dorin is a partner in the banking and finance and global projects practices of Mayer Brown's Paris office, and regularly advises on international asset and project finance transactions. He has advised clients on financing transactions in most Francophone African jurisdictions and his experience extends to advising on all types of major projects related to Africa.

Alban is continually recommended and ranked by legal directories and has in particular been singled out since 2019 as a Next Generation Partner both in Banking and Finance and in Mining, Oil and Gas and Natural Resources by *Legal 500 EMEA*. He is described in the guide as "very knowledgeable" and "familiar with Francophone Africa laws and regulations".

In addition to his native French, Alban is fluent in English.

Simon Fisher

Partner, Mayer Brown International LLP

sfisher@mayerbrown.com

Simon Fisher is a partner in the banking and finance group of the London office of Mayer Brown International LLP.

Simon's practice is primarily focused on secured asset-based lending (ABL) transactions – particularly large syndicated cross-border and transatlantic ABL transactions – and multi-jurisdictional trade receivables financings, representing some of the world's largest banks and financial institutions as well as credit funds. He has extensive experience in structuring and implementing complex and innovative cross-border transactions and regularly works in conjunction with counsel in the United States and multiple European and Asian jurisdictions.

Simon also represents financial institutions and corporates across a broad spectrum of domestic and international commercial financing transactions, as well as acting for sponsors, corporates and financial institutions in connection with funds finance credit facilities.

Pablo Gayol

Partner, Marval, O'Farrell & Mairal

pg@marval.com

Pablo Gayol joined Marval, O'Farrell & Mairal in 1997. His practice in the firm is centred on capital markets, banking and derivative regulations.

He graduated as a lawyer *cum laude* from the Pontifical Catholic University of Argentina in 1996 and obtained a master of laws from the University of Chicago Law School in 1997 and a master of finance from the University of CEMA in 2002. Pablo has also been a CFA charterholder since 2012.

Pablo is a professor of derivatives law at Torcuato Di Tella University and a professor of foreign exchange regulations at the University of San Andrés. He is also a professor at the University of CEMA.

Pablo is ranked in Band 1 by *Chambers & Partner*s and as a Leading Individual by *Legal 500*, among others.

Dominic Griffiths
Managing partner, London, Mayer Brown
International LLP
dgriffiths@mayerbrown.com

Dominic Griffiths is managing partner of Mayer Brown, London, a leading international law firm pre-eminent in the financial services sector. He has spent over 25 years in City law firms, with two of those years working in Milan, Italy. Dominic's practice is concentrated on complex cross-border lending, including asset-based lending (ABL) and receivables finance, as well as structured finance transactions for the world's leading banks and credit funds. He is ranked as a leading individual in *Legal 500* for both ABL and securitisation and has won many awards for his work, including receiving the Client Choice Award 2013 for Banking Law and Banking Lawyer of the Year for the United Kingdom in 2021, as well as multiple year entries as a world-leading practitioner in *Who's Who Legal* for Capital Markets/Structured Finance.

Dominic was educated at the University of Bristol and The College of Law and is dedicated to the promotion of diversity and social inclusion in the workplace, including through his position as director and advisory board member of One Million Mentors.

Andrew Hepner
Partner, Mayer Brown International LLP
ahepner@mayerbrown.com

Andrew Hepner is head of the real estate practice and co-head of the real estate finance practice in the London office of Mayer Brown.

He has extensive experience acting for banks, financial institutions, funds, investors and corporate clients. Andrew has a particular focus on structured real estate finance advising both lenders and sponsors in relation to investment and development facilities. He also acts for banks, private equity and opportunity funds and other participants in the acquisition, disposal and restructuring of performing and non-performing debt portfolios secured on real estate.

Andrew has represented clients on many high-profile transactions in the real estate finance market.

Andrew is recommended and ranked as a key individual by *Chambers UK* and *Legal 500*. He joined Mayer Brown as a trainee in 1998 and qualified in 2000.

Przemek Kozdój
Partner, Wolf Theiss
przemek.kozdoj@wolftheiss.com

Przemek Kozdój is one of the leading Polish finance lawyers, with more than 20 years of professional experience. He has worked in international law firms in Poland, the United Kingdom and the Czech Republic, as well as in a financial institution in Germany. He is a partner at Wolf Theiss and heads the banking and finance practice in Poland. He is well known for his achievements in real estate finance, advising investors and banks on numerous complex transactions in Poland and Russia. Przemek advised on the takeover of a leading financial institution, managing crucial financial aspects of the transaction, such as a multi-billion, multi-currency credit line providing back-up financing for a mortgage loan portfolio. He also counselled on the transfer of an enterprise of a bank to a branch of its holding company, as well as on the financial restructuring of Polish companies with subsidiaries in several jurisdictions. Przemek regularly advises fintech companies.

About the authors

Katerina Kraeva
Partner, Wolf Theiss
katerina.kraeva@wolftheiss.com

Katerina Kraeva heads the banking and finance team of Wolf Theiss in Sofia and is a widely recognised finance lawyer with more than 20 years of professional practice. She has extensive experience advising both lenders and borrowers on acquisition finance, real estate finance, project finance and restructurings. She serves in advisory roles in a wide range of cross-border and local lending projects, and advises clients on regulatory issues in the financial services sector on acquisitions, sales, operations establishment and regulatory compliance and licensing. Her expertise covers aircraft financing, Islamic finance and financial derivatives transactions. Prior to joining the firm, Katerina held senior positions at international law firms and was an in-house legal adviser and chief legal adviser to Bulgarian banks for more than five years. For six consecutive years (2016–2021), *Legal 500* has distinguished her as one of the leading legal experts in the practice area of banking and finance in Bulgaria.

Cecilia Mairal
Partner, Marval, O'Farrell & Mairal
cmm@marval.com

Cecilia Mairal is one of the most experienced partners in Marval O'Farrell Mairal's banking and finance department.

She has extensive experience and is highly active in advising banks on their private banking and investment banking businesses; multinational companies and family offices on the creation of investment vehicles; as well as cross-border bank financings, international securities transactions and debt restructurings. She also has niche expertise in sensitive regulatory work and complex international banking litigation cases.

Cecilia is the client relationship partner for several of the firm's key clients and leads the teams advising them on complex multi-disciplinary matters.

She has been recognised by many of the most prestigious legal publications. *Chambers Latin America 2017* described her as "an excellent lawyer". In 2017, Cecilia was recognised as the Best Finance Lawyer in Latin America in the Americas Women in Business Awards organised by *Euromoney*.

Charles Malpass
Partner, Mayer Brown International LLP
cmalpass@mayerbrown.com

Charles Malpass has a wide-ranging practice which focuses primarily on real estate and real estate-backed transactions. He has been practising for more than 25 years at leading international and City law firms, and has been a partner for over 15 years.

His practice includes all aspects of real estate transactions (acquisition, financing and disposal across all asset classes), non-performing loan transactions, securitisations, senior and mezzanine loan origination, and loans backed by consumer, residential mortgage and commercial mortgage debt.

He has worked on some of the highest-profile deals in the European market, including major developments, acquisitions and financings of large portfolios of properties and hotels, and distressed situations/restructurings.

He is a leader in his field and is widely recognised for his complex multi-jurisdictional work. He frequently advises on transactions across Europe and in Russia, the Middle East and the United States.

Jane Man
Senior associate, Mayer Brown
jane.man@mayerbrown.com

Jane Man is a senior associate in the asset finance team of Mayer Brown's Hong Kong office. Her practice covers a wide range of transactions in the aviation sector, including the acquisition of new aircraft from manufacturers; the sale and purchase of used aircraft; and the negotiation of leases (including operating leases and sale and leasebacks). She also advises on performance guarantees and warranties relating to new aircraft and engines; long-term engine maintenance agreements; inventory management arrangements; cabin product development agreements; in-flight entertainment supply agreements; ticket sales agency arrangements; and codeshare arrangements. Jane also has experience on a wide array of commercial and bespoke deals in the aviation industry. She has advised top-tier airlines, aircraft and engine lessors, as well as maintenance and repair organisations.

Shri Maski
Partner, Mayer Brown LLP, Tokyo
shri.maski@mayerbrown.com

Shri Maski is a partner in Mayer Brown's banking and finance and global projects and infrastructure practice in Tokyo. He focuses on project financings and has advised sponsors, lenders (including European and Asian export credit agencies) and public authorities on projects across sectors such as energy, mining and infrastructure (including Private Finance Initiative/public-private partnerships (PPPs)).

Prior to joining Mayer Brown, Shri worked at leading international law firms in Japan, the United Kingdom and the Middle East. Shri has lived in Japan for over nine years and has completed secondments to the Japan Bank for International Cooperation in Tokyo and the Export Import Bank of Korea in Seoul, where he advised on project and finance documentation for transactions in Australia, Southeast Asia, Europe and Latin America.

Ashley McDermott
Partner, Mayer Brown International LLP
amcdermott@mayerbrown.com

Ash McDermott is a partner in the London office of Mayer Brown. His practice mainly involves syndicated loan financings in emerging markets – particularly export, project, sovereign, structured trade and multilateral financings. He has experience of many different jurisdictions and cultures, having previously worked in Moscow, Hong Kong and Tokyo. Ash wrote the Loan Market Association's first facility agreement for use in export finance and is regularly consulted and published in relation to topical issues such as debt sustainability in emerging markets and London Interbank Offered Rate transition.

Ignacio Mirasol
Senior associate, Mayer Brown International LLP
imirasol@mayerbrown.com

Ignacio Mirasol is a senior associate in the banking and finance practice of Mayer Brown's London office. He has experience advising lenders, private equity sponsors, sponsor portfolio companies and corporate borrowers on a wide range of transactions, including cross-border acquisitions, recapitalisations, refinancings, public-to-private takeovers and general corporate financings. He has a particular focus on sponsor-backed cross-border acquisition financings.

Prior to joining Mayer Brown in 2019, Ignacio completed his training contract and qualified into the debt finance practice of a large international law firm in London. In 2017, he undertook a secondment in the financial services legal team of The Royal Bank of Scotland plc.

Ignacio attended the London School of Economics for his LLB and completed the LPC at The University of Law, London.

Luis Otero Montes
Partner, Tauil & Chequer Advogados in
association with Mayer Brown
lmontes@mayerbrown.com

Luis Otero Montes is a partner in the São Paulo office of Tauil & Chequer Advogados in association with Mayer Brown and a member of the finance and capital markets practices. He focuses on project finance transactions and construction law, representing multilateral institutions, commercial banks, institutional lenders and project sponsors in infrastructure, energy and natural resources projects. Luis has significant experience in corporate, finance and capital market law, and has participated in significant lending transactions and projects structuring in Brazil and Latin America, including the construction and financing of energy and infrastructure projects; equity and debt offerings (both domestic and offshore); and banking regulation – in particular, banking products, derivatives and regulatory aspects.

Luis holds a bachelor of law degree (JD equivalent) from the University of São Paulo and an LLM from *Fundação Getúlio Vargas*. He is ranked as a Leading Individual in different legal directories.

Juan Pablo Moreno
Partner, Mayer Brown LLP
jmoreno@mayerbrown.com

Juan Pablo Moreno is a partner in Mayer Brown's banking and finance practice and the Latin American and Caribbean group. Juan Pablo regularly represents financial institutions and large corporates involved in cross-border transactions in Latin America with a focus on structured finance, project finance, corporate finance and capital markets transactions, including lending and securities offerings in the form of private placements or under Rule 144A/Regulation S offerings. Juan Pablo has a unique background, having been admitted to practise in both the United States and Colombia, and having practised as a lawyer in France, Colombia and the United States.

Mark Prinsley
Partner, Mayer Brown International LLP
mprinsley@mayerbrown.com

Mark Prinsley is a partner in the London office of Mayer Brown. He heads the intellectual property and technology practice in the firm's London office and has many years of experience in the intellectual property and personal data aspects of transactions, acting for sellers, buyers and lenders.

Mark's transactional and licensing experience spans a wide variety of sectors and industries, including fast-moving consumer goods, chemicals, retail, technology, travel and leisure, professional services and e-commerce. He has extensive experience of multinational transactions, including in particular the treatment of personal data in arrangements which involve international data transfers.

Ariel Ramos
Partner, Mayer Brown LLP
aramos@mayerbrown.com

Ariel Ramos is a partner in Mayer Brown's finance and energy practice groups based in the firm's Mexico City office, focused on energy, infrastructure and projects. Ariel also has extensive experience in structure finance, lending and credit transactions, project finance, M&A, regulatory matters and governmental procurement. Among others, he has represented international and national conglomerates in acquisition transactions in different sectors, including steel, telecommunications, energy and infrastructure. He has also represented investment funds and institutional investors in financing and acquisition transactions.

Ariel has been ranked as a top lawyer in Energy, Infrastructure, Projects, Project Finance, Natural Resources and Government Procurement by international publications such as *Chambers Latin America: Energy & Natural Resources* and *Chambers Global*.

Loreto Ribera

Senior associate, Carey y Cía
lribera@carey.cl

Loreto Ribera is a senior associate at Carey y Cía, where she is a member of the banking and finance practice. She advises clients on local and foreign project financing in various industries, including energy and mining projects, lending transactions and banking law. She also has experience in commercial and corporate law matters, such as M&A, due diligence coordination, contract negotiation and corporate governance.

Gabriela Sakamoto

Partner, Mayer Brown LLP
gsakamoto@mayerbrown.com

Gabriela Sakamoto is a partner in Mayer Brown's Washington DC banking and finance practice, and a member of the Latin America and global projects groups. Gabriela's practice focuses on advising commercial banks, multilateral agencies and other financial institutions – as arrangers, lenders and agents – on cross-border project finance, structured finance, capital markets and

acquisition financing transactions, particularly in Latin America. Her Latin American experience is extensive and includes transactions in more than 10 countries in the region – including Argentina, Brazil, Chile, Colombia, Mexico and Peru – and across a wide range of sectors, including energy, oil and gas and infrastructure.

Luis Schrader

Associate, Mayer Brown LLP
lschrader@mayerbrown.com

Luis Schrader is an associate in Mayer Brown's banking and finance practice and the Latin American and Caribbean group. Luis has extensive experience representing financial institutions and large companies in cross-border transactions in Latin America, with a special emphasis on structured finance, project finance, corporate finance and capital markets transactions, including lending transactions and securities offerings in the form of private placements or under Rule 144A/Regulation S offerings.

Aimee Sharman

Partner, Mayer Brown International LLP
asharman@mayerbrown.com

Aimee Sharman is a partner in the banking and finance practice of the London office. She has a broad client base across multiple fund and asset classes (eg, private equity funds, credit funds, infrastructure funds, secondary funds, real estate funds, emerging market funds and hedge funds), acting for both borrowers and lenders on a wide range of financing products across the fund finance sector. Her extensive experience includes advising on bridge financing, GP support or co-investment facilities, fund of funds financing, net asset value/asset-backed facilities or hybrid facilities and preferred equity solutions.

About the authors

Gary Silverman

Counsel, Mayer Brown International LLP

gsilverman@mayerbrown.com

Gary Silverman is counsel in Mayer Brown's banking and finance practice in London. Gary holds an LLM in banking and finance law from University College London and has specialised in advising corporate trustee and loan agency houses on a broad range of banking and debt capital market products for over 15 years, including securitisations and other forms of asset-backed and secured finance lending. He has significant experience advising on pre- and post-completion matters, including exercise of trustee discretion.

Rachel Speight

Partner, Mayer Brown International LLP

rspeight@mayerbrown.com

Rachel Speight is a partner in the banking and finance and global projects and infrastructure practice of the London office. She represents banks and sponsors in international structured and project financings. She particularly focuses on the mining finance sector and has experience in infrastructure finance in areas including road, rail and healthcare, including work on PPP projects.

Consistently recommended and ranked as a key individual by the legal directories, Rachel is recognised as a Leading Individual and "is recommended for advising banks and sponsors on cross-border project financings, particularly in Africa markets" (*Legal 500 UK*). Rachel has also been listed in *The 100 Global Inspirational Women in Mining* and has been named as one of the Hot 100 Lawyers by *The Lawyer*.

Rachel joined Mayer Brown in 1999 and has spent some time on secondment to both The Royal Bank of Scotland and WestLB.

Richard Stock

Partner, Mayer Brown

richard.stock@mayerbrown.com

Richard Stock is a partner in Mayer Brown's Hong Kong office. He is a co-leader of Mayer Brown's banking and finance practice and a leader of the firm's asset finance team. He focuses his practice on the aviation industry, with nearly 30 years' experience assisting airlines, lessors and financial institutions in documenting aircraft and aviation transactions.

Richard's practice covers the lifecycle of an aircraft, including aircraft purchase arrangements (he has documented original equipment manufacturer purchase agreements for the purchase of aircraft with a total value exceeding $30 billion); aircraft finance arrangements (including commercial debt, export credit agency supported debt, tax leases, operating leases and sale and leaseback transactions); aircraft maintenance and operational support arrangements (including long-term engine maintenance agreements and inventory technical management agreements with total revenues exceeding $7 billion); aircraft leases, sub-leases, charters and wet leases; and aircraft disposals and parting out arrangements. These arrangements have concerned both commercial aircraft and corporate jets.

Charles Thain

Partner, Mayer Brown International LLP

cthain@mayerbrown.com

Charles Thain is a partner in Mayer Brown's banking and finance practice in London. His work is focused on asset-based lending, receivables finance, payables finance and trade finance; and he represents financial institutions, sponsors, corporates and fintechs in both domestic and cross-border transactions.

Having managed legal due diligence projects relating to receivables/payables/trade finance products in over 70 jurisdictions, Charles has a unique breadth of knowledge in this area. He is a trusted and go-to adviser for these products and has drafted standard form documentation for these products for a number of financial institutions and fintechs.

Before qualifying in law, Charles obtained a master's degree in chemistry.

Sarah Walters

Professional support lawyer, Mayer Brown International LLP
swalters@mayerbrown.com

Sarah Walters joined Mayer Brown's London office as a professional support lawyer in the banking and finance practice in 2019. She is responsible for developing the knowledge strategy; helping the practice stay abreast of cutting-edge issues and products; organising thought leadership; developing precedent documents and other practice resources; training lawyers; and assisting in the implementation of technology to allow the practice's lawyers to leverage internal and external knowledge to deliver excellent client service.

Prior to becoming a professional support lawyer, Sarah gained extensive experience at leading firms in London acting for lenders, borrowers and financial institutions in relation to corporate finance, acquisition and leveraged finance transactions.

Conor Warde

Partner, Mayer Brown
conor.warde@mayerbrown.com

Conor Warde is a partner in the Hong Kong office of Mayer Brown and is Mayer Brown's head of ship finance and maritime transactions. He has a diverse practice advising clients on transactional,

corporate, regulatory and policy matters, with particular experience in ship finance and maritime transactional matters. He represents companies, commercial lenders, lessors, lessees and investors in international financings, M&A, restructurings and other corporate transactions across multiple industries and involving a broad range of corporate finance and investment issues, including senior and subordinated debt financings, asset-based lending transactions and private equity investments.

Conor is recognised as a Leading Individual in Asset Finance (Hong Kong) by *Legal 500 Asia-Pacific*; a Leading Individual in Ship Finance (International Firms): China by *Chambers Asia Pacific*; and an Expert Based Abroad in China in General Business Law, Marshall Islands by *Chambers Asia Pacific*. Clients report that he "thinks ahead, is extremely organised [and] extremely well plugged into the industry", "is very professional" and "provides commercial insights into the shipping industry and shipbuilding".

Matt Wargin

Partner, Mayer Brown LLP
mwargin@mayerbrown.com

Matt Wargin, a partner in Mayer Brown's restructuring practice group, represents institutional lenders, bank groups, hedge funds and other creditors in out-of-court workouts, bankruptcy proceedings and other distress situations, including advising corporate clients on distressed asset sales and acquisitions and on structuring considerations in complex debt transactions.

Matt's experience includes representing debtors and other stakeholders in Chapter 11 proceedings and also includes a variety of matters representing corporate trust clients in connection with restructurings, litigation and other special situations.

Matt has advised clients in connection with transactions and disputes involving a wide variety of industries, including telecommunications, oil and gas, manufacturing, life insurance and financial services. Matt regularly litigates matters in federal bankruptcy and district courts and has significant experience working with expert witnesses and litigating contested valuation issues.